S0-BYE-604

# THE DEATH OF OLD MAN RICE

TRH
IF 28/XII/94

To Dick
at Xmas 1994, a part
of our family history!
from
Ted

BY THE SAME AUTHOR

*Detention before Trial*
*Double Jeopardy*
*Courts and Trials: A Multidisciplinary Approach*
*Access to the Law*
*Cases and Materials on Criminal Law and Procedure* (with K. Roach)
*National Security: The Legal Dimensions*
*The Trials of Israel Lipski: A True Story of a Victorian Murder in the East End of London*
*A Century of Criminal Justice*
*The Case of Valentine Shortis: A True Story of Crime and Politics in Canada*
*Sanctions and Rewards in the Legal System: A Multidisciplinary Approach*
*Securing Compliance: Seven Case Studies*
*Regulating Traffic Safety* (with M.J. Trebilcock and K. Roach)
*Rough Justice: Essays on Crime in Literature*

Martin L. Friedland

# The Death of
# Old Man Rice

## A TRUE STORY OF
## CRIMINAL JUSTICE
## IN AMERICA

UNIVERSITY OF TORONTO PRESS

Toronto and London

© University of Toronto Press Incorporated 1994
Toronto London
Printed in Canada

ISBN 0-8020-2941-8 (cloth)

Printed on acid-free paper

Canadian Cataloguing in Publication Data

Friedland, M.L. (Martin Lawrence), 1932–
   The death of old man Rice : a true story of
   criminal justice in America

   ISBN 0-8020-2941-8

   1. Patrick, Albert T. – Trials, litigation, etc.
   2. Rice, William Marsh, 1816–1900.   3. Trials
   (Murder) – New York (N.Y.).   4. Criminal justice,
   Administration of – United States.   I. Title.

   KF224.P37F7 1994      345.73′02523      C94-930898-6

This book has been published with the help of a grant from the Social
Science Federation of Canada, using funds provided by the Social
Sciences and Humanities Research Council of Canada.

# Contents

# PART TWO: THE TOMBS

# PART THREE: THE PROSECUTION

## PART SEVEN: CONCLUSION

# Preface

WILLIAM MARSH RICE, the founder of Rice University in Houston, Texas, died in New York City in the year 1900. The trial of Albert T. Patrick, a lawyer, for his murder was described by one newspaper at the time as 'America's most remarkable murder case'[1] and by another as 'one of the most remarkable trials in all history.'[2] It is surprising, therefore, that no book has yet been written about the case, although it has been included in a number of anthologies and encyclopedias of crime.[3]

This book is the third that I have written in which I have reconstructed a murder case and attempted to place it in its social, political, and economic context. The first book, *The Trials of Israel Lipski*,[4] published in 1984, dealt with a murder case in Victorian England. The second, *The Case of Valentine Shortis*,[5] published in 1986, explored a Quebec case that was tried in 1895. I then deliberately set out to find a turn-of-the-century American case – preferably one that took place in New York City – that would enable me to gain an understanding of the administration of criminal justice in the United States. *The Death of Old Man Rice* is the result.

As it turned out, each book appears to capture the essence of the society in which the case occurred. The Lipski story is one of class and prejudice in England; Shortis is about race and religion in Canada; and the Patrick/Rice case is about wealth and ambition in the United States.

All three cases show the inherent frailty of the criminal process and the many nonlegal factors that may influence any criminal trial, then and now. A trial may in theory be an objective pursuit of truth, but in practice there are many subjective factors which influence the course of events. Justice may in theory be blind, but in practice she has altogether too human a dimension.

The story also enables us to learn much about criminal justice in the United States, then and now: the practice of law; the functioning of the

police and the courts; the advantages of wealth; the influence of the popular press; the role of expert witnesses; the problems of delay and mul-
tiplicity of appeals; the issues of capital punishment and the pardoning
process; and the inadequacy of penal institutions.

I was fortunate in that there are very extensive records of the Patrick/
Rice case. The archives at Rice University contain a roomful of documents pertaining to the case from the perspective of the prosecution,
deposited there by a prominent character in the story, James A. Baker,
Jr, the grandfather of the former secretary of state. And the papers in
Albany of former governor David B. Hill, who acted for Patrick, show
aspects of the case from the defense perspective. Moreover, there was
a full transcript of the proceedings available, as well as district attorneys'
and court files. There were also very detailed newspaper accounts of
the case. Indeed, one paper remarked that more had been written about
Patrick by the press than about any other individual,[6] with the possible
exception of the president of the United States. All the dialogue in the
book has been taken from the transcript, the newspapers, and other sources. Nothing has been made up.

I am grateful to a great number of individuals and institutions for
their help and support. Former dean Robert Prichard, now the president
of the University of Toronto, and his successor, Dean Robert Sharpe,
actively encouraged my work on this project. Over the past few years
I was assisted by several Social Sciences and Humanities Research Council
grants administered through the university and by the Ontario Law Foundation's block grant to the Law School. I have been fortunate in having
had a succession of exceptionally able summer research assistants: Tim
Endicott helped me find the case; Freddie Pletcher, Jennifer Webster,
and Craig Godsoe in turn helped me gather material on it; and finally,
Paul Michell helped me check the accuracy of the manuscript. In addition,
I am indebted to the Canadian Institute for Advanced Research and its
president, Dr Fraser Mustard, for their continuing support.

Librarians and archivists were, as always, helpful and considerate. I
would like to mention in particular the staff at the Faculty of Law and
at the Robarts Library at the University of Toronto; Barbara Halbert,
Nancy Boothe, and other staff members at the Woodson Research Center
at Rice University; Kenneth Cobb and his staff at the Municipal Archives
of the City of New York; Jim Corsaro and others at the New York
State Library in Albany; Professor Ellen Gibson, the librarian, and her
staff at the University of Buffalo Law School; and staff at the New York
Public Library, the New York Historical Society, the Association of the

Bar of the City of New York Library, New York University Law Library, the Albany Institute of History and Art, the George Arents Research Library at Syracuse University, the New York Court of Appeals, the Manuscript Division of the Library of Congress, and the National Archives, Washington, as well as public libraries, archives, court offices, and newspapers in St Louis, Austin, Houston, Denver, Tulsa, New Orleans, Schenectady, Philadelphia, Orlando, and many other cities across the United States.

A number of knowledgeable individuals read all or parts of the manuscript. Their comments helped shape this final version. My colleagues Kent Roach, Bob Sharpe, and Steve Waddams were, as usual, perceptive critics, as were criminal lawyers Larry Fleischer of New York City, Michael Code and Eddie Greenspan of Toronto, and Mark Mahoney of Buffalo, historians Ted Hill of the University of British Columbia and Ken Lipartito of the University of Houston, and law professors Peter Kutner of the University of Oklahoma, William Nelson of New York University, and Richard Uviller of Columbia University. I also benefited greatly from the advice of a number of medical experts: Frederick Jaffe, the former chief pathologist at the Centre of Forensic Sciences in Toronto; Alan Von Poznack, Department of Anaesthesiology and Pharmacology at Cornell Medical Center; and Charles Hirsch, the chief medical examiner of the City of New York. Insights into other specialized areas were provided by Janet Masson, a handwriting expert from Houston; Edward and Gail Johnson, embalmers from Chicago with an interest in the history of embalming; and Paul Faris, an embalming instructor at Humber College, Toronto, who allowed me to observe a number of embalmings.

At a very early stage of my research I presented an outline of the case at a University College symposium at the University of Toronto on 'Fakes, Frauds and Forgeries' and in November 1992, at a much later stage, I had the opportunity to discuss the case at Professor William Nelson's Legal History seminar at New York University. Both occasions helped significantly to shape my final presentation of the story.

Many others assisted me in various ways. Joseph Levy of Albany, Tornes Mock of Houston, and Philip Ower of the Robarts Library in Toronto assisted me with the reproductions of photographs. My son, Tom, now a lawyer in Toronto, helped with a number of tasks, including tracking down the locations of the various New York places mentioned in the manuscript and discovering what structures now occupy the sites. A succession of excellent secretaries – Kathy Tzimika, Julia Hall, Pauline

Yan, and Rochelle Vigurs – helped produce this long and complex manuscript. Finally, I would like to thank Jack Robson, professor of English at the University of Toronto, who read an earlier draft of the entire manuscript with great care, Virgil Duff and Bill Harnum of the University of Toronto Press and Niko Pfund of New York University Press for their editorial guidance, and Lorraine Ourom for her expert copy editing. To all of the above, I offer my sincere appreciation and thanks.

The book is dedicated to my late father, Jack Friedland, who grew up in New York City in the early years of the century before moving to Toronto. Whether the family ever discussed the Patrick/Rice murder is not known.

# Cast of Characters

| | |
|---|---|
| ACHESON, Harold | New York correspondent of the *Houston Post* |
| ADAMS, Charles T. | friend of Rice in New York |
| ADAMS, Robert | deputy sheriff of Galveston County |
| AURICH, Robert H. | in charge of autopsy department at morgue |
| BACON, William | supplied information to Hornblower, Byrne |
| BAKER, Graham | James A. Baker's eldest son |
| BAKER, James A., Jr | senior partner with Baker, Botts, Houston |
| BAKER, James A., II | son of James A. Baker, Jr |
| BAKER, Jules J. | Texas Ranger |
| BARNES, Dr Carl | head of Barnes School of Embalming in Chicago |
| BARTINE, Judge John D. | executor of Rice's 1896 will |
| BARTLETT, Edward | judge of New York Court of Appeals, 1893–1910 |
| BATTLE, George Gordon | Jones' New York lawyer |
| BELL, Clark | lawyer and president of the Medico-Legal Society |
| BENNETT, Dr Thomas L. | anaesthetist at New York Hospital |
| BIGGS, Dr George | pathologist at New York Hospital |
| BILLMEYER, Frank | juror |
| BLACK, Frank | lawyer and governor of New York, 1897–8 |
| BRANN, Magistrate | New York magistrate who conducted preliminary inquiry into forgery charges |
| BRINDLEY, Nicholas T. | New York police officer guarding Jones |

| BROCKMAN, James B. | Houston defense counsel |
| BROWN, Charles F. | lawyer and former judge of the Court of Appeals |
| BRYANT, Dr Joseph | president of the Medical Society of New York |
| BYRNE, James | partner of Hornblower, Byrne, New York City |
| CAMPBELL, Frank E. | New York embalmer |
| CAMPBELL, John J. | juror who became ill |
| CANTWELL, Thomas W. | defense handwriting expert from Albany |
| CANTWELL, William | Robert M. Moore's law partner |
| CAREY, Arthur | New York detective sergeant handling homicide cases |
| CARPENTER, Isabel | friend of Rice in New York |
| CARVALHO, David | New York City handwriting expert |
| CHURCH, Colonel William C. | foreman of the grand jury |
| CLEVELAND, Grover | president of the United States, 1885–9, 1893–7 |
| COHN, Arthur | William M. Rice's employee in Texas |
| COLEMAN, John | lawyer and friend of Patrick from Houston |
| COSTELLO, Elizabeth | cook at Mrs Francis' boarding house |
| CRAVATH, Paul | one of the founders of the present Cravath, Swaine law firm |
| CREED, Nellie | girlfriend of Charlie Jones |
| CULLEN, Edgar M. | chief judge of New York Court of Appeals, 1904–13 |
| CURRY, Walker | physician who signed death certificate |
| DAY, William Rufus | justice of United States Supreme Court, 1903–23 |
| DE FORD. William A. | assistant district attorney in New York City |
| DE MEULES, Edgar | Oklahoma lawyer |
| DEVERY, William | New York police chief in 1900 |
| DINES, Tyson S. | Milliken's St Louis lawyer |
| DIX, John A. | governor of New York, 1911–12 |
| DONLIN, Dr Edward | coroner's physician, New York City |
| ECKELS, Howard S. | professor of embalming in Philadelphia |

| | |
|---|---|
| ELLIOTT, Mabel | boarder at Mrs Francis' house |
| EWING, Dr James | professor of pathology at Cornell Medical School |
| FANE, John | keeper of the morgue |
| FITZGERALD, Judge | surrogate court judge |
| FLINT, Dr Austin | professor of physiology at Cornell Medical School |
| FORD, Thomas W. | Texas lawyer who met Patrick in New York in August 1900 |
| FRAME, John | Houston police officer |
| FRANCIS, Addie | Patrick's landlady and, later, his second wife |
| FRANCIS, W.H. | former New Jersey judge |
| FRENCH, Charles | defense handwriting expert from Boston |
| FULLER, Melville W. | chief Justice of the United States Supreme Court, 1888–1910 |
| GAILLARD, Minnie | Texas schoolteacher |
| GALVIN, Lucy | waitress at Mrs Francis' boarding house |
| GANS, Howard | assistant district attorney in charge of Appeals Bureau |
| GARDINER, Asa Bird | New York district attorney, 1897–1900 |
| GARVAN, Francis P. | assistant district attorney in New York City |
| GAULE, Margaret | a New York City spiritualist |
| GAYNOR, William | justice of the Appellate Division of New York, later New York mayor |
| GERARD, James W. | New York lawyer with Bowers and Sands |
| GILLETTE, Judge J.A. | friend of Jones' family in Texas |
| GIRDNER, Dr John | performed experiments using chloroform |
| GOODRICH, George C. | New York mining promoter |
| GOFF, John | recorder of New York |
| GRAY, Henry G. | assistant district attorney and son of Judge Gray |
| GRAY, John C. | judge of New York Court of Appeals, 1888–1913 |
| GRINNELL, Dr Ashbel P. | specialist in medicolegal issues |
| GROSSMAN, Moses | partner of Frederick House |

GROTTY, Adolphus              alias William Bacon
HAIGHT, Albert               judge of New York Court of Appeals,
                             1895-1912
HAMILTON, Albert H.          forensic expert from Auburn
HAMILTON, Dr Allan
  McLane                     president of the Psychiatrical Society
HARBY, Max                   New York City lawyer with Hogan,
                             Demond, and Harby
HARE, Dr Hobart              professor of therapeutics from
                             Philadelphia
HARMAN, W.F.                 bookkeeper at the Swenson Bank
HART, Edward                 New York City coroner in 1900
HEARST, William Randolph     publisher of New York *American* and
                             *Evening Journal*
HELLMUTH, I.F.               Ontario lawyer
HIGGINS, Frank               New York governor, 1905-6
HILL, David B.               former governor of New York (1885-91)
                             and United States senator (1891-7)
HILL, Leonidas               from Denver, married to Albert Patrick's
                             sister
HOLT, Orren Thadeus          Houston lawyer who prepared Mrs
                             Elizabeth Rice's will
HORNBLOWER, William B.       senior partner in Hornblower, Byrne,
                             New York City
HOUSE, Frederick B.          defense counsel, New York City
HOWE, William F.             member of New York law firm of Howe
                             and Hummel
HUFFCUT, Ernest W.           dean of Cornell Law School and legal
                             counsel to New York governors
HUGHES, Charles Evans        governor of New York (1907-10) and
                             later chief justice of the United States
                             (1930-41)
HUMMEL, Abraham              member of New York law firm of Howe
                             and Hummel
HUNCKE, Max                  embalming fluid manufacturer
HUTCHESON, J.C.              Houston lawyer and former congress-
                             man
JENKS, Almet F.              justice of the Appellate Division of New
                             York, 1901-21

JEROME, William Travers    judge of Court of Special Sessions and later the district attorney of New York City, 1902–9

JOHNSON, Addison    warden of Sing Sing

JONES, Charles (Charlie)    Rice's valet

JONES, Lafayette    Charlie Jones' brother in Texas

JORDAN, Joe    knew Jones in Texas

KEMP, Dr Robert Coleman    professor at New York Clinical School of Medicine

KENNEDY, Dr Samuel    charged with murder in New York City

KINSLEY, William J.    New York City handwriting expert

KOHLER, Edgar    New York City lawyer, brother of Max

KOHLER, Max    New York City lawyer, brother of Edgar

KOHLSAAT, H.H.    Chicago publisher

KOSER, E.    friend of Charlie Jones

LACOMBE, Henry    judge of federal Circuit Court of Appeals

LANDON, Judson S.    former judge of the New York Court of Appeals, 1900–2

LEDERLE, Dr E.J.    chemist

LEE, Dr Edward Wallace    defense medical expert

LEE, Fayette    knew Jones in Texas

LEUF, Dr Alexander H.P.    expert on lung diseases from Philadelphia

LINDSAY, William    lawyer and former United States senator from Kentucky

LOGAN, Frank G.    Chicago businessman

LOOMIS, Dr Henry P.    professor of diseases at Cornell Medical School

LOVE, Dr Isaac Newton    St Louis physician

LOVETT, Robert S.    partner in Baker, Botts, Houston, later president of Southern Pacific

LOW, Seth    president of Columbia University and mayor of New York in 1902

MACFARLANE, Wallace    former United States district attorney, New York City

MACHELL, James    juror

MARSHALL, Louis    New York City lawyer

MAYER, Joseph    Patrick's office boy

| MCALLISTER, Dr John Downs | pathology teacher working at the morgue |
| MCCLUSKEY, George | head of New York City Detective Bureau |
| MCDONALD, William L. | New York lawyer and classmate of Patrick |
| MCLAUGHLIN, Chester | judge of the Appellate Division of New York |
| MCMAHON, Judge | New York judge in General Sessions Court |
| MELDRUM, Norman S. | Texas railway official |
| MEYERS, Morris | lawyer in Patrick's office whose name appeared as a witness to the 1900 will |
| MILBURN, John G. | Buffalo lawyer, later moved to New York City |
| MILLICAN, Dr Kenneth | associate editor of the *New York Medical Journal* |
| MILLIKEN, John T. | Patrick's brother-in-law from St Louis |
| MILLIKEN, May | Patrick's sister and the wife of John T. Milliken |
| MOLINEUX, Roland | charged with murder in New York City |
| MOORE, Robert M. | New York defense counsel |
| MORTIMER, Maude | girlfriend of Charlie Jones |
| MOTT, Magistrate | New York magistrate |
| MOTT, J.L., Jr | Houston detective |
| MURPHY, Charles F. | 'Boss Murphy' of Tammany Hall |
| O'BRIEN, Dennis | judge of New York Court of Appeals, 1889–1909 |
| OLCOTT, William M.K. | law partner of Frank S. Black |
| OSBORN, Albert S. | handwriting expert from Rochester |
| OSBORNE, James W. | assistant district attorney, New York City |
| PARKER, Alton B. | chief judge of the New York Court of Appeals, 1898–1904 |
| PARKER, Edwin B. | partner in Baker and Botts, Houston |
| PATRICK, Albert T. | Texas lawyer, practicing in New York City |
| PATRICK, Emma | Albert Patrick's younger sister |
| PATRICK, Henry D. | Albert Patrick's father |
| PATRICK, Lillian | Patrick's younger daughter |

| | |
|---|---|
| PATRICK, Lucille | Patrick's elder daughter |
| PECKHAM, Rufus | justice of United States Supreme Court, 1895–1909 |
| PHILBIN, Eugene | New York district attorney after A.B. Gardiner |
| PLOWRIGHT, Charles | Manhattan undertaker |
| POTTER, John | embalmer who worked for Charles Plowright |
| POTTS, John R. | lawyer who rented space from Patrick |
| PULITZER, Joseph | publisher of New York *World* |
| RAILLEY, Judge | formerly justice of the peace in Houston |
| RAMSEY, George S. | Oklahoma lawyer |
| RANSOM, Henry L. | Texas Ranger |
| RAPHAEL, Emmanuel | secretary of the Rice Institute |
| RECORDS, Edward | intermediary between Jones and Baker |
| RICE, Baldwin | nephew of William M. Rice and mayor of Houston |
| RICE, Elizabeth | William M. Rice's deceased wife |
| RICE, Frederick A. | William M. Rice's brother |
| RICE, William Marsh | Texas millionaire, living in New York |
| RICE, William M., Jr | nephew of William M. Rice |
| ROGERS, Judge | justice of the New York Supreme Court |
| ROOSEVELT, Theodore | governor of New York (1899–1900), later president of the United States (1901–9) |
| SCHIRMER, Gustav F. | juror |
| SCHULTZE, Dr O.H. | prosecution expert on chloroform |
| SCOTT, Joseph F. | superintendent of New York Prisons |
| SCOTT, Maria | Rice's housekeeper |
| SHARP, L.P. | New York detective |
| SHENSTONE, Archibald | New York lawyer |
| SHORT, David | person close to Patrick whose name appeared as a witness to the 1900 will |
| SMITH, Dr William | anatomy professor in Missouri |
| STANBERY, Alexander | friend of Charlie Jones from Texas |
| SWENSON, S.M. | principal of the Swenson Bank |
| TAYLOR, Robert C. | New York assistant district attorney |
| THAYER, Dr Alfred E. | instructor of pathology at Cornell Medical School |

THOMAS, Samuel Bell          lawyer friend of Patrick and secretary of
                             the Medico-Legal Society
TINSLEY, Charles             businessman in Texas
TOLMAN, Henry                handwriting expert from Chicago
TOMLINSON, John C.           New York City lawyer
TRAIN, Arthur                author and assistant district attorney in
                             New York
TRUESDALE, John              handwriting expert from Syracuse
TYRELL, John                 handwriting expert from Milwaukee
TURNER, Frank D.             defense counsel from Chicago
UNTERMEYER, Samuel           partner of Guggenheimer, Untermeyer,
                             and Marshall, New York City
VALLELY, James               detective sergeant with New York Police
VANN, Irving                 judge of New York Court of Appeals,
                             1896–1913
WALDRON, John M.             Milliken's Denver lawyer
WALKER, Joseph               New York stock broker
WALLACE, John                cashier at the Swenson Bank
WELLMAN, Francis L.          New York City lawyer
WERNER, William              judge of New York Court of Appeals,
                             1900–16
WESTON, Dr Albert T.         coroner's physician, New York City
WETHERBEE, Walter            head clerk at the Swenson Bank
WHERRY, William              junior lawyer in Hornblower, Byrne
WHITE, Horace                acting governor of New York, 1910
WHITE, Isaac De Forest       New York *World* reporter
WHITMAN, Charles S.          district attorney and later governor of
                             New York, 1915–18
WHITNEY, Mabel               girlfriend of Charlie Jones
WHITTLESEY, John             friend of William M. Rice
WILLIAMS, Dr Hamilton        coroner's physician, New York City
WITTHAUS, Rudolph A.         professor of toxicology at Cornell
                             Medical School
WYETH, John A.               president of the American Medical
                             Association

Albert T. Patrick with his first wife and elder daughter, Lucille, about 1895.

# PART ONE
# Arrest

William Marsh Rice in his later years.

The Berkshire Apartments, 500 Madison Avenue, now the site of the Omni Berkshire Place hotel: New York *Herald*, 7 October 1900.

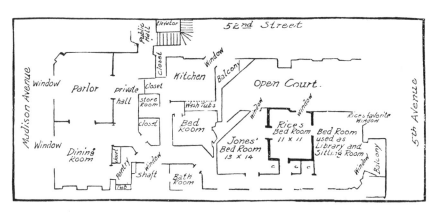

Plan of Rice's apartment: New York *World*, 7 October 1900.

Charles Jones: New York *World*,
27 September 1900.

Albert T. Patrick: New York *World*,
7 October 1900.

Captain George McCluskey: New York
*Evening Journal*, 8 October 1900.

Mrs Addie Francis: New York
*Evening Journal*, 18 January 1902.

Form No. 291.

THE WESTERN UNION TELEGRAPH COMPANY.

——— INCORPORATED ———

21,000 OFFICES IN AMERICA. CABLE SERVICE TO ALL THE WORLD.

THOS. T. ECKERT, President and General Manager.

| Receiver's No. | Time Filed | | Check |
|---|---|---|---|

SEND the following message subject to the terms on back hereof, which are hereby agreed to.

189

Houston, Texas, Sept. 24, 1900.

To____C. F. Jones,
C/o W. M. Rice,
500 Madison Ave.,
New York, N. Y.

Please make no disposition of Mr. Rice's remain
until we arrive. We leave tonight, reach New York Thursday morning.

F. A. Rice,

Jas. A. Baker, Jr.

☞ READ THE NOTICE AND AGREEMENT ON BACK. ☜

Telegram dated 24 September 1900 from F.A. Rice and James A. Baker, Jr, to Charlie Jones.

The Gibbs Building, Houston, where Baker had his law office, 1893.

James A. Baker, Jr: New York *World*, 29 January 1902.

The still standing Broadway Chambers Building at 275 Broadway and Chambers Street, where Patrick had his law office: New York Historical Society.

Herald Square, at Broadway and 34th Street, about 1900; New York Herald building in foreground and Hotel Normandie in background: New York Historical Society.

# 1. A Death on Madison Avenue

At about ten o'clock on a balmy Sunday evening in late September 1900, Charles Plowright, a Manhattan undertaker, arrived with his assistant at 500 Madison Avenue. He had been telephoned by the superintendent of the apartment building about an hour earlier and asked to make the necessary funeral arrangements for the remains of William Marsh Rice, a wealthy, aged Texan living in New York.

The stately, chateauesque Berkshire apartment building on Madison Avenue and 52nd Street, now the site of the luxurious Omni Berkshire Place hotel, was one of the finest in New York, just one more example of the gilded elegance of turn-of-the-century New York City.[1] It was a time of great wealth and privilege for some – in contrast to the extreme poverty of the many immigrants arriving in New York at the time. The city was a great magnet – the leading centre of commerce, society, and culture in North America – drawing people from all over the continent.[2]

Rice had lived in a large, sparsely furnished, fifth-floor apartment with his twenty-five-year-old valet, Charlie Jones, for the past four years. There were no pictures on the walls – only a large map of the world hanging in the parlor.

The superintendent introduced Plowright to Albert Patrick, a lawyer, who was clearly in charge of the arrangements, and to Dr Walker Curry, Rice's physician. Dr Curry asked the undertaker for a blank death certificate, which the doctor then filled out. Dated Sunday, 23 September 1900, the certificate stated:[3]

William Marsh Rice
84 years, 6 months, 9 days
widowed
retired merchant
resident in City of New York: 17 years

'I hereby certify,' Dr Curry wrote at the bottom of the form, 'that I attended deceased from April 16th, 1900 to September 23rd, 1900, that I last saw him alive on the 23rd day of September, 1900, that he died on the 23rd day of September, 1900, about 8 o'clock, P.M., and that to the best of my knowledge and belief the cause of his death was: Old age and weak heart; immediate cause, indigestion followed by collicqotue [sic] diarrhoea with mental worry.'

Patrick asked that the body be cremated as soon as possible, without embalming. The undertaker explained, however, that at least twenty-four hours would be required to get the furnace at the crematorium to the required temperature. New York was experiencing Indian summer weather at the time. Something would have to be done in the meantime, Plowright said, to prevent the body from decomposing:

'What would you suggest?' Patrick asked.
'Embalm it,' replied Plowright.
'Go ahead and do it,' Patrick ordered.[4]

For Plowright's assistant, John Potter, this would be a very routine job, just one more in the close to one thousand embalmings in his six-year career. It would, however, turn out to be perhaps the crucial event in the later murder charge against Albert T. Patrick.

Embalming was an increasingly important activity in the United States, unlike in Europe, where it was still infrequently used. Embalming had gained respectability during the American Civil War when the government paid for the embalming of dead soldiers to preserve their remains while they were being transported to their hometowns for burial. It was given even greater legitimacy when Lincoln's body was embalmed.[5]

Potter lifted the 120-pound Rice from the couch onto the embalming board that he had brought with him. A small incision was made in the artery on the underside of the right arm above the elbow. Three pints of Falcon embalming fluid, a commercial mixture primarily of formaldehyde and water, were pumped into Rice's body through the right brachial artery, using the then standard manual injection pump with its elongated hollow needle.[6] The vein was not opened to allow the blood to be removed, as was usually done. The effect, therefore, was to force the blood into the heart and other cavities. The whole procedure took less than thirty minutes. Potter arranged to call back the next day with a casket and to have the cremation certificate signed.

The undertakers left and Patrick returned to his boarding house at West 58th Street, telling the young elevator operator as he left that Rice had remembered him in his will. Jones reluctantly stayed alone in the apartment, with 'old man Rice,' as he was often referred to, lying on the embalming board.

# 2. Certifying Checks

On Monday morning, Potter returned to Rice's apartment with a black coffin. Albert Patrick was already there. Although Rice had not been religious, arrangements were made to have a 'proper Christian' funeral in the apartment at ten o'clock the next morning and to have the body taken to Long Island for cremation at noon. Patrick signed the cremation certificate.

Patrick had four checks in his possession totaling $250,000 made out to himself. They were all signed 'W.M. Rice' and were dated 22 September, the day before Rice died. Patrick had to move quickly to have the checks certified before the institutions on which the checks were drawn learned of Rice's death. Both Patrick's office assistant as well as the young lawyer in his law office were not at work that morning as they were Jewish and it was the Jewish New Year. Patrick, however, had sent a telegram earlier that morning to John Potts, a lawyer who rented office space from him, requesting that he meet him at his boarding house. Both Potts and Patrick were originally from Texas, and they had known each other since they were very young children growing up in Navasota, about fifty miles northwest of Houston. Patrick gave Potts a check for $25,000 drawn on the Fifth Avenue Trust Company. Potts had no difficulty having it certified at the trust company.

Patrick had also arranged for a message to be left under the door of David Short's house in Brooklyn, asking Short to meet him at his office on lower Broadway as soon as possible. Short, although not a lawyer, rented space from Patrick. Patrick gave Short a check for certification for $25,000 drawn on the Swenson Bank. Short – from Wichita, Kansas, and a resident of New York for five or six years – was a promoter of various borderline schemes. He was involved in Cuban land speculation, promoted a device called 'The Bust Developer,' and sold stock in the Dr Hortelius Medicine Company, which produced medicines for 'lost manhood.' His main enterprise at this time, however, and one with which Potts was associated, was the 'U.S. Health Reports.'[1] Not only did these reports falsely appear to be emanating from a government department (the documents had a picture of the US Capitol and claimed to come out of Washington), but no reports were, in fact, ever published. Very laudatory articles were prepared by Short and others on various commercial products and shown to the manufacturers named, who were usually more than pleased to order reprints of the articles ('reprinted from the U.S. Health Reports') to use for their own promotion purposes. The operation had been going on for a number of years, but an issue of the reports had yet to appear.

At about eleven o'clock, Short entered the second-floor office of the Swenson Bank at 15 Wall Street, the old Drexel Building. (Like most of the buildings mentioned in this story, the Drexel Building was later torn down and replaced by a larger structure, in this case the New York Stock Exchange.) The Swensons, like Rice, were originally from Texas, and Rice had over the years done much of his banking with the firm.

Short laid the check on the counter. Following his normal practice, the cashier took the check to the rear office of the head clerk, Walter Wetherbee, for his approval. Wetherbee, also a former Texan, had handled Rice's banking at Swenson and Sons for over fifteen years and the cashier had cashed Rice's checks for over twenty years. They were suspicious. Neither had ever seen the person presenting the check and neither knew Albert Patrick.

Wetherbee had reason to believe that those close to Rice were interested in improperly securing part of his great wealth. On New Year's Day, 1900, about nine months earlier, Wetherbee had gone to see Rice on a personal basis to borrow money from him, but Rice had refused the loan. Two days later, however – according to Wetherbee – Rice's valet, Charlie Jones, went to Wetherbee's house in Brooklyn and made a proposition to him: if Wetherbee would be an executor and arrange a witness to a new will of Rice's – Wetherbee had witnessed the then existing 1896 will – the beneficiaries of the new will would assist Wetherbee financially. Wetherbee refused the offer and the next day reported the incident to the Swenson Bank. Rice was never told of the matter, but a notarized affidavit was later prepared by Wetherbee about his conversation with Jones.

The body of the check to Patrick was clearly in Jones' handwriting, as was usually the case with checks by Rice. But was the signature in fact Rice's? Wetherbee and the cashier hastily compared Rice's signature with a large number of canceled checks that had previously been signed by Rice. Short tapped nervously on the counter in the main office. The cashier stuck his head out of the back office: 'Sorry to keep you waiting. The person to sign the certification is not here just now. Sit down and make yourself comfortable.' He disappeared again into the back room. When carefully examining the check, they noticed that it was endorsed 'Albert T. Patrick' but had actually been made out to 'Abert T. Patrick.' The 'l' had been omitted from 'Albert.' The cashier returned the check to Short uncertified and told him to get Rice to prepare a new and proper check.

Short returned about half an hour later with a second endorsement on the check – 'Abert T. Patrick.' Swenson was shown the check. It was again compared with earlier ones. 'I want to speak to Rice,' Swenson said. The cashier called 500 Madison Avenue. The telephone was in the lobby and was answered by the bellboy, who handed the phone to Jones, standing nearby as if waiting for a call. 'That cheque is all right and you must pay it,' Jones assured the cashier. 'We want to speak to Rice personally.' 'That would be difficult,' Jones replied; 'he is hard of hearing and also has trouble coming to the phone.' The cashier was insistent: 'Jones, Mr. Swenson would like to speak to Mr. Rice immediately.' Jones hung up and called Patrick for instructions. The Swenson clerk phoned back: 'Bring Rice to the phone.' 'Mr. Rice is dead,' Jones replied: 'He died last night.' The check was returned to Short uncertified.

Patrick and Potts called in person on Swenson, who had refused to discuss the matter with Patrick over the phone. 'Our mutual friend is dead,' Patrick told Swenson, and explained that he had not told Swensons about Rice's death because he knew that the check would not be certified if Swensons knew the full facts. The certification of the check was unimportant, Patrick said, showing Swenson a document, purportedly signed by Rice and dated 7 September 1900, giving Patrick an assignment of all of Rice's property 'real, personal and mixed, of whatever nature and wherever situated.'[2] The funeral, Patrick said, would be the next day and Rice would then be cremated. He died, Patrick added, from eating too many bananas.

Later that day, Short had another check, drawn on the Fifth Avenue Trust Company, certified for $135,000. 'All right,' Patrick is reported to have said, 'I guess I can get along now.'[3]

Immediately after Patrick and Potts left Swensons, the bankers called on their lawyers, Bowers and Sands, who advised them to contact at once Rice's lawyer in Houston, Texas, James A. Baker, Jr.

# 3. Houston, Texas

Houston, now the fourth largest metropolis in the United States, was then a city of under fifty thousand.[1] Named after Sam Houston, the first president of Texas and the legendary figure who had defeated Santa Anna and the Mexican forces in 1836 just outside Houston at the battle of San Jacinto, the city slowly emerged as a vital force in the economic development of Texas. Houston was connected to the coastal city of Galveston, forty miles to the southeast, by a waterway that could be used by barges and small craft. (The canal was made navigable in 1913, and Houston is now the third largest port in the United States.) Moreover, the city was an important rail junction, not only on the north–south axis between the Gulf of Mexico and St Louis, but, more importantly, on the Southern Pacific line connecting Los Angeles with New Orleans.

The city surpassed Galveston in population for the first time in the year 1900 and would double its population in the next ten years, while Galveston's would actually decline. The major reason for Galveston's decline was the devastating hurricane there on 8 September 1900, two weeks before Rice died. Over six thousand people perished in what was – and still is – the greatest natural disaster in US history. Houston, being away from the coast, was much less seriously affected. Its natural growth was later spurred by the major oil discovery at Humble, just north of Houston, in 1904.

William Marsh Rice had actively participated in the growth of Houston.[2] In 1838, at the age of twenty-two, he had left Springfield, Massachusetts, where he had been born and raised, for Texas. The depression on the east coast at the time and the prospect of becoming a successful merchant in the newly independent Lone Star State made the move a natural one. Unfortunately, all his goods were lost at sea on the voyage to Galveston. Nevertheless, he prospered in a number of different fields. Indeed, by the year 1860 he was the wealthiest person in Houston, worth over $750,000, and was possibly the second wealthiest person in all of Texas.

When Rice died in 1900 he was probably the wealthiest Texan in the United States. He had been engaged in a great variety of activities: a merchant, supplying liquor to taverns and hotels, even though he was a teetotaler; a shipowner, bringing ice from New England to Texas; a cotton planter, owning at least fifteen slaves before the Civil War; a railroad entrepreneur, participating in the early 1850s in the financing and construction of the first railroads in the Houston area; and many others, such as a timber merchant, vegetable-oil processor, rancher, hotel owner, and moneylender. Rice's advice to a friend the month before he died illustrates his careful approach in business and why his investments were usually successful: 'Money should only be loaned upon undoubted security,' he wrote. 'The papers should be drawn by a good lawyer of your own selection and the borrower should pay the lawyers fee for attending to it. The property given as security should be of fifty percent more value than the money loaned.'[3]

For many years, Rice relied heavily on James A. Baker and his firm, Baker and Botts,[4] for legal advice. Baker had known Rice since 1877. His father, Judge Baker, had been involved with Rice's affairs ever since moving with his family from Huntsville, Texas, to Houston in 1872 to join the law firm of Gray, Botts, and Baker. Even before that, Judge Gray, the senior partner in the firm, had handled Rice's transactions, possibly starting in the early 1840s. So, the association with the law firm had been a very long one.

The forty-three-year-old Baker was known as a 'hardworking, methodical, exact and thorough lawyer' with a 'vigorous, powerful, firm, almost imperious nature'[5] – qualities not unlike those of his grandson, James A. Baker III, the former secretary of state. Baker's 'impeccable dress, erect carriage, and finely chiseled features'[6] were also like those of his grandson.

Baker had been born in Huntsville, Texas, in 1857, attended school there, and then graduated with an AB from the Texas Military Institute in Austin. Because of his military background in college he joined the socially desirable Houston Light Guards,[7] later becoming a captain. Throughout his life he was known as Captain Baker, although he never served in the full-time army. He did not attend a law school – the University of Texas Law School did not open until 1883[8] – but instead learned law in his father's law firm in Houston, which he entered in 1877, and was admitted to the Texas Bar in 1880. He was associated with Baker and Botts for sixty-four years, until his death in 1941. (His son, James A. Baker II, was later also a member of Baker and Botts, but his grandson, James A. Baker III, could not join the firm because of an antinepotism policy developed in the 1930s, and instead went to the rival Houston firm of Andrews and Kurth.)

Baker and Botts was a four-man law firm in the year 1900, not unlike other important corporate/commercial law firms at the time in New York, Chicago, or Toronto.[9] The firm was not a collection of self-practitioners, as many firms were, but an example of the new breed of law firm then emerging[10] – a true partnership in which all the members of the firm shared responsibility for the work. Today, with its offices on ten floors of the fifty-story One Shell Plaza, dominating the Houston skyline, and over four hundred lawyers and offices in Washington, New York, and other major cities, it is also not unlike other corporate/commercial law firms in New York, Chicago, or Toronto.

The firm was then the oldest as well as the dominant corporate firm in Houston. Known as the 'lawyers in three-piece suits,'[11] their major client since 1893 was the Southern Pacific railroad, which had acquired Rice's Houston and Texas Central Railway in 1885 in its development of a southern route from California. The firm handled all of the litigation, corporate, administrative, and lobbying work in Texas for the Southern Pacific railroad.

Rice was, of course, a very major client and the litigation that stemmed from his death dominated the firm's activities for many years. Baker's partner, R.S. Lovett, said several months later that 'the Rice case is of course the most important that we have ever had or are likely to have.'[12] This may still be true, although the firm's recent successful handling of the Pennzoil multibillion-dollar action against Texaco might well be a rival for that honor.[13]

# 4. Telegrams

Sometime between three and four o'clock in the afternoon Houston-time, on Monday, 24 September, a telegram from Charlie Jones was delivered to James A. Baker, Jr, at his law office in the Gibbs Building in downtown Houston:[1]

Mr. Rice died 8 o'clock last night under care of physician. Death certificate old age, weak heart, diarahue. Left instructions to be interred at Milwaukee with wife. Funeral ten A.M. to-morrow, at 500 Madison Avenue. When will you come?

C.F. Jones

A similar telegram was sent to Rice's only living brother, Frederick A. Rice. Nothing was said about cremation. Other telegrams were sent to relatives and friends throughout the United States telling them of the funeral. (The long-distance telephone was not commercially developed for such lengthy distances until 1915.) Baker wired his reply:

Dispatch just received. I suppose you will accompany remains to Milwaukee. In that event, please place all papers and the apartment in charge of N.S. Meldrum, who is now in New York and who will call on you at once. Please co-operate with Mr. Meldrum in preserving everything intact until I can reach New York. I leave tonight. Please meet me there as soon as you can. Answer.

Jas. A. Baker, Jr.[2]

Meldrum was a Texas railway official, then in New York on business.
(Throughout this story, the reader will no doubt be struck – as I was
– with the apparent ease with which people traveled across the continent.)

It was clear that Captain Baker had to go to New York to settle Rice's
affairs. He had prepared a will for Rice in 1896 and was named in it
as one of the executors. The will had been sent by Baker to Rice in
New York in September 1896 for execution and as far as Baker knew
was in Rice's safety deposit box in Manhattan.

The will had made a number of specific bequests to relatives and others
and then had left the residue of Rice's estate, worth well over five million
dollars, to the Rice Institute. Baker had incorporated the institute in 1891,
with a $200,000 initial endowment from Rice, payable on Rice's death,
and had been named the chairman of the board. For the next fifty years,
until he died in 1941, Baker remained chairman of Rice University, as
it was renamed in 1960.[3] (In July 1990 the university attracted international recognition when it hosted a meeting of the leaders of the seven
western industrial nations.)[4]

The law firm had been keeping in close touch with Rice, who seemed
to have been in reasonable health and able to deal with his business affairs.
Baker had corresponded with him concerning damage arising out of the
Galveston hurricane and the later destruction by fire of Rice's Merchants
and Planters Oil Company in Houston. Exactly one week before Rice
died Baker had wired him the news: 'Merchants and Planters Oil Mill
entirely destroyed by fire at noon to-day. Believed to be fully insured.'[5]
And the following day Baker sent another telegram: 'Directors of the
Merchants and Planters Oil Co. are unanimous in opinion that Company's plant should be rebuilt without delay. What are your views? Answer quick.'[6] Rice favored rebuilding and authorized the use of most
of the cash he had on deposit in New York for this purpose. Drafts
had started arriving at the end of the week for Rice's signature. A draft
for $25,000 upon Swenson and Sons was brought to Rice's apartment
for his signature on Saturday, 22 September, but Jones asked the caller
to put off the transaction until Monday on the ground that Rice was
not well.

The two other senior members of the firm, Lovett and Parker, had
recently spent time with Rice in New York and they had both found
Rice in good health. R.S. Lovett[7] – or Judge Lovett as he was known,
although he was never a judge – was born at San Jacinto and raised
on a farm. Called to the bar in 1882, two years after Baker, he worked

for railways in Houston until he joined Baker and Botts in 1892. (Railways were his life, and in 1904 he moved to New York to become general counsel for Southern Pacific and Union Pacific and all their affiliated lines in the Harriman system. In 1909, when Harriman died, Lovett became president of both Union Pacific and Southern Pacific.)

Lovett had visited Rice twice in September when he was in New York in connection with the affairs of the Southern Pacific. The first visit early in the month was a social call, at which time Rice claimed his health was very good, although he had only been out of the house once since the beginning of the year. The subsequent visit, five days before Rice's death, was in response to Baker's request to have Lovett ascertain Rice's intentions with respect to the rebuilding of the mill. On this occasion, according to Lovett, Rice seemed even stronger than on the previous visit. Lovett had left New York on Friday, arriving in Houston early Monday morning. The telegram to Baker was, therefore, the first that Lovett had heard of Rice's death.

The third member of the firm, Edwin B. Parker,[8] had joined Baker and Botts in 1897. Unlike Baker and Lovett, he had attended a law school, graduating from the University of Texas in 1889 and then returning to his home in Missouri to work for various railroad interests there. Parker had spent two hours talking with Rice in New York at the end of August. 'In the course of the conversation,' Parker later wrote, 'Mr. Rice remarked that his general health was very good, and that the only trouble he experienced of late was a lameness in one of his arms, due to an old injury which he had suffered in a railroad accident years ago.'[9]

Although there was some concern by Baker and the other members of the firm that Rice's health had deteriorated so quickly, there was nothing concrete to cause suspicion – until the cable from S.M. Swenson and Sons arrived later in the afternoon. It read:

Jones telephoned this morning Mr. Rice died last night. A lawyer here presented draft for large amount and assignment to himself of all securities and moneys in our hands. He informed us funeral tomorrow body to be cremated. Have consulted Bowers and Sands lawyers thirty one Nassau Street. Think you should have them represent you at once. We have seen them. Answer them and us instantly. Wire Bowers and Sands authority from some relative about disposition of body. Address Bowers and Sands tonight care James W. Gerard Seventeen Gramercy Park, New York City.[10]

Patrick was not identified in the telegram.

Baker and Rice's brother, Frederick, boarded the Monday evening 7:25
p.m. Southern Pacific from Houston, due to arrive in Manhattan at 6:30
a.m. Thursday morning. Before leaving, they dispatched a series of telegrams to New York. Norman Meldrum was asked to see Jones and
take charge of Rice's papers: 'I have asked Jones to place all papers and
the apartment in your charge until I reach New York ... Please see him
at once and wire answer.'[11] Meldrum was just starting out with a party
to the theatre and wired back that he would see Jones in the morning.

The law firm of Bowers and Sands was asked to 'see Meldrum and
Jones at once and do what you can to preserve papers' until Baker's
arrival; and the firm of Swenson and Sons was instructed to cooperate
with Bowers and Sands and 'under no circumstances recognize any drafts
or assignments.' The safety deposit company was asked not to let anyone
into Rice's box. Finally, instructions were sent not to dispose of the
body. F.A. Rice wired Bowers and Sands: 'As the only surviving brother
and nearest relative of William M. Rice, I request that his body be held
until I reach New York.' And both Baker and F.A. Rice told Jones:
'Please make no disposition of Mr. Rice's remains until we arrive. We
leave tonight, reach New York Thursday morning.'[12]

# 5. The Authorities

James W. Gerard of Bowers and Sands had no doubt that the authorities
should be notified of possible wrongdoing. Swensons, however, were
reluctant to do so as they felt they might be sued for malicious prosecution. Gerard said he would personally go to see the district attorney
on his own responsibility.[1]

Gerard came from an old, respectable, and wealthy New York family.
His maternal grandfather had been a captain in the Revolutionary Army
and his paternal grandfather had been a lawyer who had established Bowers and Sands in 1812. The family mixed with the Astors and Belmonts,
and Gerard was a noted polo player. He was known for his bluntness
and frankness, characteristics which later made him popular throughout
the United States as the US ambassador to Germany during the crucial
years 1913-17 and subsequently when he was frequently mentioned as
a possible Democratic candidate to succeed Woodrow Wilson.[2]

Late Monday afternoon, Gerard went to see the district attorney at
the Court House. He knew District Attorney Gardiner reasonably well,
although Gardiner was much older than the thirty-three-year-old Gerard.
Both were active Democrats (the Democratic Tammany Hall organiza-

tion was then in control of New York City) and both were military men. Gerard was active in the New York National Guard, having recently served in Cuba in the Spanish-American War, emerging as a major. Asa Bird Gardiner[3] had served with the Northern Forces in the Civil War and had been awarded a Congressional Medal of Honor for 'conspicuous bravery and distinguished conduct during the Gettysburg Campaign.' Colonel Gardiner remained in the army until 1888 as a professor of law at West Point and had been elected district attorney of New York in 1897. In December 1900, however, he was removed as district attorney by the Republican governor Theodore Roosevelt for ignoring all charges against gamblers and for not prosecuting the corrupt chief of police, 'Big Bill' Devery, who had been indicted by the grand jury.[4]

Gardiner agreed with Gerard that the case looked highly suspicious and called the Detective Bureau. Detective Sergeant James Vallely[5] was assigned to the case.

The Detective Bureau, headed by George McCluskey,[6] who was out of town on vacation at the time, was located at police headquarters or, as it was called, Central Office, a since-destroyed old gray four-story building on Mulberry Street, just north of Houston Street.[7] In spite of the poor reputation of the force during Devery's reign, the Detective Bureau itself was highly regarded. Established by the well-respected Thomas Byrnes in 1880, it had forty detective sergeants.[8] Byrnes always maintained that he had a better department than Scotland Yard. Vallely had joined the bureau in 1884 and at age forty-six was one of the most senior detectives there. The following year he would gain notoriety as the chief of detectives for the Pan-American Exhibition in Buffalo who personally captured the assassin of President McKinley. Byrnes' formula for success was to appoint persons who were good judges of human nature and who coupled that with the habit of close observation.[9] The Byrnes-trained Vallely immediately assigned a person to observe Rice's apartment.

Gerard, accompanied by a uniformed police sergeant, first called on Dr Curry on East 61st Street. The sixty-five-year-old Curry was a prominent New York doctor, described in a contemporary publication as 'greatly esteemed by his professional brethren.'[10] A native of Georgia and a graduate of the University of Pennsylvania Medical School, he had been a surgeon for the Confederacy during the Civil War with upward of forty thousand sick and wounded soldiers under his charge. Curry had been Patrick's doctor for over five years and in the spring of 1900 had treated Jones, who was then in the hospital with pneumonia.

Patrick, he assured his callers, was a fine gentleman whom Rice greatly trusted.

Rice died from natural causes, Curry said. He had examined him Sunday morning in Rice's sitting room overlooking 5th Avenue and had found him to have had a weak pulse and irregular breathing, but otherwise to be in fair health. Rice had been his patient for over six months and he had been seeing him regularly. Indeed, Curry had seen him on each of the four days before he died. Rice's condition, he said, was aggravated by worry over the consequences of the Galveston hurricane. It was, however, eating bananas, Curry added, that was the major cause of death. Several days before he died, a friend had recommended bananas and Rice had eaten four or five cooked bananas and the same number of raw ones. The result was a very weakened condition caused by indigestion and diarrhoea.

Gerard's next stop was the business office of the U.S. Cremation Company. Cremation was still considered an extraordinary procedure in the United States in the year 1900. The first crematory in America had been constructed in 1876 and the first in New York was built on Long Island by the U.S. Cremation Company in 1885.[11]

The order for cremation, Gerard saw, had been signed by Patrick, and a letter to Patrick purportedly signed by Rice, dated 3 August 1900, had been given by Patrick to the company:

Concerning the matter of cremation. I sent down to the United States Crematory office for information and got two circulars which are very interesting. I will show them to you when you come up ... It seems to me that the law should not allow dead bodies to be buried all over the country, after dying of all kinds of deseases [sic]. I would much rather have my body burned than eat [sic] by worms or stolen by some medical student and carved to pieces. If I should die I want you to see that I am not embalmed as they fill you with chemicals when they embalm you, but I want you to have my body cremated at once and my ashes put in an urn and interred with my late wife Elizabeth B. Rice.[12]

The cremation was scheduled for Tuesday morning, directly after the funeral.

# 6. Monday Evening

Gerard and Detective-Sergeant Vallely were waiting in Reisenweber's restaurant in nearby Columbus Circle when they received word from a detective that Patrick had arrived back at his boarding house. Gerard had gone to the house a few hours earlier, but a servant had said that 'Mr. and Mrs. Patrick were not at home.' At about ten o'clock, Gerard and Vallely knocked at the front door. A tall woman in black opened the door. 'Is Albert Patrick in?' Vallely asked. The woman went to the back room and called Patrick. Vallely helped her light the gas lamp in the front room. Patrick emerged.

'This is Mr. Patrick,' the woman stated.

'I am James Gerard from Bowers and Sands, and,' indicating Vallely, 'this is my assistant at the firm, McAndrew.' Gerard later wrote that Vallely's 'very detective air and thick shoes would have proclaimed his calling to a child.'

'Swensons,' Gerard went on to say, 'are concerned about the unusual events today. The firm wants to avoid any possible misunderstandings.'

'I do not intend to take action,' Patrick said: 'I needed the money then, but have now made other arrangements and so I don't need it now.' 'I should tell you,' Patrick went on, 'that I have a will by Rice naming me an executor and also possess an assignment of all of Rice's property.'

'Are you a beneficiary under the will?' Vallely asked.

'No, I don't get one cent.' 'But Swensons will handle all the financial matters,' Patrick added.

'What was the use of a will,' Gerard asked, 'if you had an assignment?'

'That is a secret,' Patrick replied.[1]

The conversation turned to Rice's death. Patrick told them that he had died from eating bananas. 'An old woman had come to the house,' Patrick said, 'and told him bananas were a good thing for him to eat. He ate nine of them. This caused or at least hastened his death.'

Gerard asked what would happen to Rice's remains, knowing, of course, that arrangements had been finalized to have the body cremated the next day. 'The body will be kept until the relatives arrive on Thursday and will then be buried in Wisconsin,' Patrick replied.

Gerard went home, but Vallely went on to the Berkshire Apartments. Jones had just said good-bye to some of Rice's old family friends who had called to pay their respects and was getting ready for bed when the elevator boy knocked to say that four lawyers from downtown were

there to see him. The four 'lawyers' were Vallely and three other detectives. Jones invited them to come up to the apartment.

All the funeral arrangements, Jones said, were in Patrick's hands. 'Why
did you obey Patrick?' Vallely asked. 'Mr. Rice had told me to obey
Mr. Patrick the same as if Mr. Rice had given the order,' Jones replied.
The detectives left about two o'clock in the morning. Vallely warned
Jones not to let anybody touch the body, adding that he would be back
early in the morning and would very much like to have breakfast with
Jones. 'Would you like to see the body before you leave?' Jones asked.
Vallely declined the invitation.

While the detectives were there, a representative of the *Houston Post*
called on Jones. The *Post* had wired the reporter to gather material for
an obituary for the morning paper. Jones referred the reporter to Patrick
for details and the newspaperman phoned Patrick. 'Rice will be buried
in Wisconsin,' Patrick said, and added that Rice's life was uneventful
and unworthy of newspaper notice.[2]

Norman Meldrum, who had been asked by Baker to see Jones, arrived
after the theatre. 'All of Mr. Rice's papers were in Mr. Patrick's hands,'
Jones said: 'Patrick was in charge of everything.' Meldrum left, knowing
something was wrong. He had heard of Patrick and knew that he represented a party that was then in litigation with Rice. Meldrum immediately wired Baker in Houston: 'Called on Jones since wiring. He says
all papers turned over to A.T. Patrick on Rice's written request. Will
see Patrick in morning.'[3]

# 7. The Funeral

The Tuesday morning newspapers contained no hint of possible wrongdoing. The New York papers simply contained a routine notice under
the 'Died' column:

> RICE – On Sunday, September 23, 1900,
> WILLIAM MARSH RICE,
> 84 years, 6 months, 9 days.
> Funeral from his late residence, 500 Madison av.,
> on Tuesday, September 25, at ten A.M.
> Relatives and friends are invited to attend.[1]

Detective Sergeant Vallely was at the Berkshire before seven in the
morning. He had already received a detective's report that Patrick had

gone to his office on the thirteenth floor of the newly constructed – and still standing – Broadway Chambers Building,[2] at 275 Broadway, late Monday night and had attracted the night watchman's attention when the toilet, clogged with papers, overflowed to the floor below. Patrick later called on Jones before returning to his boarding house in the early hours of Tuesday morning.

Vallely and Jones went to a nearby restaurant for breakfast. When they returned to the apartment, Patrick confronted Vallely:

'What does all this mean? You are not a lawyer; you are a Central Office man.'
'Nothing like that. Do I look like one?'
'There is nothing wrong here. I do not see why you people are around.'[3]

At ten o'clock, an assistant minister from the 5th Avenue Episcopal Church of the Heavenly Rest[4] began the service. About twenty persons sat staring at the open black casket. Several nephews had come down from Springfield, Massachusetts, where Rice was born, and a few old friends had come over from New Jersey, where Rice and his late wife had lived for many years before moving to Manhattan. Patrick greeted them when they arrived and assured them that they had been remembered in the will. Mrs Van Alstyn, a friend of Rice's first wife and the person who had suggested that Rice eat bananas, was there, as were Dr and Mrs Curry, Potts, Meldrum, and Gerard. Vallely and three other detectives tried to blend in with the mourners.

When the very brief service was over, Detective Vallely stepped forward and ordered Potter, who was in charge of the funeral arrangements, not to touch the body: 'there is a coroner's warrant for an autopsy,' Vallely said. Earlier that morning, Coroner Edward Hart had consulted with District Attorney Gardiner about what to do. 'You have all the authority you need,' was the DA's advice.[5] The horse-drawn morgue wagon was waiting downstairs. 'As the services were beginning,' the New York *World* reported the next day, 'there appeared in Madison Avenue a vehicle seldom seen in that neighborhood. It was a dilapidated, soiled affair, weather-beaten and suggestive in many ways of the slums.'[6] Potter persuaded Cusick, the driver, to permit Rice's body to be taken to the morgue in the undertaker's more-fashionable wagon, which was then summoned from Plowright's funeral home. The wagon had not been waiting at the Berkshire because in the middle of the night Patrick had telephoned Potter to delay the cremation until Rice's brother arrived.

As the casket was being carefully taken into the elevator, Vallely said to Patrick and Jones: 'You are requested to come down to the Central Office for a talk.'

# 8. En Route

James A. Baker and Frederick Rice, on Southern Pacific's train no. 36, had now passed through New Orleans and while the funeral was taking place in New York were about to head north. At Mobile, Alabama, a telegram from Baker's partner, R.S. Lovett, was handed to them by the stationmaster: 'Telegram from Meldrum reads as follows: Called on Jones. He says all papers turned over to A.T. Patrick on Rice's written request. Will see Patrick in morning.'[1]

Both Baker and Frederick Rice knew the thirty-four-year-old Patrick, as did members of the Baker and Botts law firm. Lovett in Houston had immediately wired Meldrum and Gerard in New York: 'A.T. Patrick, a lawyer now living in New York, formerly resided here. He has never represented Mr. Rice, but on contrary, has been employed adversely to him in litigation growing out of Mrs. Rice's will. We know he did not have Mr. Rice's confidence.'[2]

Mrs Elizabeth Rice – Rice's second wife, whom he had married in 1867 – died in 1896 leaving a will which attempted to dispose of a large part of her husband's property to members of her own family and to various charities. She was entitled to do so under the Texas community property law if, and only if, Rice was domiciled in Texas at the time of her death.[3] Rice was furious and through his lawyer, Baker, contested the will, claiming that for over twenty years he had been domiciled in New York. Four years later, however, the case had still not been tried or settled. Orren Holt,[4] a prominent Houston lawyer and later mayor of Houston, acted for the relatives of Mrs Rice. He had drafted the will and was named as the executor, with a very generous compensation provision (10 percent of all funds taken in and expended). Much of the evidence relating to Rice's domicile was necessarily taken in New York. Holt's legal representative there was Albert T. Patrick.

In the fall of 1899, Baker had had considerable contact with Patrick when Baker had spent several months in New York in connection with the case, staying at Rice's apartment. There were frequent meetings between Patrick and Baker as they examined witnesses. There was also talk of settlement. Holt and Patrick had offered to settle the case for

$250,000, but neither Rice nor Baker would consider it. The most that Baker would offer on Rice's behalf was $50,000.

Frederick Rice had known Patrick for many years. Patrick's father had been a Confederate captain and quartermaster of Gould's Battalion in Walker's Texas Division in the Civil War.[5] Captain Patrick had later been the agent of Rice's Houston and Texas Central Railway in Navasota and still later in Austin. In the summer of 1880, Patrick, who was then fourteen, had received a railway pass from Frederick Rice. Patrick later stated that this pass had been made out to 'A.T.' Patrick rather than to Albert and from that time on he used the initial 'T' as his middle name.[6]

Patrick had graduated from engineering at Texas Agricultural and Mechanical College in 1883 and had worked for a time as a surveyor for Rice's Houston and Texas Central railroad. He then entered the University of Texas Law School in Austin, graduating in 1886, without distinction.[7] While at law school, Patrick had joined the Austin Grays, the governor's bodyguard; in 1888 he became the brigade quartermaster-general and in 1889 he was made the brigade inspector-general. It is likely that Baker, as a captain in the Houston Light Guards, would have had some involvement and even perhaps rivalry with Patrick during this period through the annual drill competitions.[8]

In 1890 Patrick moved his law practice from Austin to Houston. He established a reputation as an aggressive lawyer and was involved in politics, at least to the extent of helping to defeat the election of a corrupt judge. Every lawyer in Houston knew about another controversy involving Patrick. In 1893 he became involved in a lawsuit in which a US congressman, J.C. Hutcheson,[9] appeared for the other side.[10] Patrick claimed Hutcheson was involved in sharp practices in acting when he had a conflict of interest and he attempted to have Hutcheson barred from practicing in the federal courts and from continuing as a congressman. In the end, Hutcheson was cleared and charges of unprofessional conduct were threatened against Patrick. It was about this time that Patrick decided to move permanently from Texas to New York.

A second telegram from Meldrum, forwarded by Lovett, was given to Baker when the train pulled into Montgomery, Alabama; it read: 'Have deferred burial until Baker arrives. Patrick holds assignments to everything. Safe deposit vault and Swenson Bank balance cannot be disturbed until Baker arrives.'[11] Nothing was said about a new will. Baker was understandably worried that Patrick might have a new will revoking the

1896 one, which, it will be recalled, had left the bulk of the estate to the Rice Institute. Baker wired Lovett from Montgomery: 'Messages to Mobile and Montgomery received. Is Patrick in possession of a will?'[12]

Baker had drafted the 1896 will shortly after Rice's wife died. New York law limited a testator's right to give more than half of his or her estate to charity if there was a spouse or child surviving.[13] This limitation now no longer applied to Rice. 'I think I had better have a will drawn up and sent to me to be executed,' Rice wrote to Baker from New York on 15 September 1896: 'It need not be long and can be easily changed if necessary.'[14] Baker prepared a will according to the simple instructions Rice had given and sent it to New York for execution. Several weeks later, Rice informed Baker by letter: 'I have completed the will and placed it in my box in vault of New York Deposit Co., Corner Liberty St. and Broadway. You are the only person other than myself who can have access to it – when you have the combination. Have made no change in the Will.'[15]

Baker had never in fact seen the executed will. He must have said something to Jones about it when he was in New York in the fall of 1899, because Jones sent the following letter to Baker on 18 January 1900:

I have seen the will. It is now in the house and has been opened, is all in your hand writing except 10 or 12 words. Is witnessed by W.O. Wetherbee, and W.F. Harmon, both of Brooklyn and employed by the Swensons. I do not like to assume the responsibility of sending it but if you insist I will do so, or send you a copy of it as we are expecting you here soon. Any letters concerning this will reach me addressed c/o E. Koser, 248 East 52nd Street.[16]

This letter is surprising because Baker is obviously having dealings with Jones behind Rice's back, with correspondence not sent to Rice's apartment, but to a friend of Jones'. The letter, contained in the Rice archives, was never made known to the defense or made public. It raises, of course, questions about Baker's personal relationship with Jones, a relationship that becomes important later in the story.

On Wednesday morning, Lovett sent a further telegram from Texas to Baker at Danville, Virginia: 'Nothing since telegram sent you at Montgomery. New York dispatches morning paper show authorities are holding autopsy, and also that Patrick presented checks for large amounts which were not paid; also indicating that Jones is weakening and I apprehend will disclose all facts. Nothing said about will.'[17] Lovett had not seen the later dispatches discussing the so-called Patrick will when this telegram was sent.

# 9. Probings

After the funeral, Patrick and Jones waited in Captain George McCluskey's office at police headquarters for someone from the district attorney's office to arrive. McCluskey, the head of the Detective Bureau, was still out of town. Patrick took possession of the large leather sofa. At about two o'clock – almost two hours later – Assistant District Attorney James Osborne entered the room.

Osborne was at the time New York's best-known prosecutor.[1] The previous year he had obtained murder convictions in two highly publicized murder cases: against a dentist, Dr Samuel Kennedy, for bludgeoning a woman to death; and against Roland Molineux for killing a woman by poison.[2] A Southerner from Charlotte, North Carolina, he graduated from Columbia Law School in 1885 and a few years later joined the district attorney's office. The forty-one-year-old Osborne had political ambitions and a few years later would run as the Democratic candidate for the office of district attorney for New York. The Rice affair had obvious possibilities for further enhancing his reputation.

Patrick denied that there was anything to warrant an investigation. It was an outrage. He had been Rice's lawyer and had had Rice's complete confidence. Rice, Patrick said, had died a natural death. The new will, Patrick went on, was to carry out Rice's benevolent intentions. Patrick fielded all the questions. Jones said very little. Osborne thanked them and said that, of course, he was only interested in this matter if a crime had been committed and that everyone would have a better idea of where they stood after the autopsy report. As they were leaving the office, Osborne asked Jones if he could have a word with him in private. Jones reluctantly agreed. Why had Jones gone to see Wetherbee the previous January? Osborne asked. What was Jones' proposal to Wetherbee? Jones gave some noncommittal answers. The experienced Osborne knew that he had found a weak link.

The morgue was in a one-story structure on the grounds of the Bellevue Hospital on the East River.[3] Rice's body was laid on one of the four marble slabs. Dr Edward Donlin had been assigned by Coroner Hart to conduct the autopsy.[4] (The office of coroner no longer exists in New York City, having been replaced in 1918 by the office of chief medical examiner.)[5] If Osborne was the best-known lawyer in the DA's office, Donlin was the best-known physician in the coroner's office. A graduate of New York University and the Bellevue Hospital Medical College, he had been a coroner's physician since 1889 and had conducted several thousand autopsies, including the autopsy in the Molineux case.[6]

Donlin performed the hour-long autopsy in the usual way. A long incision was made on the front of the body as well as in the head. Donlin called out his observations to Dr Hamilton Williams,[7] a sixty-year-old Irish-trained doctor who had been a coroner's physician in New York for the past four years. Professor Rudolph Witthaus,[8] professor of toxicology at the Cornell Medical School in Manhattan and the author of a four-volume work on medical jurisprudence, also attended, in case any organs required later chemical analysis. Vallely and three other detectives waited outside the autopsy room for the results.

The brain, heart, liver, spleen, and kidneys, Donlin observed, all appeared normal for a person Rice's age. It was difficult to comment on the stomach and the intestines, he said, because they were greatly affected by the embalming fluid, although they also seemed normal. Incisions in the lungs revealed, however, that they were both somewhat congested with an excess amount of blood and that there was a slight area of consolidated lung tissue in the lower lobe of the right lung.

Professor Witthaus was invited to take whatever organs he wanted for chemical analysis. A graduate of Columbia, the Sorbonne, and the New York University Medical School, the highly respected chemist was the person usually called in by the coroner for such examinations and had been involved in most of the well-known poisoning cases in New York. The intestines and stomach were placed in one jar and the liver, kidneys, and heart in another. These were sealed and placed in an icebox.

'What did you find, Doctor?' Coroner Hart asked Donlin.
'I was unable to discover the cause of death. It is up to Dr. Witthaus.'

Donlin prepared his subsequent report to the coroner from Williams' notes. The 'cause of death' was left blank. Williams is said to have told the office staff: 'There's nothing to it. The old boy died of old age. He ought to have died years ago.'[9]

Detective Vallely returned to police headquarters with the results of the autopsy. Rice's remains were returned to 500 Madison Avenue.

# 10. The Press

The press now knew of the story. Although, according to Meldrum, 'greatest effort is being made to keep yellow journals away,'[1] proceedings at the morgue were routinely covered by the press and it would have been very difficult to keep the events secret, even if the activities at police headquarters had escaped their notice. Reporting of crime at the turn-of-the-century was given even greater prominence than it is given today.[2]

On Wednesday morning, 26 September 1900, newspaper headlines with detailed stories appeared.

The *Times* assigned three reporters to the case. Its headline read:

INVESTIGATING A MILLIONAIRE'S DEATH
AUTOPSY HELD ON THE BODY OF WILLIAM M. RICE
LAWYER PATRICK'S BIG CHECKS.

The *Herald*'s headline stated:

MYSTERY ENSHROUDS MILLIONAIRE'S DEATH
BANKERS, SUSPICIOUS WHEN $25,000 CHECK IS PRESENTED,
NOTIFY CORONER,
AND CREMATION OF WILLIAM MARSH RICE'S BODY IS
STOPPED.
PROFESSOR WITTHAUS WILL MAKE A CHEMICAL ANALYSIS.

Pulitzer's New York *World* had a similar headline:

MILLIONAIRE'S BODY SEIZED BY CORONER
FUNERAL SERVICES OF WILLIAM MARSH RICE INTERRUPTED
IN FASHIONABLE APARTMENT AND THE REMAINS TAKEN TO
THE MORGUE
HIS BANKERS WERE SUSPICIOUS.

Isaac De Forest White, 'one of New York's great reporters,'[3] was assigned by the *World* to the case. The Yale University graduate had a reputation for solving murders the police could not solve.

Hearst's *Evening Journal* – Pulitzer's rival – missed the Tuesday paper, but made up for it with an eight-inch headline on Wednesday evening:

KEPT RICH MAN'S DEATH A SECRET FROM BANKER
CHECKS AT THE CASHIER'S WINDOW FOR A FORTUNE
DETECTIVES PROBE THE MYSTERY
CHEMISTS WILL EXAMINE THE BODY.

Every person with a possible connection to the case was visited and, with the exception of Gerard, everyone was willing to comment on the events. (This form of 'trial by newspaper' would be treated as contempt of court and would not be permitted in England or Canada.)[4] The newspapermen themselves became part of the story and later testified at the trial about statements made by the participants.

Dr Donlin was seen by reporters at his home Tuesday night. 'At present the autopsy has revealed nothing to indicate the probability of foul play,' Donlin stated: 'Professor Witthaus has the viscera and will make a chemical analysis. I do not yet know the ingredients of the embalming fluid.' Dr Curry told the reporter: 'It seems to me that I should have been at the autopsy, but I wasn't.'

Every possible detail was explored. The *Times* reported the opinion of doctors at Bellevue Hospital 'that an analysis under the circumstances would be of little or no value, as the embalming fluid ... contained arsenic, which, being a powerful mineral poison, would destroy any trace of any vegetable poison.' The enterprising *World*, however, discovered the manufacturer of the embalming fluid and interviewed him: 'President Max Huncke of the company said yesterday that the ... Falcon embalming fluid ... does not destroy the original poison. On the contrary the fluid helps to preserve the original poison.'

Chief of Detectives George McCluskey had cut short his vacation and returned to New York. He told reporters on Wednesday: 'There is a great deal to be explained before this matter can be allowed to rest. We have begun a systematic investigation that will be far reaching. There is nothing in the autopsy to suggest foul play in connection with the old man's death, but we have yet to hear from the chemical analysis of the viscera.'[5]

District-Attorney Gardiner was noncommittal: 'No facts in the Rice case have so far been laid before me. Should the facts warrant it, when they are placed before me, I shall act vigorously. As far as I and my assistants are concerned, we know nothing derogatory to Albert T. Patrick, the dead man's counsel. As far as we have heard, he has an excellent professional standing.'[6]

# 11. Explanations

The press descended on Patrick and Jones. The *World* provided a description of Patrick: 'A tall, stoutly built man about forty-years old [in fact, he was only thirty-four], bald-headed and with a closely-cropped red beard ... A man of solid and dignified appearance and courteous in his manner.'[1] Jones was described by the *World* as a 'tall, slender and very intelligent young man ... with clean-cut features, a soft, well-modulated voice, and gentle, unobtrusive manners.'[2] The *World* and other papers sent artists to sketch Patrick and Jones.

Patrick was first seen by the press at his boarding house on Tuesday evening. He had just returned from a long discussion with Meldrum at the Waldorf – at Meldrum's request. Patrick explained to Meldrum that 'Mr. Rice had taken a very strong liking to him' and 'had the utmost confidence in his judgment.' Although under the new will Patrick 'was not legally bound to give anything to anybody ... he had talked over matters generally with Mr. Rice and he thought he had a general idea of what Mr. Rice wanted.' Patrick told Meldrum that he and Jones had been down to police headquarters and that the following day's papers would have quite a write-up about it. The problem, Patrick said, is that with this publicity Holt 'would probably back out' of the agreement to settle the litigation over Mrs Rice's will. Patrick suggested that perhaps he, Patrick, should go down to Washington to meet Baker's train. In any case, he wanted to see Baker before Gerard and Swenson confused him with irrelevant ideas.

At first, Patrick refused to say anything to the waiting press, but when the reporters told him about the stories they were running the next day he agreed to give an explanation of the events. 'I had known Mr. Rice for a great many years,' the *Times* reported Patrick as saying, 'and was his legal adviser ... It was legal for me to have the check certified before the bankers were notified of Mr. Rice's death[3] ... The reason that I wanted the checks certified was that if there should be any litigation over the estate I would have at my disposal money belonging to the estate with which to defend or institute suits. Everything was done in a legal manner.' He also told the reporters that 'Mr. Rice died from natural causes' and repeated the story that he had taken ill after eating nine bananas, 'five baked and four raw.' 'I am not a beneficiary to the extent of one penny,' the *World* reported Patrick as stating: 'The only persons who came in contact with Mr. Rice were Jones, the cook, Dr. Curry and myself. None of these are beneficiaries. Jones and the cook

have lost their positions, the doctor has lost a patient and I have lost
a client.' The checks totaling $250,000 were 'to facilitate certain pending
transactions ... the nature of which I am not at liberty to divulge without
the consent of the heirs.'

Over the next few days, Patrick's career was put under the journalistic
microscope. He had practiced law in New York since 1892, they discovered, and his formal application for membership in the New York
Bar included an affidavit by the chief justice of Texas stating that Patrick
was 'a person of good character and qualifications.'[4] Dispatches from
Texas told of Patrick's unsuccessful attempts to have Congressman Hutcheson, the Texas lawyer mentioned earlier, disbarred from practice and
impeached by Congress. A 'whitewash,' Patrick told the inquiring reporters. The Texas dispatches also referred to a divorce case in Texas
in which Patrick acted for a husband in a successful alienation-of-affection
action against a third party and then acted for the wife in suing the
husband for a divorce. There was nothing improper in such actions, Patrick told the reporters.

The *World* dug up a story about how Patrick had broken a lease on
an apartment by subletting the apartment to 'a negro Republican club,'
which caused the other tenants to move out. 'Patrick then sent me word,'
the landlord is reported as stating, 'that if I would pay him $1,000 he
would take the negro club away. I consulted a lawyer and offered Patrick
$500, but he refused it, and said he wanted $1,000. I held off for a
time, but under advice of counsel I finally agreed to pay the $1,000.
Then Patrick declared I must pay him $2,000 or he would keep the
club there. Before he could put up his price again I paid the $2,000.
He then surrendered the keys of the apartment to me and the club moved.'

Charlie Jones was seen by the press at 500 Madison Avenue. On his
way back from police headquarters, the police observed that he had
stopped at Bloomingdales to tell Miss Mabel Whitney, whom he saw
every Tuesday evening, that he could not see her that night. Earlier
in the year, she had threatened to bring a breach-of-promise suit and
Patrick had advised him to see her once a week. Jones was also seeing
Mabel Whitney's cousin, Maude Mortimer. Indeed, he was to have seen
her on the evening Rice died, but had sent her a telegram that morning:
'Yours received. Cannot call this evening. See letter this date. Charles.'

These amorous activities of Jones were not revealed by him to the
press. Nor did he tell them that another girlfriend, Nellie Creed, had
slept in Rice's apartment on many occasions, including the Friday evening
before Rice died. Rather, the twenty-six-year-old valet told about grow-

ing up on a farm just outside Houston, working on boats and as a locomotive fireman and then in a flour mill in Galveston. It was through Rice's previous valet that he had obtained his position with Rice. His friend, Alex Stanbery, who had worked with him at the flour mill, had been in Wisconsin with Rice's wife, who had gone there for her health, where she had her third stroke and died. Stanbery had arranged her burial there and then shipped her belongings to Jones in Galveston. Jones brought the trunk to Rice in Houston, who was so impressed with Jones' honesty that he offered him a job at his hotel in Houston, the Capitol Hotel, and then invited him to come to New York as his valet in early 1897.

Jones described to the press Rice's last day on earth. The *Times* reported the next day:

Charles F. Jones still lives at the apartments occupied by his late employer. Last night he said that his employer retired to bed about 5 o'clock on Sunday afternoon. Jones then went and had his dinner. On his return at 8 o'clock, he said, he carried a jug of water to Mr. Rice's room, and asked if he wanted a drink. He received no response, and when he picked up Mr. Rice's arm he found that it was limp. He says he then sent for Dr. Curry. When the latter arrived he found that the body was still warm, and said that Mr. Rice had been dead about twenty minutes.

Patrick told a *World* reporter: 'When Captain Baker arrives, a full, and I promise you a satisfactory statement will be made respecting the trust executed to me; but until then, for good and sufficient reasons, my lips are sealed on that point.'

# 12. Baker Arrives

Baker and Frederick Rice arrived at the Pennsylvania Railroad depot in New Jersey early Thursday morning and crossed over the Hudson River into Manhattan by ferry. (The tunnel under the Hudson River was not completed until 1906 and Pennsylvania Station in midtown Manhattan was not opened until 1910.) On Wednesday, they had received en route a telegram from Meldrum, asking them to meet him for breakfast at seven at the Waldorf (then on the site of the present Empire State Building.) The meeting, which included Gerard and Swenson, went over the developments during the past several days.

Shortly after nine, Baker, Meldrum, and Frederick Rice arrived at 500 Madison Avenue. They were met by Jones.

'Why didn't you inform me immediately of Mr. Rice's death?' Baker asked, glancing over at the closed casket.

'Mr. Patrick was in charge of all of Mr. Rice's affairs,' Jones replied: 'I took my instructions from him.'[1]

Jones insisted that he had written to Baker about Patrick's involvement, but Baker said he had never received such a letter.

Patrick entered from a back room. Baker and he looked at each other for a moment in silence.

'I suggest that you and I go into the back room for a private conversation,' Patrick stated.

'That would be fine; I don't suppose you would object to Mr. Meldrum being present.'

'I would prefer that we be alone,' Patrick replied.

They went into the back room of the apartment. Patrick closed the door. The two adversaries talked for about half an hour.

'I suppose you are surprised to find me in charge,' Patrick stated.

'Yes, quite.'

'I believe I owe you an explanation,' Patrick went on.

'I would be pleased to hear one.'

'Well, when you left New York about a year ago,' Patrick explained, 'I thought that I should try to bring about a settlement of the Holt litigation with old man Rice himself. Of course, I knew that if I just called on him in the usual way he wouldn't see me.'

'Mr. Rice didn't like you or Holt,' Baker interjected, 'particularly after your scandalous questioning of a friend of Mr. Rice, suggesting she had given birth out of wedlock.'

'No doubt that was true. In any event, last winter,' Patrick went on, 'I placed notices in some of the New York papers asking: "Will former acquaintances of Mrs. William M. Rice, deceased, please address Justice" and gave an address on Lexington Ave. for reply. The notice came to the attention of Rice who replied to it. I called on him and we eventually became friends. I became his counselor and advisor in all matters except the Holt litigation. Rice, I must tell you, had lost confidence in you and your law firm and wished me to handle all of his affairs.'

'What caused him to lose such confidence in me?' Baker asked.

'In part it was that the Holt litigation was dragging on too long. Rice wanted it settled before he died. Also, Rice didn't like the fact that while testimony was being taken here in the apartment you invited Holt to join you for lunch. I explained to Rice that this was common practice for lawyers but I couldn't change the old man's view.'

At about this point, Detective Vallely came to the apartment to see Baker. After a brief private discussion, they arranged to meet later that afternoon at the office of the lawyers, Bowers and Sands, on Nassau Street in downtown Manhattan. Baker rejoined Patrick.

'You should also know,' Patrick said, 'that I have a will Rice made in June 1900 making me the residuary legatee of nine-tenths of his estate.'

'How is it that he would leave you the bulk of his estate?' Baker asked.

'Well, as I explained to you, Mr. Rice and I were friends and to be frank with you, the old man became, as it were, stuck on me; He thought I was the most wonderful man in the world.'

'What do you intend to do with all that money?'

'Rice and I had discussed the matter in great detail. It was Rice's purpose – though there was no legal obligation on me to do so – to distribute it in great measure to charities and to exploit the name of William M. Rice throughout the world. I intend to quiet the voice of suffering wherever I hear it – in the name of William M. Rice. I know that Rice thought a great deal of the William M. Rice Institute and I am willing to give several million to it, whatever you think is right. Indeed, I would like to become a director of the Institute.'

Patrick said that he and Rice had agreed to settle the Holt litigation for $250,000:

'That was the reason he had sent me those checks amounting to that sum. His death was a great misfortune to me. I had an assignment of all of his property and we were going to go to his vault Monday morning, the day following his death, and he was to turn over to me all his bonds, stocks and other personal property. If Rice hadn't died, I would now be in possession of all his property.'

'But why would Mr. Rice assign all his property to you?' asked Baker.

'Simply because he was tired of looking after all his affairs. I had undertaken to give him $10,000 a year for the rest of his life and to spend $5,000 on a suitable headstone after he died.'

'Did Mr. Holt know of the settlement?'

'No, only Rice and I knew of it. We kept it a secret from Holt, just as we kept it a secret from you. I have wired Holt for his confirmation of the arrangement,' Patrick stated.

'Don't worry,' Patrick assured Baker, 'You will do well from all this. I want you to continue to handle all of Rice's Texas affairs; and you and Rice's nephew are named as executors of the estate and it would be expected that you would get the bulk of the 5% commission provided in the will for the executors – a round sum. Of course, I am also an executor, but will decline compensation.'

'What about all the work my firm has already done in the Holt litigation?' Baker asked.

'It goes without saying that you will bountifully be compensated for your services,' Patrick replied.

Baker wrote to Lovett, shortly after this conversation, that Patrick 'threw out abundant baits for me to swallow with the hope that I would be satisfied.'[2]

'Could I see the two wills?' Baker asked.

'Yes, we can go to my home later, but first we should take care of the arrangements for the cremation.'

Potter, the undertaker, had arrived to take the body to Long Island for cremation. He told Jones that the retort had been fired at the crematory and that unless the body arrived soon they would have to let the retort cool off and then reheat it. Jones interrupted Patrick and Baker's discussion to inform them of this fact.

'Do you agree to the cremation?' Patrick asked Baker.

'I will leave that decision to Frederick Rice,' Baker replied.

Frederick Rice was shown his brother's letter requesting cremation: 'I care to have nothing to do with the question,' Frederick Rice stated: 'I neither oppose nor authorize any action in the matter.'

Patrick ordered Potter to take the body for cremation, but regretted that owing to other pressing business he could not accompany it. Baker and Rice's brother also chose to stay behind. The funeral cortege for one of America's wealthiest citizens consisted of only Jones, Dr Curry, and three detectives. The horse-drawn hearse crossed the Brooklyn Bridge – at the time the only bridge over the East River – and then traveled through Brooklyn into Queens. The Fresh-Pond Crematory building in Middle Village in Queens was – and is – in the form of a Grecian temple with an ornamental marble front.[3] The retort had reached the desired temperature of 2,700 degrees Fahrenheit when they arrived. The body, apparently unadorned with a single flower, entered the retort. Jones and Curry immediately returned to Manhattan.

# 13. Gathering Documents

When Jones returned to the apartment, Baker, Meldrum, and Patrick had already left for Patrick's boarding house, where Patrick had said the two wills were kept.

At the boarding house, Patrick showed them the original of the will of 1900, purportedly signed by Rice and witnessed by David Short and Morris Meyers, the young lawyer in Patrick's office. 'The signature,' Baker subsequently wrote Lovett, 'looks like Mr. Rice's, but I believe it is a forgery.'[1] 'May I keep the will?' Baker asked: 'As an executor named in the will, I have as much right to it as you.' Patrick declined to let him have the original or, at first, even a copy. Baker objected: 'As Rice's counsel and an executor of the 1896 will, it is my duty to make a full and fair investigation.'[2] Patrick relented and gave him a carbon copy of the 1900 will, but refused to certify that it was a true copy. Baker also received a copy of the 7 September assignment of all of Rice's property to Patrick.

Baker asked for the original 1896 will, handing Patrick a copy of it that he had brought with him. To Baker's surprise, Patrick gave him the original. Baker and Meldrum left, having arranged to meet Patrick later in the day at Patrick's office.

Baker telegraphed Lovett: 'Have possession will ninety six. Patrick in possession purported will dated June last naming Rice Jr., Patrick and myself executors. Am trying to get possession of all property which I think I can do.' Lovett wrote back: 'rejoiced to receive your telegram.'[3]

Clutching the 1896 will, Baker and Meldrum went straight to the offices of Bowers and Sands. Gerard was there with Vallely and two other senior detectives, including Arthur Carey, later New York's deputy inspector in charge of homicide.[4] An assistant district attorney attended in place of Osborne. Baker, the meeting decided, should obtain as many documents as possible with Rice's signature on them for handwriting analysis. Special arrangements were made with the New York Safe Deposit Company to stay open until 7 p.m. to receive any documents Baker obtained.

When Baker arrived at Patrick's office late in the afternoon, Patrick was just concluding a lengthy meeting with the press. Baker was not unhappy to see Patrick giving interviews. As he later wrote to Lovett, 'Patrick has talked himself to death.'[5] Baker meant it figuratively and, he hoped, literally. Baker himself declined to comment on the case: 'I have only been here since morning,' he said, 'and I am not in a position to talk. A thorough investigation is being made, and if there is anything that the public should know it will be given to the newspapers.'[6]

Patrick had given the press a prepared statement referring to the 'secret negotiations' he had conducted with Rice resulting in the four checks amounting to $250,000. 'I understood Colonel O.T. Holt to authorize a settlement of all claims for $250,000,' the statement read. He was questioned by the reporters:

'Is it true that you have offered to turn over the four checks?' he was asked.
'You can say that I decline to deny or affirm any such report.'
'Will Holt accept the settlement?' a reporter asked.
'I don't yet know,' Patrick replied.
'Do you expect to be placed under arrest?'
'No,' said Patrick emphatically.[7]

After the press left, Patrick produced a large satchel of Rice's papers and some personal effects for safekeeping. The four checks and the 1900 will were not included, however. It was now after 7 p.m. and the safety deposit company was closed. He and Baker agreed to deposit the documents overnight in the safe of the Hotel Normandie at 5th Avenue and 38th Street, where Baker was staying. While waiting for a streetcar to take them to the hotel, Patrick turned to Baker, saying:

'We are all together here, now, and you have Gerard with you; cannot we get into a room together and settle up this whole business?'
'I guess not,' Baker replied.[8]

# 14.  Orren T. Holt

That same evening, Orren T. Holt was seen in Houston by a reporter for the *Houston Post* at the Capitol Hotel, soon to be renamed the Rice Hotel. (The hotel is still standing – unoccupied.)[1] The fifty-one-year-old Texas-born Holt was a prominent Houston lawyer – a graduate of the University of Michigan Law School – who would become the mayor of Houston in 1902.[2] He was asked about Patrick's statement in New York earlier that day concerning a proposed settlement for $250,000. 'He cared to make no comment on the statement,' the *Post* reported, 'further than that he had agreed to settle the claims of his clients under the will of Mrs. Rice for the sum of $250,000, but that Mr. Baker had turned the proposition down.' 'The proposition was made,' Holt stated, 'on the proviso that it would have to be approved by the beneficiaries under Mrs. Rice's will. The statement of Mr. Patrick is not correct in some particulars, but I do not care to discuss the matter.'

Patrick had written Holt several letters about a week before Rice died saying that Rice had agreed to a $250,000 settlement. 'Rice is growing very weak and cannot live very long,' Patrick wrote: 'Whatever was to be done would have to be done at once.'[3] There is no record of Holt's responses.

The story then unfolds hazily through telegrams passing back and forth between Houston and New York. Some of the ones that later became known are set out here. No doubt many others, not now available, were also sent. Patrick had wired Holt of Rice's death, telling him about the checks, totaling $250,000. Holt wired back on Tuesday: 'Telegram received. Is it necessary for me to come and why. Answer.'[4] This was followed by another telegram from Holt informing Patrick that Baker had left Houston: 'James A. Baker left here for New York last night.'[5]

The Wednesday morning papers, as we have seen, contained detailed accounts of the suspicious circumstances surrounding Rice's death. Patrick immediately wired Holt: 'Place no credence in absurd stories afloat. Am preparing long telegram for your confidential information which will follow in a few hours.'[6] A lengthy telegram was then sent to Holt: 'Opened personal negotiations with Rice several months ago for compromise. He would not hear to large sums. I finally told him that in negotiations last Fall you had rejected all sums less than two hundred and fifty thousand dollars but had authorized compromise at that figure.'[7] Patrick then outlined in detail an arrangement ('the best contract that I could get out of him') whereby the parties would continue to try to resolve the dispute through litigation, but if Rice died before the case was decided his estate would pay Mrs Rice's relatives $250,000.

Later news reports received in Houston on Wednesday mentioned the new 'Patrick' will. Holt no doubt suspected his telegrams were being monitored and he used Patrick's friend, John M. Coleman, to send a telegram: 'Newspapers full all sorts reports. Wire me briefly names executors and provisions new will. Do nothing mentioned in your telegrams today [these telegrams are missing and it is not clear what Patrick was proposing]. You will be fully advised upon receipt full information.'[8]

John Coleman, who had been a year ahead of Patrick at the University of Texas Law School, was a good friend of Patrick's.[9] Coleman had started practicing law in Houston in 1890, and when Patrick moved to New York in 1893 he had placed his Texas files in Coleman's hands. Patrick replied to Coleman through his landlady and 'friend,' Addie Francis.

Mrs Francis, a forty-one-year-old widow with a son in the Klondike, had lived in New York for twenty years. She had known Mr and Mrs Patrick and their daughter Lucy since 1893, when they all lived in the Lennox Hotel on 5th Avenue.[10] Mrs Francis was then in charge of a clothing manufacturing business, 'Mother's Friend.' The following year she retired from business because of poor health and opened a boarding house.

Mrs Patrick gave birth to another daughter, Lillian, in 1895, but then died of consumption in her hometown of Napoleonville, Louisiana, where she had gone because of her condition.[11] Patrick returned to New York with his sister Emma and his two children and took rooms at Mrs Francis' boarding house. Patrick's sister and his two children later returned to Texas to stay with his parents in Austin. Patrick continued to stay in Mrs Francis' boarding house. They became very close, indeed so close that persons in the boarding house, as noted earlier, referred to them as Mr and Mrs Patrick. The press, however, never referred directly to this relationship.

Mrs Francis' long telegram to Coleman on Wednesday, prepared by Patrick, sets out the terms of the 1900 will and then states, in part, that Patrick

anticipates perfect co-operation Baker and relatives. Needs Holt's help pay debts legacies take immediate charge. If Holt does not ratify will be compelled, owing public pressure, turn everything over Baker and await result litigation. If Holt's answer favorable, checks explained to-morrow and public clamor abated. At request bank checks today placed escrow. Waiting Holt's answer morning, otherwise to executors.[12]

On Thursday, Patrick was pleading with Holt to ratify. Mrs Francis wired Holt through Coleman: 'Telephones that unless Holt ratifies today, compelled to deliver checks tomorrow morning to Baker and wash hands whole affair. Everything else turned over now.' Coleman replied: 'Executor powerless until ratified by Court and legatees. My advice, hold funds touching settlement until time for ratification. My telegram morning [this telegram is no longer in existence] concerns other features, which you seem not to understand.' No doubt Holt and Coleman were referring to the possibility of forgery or murder charges.

Patrick wired directly to Holt: 'Wire instructions to me to hold compromise open to enable you to secure ratification of court and legatees.' No such instructions, however, were sent by Holt or Coleman. Patrick was therefore on his own.

# 15. Hornblower, Byrne

The next morning, Patrick was the model of cooperation. He and Baker itemized the documents that had been placed in the safe at the Normandie. Baker deposited them in the National Deposit Company under his sole control, using the password 'Houston.' Patrick also agreed that Baker should take control of Rice's Texas affairs.

'I fully concur in the appointment of Baker as temporary administrator,' he wired Lovett in Houston,[1] and that afternoon the probate court of Harris County, Texas, made the appropriate order. But most importantly, Patrick handed over to Baker the two checks Rice had purportedly drawn on the Swenson Bank, and he later deposited with the solicitors for the Fifth Avenue Trust Company the certified check for $135,000 drawn on that institution. The $25,000 that had been received when the second Fifth Avenue Trust Company check was cashed was not turned over, however.

Patrick refused to talk to the reporters waiting outside his office; instead he posted a notice on his door:

From this time I shall neither deny nor affirm any statement made concerning me nor make any statement, except in the form of a written statement handed out by me to the press. I do not contemplate making any such statement.

I am forced to this position on account of false statements heretofore imputed to me.

I thank the members of the press for their courtesy to me, and trust they will not disturb me further by attempting to interview me.[2]

Baker now had the disputed checks. He needed advice on how to proceed. Instead of going back to the law firm of Bowers and Sands,

Baker went to the firm of Hornblower, Byrne, Miller, and Potter, the law firm that normally handled Baker and Botts' affairs in New York. The ten-member firm at 30 Broad Street was one of New York's largest and most-prestigious firms.

Forty-nine-year-old William Hornblower, from an old and distinguished legal family, had graduated from Princeton University and Columbia Law School and had at one time been a member of the famous Carter firm that had included Charles Evans Hughes, later the chief justice of the United States Supreme Court, and Paul Cravath, one of the founders of the present Cravath, Swaine, and Moore firm. In 1888, Hornblower and Byrne had founded their own firm, representing clients such as the New York Central Railroad, the New York Life Insurance Company, and Joseph Pulitzer. 'At the age of forty,' Benjamin Cardozo later wrote, Hornblower 'was an acknowledged leader of the bar.' In 1893, President Grover Cleveland nominated Hornblower to be a member of the US Supreme Court, but the Senate refused to confirm the nomination. 'The rejection,' Cardozo wrote, 'was not an estimate of fitness, but a measure of reprisal.' The reprisal was by Senator David B. Hill, because of the position that Hornblower had taken on behalf of the New York Bar to block a judicial appointment favored by Hill.[3] Ironically, David B. Hill will later play a major role in our story, acting on behalf of Patrick.

The forty-three-year-old James Byrne[4] – born within a week of Baker – was to spend the bulk of his time on the case for at least the next year. Byrne, whose parents had emigrated from Ireland, had graduated from Harvard College and Harvard Law School. Years later he became the first Catholic ever elected to serve on Harvard's governing board, and in 1917 he donated $150,000 to establish the Byrne Professorship of Administrative Law at the Law School.[5]

Baker wrote to Lovett: 'I thought it decidedly best that Hornblower's firm should be retained and have spoken to Mr. Byrne. Our understanding is that he should take hold of the matter now and the question of fee is to be hereafter arranged.'[6] Baker wanted Lovett to obtain a resolution of the board of the Rice Institute authorizing any reasonable expenditure of funds. Under the 1896 will, Baker wrote, the institute gets nine-tenths of the money; under the 1900 will Patrick gets nine-tenths: 'Under these circumstances, the Institute is more largely interested than any other person or Institution. It must make the fight against Patrick and put up the necessary money to do so.'

Lovett wrote back: 'I am sure it could not be in safer or more careful hands,' adding that 'it would be well to have an agreement with him about compensation, since it seems to me in [an earlier case] he was altogether unreasonable.' Lovett also added some observations on Patrick's activities: 'Every one here seems to be amazed at Mr. Patrick's performance, and I have yet found no one who did not entertain the opinion that any will or other papers in Patrick's favour were either forgeries or otherwise fraudulent.'[7] Lovett was sure that Patrick was also guilty of murder, stating: 'Dispatches in the papers here indicate that the New York police do not consider there was any foul play in connection with Mr. Rice's death, but I don't care what their opinion is, I am convinced that he was murdered ... It would be a very simple matter to smother him with a pillow at his age without leaving any signs of violence.' Baker's other partner, Parker, shared this view – pointing out that a fellow lawyer who was a year behind Patrick at law school 'does not hesitate to say that in his opinion Mr. Rice was murdered.'

# 16. McCluskey

It did not take McCluskey's Detective Bureau long to learn that Patrick had turned over the Swenson checks to Baker. McCluskey sent word that he wanted to meet with Baker.

At ten o'clock Friday evening, McCluskey called on Baker at the Hotel Normandie. (The since-demolished Normandie was a two-hundred room hotel at the corner of Broadway and 38th Street, noted in the guidebooks of the time as having an excellent restaurant and first-class 'appointments.')[1] McCluskey took the elevator up to Baker's room, while his subordinates waited on the sidewalk outside the hotel.

Captain George McCluskey, the product of Captain Byrne's Detective Bureau, was not out of place in such surroundings. He was often referred to as 'Gentleman George' because of his ability to blend in with the crowd while on duty in evening dress at gala entertainments. With slicked-down hair and a well-groomed mustache, he looked and acted the part of a prosperous Wall Street broker. One of his sergeants later wrote that he 'made his unofficial headquarters at Delmonico's famous café. Here he mingled with the moneyed crowd while casting an inquisitive eye at the easy-money men who follow the trail of wealth.' He would shortly also be known as 'Chesty George,' after the chief of police, Devery, had him transferred temporarily to the relatively unimportant Grand Central substation because he was thought to be 'too chesty.' As captain of the Detective Bureau and later as the youngest inspector in New York, he was probably New York's best-known policeman. He died in 1912 at the age of fifty-one, worth a million dollars.[2]

McCluskey went up to Baker's room. Hornblower, Byrne, and Gerard were waiting with Baker. 'I understand that you have the two cheques on Swenson and Sons,' McCluskey stated. 'May I see them?' Baker handed them to him. 'There is a wonderful similarity in the two signatures,' McCluskey observed. Then, placing them under his magnifying glass, he repeated: 'Yes, a wonderful similarity. I would like Mr. Kinsley to examine them. He acts for us in all such cases and was our chief expert in the recent Molineux case.'[3] Byrne said that he would be pleased to make the necessary arrangements.

The press were waiting for McCluskey to reemerge from the Normandie.

'There is nothing new in the case tonight from a police standpoint,' McCluskey said. 'We are still at work, however, and one can never tell what may happen.'

'Do you contemplate making any arrests?' a reporter asked.

'All things are possible in this world,' replied the Chief of Detectives.[4]

# 17. More at the Normandie

The next morning, Patrick was at the Normandie waiting for Frederick Rice to emerge from his breakfast in the dining room.

'I want to talk to you,' Patrick said.

'We can talk in the gentlemen's reading room,' Rice suggested.

'I want to talk to you privately,' Patrick insisted. 'Can't we go to your room?'

As they approached the elevator, Patrick remarked: 'All the notes of your son's held by Mr. Rice are settled. They will never be presented by the estate for payment.'[1]

When they entered Rice's room, Patrick said: 'Please lock the door. I am feeling very ill. I did not sleep at all last night. Can't I lie down?' Patrick stretched himself out on the lounge and closed his eyes. He lay there for some time, but all at once he sat up and, according to Rice's memorandum of the conversation, said, 'What's that?' Rice explained that it was the noise made by the elevator. 'We don't want any listeners,'

Patrick said. He noted that the transom was open and got up and closed it, saying, 'I want no listeners here.'

Patrick lay down again and asked Rice to order up some ice water. After it arrived, Patrick discussed the will of 1900, telling Rice why his brother had lost faith in Baker ('Baker was putting off the will case too long') and how Patrick's relationship with Rice had emerged. Patrick took out a bundle of at least thirty letters, dated from January 1900 to August 1900, purported to be signed by Wm. M. Rice, and started reading them to Frederick Rice. Some of them discussed a compromise of the suit brought by Holt. Others found fault with Captain Baker.

'You are going to show these letters to Captain Baker,' Frederick Rice said.

'I am not,' Patrick replied: 'He is fighting me and I am not going to show him anything.'

When Patrick got up to go, he said: 'Now I want you to understand that you can have all the money you want for the Institute, three, four or five million if you want it.'

Frederick Rice's notes of the interview ended by stating: 'Patrick was very nervous during the whole time he was in my room and would frequently hesitate, wait a minute or two and then ask, "What was I saying?" or "Where did I leave off?"'

During the session, Baker came into the room to discuss with Patrick the arrangements for the opening of Rice's safety deposit box, containing securities and possibly another will. Neither Patrick nor Baker had the combination and so it was arranged to meet later in the week at the security company when the box would be opened in the presence of both Baker and Patrick. After Baker had left the room, Patrick said to Rice: 'I feel better; it always strengthens me when I come in contact with an antagonist.'

Patrick refused to talk to the press. Instead, he gave out a typewritten statement, referring to the $250,000 compromise he said he had arranged with Rice: 'When this has been formally ratified ... I shall speak freely upon all subjects. Until then my lips are sealed.'[2]

# 18. Handwriting Experts

Over the weekend, Byrne contacted a number of handwriting experts, who, in the next few days, examined the Swenson and Fifth Avenue Trust Company cheques. Baker wrote to Lovett: 'we are working under cover as far as we can. It would be unfortunate for the information to get out that we had obtained an opinion from writing experts.'[1] In particular, Baker did not want Patrick to learn of their activity and cease his cooperation.

William J. Kinsley, whom Captain McCluskey had wanted to examine the checks, quickly declared them 'clumsily done' forgeries.[2] Kinsley, like most other handwriting experts at the time, had been a teacher of handwriting for many years. The editor of *Penman's Art Journal*, he had, for the past ten years, taken a special interest in disputed handwriting and had appeared as a witness, principally for the prosecution, in almost four hundred court cases.[3] 'To a practised eye,' he told the press later in the week, 'it did not even take a microscope to detect the forgery.' The similarities in the two Swenson checks, he said, showed that they could not be genuine. The two signatures measured exactly alike in every particular, which, he went on to say, was absolute evidence that they had been traced from the same model. The tracings were probably done directly, using an electric light under the original. The Fifth Avenue Trust Company checks, however, were 'free-hand forgeries and evidently the work of a novice.'

Another expert, David Carvalho,[4] described by one of his colleagues as the 'Paul Bunyon of document examiners,'[5] examined the two Swenson checks on Monday morning. The fifty-year-old Carvalho had acted for the district attorney's office in numerous cases in the past, appearing for the prosecution in many of its most important cases. His letterhead advertised that for the past eighteen years he was the 'Grand Jury Expert of New York City.' He had also given an opinion on the validity of Alfred Dreyfus' signature in the famous Dreyfus case.[6] He had studied organic chemistry and photography at New York College and was the author of *Forty Centuries of Ink*.[7]

Carvalho also had no doubt that the Swenson checks were forgeries. Displaying blown-up photographs of the two checks, he explained to the press that they were 'absolutely alike in every particular.'[8] Taking a compass, he demonstrated that the distance from any point to any other point of the signature was exactly the same on each check. Superimposed, one over the other, he pointed out, the signatures fit exactly, except on the final stroke or curl of the letter 'e' in 'Rice' where the tracer apparently lost his caution. No doubt, he went on, the tracer used a light under a glass, with the genuine check on the glass, first tracing the signature with a dry pen. Carvalho expounded his theory to the press:

Where two signatures have been shown to be exactly alike in every particular, and where they occupy exactly the same position on two instruments of the same character, the courts have held that ipso facto, one must be a forgery. Now it is absolutely impossible for a man to write his name twice and get the signatures to tally as to characters and size and position in both cases.

The best evidence of this, he said, is to examine genuine checks. He had looked at fifteen of them and no two of them were absolute reproductions of each other and no two when superimposed would fit each other. 'No man who stopped to think would use a model for two forgeries in exactly the same way.'

'The signatures,' Carvalho stated, 'are such palpable tracings that their character could not be mistaken.' One could easily see the halts in the writing when the tracings were being filled in. Moreover, he said, the traced signatures look flat and dead:

There is no life, no motion to them, as is plain in the originals, where the handwriting flowed naturally. The tracer is a mere machine, and his attention being given entirely to get the signature exact he gets the same effect that one would get from an automatic piano in contrast with the same music played naturally by an artist. The automatic playing is too perfect, there can be no mistake, but the effect is flat and dead. It is very much the same with a signature that is traced.

Later in the day, Carvalho examined the Fifth Avenue Trust Company checks and concluded that they were 'probably not genuine.' These checks, he said, were forged, but without tracing. The checks had distinct pinholes in the corners, which Carvalho thought may be the result of somebody contemplating tracing, but then forging them freehand.[9] 'Can you tell whether Jones or Patrick wrote the signature?' he was asked. 'It would be hard to do, but by no means impossible,' was his reply. 'I have not examined the writings of the suspected persons closely enough to make any positive assertions.' Other experts – Hagan from Troy, New York, and Gumpel from San Francisco, who was in New York City at the time – also took the view that the four checks were forged.

Byrne, the lawyer, reported these opinions to Captain McCluskey, who then arranged a conference with the experts. At the conclusion of the Thursday morning meeting, and after consulting Assistant District Attorney Osborne, McCluskey ordered that Patrick and Jones be arrested for forgery – although he wanted Patrick's arrest delayed until after Rice's safety deposit box was opened later that afternoon.

The charge would be forgery, not murder. Dr Witthaus had not yet reported the results of his chemical analysis. He was, he said, moving 'very slowly and cautiously.'[10] He was having difficulty in analyzing the stomach contents because of the presence of arsenic and sulfate of zinc from the embalming fluid. McCluskey knew that Patrick and Potts had visited the coroner's office the previous evening to see what progress was being made by Witthaus.

# 19. Arrests

At 4:30 on Thursday afternoon, 4 October, as arranged, Patrick and Baker met at the office of the New York Safe Deposit Company at 140 Broadway. It was agreed that if a will was found it would be delivered to the Surrogate Court. Neither Baker nor Patrick had the combination – Baker had wired Lovett to search their safe for one, but nothing was found – and it was therefore necessary to drill a hole through the side of the box so that the lock inside the safe could be sprung by hand. It required three hours for two workmen to drill a small circle of holes through the steel partition. It took another two hours to examine and list the more than two million dollars' worth of securities in the box. The largest item was a half a million dollars' worth of Atchison, Topeka, and Santa Fe bonds and stocks. No will was found, however; nor was there any reference to a will in the box. The documents were placed in another safe to await a court order and Baker, Meldrum, and Gerard left for a late dinner.

Patrick, accompanied by his friend Potts, stayed to talk to the press assembled outside the depository. 'I was not disappointed in the aggregate value of the securities found,' he said: 'For my own part, I do not anticipate any litigation over the property, as Mr. Gerard, Mr. Baker and myself seem now to understand each other very well.'

'Was another will found?' he was asked.

'No will was found,' Patrick replied.

'How about the will Mr. Rice is supposed to have made a few months ago?'

'I have not said anything about another will and do not intend to talk about wills at all,' said Patrick.[1]

Waiting for the interview with the press to be concluded was Detective Sergeant Arthur Carey, who worked exclusively on homicide cases for McCluskey. (An Irishman, his father had been a policeman on the New York force and two of his own sons would become New York policemen. Carey, several years later, would set up the Homicide Bureau in New York City and for almost a quarter of a century would be its chief.)[2] 'You're under arrest for forgery,' Carey announced. Patrick smiled at Carey and then at Potts: 'Call up House,' Patrick instructed Potts. 'And wire my father that everything will turn out well.' The next day Patrick's father in Austin, Texas, received a telegram from Potts: 'Be not alarmed by newspaper reports. Albert will triumph.'[3]

When they arrived at police headquarters on Mulberry Street, Jones was already there and had concluded a two-hour interview with McCluskey. Detective Sergeant Vallely had been assigned to bring Jones to headquarters. He had missed him at Patrick's office earlier in the day when Jones had slipped out through the barbershop on Chambers Street after the elevator operator had advised him that Vallely was looking for him. Vallely was waiting for Jones at 500 Madison Avenue in the late afternoon.

'I'm afraid that you are under arrest for forgery,' Vallely said.

Jones turned pale. 'Where's Mr. Patrick?' Jones finally asked.

'He's being arrested, too. Captain McCluskey would like to ask you a few questions.'[4]

'Gentleman George' McCluskey gently questioned Jones about the events surrounding Rice's death, his wills, and the questioned checks. No *Miranda*-style warning was given.[5] A stenographer took down the interview. Jones maintained throughout that Rice had signed the four checks.

'What did Mr. Rice say to you when he told you to draw these cheques?'

'He told me to draw one for twenty five thousand dollars on Swenson and Son, which I did. I brought it to him and he told me to draw the one for sixty five thousand, which I did. Then I brought both these checks to him.'

'Did you see him sign them?'

'Yes, sir, I did.'

'Are you positive of that?'
'Yes, sir.'[6]

McCluskey walked around the room with his fingers in his vest, quickly changing from one topic to another:

'Is it not true that Mr. Rice had the greatest confidence in Captain Baker and trusted him fully?'
'I think Mr. Rice trusted him as an attorney in all his matters, that is papers, etc., but I do not think that Mr. Rice trusted anybody.'
'Do you think Mr. Rice trusted Mr. Patrick?'
'Mr. Rice trusted Mr. Patrick in a business way, just as he did Captain Baker himself, or anybody else.'

Jones ended the interview protesting his innocence:

'Did Patrick ever talk to you about the will?'
'No sir, I don't believe that he ever said half a dozen words to me about the will. He would generally say to me, you give these papers to Mr. Rice, and Mr. Rice would give me papers to give to Mr. Patrick, that was the substance of our conversation.'
'You saw Mr. Rice sign these cheques on Swenson and Son and the Fifth Avenue Trust Co.?'
'Yes Sir.'

Patrick arrived at police headquarters accompanied by Detective Sergeant Carey and John Potts. He expressed outrage to McCluskey, who later permitted him to talk to the waiting press:

'If these cheques which were brought to me the Saturday before Mr. Rice's death are forgeries, I cannot conceive that they are so. I freely and willingly turned them over to Captain Baker for his investigation and I have never made any request to him other than that he probe the matter to the bottom.'
'His death fell upon me like a thunderbolt. These accusations against me are most unfair and contemptible.'
'I have retained Frederick B. House as my attorney and have instructed him to get out a writ of habeas corpus tomorrow morning and I shall lay the whole matter before the court. I expect to be free before the setting of the sun.'[7]

# PART TWO
# The Tombs

The Tombs Prison and the Criminal Law Courts in the 1890s.

Assistant District Attorney James W. Osborne: New York *Evening Journal*, 15 April 1901.

Defense Counsel Frederick B. House: *Tammany Times*, 27 July 1907.

Patrick and Jones arraigned before Magistrate Mott on charge of forging Rice's signature; Captain Baker in background: New York *World*, 6 October 1900.

Patrick, Morris Meyers, and Mr and Mrs David Short: New York *Journal*, 3 April 1901.

tate, and such portion shall enure to the said Albert T. Patrick.

Eleventh: I give, devise and bequeath to Albert T. Patrick, formerly of Texas, now of New York, all the rest
and residue of my estate, real, personal and mixed, heretofore or hereafter acquired and wheresoever situated.

IN TESTIMONY WHEREOF, I, the said William M. Rice,
to this my Last Will and Testament, have subscribed my
name and affixed my seal in the presence of *Morris
Meyers* and *David L. Short*
as subscribing witnesses, who sign the same as subscribing
witnesses at my request, in my presence and in the presence
of each other this 30th day of *June*, A. D. nineteen
hundred (1900).

_____ *W. M. Rice* (Seal)

Signed, sealed, published and declared by the said
William M. Rice, as, for and to be his last Will and Testament, in our presence, and we, at his request and in his
presence and in the presence of each other, have hereunto
signed our names as witnesses this 30th day of *June*
A. D. nineteen hundred (1900).

| Name. | Occupation. | Address. |
|---|---|---|
| *Morris Meyers* | *Lawyer* | *168 Henry St Manhattan, N.Y.C.* |
| *David L. Short* | *Publisher* | *404 Bradford St Brooklyn N.Y.* |

The last page of the disputed will dated 30 June 1900.

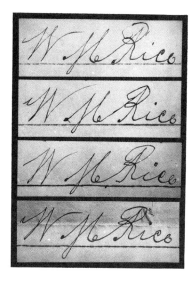

Rice's disputed signatures on the four pages of the will dated 30 June 1900.

Bellevue Hospital ambulance, about the turn-of-the-century: Museum of the City of New York.

# 20. Arraignment

At one in the morning on 5 October 1900, Patrick and Jones were lodged in separate cells at police headquarters. 'The cells in the present Police Headquarters,' a chief of police wrote, 'have officially been adjudicated as the worst in this State.'[1]

Early the next morning, Frederick B. House[2] came to police headquarters to see Patrick. Born in Cooperstown, New York, the forty-one-year-old graduate of New York University Law School was considered 'one of the ablest criminal lawyers in the city.' A Republican member of the State Legislative Assembly at the age of twenty-three, he later became prominently allied with New York City's Democratic Tammany Hall.

Jones was requested to join them in the waiting room. House told Jones that he was representing Patrick.

'Do you want me to represent you as well?' he asked.

'I have no money,' said Jones.

'Mr. Patrick said that he could look after that for you.'

'I accept your offer,' Jones replied.[3]

(Representing both Patrick and Jones would today be held to be a conflict of interest and a violation of the accused's right to the effective assistance of counsel.)[4]

House and District Attorney Osborne agreed that the arraignment at the Centre Street Police Court would be delayed until three o'clock that afternoon to enable Osborne to prepare the necessary documents.

For the next two hours, Osborne met with McCluskey, Baker, Byrne, Gerard, and a number of the handwriting experts in his crypt-like office on the third floor of the Centre Street Criminal Court Building. The safest course, it was decided, was to proceed only on charges of forgery of the Swenson checks. The experts had no doubt about those two checks being forged. Osborne emerged and told the press that he would not say anything until after the court hearing: 'Until after the Tombs Court hearing the case is in the hands of Captain McCluskey. I shall take no action until the Magistrate has passed on the case.'[5] McCluskey expressed supreme confidence: 'We have a dead open-and-shut case on the Swenson cheques.'[6]

At three o'clock, the case of Patrick and Jones was called at the Tombs Court presided over by Magistrate Mott in the Tombs Prison, connected to the Criminal Court Building by the so-called Bridge of Sighs. House and his partner, Moses Grossman, appeared for the accused. Captain Baker took a prominent position at Osborne's side for the prosecution. Detective Carey presented the charge in the form of an affidavit based on information and belief, charging Patrick and Jones jointly with forgery of the two Swenson checks.

'In view of the importance of this matter, Your Honour,' Mr. Osborne said, 'I request that bail be fixed at $10,000 for each defendant.' House thought that $5,000 would be quite sufficient and then proposed that they split the difference and make it $7,500 in each case. But Osborne was firm at the $10,000 figure and Magistrate Mott agreed with him. House said that he would not proceed with a habeas corpus proceeding, but rather that bail would be provided. The magistrate adjourned the proceedings until Monday, 8 October, at 3:30. The defendants returned to the Tombs Prison.

The *Times* reported the next day that 'the defendants were perfectly cool.' The *World*, however, stated that Patrick 'perspired profusely and in many other ways showed evidence that he was greatly worried at the position in which he found himself.'

The press wanted to know if murder would be added to the charges. Osborne replied: 'in present circumstances I have no intention of acting on an idea that death was not due to natural causes.'[7] McCluskey said that he was 'busy with the question of Mr. Rice's property,' but went on to speculate that Rice died too soon to fit in with a murder theory: 'If Mr. Rice did not die a natural death his end was so inconveniently sudden as to force the hands of those who appear at present to have committed crime to get his wealth. I can't base murder theories on suspicion. I want facts and as yet I have not got facts.'

House expressed optimism at the outcome. 'I am confident,' he said, 'that Mr. Patrick will come out of the case all right. I have the utmost confidence in his defense, despite the remarkable condition of affairs and the peculiar combination of circumstances.'

# 21. The Tombs

Completed in 1840 on a former pond on what is now Centre Street, the Tombs Prison was modeled after an Egyptian tomb near ancient Thebes. Its massive gray walls and funereal appearance reinforced the image. Charles Dickens described it in his *American Notes* as 'bastard Egyptian,'[1] but others found it 'the finest specimen of Egyptian architecture outside of Egypt.' Whatever its architectural merit, the front portion of the Tombs was demolished in 1896, shortly after the new Criminal Court Building was completed, and was replaced by a new structure on the site, also called 'the Tombs,' although bearing no resemblance to an Egyptian tomb. The remaining parts of the old Tombs were finally emptied of inmates in 1902 and all prisoners transferred to the new structure.[2] This new Tombs and the courthouse beside it were later replaced by the present massive gray building and adjoining structures at 100 Centre Street in Lower Manhattan. The detention facility is still popularly known as 'the Tombs' and the walkway connecting it to the courts as 'the Bridge of Sighs.'

Patrick and Jones were on different tiers of the old structure, Patrick on the second and Jones on the third. The press reported that they spent Sunday reading the newspapers and watched the Sunday afternoon service 'with interest.' The service was largely choral because, as the *World* reported, 'experience has taught the evangelists who visit the Tombs that the inmates of the prison receive with disfavor extended sermons and lengthy prayers.' Patrick was reported to have been shocked at the antics of the other prisoners when 'they broke into a storm of applause and lustily yelled for an encore' from the soprano.

On Monday afternoon, the two prisoners, according to the *Times*, looking 'well groomed,' were brought from the Tombs by Detective-Sergeants Carey and Vallely over the Bridge of Sighs into the adjoining Criminal Court Building. All parties agreed to a one-week adjournment. Patrick and Jones were represented by House and his partner, Grossman. The press speculated that House 'will have associated with him in the near future several lawyers of national reputation.'[3]

Over the weekend, Coroner Hart stated that Dr Witthaus' 'quick test' had failed to discover any traces of poison and that the 'slow test' would now be used.[4] The press asked Dr Witthaus for his comments. He replied: 'I know nothing about slow tests or quick tests. There is only one test to discover traces of poison in a matter of this kind. That is the one I am making and it will be a week or ten days before it is completed. Until the work is finished and I have made my report to the proper authorities I will say nothing.'[5]

The *World* and the *Herald* discovered over the weekend that Jones had taken hypnotism lessons in the spring from the American School of Hypnotism. The principal of the school said that Jones had paid $100 for twelve lessons. 'He was an apt pupil,' the principal, Dr Ferris, told the *World*, 'and I would have no hesitancy in saying that he was in a position and held the power to influence a man through a suggestive action without the latter realizing that he was being influenced. He could easily have controlled an old man like Rice, and may have had equal power over his physician.' For days, the *World* ran front-page stories showing, through diagrams, the knowledge of hypnotism Jones is said to have possessed ('Lessons in Hypnotism Dr. Ferris Says He Gave to Millionaire Rice's Valet, Jones'), reproducing a portrait of Jones' eyes with the caption 'Valet Jones's Hypnotic Eyes,' and suggesting that 'Jones may even have exercised his hypnotic power on Lawyer Patrick.' McCluskey noted that 'in the hypnotic state a person might be induced to sign his name to any kind of a document.' The *World* arranged for handwriting expert Kinsley to conduct further tests: 'the handwriting of old Mr. Rice or any other person,' Kinsley reported, 'would have the same characteristics, hypnotism or no hypnotism.'[6] Osborne, the prosecutor, commented: 'So hypnotism has got into the case? Well, I have no knowledge on that point, but it was to be expected.'[7] Jones himself indignantly told the press: 'I don't know the doctor. I never saw the man in my life. Dr. Ferris is a liar.'[8] Osborne arranged for Dr Ferris to see Jones in the Tombs, and Ferris reported his great embarrassment that he could not positively identify Jones as the man to whom he had given lessons in hypnotism. The *World* dropped the hypnotism story, but the *Herald* continued to believe that hypnotism was involved, claiming that Jones had told his lawyer that he had made a private study of hypnotism for eight years for his own amusement.[9]

Neither Patrick nor Jones was able to raise the $10,000 bail that had been set. House put the blame on Osborne: 'I will make no attempt at all to furnish bail for my clients, as I suspect that the D.A. or the police are prepared, in case my clients should be released on bonds, to have them immediately rearrested.'[10] Osborne, however, countered: 'I really have no intention to re-arrest Patrick and Jones in case they should be able to furnish bail. There are no other charges pending against these two defendants – at present.' A bondsman came forward later in the week as a favor to House but was rejected by the magistrate because of an unsatisfied judgment against his property – in spite of the fact that he claimed he still had an equity of almost $70,000 in the property.

Patrick himself had no money. His friend, John Potts, had had to lend him $100 several weeks earlier. The $25,000 check on the Fifth Avenue Trust Company, which Patrick had cashed, could not be used because it had been placed in trust. Baker wrote to Lovett: 'While Patrick cashed one of the Rice cheques for $25,000, my understanding is that he deposited it for the benefit of whomsoever might be thereafter entitled to receive it, and in that way has cut himself off from putting up the money as security for the appearance of Jones and himself.'[11] Coleman in Texas declared that 'Patrick let his foot slip in declaring that the money represented by the cheques was a trust fund. He could not personally use this money, although he seemed to be sorely in need of money.'[12]

The press pointed out that one of Patrick's sisters had recently married a millionaire in Denver, Colorado, and another was married to a wealthy St Louis wholesale druggist. Both brothers-in-law were coincidentally named Milliken, but they were not related. The St Louis Milliken came to New York to see Patrick later that month, but did not put up bail. Baker wrote to Lovett:

My information is that Patrick has a rich brother-in-law in St. Louis, a Mr. Milliken, a drug manufacturer of high standing financially and otherwise. He was here for ten days or two weeks. I understand that Patrick and his attorneys attempted to induce Milliken to finance their scheme, but that Milliken left without doing anything, stating in effect, that while he had married Patrick's sister, he did not marry the whole family.[13]

# 22. Short's Story

On Saturday, 6 October – the day after Patrick and Jones were lodged in the Tombs – Captain McCluskey invited David Short, a purported witness to the contested will of 1900, to police headquarters on Mulberry Street for a further discussion. In an earlier interview with McCluskey on 28 September, Short had explained how he had become involved with Patrick and had become a commissioner of deeds for the State of Texas. He, Short, had been renting space in John Potts' office and had met Patrick there about a year earlier. According to Short, Patrick told him that a number of Patrick's clients, who owned considerable property in Texas, had been looking for a commissioner of that state and if he, Short, were appointed a commissioner 'he could add a few dollars to his small income.' Potts arranged for the mayor's endorsement, which permitted Governor Roosevelt to recommend the appointment to the governor of Texas.

Short said in this earlier interview that Patrick had called on him a number of times to go to Rice's apartment to acknowledge or witness some document. McCluskey asked him about Rice's will:

I witnessed his will on the 30th day of June, 1900. Meyers read it over to him and Mr. Rice asked him to read over some certain page or section. I remember that day very well. Mr. Patrick telephoned for me to come up to his office and accompany Mr. Meyers up to 500 Madison Avenue and acknowledge some papers. I went to Mr. Patrick's office. Mr. Meyers, I and a friend of Mr. Meyers, a Hebrew, – I don't remember his name, never met him until that day – and we all went up together. We got up there and the old man was there and we acknowledged some papers, etc. He kept us there a while and said 'While you gentlemen are here I wish to have you witness my last will.' He went over and brought down a document covered with paper, brought it down and laid it down on his desk, in front of Mr. Meyers. He turned it over and ran through the pages himself, and then handed it to Mr. Meyers. Then he took it back again and signed it and I believe put his initials on the pages after he signed it, and then looked it over again. Then he asked Mr. Meyers and I to sign it. That was the first time I had any experience in signing wills and that is why I remember it. I signed it and Meyers read it just as the old man requested. There was some clause that the old man wanted a clear understanding on. Then we witnessed it. There was a number of typewritten pages, I could not imagine how many there were. Then he said 'Now boys, I want to ask one thing of you gentlemen. I want you to keep this quiet. Don't tell anybody, do you understand? I don't want you to tell anybody. I want you to promise one thing, keep this quiet, don't breathe it to anybody, I don't want you to tell a soul on earth. Don't talk about this.'[1]

McCluskey asked what they did with the will. Short said that he 'brought the will back to Mr. Patrick, carried it down and gave it to Mr. Patrick in his office.' He claimed he never read the will: 'I carried it down without reading it. Never opened it. It is against my principles. I was a sort of a secret trust and it was against my principles to read it.' Short said that while he was with Patrick a big ship fire occurred in the river. 'The bells began to ring. Everybody started to run on the street. I went from his office and went up to my printing office building, where my printing is done. Went up on the roof and saw the fire.'

The 30th of June was in fact the day of the great fire on the New Jersey side of the Hudson River. Over two hundred people died. The New York *Times*, which the next day devoted its entire first two pages to the tragedy, stated that the fire started 'at 4 o'clock yesterday afternoon, and in less than fifteen minutes covered an area a quarter of a mile long ... and caught four great ocean liners and two dozen or more smaller harbour craft in its grasp.'

Short did not say anything to McCluskey at the first interview about his role in attempting to certify the Swenson checks. At the second session with McCluskey on 6 October, Short was asked about the Swenson check and described the events at Swensons. McCluskey asked why he had omitted mentioning these facts earlier:

A. Well, Captain, I really did not remember it.
Q. You did not tell me all you knew that day, did you?
A. Well, I thought I did.
Q. Well you did not. Did you not think it was important to carry a cheque for twenty-five thousand dollars down to Swenson and Sons?
A. Well I did not think it was so important, or if I did I would be glad to tell it to you.
Q. Then everything you told me is the truth?
A. Absolutely the truth.

McCluskey asked again about the will.

Q. Did you see Mr. Rice sign that will, and you witness it?
A. Yes sir.
Q. And you witnessed it?
A. Yes sir.
Q. You saw him take the pen, dip it in the ink well and sign it?
A. Yes sir. I saw him sign a number of other papers too and always sat beside him when he did sign each. About the cheques I don't know anything. When I don't see a man sign his name I cannot swear that he signed it?
Q. Do you ever remember witnessing any papers that you never saw a man sign?
A. No sir, I would not do it. If I knew a man a thousand years I would not do it.

Short had still said nothing about certifying the check for $135,000 at the Fifth Avenue Trust Company. Osborne raised the issue towards the end of the interview:

Q. Well, you did not tell me about going up to the Fifth Avenue Trust Co. when I asked you if there was anything else that you did not tell me?
A. No sir, I did not tell you because I did not remember it.
Q. You recollected it, and why did you not tell me?
A. Because I did not think there was anything in it.
Q. Do you recollect anything now that you have not told me, that you ought to tell me?

A. No, Captain, I do not recollect anything more that I can tell you. This is a whole complete record of the transactions.

Q. Did you ever see Mr. Patrick in Mr. Rice's house?

A. Not during his lifetime.

That ended the interview. It was obvious that McCluskey was more than suspicious about what Short had told him, although he told the press that Short 'talked freely and frankly and apparently had nothing to conceal.'[2]

# 23. Jones' Story

Charlie Jones was attracting as much press notice as Patrick. Indeed, the *Herald* claimed that Jones attracted more interest: 'Of all the more than three hundred prisoners now in the Tombs he who has excited by far the most interest is Charles F. Jones. No day passes without a score of women making attempts to see him.'[1] In line with the hypnotism stories, the *Herald* reporter then described Jones' eyes:

While the observer is taking stock of the facial features of Jones he is impressed with the fact that he is looking into a pair of eyes that have great penetration. It is almost impossible to give an accurate description of those eyes. They sometimes appear to be almost gray and at another time are so dark as to approach blackness. Once they are veiled and dull and again they shine like black diamonds. They are always steady. Jones is ever ready to look any man in the face, a trait which some say betokens honesty.

Shortly after the arrests, Baker received a letter regarding Jones' honesty from a Judge Hamblen in Houston: 'I have known him since infancy, and knew his father from his childhood, and served with him in the army; he was a gallant soldier, a true, good man, and has always borne a splendid character and reputation, and Charlie was always considered a good boy, honest and honorable in all his dealings.' The judge urged Captain Baker to help Jones: 'If there is anything wrong, I am satisfied that he has been made the tool of other parties, and for the sake of his parents, as well as for himself, I ask you to protect him as far as possible from criminal prosecution.'[2]

During their first week in custody, Jones and Patrick saw House and his colleague Grossman nearly every day in the consultation room of the Tombs. With the help of his lawyers, Jones prepared a seventy-page

statement, the initial part of which was released to and reproduced by
the press:

I was born near Lynchburg, Texas. That is a village built at the mouth of the
San Jacinto River where it joins Buffalo Bayou. I was raised on a farm about
three miles from Lynchburg. My father's name is Lafayette W. Jones. He is a religious enthusiast, and my mother is nothing less. As a boy I was reared in the
fear of God and have never neglected my duties as a Christian. I am greatly impressed by a letter just received from my father, who expresses his full confidence in my innocence and his firm believe that God will care for and protect
me.
     I believe that I can get a certificate of good character from each official of Har-
ris county, where I was born. I have done no wrong, and I cannot understand
why I have been arrested.[3]

     The rest of the statement was not released to the press. In it, Jones
outlined how he had worked in Rice's Capitol Hotel in Houston and
had been asked to accompany him to New York in 1897. His responsibilities, he wrote, were 'to open mail, write letters, carry check deposits
to the bank, general assistant, go out and buy any little things he wanted,
and attend to his wishes and wants in general':[4]

Under the arrangement that I had with Mr. Rice it was understood that I was to
keep in touch whenever he needed me, such as to open his mail in the morning
and attend to those matters. I have never been away more than a day at a time. I
have been away over night only a few times, with his consent, but without his
knowledge at the time; that is he never said anything about it. I generally stayed
out around the City at different Hotels with women. I have never been married,
but I have had several love affairs.

For the next four pages of the statement Jones gave details of his various
girlfriends. No doubt his lawyers were seeking this information to assess
what incriminating evidence the prosecutor might be able to garner
against Jones:

I have several girls now, one of them is Nellie Creed, of 35 West 127th St., and
the other is Mabel Whitney, of 115 Jamaica Avenue, Astoria, Long Island. I have
known Nellie since January, 1900. I met her at Sulzer's Harlem River Park, at a
Ball. I have known Mabel since April 1898. She was a friend of a waitress who
used to bring up meals, and in that way I was introduced to her at the Berkshire

flat. I never slept with Mabel, but she has been in the house quite frequently. She threatened to sue me for breach of promise; and under Mr. Patrick's advice I gave her one evening every week – that is the hole I am in now. I never promised to marry her. Nellie slept in the house a number of times. She slept in the house on the Friday before Mr. Rice's death, and she saw his condition.

The statement then discussed Jones' relationship to Wetherbee of Swensons. Wetherbee propositioned him, Jones said, not the other way around; and he had told Rice about the proposal. Rice, according to Jones, was not surprised, as he, Rice, believed Wetherbee had stolen a bond. Several months later, Jones said, the bond reappeared.

Jones' counsel asked him about the events on 30 June, when the new will was said to have been executed:

To the best of my recollection, Mr. Rice's last Will was signed June 30th, 1900. There were negotiations going on between Mr. Patrick and Mr. Rice, from March until his death, and so they talked about Wills and compromises and many other matters. Mr. Rice never asked me to typewrite or re-typewrite the Will, he had made. Whatever changes were made, Rice made himself. I took the Will down to Patrick's office several times, with corrections made. I suppose the only reason why Mr. Rice did not give me the Will to change on the typewriter, was because he did not want me to know what the Will contained.

Jones described how the execution of the will took place: Meyers and Short, he said, came to Rice's apartment to witness his signature to some documents, and just as they were about to leave Rice asked if they would witness another document. Jones went on:

While Rice was reading it, and in the act of executing it, I glanced over his shoulder and looked over the Will, and saw that my name was not mentioned in it. I saw Mr. Rice sign the Will, and he then asked Mr. Meyers as to how the Will should be executed, and Meyers told him where to sign it. He said 'Sign on the foot of this page, and on the foot of this page,' and Mr. Rice signed his name at the foot of each page of the Will, and also at the end of the Will. He then asked Mr. Meyers and Mr. Short to sign it, and asked Mr. Meyers to be sure that it was correctly done. At that time, the old man was in fairly good physical condition. He knew what he was about, and understood perfectly the transaction that was going on. He signed the Will on the table in the dining room.

Patrick, Jones said, had Rice's complete confidence:

From January, 1900, after Mr. Patrick began calling at Mr. Rice's house, Mr. Rice, a number of times, in fact frequently spoke to me in the highest terms of Mr. Patrick, and said that he thought Patrick was a remarkable man and a man of great ability, and one whom he could trust, and who he liked very much, and in whom he had great confidence.

# 24. Rice's Last Days: According to Jones

In his statement to his counsel,[1] Charlie Jones described Rice's last days, including eating the allegedly fateful bananas:

About the middle of September, after the fire of the Merchants & Planters Oil Mill, Mrs. Van Alstyn called on Sunday and she told him that baked bananas were very good diet, and good for constipation, and he then asked me to get bananas for him. I tried to keep him from eating them and said that the Doctor would object to it but he said he must have them and I went and got a dozen. He baked five himself and ate them and wanted me to join. I told him that I was afraid of bananas and wouldn't try any. He then ate four more in a green state and then he took very sick. I went for Dr. Curry, at his request, but he told me not to tell Dr. Curry he had eaten baked bananas. I did tell the Doctor about it and the Doctor said he might just as well have eaten so many bricks, and that if he didn't happen to have the diarrhoea at that time it would have killed him.

According to Jones, sometime between eight and nine o'clock on Saturday morning, the day before Rice died, Rice ordered Jones to draw the questioned checks for his signature:

He told me to go and draw the first check for $25,000 on the Swenson Bank, to the order of Patrick. He was then lying in bed, with his hands behind his head. I brought the check to him, and gave him a paper or a magazine, I don't remember which, to sign it on. He sat on the side of the bed and signed it. Then he told me to draw either the $65,000 check or the $25,000 on the Fifth Avenue Trust Company, but I don't remember which one was first, but this was just after he signed the first check. He told me then to draw the one on the Fifth Avenue Trust Company, I think for $25,000. I filled out the check on the Fifth Avenue Trust Company, and gave it to him. He then told me to get the Swenson book, as he wanted to see the amount of his deposit there. I got the book, and I also got a slip of paper on which they put his balance, and he then told me to fill out his check for $65,000 on Swenson. I did so, and brought it to him, and he signed it sitting on the side of the bed, as he did when he signed the first check, – on the same paper or magazine. Then he told me to go and get a check for $135,000 and he said figure out how much more you need for $250,000. I figured out $135,000, and he said draw a check for that amount.

I said to Mr. Rice, 'What are the checks for?' and he said 'for Mr. Patrick.' I said, 'But what for?'; he spluttered and said, 'Damned, take that to Mr. Patrick, do you hear me?' I picked up the checks and took them to Mr. Patrick, and told Patrick about Rice's condition, and that Mr. Rice was very weak, and seemed to be very nervous and fretful, and Patrick sent me for a doctor. I had taken the checks to Mr. Patrick's house 316 West 58th Street, this was probably between nine and nine-thirty Saturday morning.

At about five o'clock Sunday evening, Jones said, he saw Rice alive for the last time:

I went into the back room, and he was at the window again. He seemed to be quiet, and was looking at the carriages, and called my attention to the fact that the hansoms were top heavy. We talked about twenty minutes or a half an hour. I tried to persuade him to go to bed, but he would not go for some time. Finally, he started, but was too weak. I took him up in my arms. This was about five o'clock in the afternoon, and I put him in his bed. He laughed and remarked that I had a large baby. He asked if he was heavy, and I said no, and he said it was nice to say no, even for the sake of politeness, but if I could always say no, I would get along better in life than I had. With that he laughed. I covered him, and I went out. This was about five o'clock. I returned about fifteen minutes later, and he seemed to be asleep. I then went out for my dinner, and left him alone, getting back a little after six o'clock Sunday evening. I went to his room, and found him still sleeping. I then went to send my telegram that I had written. I did not try to disturb him. I saw he was breathing.

Jones described going to 56th Street and 6th Avenue to send a telegram to Maude Mortimer saying that he could not see her that night. He returned to the apartment about seven o'clock or a little later, went into his room, and fell asleep. At about eight o'clock, he said, he awoke and went in to see Rice, who 'seemed to be resting very quietly.' He then got Rice a bottle of water, as he did every night:

I took the bottle of water in to his room, and asked him if he wanted a drink. He did not answer, and I repeated it, but got no response. I then took hold of his hand, and found it perfectly limp. I thought it was one of his former attacks of heart trouble, and I looked again, and it occurred to me that he must be either dead or had fainted away with one of his former spells that he had had. I asked the elevator man, Paul Teisch, to send some one for the Doctor, and he sent James Scott, the freight elevator man. I then telephoned Mr. Patrick, and asked him if he would go for the Doctor. He asked me if it was very serious, and I told him that I thought it was. I then went back and tried to arouse the old man, but could not. I thought then he was dead and could do no more for him, and shortly afterwards Dr. Curry and Mr. Patrick came. Dr. Curry asked how he was, and I said I thought he was dead. It almost took Mr. Patrick's breath away, and he came near falling. He went into the room, and Mr. Patrick has related exactly what has taken place. He took charge then, and has had charge ever since.

'When I was in Captain McCluskey's office,' Jones told his lawyers, 'he wanted me to confess, but I told him that all I had to confess was the story that I have related here.'

# 25. Baker Settles In

Baker was concerned that the criminal proceedings were premature. 'I am inclined to think,' he wrote to Lovett, 'that the criminal proceedings against Patrick at this time are unfortunate from our standpoint.'[1] Baker had not, in fact, wanted to report the findings of the handwriting experts to McCluskey. He explained to Lovett:

I still did not wish to report to McCluskey the conclusions of the experts, but the lawyers here seemed to think I could do nothing else. Under the circumstances I do not know that the arrests could have been avoided, but somehow I feel that if no arrests had been made, possibly we could have gotten Patrick in such a tight place that he would have been willing to release all claim he might have to the estate under the will and assignment for a nominal amount; but the game he is playing involves large stakes, and it may be that no reasonable settlement could have been made with him.

Lovett did not share this view. 'I was much gratified to observe in the Press,' he wrote Baker, 'that Patrick and Jones had been arrested for forgery ... I believe also that the crime of murder will be added to their list of misdeeds before the investigation ceases.'[2] 'I incline to the opinion,' Lovett later wrote, 'that the [Patrick will and assignment] will never appear again.'[3] Baker was less sure and was afraid that Patrick would try to probate the will in Texas: 'I am apprehensive that Patrick may not offer his will for probate here, but send it to Texas for that purpose.'[4]

Baker's Houston partners were not concerned about a fight in Texas. Parker wrote Baker: 'I have heard no one who knows the parties express themselves as giving any credit to the statements attributed to Patrick through the public print. In the present state of the public mind, I certainly should not fear the result of a contest here between the will of 1896 and that of June 30, 1900.'[5]

On Friday, 13 October, the Hornblower firm filed the original 1896 will for probate in the Surrogate Court in New York. Judge Bartine, one of the executors of that will, was the proponent. Baker explained to Lovett why Judge Bartine was put forward: 'In the so-called Patrick will, it is provided that in the event any of the legatees contest the same, they shall forfeit their legacies; while the lawyers here are clearly of the opinion that this provision does not apply to the conditions of an executor; yet it was thought best to take the safest course to have the will offered and contested by Judge Bartine.'[6] If William Rice, Jr, had filed the 1896 will for probate and the Patrick will was upheld, he might have been denied his bequest under the Patrick will and if Baker had been the one to file the 1896 will, there was a danger, it was thought, that he could not obtain executor's fees.

Lovett forwarded to Baker the documents relating to the 1896 will that he found in the Baker and Botts safe, including Rice's instructions to Baker in September 1896 respecting that will. 'You will observe in the postscript to Mr. Rice's letter of September 15th [1896], giving directions about his will,' Lovett wrote, 'that he states that if he lives several years, he might make another will.' 'While I cannot conceive of his having made another,' Lovett went on to say, 'yet that language in the letter referred to would of course present the question whether it is expedient to show the letter under these circumstances.'[7]

A rather unflattering picture of Baker appeared in the New York *Herald* and a number of other papers shortly after Patrick and Jones were arrested. Lovett commented good-naturedly on the picture: 'The edition containing your alleged picture was very soon exhausted, and I have heard of very high premiums being offered by some of your enemies. Mrs. Baker has already consulted me about a libel suit and says she will proceed if you do not.'[8]

Baker was settling in for a long stay. His firm wrote to him to devote all his energy to the Rice interests: 'You have a big fight on your hands and must command us all freely if we can serve you from this end of the line. Do not let other matters down here annoy you or take up your time or attention.'[9] Arrangements were made for Baker's secretary and his family to come to New York. Mrs Baker, the children, and a nurse arrived on 18 October, on free passes arranged by Baker and Botts – one of the perks of doing legal work for the Southern Pacific.[10] The trip had been delayed a few days because young Jim had malarial fever. Baker switched his accommodation from the Normandie to the more elegant San Remo Hotel on the west side of Central Park (the site of the present San Remo apartments).[11]

Baker had refused to discuss the contents of the Patrick will with the press. He wanted to force Patrick to produce it and thus be able to have the handwriting experts examine it. The day that the 1896 will was filed, however, McCluskey released to the press full details of the 1900 will. The contest over the two wills, the *Herald* speculated, 'promises to be one of the greatest legal battles that has ever taken place in the courts of this country.'

In mid-October, the Board of Directors of the Rice Institute met in the offices of Baker and Botts in Houston and appointed 'a committee to draft suitable resolutions touching the death of Mr. Rice, and expressing the respect and esteem in which he was held by the Trustees.'[12] Of even more importance was another resolution, unanimously adopted, giving Captain Baker full authority to act in the name of the institute:

to take all such action, employ such counsel, and incur such expenses as in his judgment may be necessary to secure the probate of the will of Wm. M. Rice, deceased, executed in 1896 ... and resist the probate of anything purporting to be a subsequent will, and to prevent the collection of any checks or the enforcement of any transfers or assignments purporting to have been executed by said Wm. M. Rice, which he may believe to be forgeries, or to have been obtained by undue or improper influence or means ...

Editorials in the *Houston Post* around the same time, arranged by Lovett, emphasized how important the issue was for the City of Houston. As Baker wrote: 'The fight is clearly between the City of Houston and Patrick.'

'Hornblower's firm have taken a very active interest in the matter,' Baker wrote Lovett, 'and most of the time I have been here pretty much the whole firm have been at work on it, including the eminent Mr. Hornblower himself.'[13] In spite of this activity, Baker had still not raised the issue of fees. Lovett agreed that it would be unwise to take up the issue at this time because 'a sum might be demanded which you would regard as altogether unreasonable, and yet it would be well nigh impossible to discharge the lawyers and get others at this stage of the proceedings.'

Lovett reported to Baker that he had seen Holt, who claimed he was 'quite as much surprised as we must have been when the papers announced Patrick's connection with Rice.'[14] At Baker's request, Lovett was having Holt watched: 'I have had an eye kept upon Holt,' he stated, 'but have observed nothing unusual in his movements. I shall observe his movements very closely.'[15] Lovett also saw Patrick's father in Austin and he 'expressed the same surprise' with respect to Patrick's involvement with Rice's affairs. Then, referring to Albert Patrick, Lovett stated that 'taking his whole performance together I am convinced that Judge Boarman [who had dismissed Patrick's attempt in 1893 to have Congressman Hutcheson disbarred] was correct when he told Patrick at Galveston that he had been wondering whether he was crazy or a villain and had made up his mind that he was both.'[16]

# 26. Magistrate Brann

The Centre Street Police Court, otherwise known as the Tombs Police Court, presided over by Magistrate Brann, was 'crowded to suffocation' for the start of the preliminary hearing on the forgery charges on 16 October. Not since the preliminary hearing in the then famous Molineux murder case[1] several years earlier had so large a crowd filled a courtroom in the Criminal Courts Building. The press noted the presence of 'several groups of women.' A tall woman 'with light hair, and rosy cheeks and handsomely dressed' told the *World* reporter that she 'had known Mr. Jones for three years. I hope they won't send him to jail. He is a very nice fellow. I know he is not guilty.' The reporter had recognized her as the person who had brought flowers to Jones in prison. She gave her name as Maude Giffton, but she was really Maude Mortimer, the person Jones was to see the night Rice died. When the magistrate's clerk announced that 'all persons having no business with the magistrate must leave the court,' she and other women dutifully left the courtroom.

Osborne called John Wallace, the cashier at the Swenson Bank, as the first witness. He described the request for certification, their suspicions, the attempt to contact Rice himself, and finally the rejection of the check as a forgery. In cross-examination, House showed the cashier a dozen envelopes with checks in them and the signature 'W.M. Rice' showing through slits in the front of envelopes. Wallace pronounced nine to be genuine and three forgeries. In fact, all the checks were genuine.

The *Times* contrasted Jones' manner during the questioning – 'he appeared at his ease, cool and collected' – with Patrick's – 'Patrick shifted about uneasily and pulled nervously at his mustache.' Patrick, according to the *Times*, was in better spirits the next day during the examination of Walter Wetherbee, the tall, bespectacled Texan who worked for Swensons: 'Patrick leaned back in his chair,' the *Times* wrote, 'with thumbs in the armholes of his vest, and laughed frequently at his counsel's sallies.' Wetherbee told Osborne that the $25,000 cheque was a forgery:

'Are you familiar with Mr. Rice's signature?'
'I am familiar with it.'
'Can you say whether the signature on the cheque for $25,000 is genuine?'
'I can.'
'What is your opinion of the signature?'
'It is a forgery.'


Wetherbee was then shown fifteen genuine Rice checks and declared the signature to be Rice's. Osborne asked permission to introduce Wetherbee's affidavit, made the previous spring, claiming that Jones had tried to induce him to prepare a new will for Rice and share part of the estate. House objected to its admission. Osborne argued that it was all part of a conspiracy to defraud Rice, and the magistrate, who was not legally trained, admitted the affidavit, stating: 'I am sitting only as a committing Magistrate, and I wish to know all about this case.'

Osborne and House squared off against each other during the examination of Wetherbee. That evening, Osborne, a Tammany Hall Democrat, was billed to make a political speech in Madison Square. This was part of Democratic presidential candidate William Jennings Bryan's campaign tour of New York. House taunted him:

'When the District Attorney speaks, kernels of wisdom drop from his mouth. He'll prove that tonight in Madison Square.'
    'Come up and learn something,' Osborne replied.

'Don't get excited,' cautioned House, 'You'll weaken your voice before night.'
'It will be weaker before this trial's over, as will be your case.'

The magistrate interceded: 'This is unseemly, gentlemen.' House apologized 'for following the bad example set by the District Attorney.'[2]

House's cross-examination of Wetherbee was designed to show that Wetherbee had stolen one of Rice's bonds worth $1,000 and that Wetherbee was accusing Jones of wrongdoing to shift blame from himself.

'When Jones proposed to you to draw a second will you were indignant, were you not?' asked House. 'You didn't show it, did you? You talked of other matters, didn't you?'

'I did, but – '

'You didn't throw him out of your house, did you? My Texan friend, you didn't denounce him for making such an outrageous proposition, did you?' shouted House, pounding the table.

'No sir.'

'When Jones said he had called you a thief you were indignant?' suggested House.

'I didn't believe him.'

'Then why didn't you tell Rice about it?'

'Because – '

'Was it because of any knowledge you knew Jones had of the theft of that $1,000 bond?' shouted House, again pounding the table.

On Thursday, the first of the prosecution's handwriting experts was called. The Hornblower firm had contacted virtually all the leading handwriting experts in the United States. Kinsley and Carvalho from New York, Tyrell from Milwaukee, and Tolman from Chicago were in court, and others were waiting to be called. Cornering the market on handwriting experts not only helped lock them into opinions favorable to the prosecution, but also tended to prevent them from later accepting a retainer from the defense.[3] The defense's lone handwriting expert in court was Thomas W. Cantwell, a former bank teller from Albany, who had appeared as a witness in many cases, but did not have a major reputation as a handwriting expert.

Kinsley and Carvalho gave evidence similar to what they had told Byrne as well as the press that the Swenson checks were forgeries because of the great similarity in the two signatures: 'The signatures of

the $25,000 and $65,000 checks,' said Kinsley, 'are lifeless and char-
acterless. If placed one above the other in the sunlight they superimpose
– that is, they correspond in every detail; therefore, one must be a forgery.
The similarity couldn't happen by accident.'[4] Magistrate Brann held the
two checks up to the light and compared the signatures. Kinsley was
unable to tell the method of tracing. Carvalho gave similar evidence,
but concluded that a dry pen had first been used.

On Friday, Tyrell and Tolman testified. John Tyrell[5] was employed
by the Northwestern Mutual Life Insurance Company of Milwaukee and
had started to appear in major cases. Because he had successfully solved
a handwriting puzzle in Kinsley's *Penman's Art Journal*, Kinsley had given
his name to Osborne for the earlier Molineux case. He would later appear
in the Leopold and Loeb cases and in the Lindbergh kidnapping case.
A week earlier, House had contacted him to join the defense experts,
but he was already committed to the prosecution side. He differed from
Carvalho in concluding that a wet pen was used. 'Experts never agree,'
interposed Magistrate Brann. Dr Henry Tolman of Chicago, described
as a microscopic expert, also testified that the two cheques were forgeries.

On Friday afternoon, Osborne unexpectedly announced that he had
completed his case. The defense asked for an adjournment and the case
was put over until Wednesday.

The prosecution did not therefore call the person who would turn
out to be their star handwriting witness, Albert Osborn,[6] who since
1880 was connected with the Rochester Business Institute, a commercial
school in Rochester, New York. (Osborn's name is today well known
to lawyers because he was the author of the still widely used classic
book on handwriting, *Questioned Documents*, with a preface to both the
first and second editions by the great master of evidence, John Wigmore.)[7]

Osborn had arranged to have photographs of the Swenson signatures
reproduced on glass to permit them to be superimposed and thus to
show that the two signatures were made from one model. 'At first glance,'
Osborn reported to Byrne, 'they seem to show more difference than
was anticipated, but a closer study shows them to be exactly alike in
those characteristics to be expected in a traced signature.'[8] Osborn measured various points in the four questioned signatures on the checks. 'A
test of these signatures,' he wrote Byrne, 'shows that these [seven] points
in the four checks are almost absolutely identical, or as near as could
be expected on a small signature ... As nearly as I am able to determine,
the probability of a concurrence would not be more than one in several
hundred million.'[9] Osborn was disappointed that he was not called. He

added a postscript to a letter to Byrne stating: 'I should consider it a special favor to be called at the Grand Jury hearing if you use outside experts at that time that I may be identified on the record of this interesting case.'

Baker, however, was not convinced that there would be a committal for trial. In a letter written after the prosecutor's case was concluded, he stated: 'I confess the Magistrate is an enigma to me. He frequently makes remarks which indicate that his feelings are all with the prisoner, and then again other remarks indicate that he believes them to be guilty. It is difficult to tell what he will do.'[10]

# 27. Committals

Contrary to the public's general expectations, Frederick House offered no defense evidence when the case resumed on Wednesday morning, 24 October. Lawyers, however, were not surprised. The test to determine whether there was sufficient evidence to warrant a committal for trial was then –and still is – a relatively easy hurdle for the prosecutor to get over.[1] There was therefore no point in needlessly subjecting the defense witnesses to cross-examination by the prosecutor. House told the magistrate that he would rest his case on the prosecution's evidence and move that the complaint be dismissed on the ground that the expert evidence did not show that the Rice signatures were forgeries and that the district attorney had adduced no evidence connecting either Patrick or Jones with the forgeries, if, indeed, they were forgeries.

Assistant District Attorney Osborne, in contrast, argued that the guilt of the defendants was obvious. 'The forgeries,' he said, 'were clumsy':

It is a pity that some criminals can't commit intelligent crime. I would like to hear of a good old-fashioned 'crook' who would give the District Attorney and the police something to do. The simplicity of this forgery shows that the perpetrators thereof are from Texas or from some other guileless country where things are done in broad open daylight, and that as criminals these defendants are decidedly not up to the metropolitan standard.[2]

Magistrate Brann reserved his decision.

'Osborne appears very confident,' Baker wrote Lovett, 'and says that the Magistrate will certainly hold the defendants to the Grand Jury and that he will eventually convict both of them.'[3] Baker himself was more pessimistic. He told Lovett:

I do not think the cases against them are as clear as Mr. Osborne seems to think. I have no doubt that the checks were forged, but have some doubt of the ability of the prosecution to establish the fact. Brann, the Magistrate, is an eccentric individual and rather cranky. It is difficult to tell what he will do. I should not be surprised if he discharged both of the defendants, though I certainly think under the evidence he ought to hold them.

Osborne told Baker that if the magistrate discharged the accused he would go directly to the grand jury. (This is still possible today.)[4] Lovett also took a positive approach in his reply to Baker: 'You seem to have some fears of success. Knowing your disposition to look on the "dark side" of things I am not so much surprised at this, but I must say that I never have entertained the slightest doubt since you secured possession of the will of 1896 that the whole scheme would collapse.'

Immediately after the court hearing, Baker and Byrne conferred with Osborne about a special delivery letter Baker had received the previous evening from an Edward Records:[5]

New York, Oct. 23, 1900

Capt. James A. Baker, Jr.
New York

Dear Sir:

I have lately had a number of conversations with Mr. Chas. F. Jones in the City Prison and I suggest to you that you see him at the earliest opportunity and before any fresh proceedings may be instituted.

When you see him let it be alone and not in the presence of either his counsel or of Mr. Patrick.

I have reasons for feeling sure that this interview will be of benefit both to Mr. Jones and yourself.

It is quite possible that Mr. Jones would himself write this letter if it were judicious for him to do so.

I trust, therefore, that you will let him hear from you and that you will see him as soon as possible.

Respectfully,

(Signed) EDW. RECORDS.

My mail address is
      room 30, 150 Broadway, New York.

Osborne advised them to see Captain McCluskey and obtain his permission to interview Jones. McCluskey's advice was that Baker should first see Records. When Baker tried to contact him at his Broadway address, it was discovered that Records was still in the Tombs (or as Baker wrote Lovett, Records 'had been stopping in the Tombs'). McCluskey arranged for Baker and Byrne to see Records there. Records told Baker that the letter explained itself. He, Records, had lived in Houston for a year, working on the *Houston Post*, and had therefore made Jones' acquaintance in the Tombs; he had frequently conferred with Jones while in the 'run-a-round' in the prison and 'had become convinced that Jones was being used by Patrick and expressed the hope that Baker would see him without delay.'[6] Jones was worried, Records said, because 'although he knew Mr. Rice really signed all the checks, yet he understood a large number of experts were unanimous in the opinion that he did not.'[7]

The district attorney's office arranged for Jones to be brought from the Tombs to District Attorney Gardiner's office. Baker had an interview with Jones alone. Captain McCluskey and an assistant DA were out-of-hearing in an adjoining room. Baker made a memorandum of the conversation several days later:[8] 'I asked him what he wished to say. He replied in effect that the situation now was so complicated that he was not in a position to talk at this time. That he was watched continuously and his foot-steps followed by those who noted his every act and deed. That if he went out on bail the following day (as he intended to do, if not re-arrested) he would then see me and talk fully with me.' 'In the course of my conversation with him,' Baker's memorandum stated, 'he told me that he knew of no will of Mr. Rice which gave Mr. Patrick nine-tenths of the Rice estate':

He said that he remembered seeing Mr. Rice execute a will the day of the large fire on the New York docks, the exact date he did not remember; that that will did not give Patrick nine-tenths or any large portion of Mr. Rice's estate; that I ought to know (knowing Mr. Rice as well as I did) that he would not make a will in which any large amount was given to Mr. Patrick, as there was no reason why Patrick should be a beneficiary under any will which Mr. Rice might make ... He repeated time and again that he knew of no will in which Patrick was a beneficiary for any large amount.

Jones described to Baker an earlier will signed by Rice:

He further stated that in December, last, E.P. Griffith of Chicago, an artist of long acquaintance with Mr. Rice, prepared a will for Mr. Rice in which William M. Rice, Jr., Charlie Adams, Albert T. Patrick and myself were named as executors. That Mr. Rice afterwards copied this will in his own handwriting and executed it in the presence of Emile Coser and himself (Jones) as subscribing witnesses. That Coser formerly worked for the Hygeia Ice Company, but is now in Europe and expected to return about the 23d of November. That he did not know what became of this will, whether it was kept by Griffith or by Coser.

The interview concluded with Jones claiming that no forgeries had been committed by Patrick or himself, or anyone else, and that all of these matters would be fully explained at the proper time.

Some of the newspapers learned of the interview and reported that Jones had made a confession. 'This is not true,' Baker wrote to Lovett the next day: 'I cannot understand why he sought the interview, unless he intended to further complicate the situation and mystify me more and more. McCluskey seems to think that Jones was preparing the way for a confession, but I was not so impressed ... The situation is very puzzling. We are up against a masked battery, not knowing what Patrick has in reserve.'[9]

House, when seen by the press at his home in Harlem, said that he could not believe that Jones had confessed. Lovett also didn't think much of Jones' story, which he found 'certainly puzzling and at the same time incredible.' The story about the will drafted by a Chicago artist was, according to Lovett, 'about as improbable as any that even Patrick has told': 'If Mr. Rice did execute a will, as Jones claims, it is inconceivable that he should have entrusted it to one of the witnesses with a foreign name or to the Chicago artist, who Jones says prepared it. It is also inconceivable that he would have engaged a painter instead of a lawyer to draft the will.'

On Saturday morning, 27 October, two events occurred. The first was that Magistrate Brann announced through the Centre Street court stenographer that Patrick and Jones would be held to await the action of the grand jury. Bail at $10,000 each would be continued.

The second event was that Dr Witthaus' report was released. Witthaus found that there was mercury and arsenic in the body and that the embalming fluid contained arsenic but not mercury. The report stated:

The stomach was found to contain arsenic in notable quantity and an unweighable minute quantity of mercury. The presence of the arsenic in this and the parts mentioned below would be accounted for if the embalming liquid, a sample of which I analyzed, had been used in preserving the body. The intestines were found to contain both arsenic and mercury. The quantity of arsenic present has not yet been determined.

The kidney contained arsenic and mercury also. The quantity of arsenic has not been determined. I would infer from the very small quantity of mercury found in the stomach and the relatively large amount found in the intestines, and particularly in the kidney, that the metal in some form of soluble combination had been introduced into the body during the life of the deceased, probably several hours, possibly days, previous to his death.[10]

District Attorney Gardiner was not satisfied with the report. It did not state, he said, whether the amount of mercury discovered in the organs was sufficient to cause death. He arranged for a meeting on Monday with Dr Witthaus. Dr Curry was questioned by the press: 'In none of the medicines prescribed by him for Rice,' he said, 'was there the slightest particle of mercury.' 'It is a well-known medical fact,' Curry went on to say, 'that mercury may remain in a person's system for years. Mr. Rice was subject to indigestion and stomach trouble, and may have taken some simple remedy, without my knowledge. In his closet were many such medicines.'[11]

Jones refused to comment on the report. Patrick simply said: 'I do not believe Mr. Rice was poisoned. It is not possible.' After meeting with his clients later that afternoon, House confidently told the press: 'Patrick and Jones will not have to face any more serious charge than that for forgery.'

Earlier that morning, Edward Records, who had been released from prison after his case was dismissed, called on Baker at the San Remo Hotel on the west side of Central Park. Jones, he said, was anxious to see Baker and would state to him truthfully all he knew concerning Mr Rice's affairs, the execution of wills by him, and the circumstances surrounding his death. This occurred before Dr Witthaus' report was received. Records saw Jones again in the early afternoon, after Witthaus' report had been released, and reported that Jones was now 'exceedingly anxious' to see Baker.[12]

Osborne advised Baker that he should see Jones and provided Baker with a sealed request to the warden to permit such a visit on Sunday afternoon. Baker and Byrne drove in Byrne's carriage towards the Tombs, discussing the advisability of the visit. At the last minute, however, they decided against it, Baker wrote to Lovett: 'At this particular time we thought it inadvisable to do so because the substance of Professor Witt-haus' report had been made public and indicated that Jones and Patrick were guilty of a greater crime than that of alleged forgery, and for this reason it would perhaps be better that I should not see him.'

# 28. Confession

Professor Witthaus prepared a supplementary report for the coroner and the district attorney. In total, he said, he found more than three-quarters of a gram of mercury. The intestines contained half a gram, the kidneys about a quarter of a gram, and there were very small amounts in the liver and the stomach.[1] The existing files do not indicate what Witthaus told the DA, but he told the press that the quantity was sufficient to cause death.

'In what form was poison administered to Mr. Rice?' Professor Witt-haus was asked. 'It would not be proper for me to discuss that matter,' Witthaus replied: 'I will only say that I found in the vital organs of Mr. Rice poison in sufficient quantity to have caused death. It is not for me to say who administered that poison or whether it was given with criminal intent.'[2]

The *Herald* interviewed an unnamed 'eminent physician' who said that mercury, 'if administered to an ordinary adult in any considerable quantity, would result in death after violent retchings, dysentery and great physical pain.' The newspaper then interviewed Rice's black house-keeper, who seemed to nail the lid on the coffin by stating: 'Mr. Rice was during the last days of his life subject to violent fits of vomiting. He suffered from dysentery, too, and in many ways was unlike himself.'

A coroner's inquest was set for Thursday morning at eleven o'clock. On Tuesday, 30 October, about noon, Jones' new friend, Edward Rec-ords, again came to see Baker to say that Jones was still very anxious to see him or the district attorney. Records said that Jones had told him that Patrick was conferring with the lawyers apart from him and that Patrick had told him that the best thing he, Jones, could do was to commit suicide. Baker and Byrne tried to find Osborne, the DA, but were unable to do so until about seven o'clock that evening. Osborne asked Records to see whether Jones still wanted to see him. Records returned from the Tombs saying he did.

Osborne, Baker, and Records went to the Tombs and met with Jones in the warden's office. Baker's memorandum of the interview states:

Mr. Osborne warned him that the law did not require him to make any confession; that if Jones desired to make any statement he must do so voluntarily and with the understanding that he (Osborne) for the people would use his statement as evidence against him (Jones). Jones was fully and completely warned and put upon his guard. He stated that nevertheless he desired to make a statement of all he knew about Mr. Rice's death.[3]

'The confession,' Baker wrote, 'was not extorted from Jones by the Police under what is known as the "third degree" process or otherwise, but was altogether voluntary on his part.'[4] Shortly after Jones commenced his statement, the DA sent for Byrne and Miller of the Hornblower firm to have them present as well. During the statement, Jones asked to speak to Baker privately and for a period the two conferred out of the hearing of the others. From 9 p.m. until 4 a.m. Osborne wrote out in longhand what Jones told him.

Jones said that Patrick had been seeing Rice once or twice a week for many months and had drafted a will for Rice. But this will, the 'genuine will,' was signed and properly witnessed on 26 May 1900, not 30 June. Jones said he did not know of the 30 June will, leaving Patrick the bulk of the estate, until after Rice was dead; indeed he was not aware of it until the day he was arrested.

Under the 'genuine will' of 26 May, Jones said, the Rice Institute was to get only one million dollars:

the remainder of his estate was then divided into four parts; the first part went to James A. Baker, the second part to Wm. M. Rice, Jr., the third part to be divided among friends and relatives, and the fourth, ($250,000) two hundred and fifty thousand dollars, to settle the Holt claim, and the balance to go to Albert T. Patrick for the benefit of the Y.M.C.A., West Side Branch. That will Mr. Rice refused to sign for some time, but did sign it on or about May 26, 1900.[5]

Throughout this period, Jones said, 'Mr. Rice seemed to have perfect confidence in Mr. Patrick.' But in early September 1900, after Lovett had visited Rice and had assured him about winning the lawsuit involving Mrs Rice, 'Mr. Rice seemed to become suspicious of Mr. Patrick's actions and asked him to return all the papers he had given to him.'[6]

Patrick, Jones said, had given Rice some unidentified whitish gray tablets to ease Rice's constipation. Rice took one of these tablets every night for perhaps two weeks, until the Friday night before his death.

On Saturday morning, after a sleepless night, according to Jones, Rice sent him to Patrick's house to tell him that 'if he did not return his, Mr. Rice's, papers he would report it to the authorities.' Patrick did not return the papers, but gave Jones a bottle containing a substance which he wanted Jones to dilute with twenty parts of water and give to Rice. Only a mouthful of the acidic-tasting liquid was taken by Rice. Jones said he threw the remainder of what he learned was poisonous oxalic acid into the toilet. Late Sunday afternoon, on the day of Rice's death, Jones – according to his statement to Osborne – phoned Patrick on Rice's instructions and told him that 'if Mr. Patrick did not come the next morning he would notify the authorities.'[7] Patrick said he would come that evening at seven o'clock.

Patrick, Jones said, came to the apartment about seven o'clock. Jones then described what allegedly followed:

He came about 7 o'clock and had a package of papers and sat in a chair by the bed and talked to Mr. Rice and Mr. Rice took the papers from him. Patrick said, Why do you wish the papers, and I don't remember Mr. Rice's answer. Mr. Rice told Mr. Patrick he was very nervous and did not wish to be troubled; please go away. Mr. Patrick said, I have some smelling salts to quiet the nerves. I do not know whether he said liniment or what. Mr. Patrick asked me for a towel and a sponge, which I got for him. He said, You must leave the room. I left the room. He said, I will remain with Mr. Rice till he goes to sleep and will go out of the side door. I heard Mr. Rice laughing a few moments after I left the room. I went to the door, saw Mr. Rice lying on his back and the towel was folded in a cone shape and was over his whole face, and Mr. Patrick was holding it over his face with his right hand. Mr. Patrick did not see me, nor did Mr. Rice. I opened the door enough to see what was going on, I opened it to see what was causing the laughter, and just as soon as I saw the position of things I went and laid down on my bed and went to sleep. When I waked up about 8 o'clock, I had been in the habit of carrying water to Mr. Rice's room since he had been sick. When I asked him if he wanted water, he did not answer. I took up his hand and found it limp and lifeless. I lit the gas, that is, I turned it up – it had been burning low – when I saw he was either fainting or dead, I sent for the doctor. I first looked all over the house for Mr. Patrick; he was not there. I then sent for the doctor and telephoned Mr. Patrick that Mr. Rice was either very sick or dead, and where have you been and how did you get away. He said nothing to the question, but said I will go by and get the doctor. The doctor and Mr. Patrick came together about half-past eight or nine o'clock, and the doctor pronounced Mr. Rice dead. Patrick said, Doctor, examine him thoroughly and see how long he has been dead.

He seemed nervous and very much excited. The doctor said he had been dead about twenty minutes.[8]

The following morning, according to Jones' statement, Patrick asked him to fill out in certain designated amounts the four questioned checks that already had the signature 'W.M. Rice' on them. The signatures on three of the checks, Jones said, were genuine; Rice was in the habit of signing checks in blank.

Baker recorded in his memorandum following the confession: 'At the conclusion of Jones' confession he said that he felt better since he had made it, and when we parted he seemed to feel easier.'[9] At 4:00 a.m. Wednesday morning Jones was returned to his cell.

For most of the following day, Baker, Byrne, and Gerard met with Osborne and McCluskey, going over Jones' statement. The crucial problem was that Patrick appeared to have a complete alibi. The police had interviewed persons in Patrick's boarding house who confirmed that on the evening of 23 September Patrick had had an early dinner, spent an hour or so accompanying his fellow lodgers on the piano while they practiced singing, and then gone to a Sunday evening Christian Endeavour meeting.

Baker wrote to Lovett: 'there are many inconsistent statements in Jones' confession and it is impossible for me to distinguish between the true and the apparent false statements.'[10]

Late that afternoon, Osborne and McCluskey summoned Jones to another meeting in Osborne's office. They told him that they did not believe him and asked him to give a further, accurate statement. Jones dictated to Osborne virtually the very same story he had told the night before. The *Times* reported that he remained with Osborne and McCluskey for two hours: 'At the conclusion of this conference Jones came out, with flushed features and closely set teeth. He breathed a sigh of relief when he was again handcuffed to the keeper.' Jones had been writing letters in his cell during the afternoon and continued to do so when he returned.

Osborne informed Patrick about Jones' statement and told Patrick that if he had anything he wanted to say, this was the time to talk. Patrick sent word back that he did not want to talk about any crime, but would like to have a talk with Captain Baker about the estate. Osborne returned word that he was only interested in facts concerning the death of Mr Rice and had no interest in the estate.

Shortly before dawn, a keeper found Jones lying in his cell in a pool of blood with his neck cut by a knife.

# 29. Bellevue Hospital

A prisoner who had his cell directly opposite Jones described the event
to the press:

'It was almost 4 o'clock when I was awakened from a sound sleep by the calling
of keepers and trustees. At first I thought the place was on fire, and then I saw
that the trouble was over Jones' cell. I saw Night Warden Curran run into the
cell and stoop over Jones, who was lying on his back on his cot. He seemed to be
dead. Blood was flowing from his neck, and the bedding was red with blood. I
heard Curran tell one of the keepers, "For God's sake, some of you get Bellevue
on the phone. Get an ambulance." '[1]

Bellevue Hospital recorded the call at 4:12 a.m. An ambulance with
a doctor was dispatched almost immediately. The seven-hundred-bed
hospital, affiliated with New York University, was – and is – situated
beside the East River.[2] The doctor found that Jones had inflicted a deep
cut on the right side of his throat and had slightly opened the jugular
vein. A small penknife with a one-inch blade was found in Jones' night-
clothes. If he had not been discovered for another fifteen minutes, the
doctor said, he could have been dead. At 5:30 in the morning, now
unconscious, Jones was placed in the prison ward of Bellevue Hospital,
guarded by two keepers.

Later that morning, Assistant District Attorney Osborne told the press
that Jones had made a full confession, implicating Patrick. (Such a statement by a prosecutor today would be considered improper.)[3] Patrick,
Osborne said, had given Jones the knife and had urged him to commit
suicide.

'Should Jones die,' Osborne was asked, 'could his confession be used against
Patrick?'

'No,' Osborne correctly replied, 'and no one better than Patrick knows that.
He is a lawyer, and he knows that dead men tell no tales.'[4]

Patrick sent a letter to the press: 'I do not believe that Jones ever
made such a statement. If he did, he simply told a mass of lies from
start to finish. I am innocent of the charges made against me, and hope
to be so proved in course of time.' Patrick denied knowing anything
about the knife. Jones, Patrick said, was 'bulldozed into talking a lot
of rubbish.'[5]

House called the conduct of the prosecuting attorneys 'high handed and outrageous.' The reason why defense counsel were not informed of the discussions and requested to be present, House said, 'was that the authorities might be left to work the famous "third degree."' Jones had told him, House said, that Baker had taken him aside and advised him 'to embrace the opportunity to help himself; if he did not, he was sure to be convicted of forgery, and might be executed.' House said he was in consultation with eminent counsel as to the advisability of presenting the entire transaction to Governor Theodore Roosevelt, requesting an extraordinary session of the grand jury 'for the purpose of investigating the matter and of determining whether the rights of an accused party are to be overridden and trampled upon by the authorities in this way.'

'Such talk,' Osborne said, 'is merely the natural outburst of a lawyer who is suddenly confronted with such a surprising performance on the part of a client as this confession. If you are prosecuting a case and a defendant sends for you and says he wants to make a confession, what are you going to do? Are you going to send for the defendant's lawyer, so the man's mouth will be shut up and he won't say anything?'[6] (Such questioning would not be permitted in New York today.)[7]

A *World* reporter claimed to have been in the corridor of the Criminal Court Building when the statement had been taken from Jones and reported the overheard conversation:

'You give me a guarantee in writing that I shall be granted immunity and I will talk. Unless you do that I will not open my mouth,' Jones is reported to have stated.

'You are foolish,' was the reply. 'Why don't you take advantage of what we are offering you? You can save 5 or 10, yes 15 years of time, if you talk to me.'

At noon, House and his associate, Moses Grossman, called on Jones, but because Jones was said to be partially delirious they did not stay long.

Edward Records had earlier called on Baker at Hornblower's office and suggested that under the circumstances Jones should obtain separate counsel. After consulting the DA and the chief of police, Baker and Miller, from the Hornblower firm, went to see Jones in the early afternoon. Baker wrote to Lovett about the meeting: 'He was conscience stricken and wept bitterly, reproaching himself that he should have permitted Patrick to make way with Mr. Rice when he (Jones) was in the adjoining room and could have prevented it. He sobbed aloud, saying that Mr. Rice was the only friend he ever had and he could not endure the thought of having been a party to his murder.'[8]

Baker suggested that Judge Hamblin or Jones' mother or father could come at Baker's expense to advise Jones, but, according to Baker, Jones said 'he could not bear to look into the faces of his parents or his old friends with the knowledge of his guilt.'[9] Several lawyers' names, including George Gordon Battle, were mentioned by Baker. Jones said he would like Mr Battle, a Southerner who had defended Molineux, to represent him.

# 30. George Gordon Battle

Battle was from an old South Carolinian family – his father had been a prosperous slave-owning cotton planter – and in 1890 he had come to New York to study law at Columbia University, where he was a classmate and good friend of Benjamin Cardozo. Battle spent the five years after graduation in the district attorney's office in New York City and then entered private practice. Throughout his career, he was active in Tammany Hall politics, eventually running, unsuccessfully, for the office of district attorney of New York in 1909.[1]

Both Southerners, Baker and Battle hit it off well: 'He is a South Carolinian by birth,' Baker wrote, 'and seems to be an excellent gentleman.'[2] Both Baker and Battle came to see Jones late Thursday afternoon. Baker was careful to ensure that formally it was Jones and not he that employed Battle. He wrote to Lovett: 'While I procured the services of Battle in Jones' behalf, I do not wish to be understood as saying that I employed Mr. Battle or am responsible or liable for the value of his services. It was thought best that no such relation should exist between him and those I represent.'[3] Nevertheless, there must have been some implicit understanding that Baker would ensure that Battle was paid, because he added in his letter to Lovett: 'Jones, I understand, has paid him a small retainer, but of this I will speak to you more in detail when I see you again.'

The next day, House and Battle together called on Jones for a brief meeting. According to Baker, 'House was glad to be relieved of the embarrassment of attempting to defend both Jones and Patrick, and expressed gratification that Battle was to take charge of Jones' defense.'

Baker went on in his letter to Lovett to state that House was in fact anxious to get out of the Patrick case:

because since Jones' confession it is difficult for him to draw the line between his duty to Patrick as a client, and his duty to Jones not to divulge information imparted to him by Jones while [Jones] sustained the relation of client to House. This is a very sensible and reasonable view for lawyer House to take, but I am uncharitable enough to believe that it is prompted more from Patrick's inability to pay a good fat fee than from any delicate professional considerations. Patrick has no money, so far as I can learn.

District Attorney Osborne was asked by the press about possible murder charges. 'I am not prepared to answer that,' Osborne replied: 'It would be with the greatest reluctance that I would proceed against Jones, as I recognize that Patrick's was the master mind in this case.'[4]

In a letter to Lovett, Baker also expressed the view that Jones would likely not be prosecuted for murder:

The District Attorney has not yet agreed to any immunity for Jones, but Battle thinks in any event he will be able to save his life, and possibly do very much better for him. If Jones tells the whole truth, and the story is consistent and can be corroborated, I believe Osborne will not prosecute him for murder, but may consent to his pleading guilty of the charge of forgery.[5]

The district attorney was specifically asked about Patrick using a cone-shaped towel and a sponge:

'Do you believe that Mr. Rice came to his death from the effects of either chloroform or ether?'

'Jones says he heard the old man laugh, and it is well known that a certain anaesthetic causes laughter,' Osborne replied.

The next day, Osborne told the press that 'the lungs of the dead man showed indications of smothering and that this theory would be fully investigated.' Coroner's Physician Donlin, however, ducked the issue, stating that 'if Mr. Rice was suffocated the embalming fluid covered up the traces forever.'[6]

Dr Curry was also questioned by the press. He detected no smell of chloroform or ether, stating:

I believe that he had been dead about twenty minutes when I arrived. The body was warm, which in the case of a very old person whose blood is thin, would not remain so above twenty or twenty-five minutes. In this case I found the limbs composed, showing no evidences of contortion. The eyeball, furthermore, gave no evidence of a violent death. I observed no odor either of ether, chloroform or other anaesthetic about the room when I entered. In my professional life I have attended thousands of operations and would immediately detect the odor of an anaesthetic. It seems to me that the odor of ether or chloroform in that room would have been perceptible for as long as twenty minutes after being administered.[7]

'I have the utmost confidence in Dr. Curry,' Osborne said, 'and not the slightest suspicion of guilt attaches to him.'

Baker had been thinking about the possibility of chloroform having been used because in mid-October, while searching through Rice's papers in the apartment, he came across an article on chloroform in the June 1900 issue of a magazine Rice subscribed to, the *Omega Magazine*. This discovery was made before Jones had said anything about Patrick administering a substance by means of the sponge and the cone. The short medical article was entitled 'Deaths from Chloroform' and it began: 'Two deaths in our midst from the use of chloroform as an anaesthetic within sixty days should arouse the profession to greater care and more discrimination in its use.'[8]

Battle saw Jones at Bellevue Hospital on a number of occasions and on 8 November took a detailed statement from him. The statement was similar to the one that Jones had previously given to Osborne with respect to Patrick killing Rice:

Patrick told me to go and get a towel and a sponge. I got a towel from a linen closet in front and sponge from same closet. Mr. Rice used the sponge for cleaning his clothes. When I returned Patrick had a bottle in his hand, which was filled with a colorless liquid and which he put on the bureau. He then wrapped the towel around his hand in conical shape, pinned it with a safety pin which he took from the bureau, took the sponge and placed it in the small end of it.[9]

But the statement differed with respect to Patrick's relations with Rice: 'Mr. Rice never knew Patrick,' Jones said; 'He knew him only as a friend of mine and never asked his name.' In the earlier statements he had detailed a long-standing relationship between Rice and Patrick. Moreover, in his statement to Battle, Jones denied that Rice had knowingly signed a will on 26 May 1900. That will, which Jones said gave the Rice Institute only a million dollars and then gave Patrick a quarter of the estate to settle the Holt claim and provide for the West Side Branch of the YMCA, was signed by Rice when he was 'half awake and ... without knowing what he did.' 'Patrick told me,' Jones said, 'that he (Patrick) would get the whole 1/4 and that the West Side Branch of the YMCA would get nothing and that he would look out for me.' The 30 June 'Patrick Will,' Jones said, was a forgery: 'It is possible that they may have had him sign the will of June 30, 1900 without my knowledge but I firmly believe it to be impossible and that they are out and out forgeries.'

On Monday, 12 November, Jones was released from Bellevue Hospital and returned to the Tombs Prison. Later that week, Judge Goff granted a motion by the district attorney to have Jones transferred from the Tombs to the more comfortable House of Detention.

# 31. Private Detectives

A number of private detective agencies were engaged by the Hornblower firm. Pinkerton's National Detective Agency surreptitiously kept tabs on Meyers, Short, and others, and an agency called Thiel's Detective Agency tried to ferret out information concerning Patrick. Fees for the detective agencies amounted to several thousand dollars a month.

A Thiel agency operative and his daughter took rooms at Mrs Francis' boarding house and reported to the Hornblower firm various conversations with Mrs Francis and others. One conversation with Mrs Francis, for example, told about a spiritualist, a Miss Margaret Gaule, who had conducted a seance at the boarding house a year earlier. Patrick had made fun of the spiritualist, who then approached Patrick and said: 'You don't believe in me, but I will tell you of a paper which you have now in your pocket. You are worrying a great deal about this paper and there will be trouble about it, but you will come out all right.' Patrick, Mrs Francis said, 'was staggered and nearly fell from his chair ... and sure enough there was trouble about this paper.'[1]

An operative was then assigned to cultivate Miss Gaule, the spiritualist. The operative attended a number of public and private sessions and provided the Hornblower firm with interesting descriptions of Miss Gaule and her operations: 'Miss G.,' one report stated, 'is a woman about 35 or 40 years of age; of rather dark complexion, large eyes, a sensual mouth, and appears to be gifted, as are all her kind, with a brazen self-confident unblushing effrontery.' In the end, however, no information was elicited from her relating to Patrick and the operation was dropped.

The Thiel agency also attempted to get information from Patrick's former secretary, a Miss Grand. A male operative called her and gave her secretarial work. The operative saw her professionally perhaps a dozen times, and on one occasion went to the theatre and to dinner with her and her mother. After several weeks, the conversation finally got around to lawyers the secretary had once worked for. The operative set out the conversation with Miss Grand:

'You'd be surprised if you knew who the man was,' Miss Grand said.
'I surprised? Why?' the operative replied.
'It was Patrick, the lawyer.'
'Patrick, what Patrick – not Patrick Henry?'
'No, you've seen his name in the newspapers; he was arrested.'
'Oh, you don't mean the man who was connected with the murder of that old fellow – Rice?'
'Yes.'

The secretary then gave her opinion of Patrick. In the words of the operative, Miss Grand said that 'Patrick was one of the "nicest men" she ever worked for, and that he seemed to be a prosperous lawyer. She said that she did not believe that he was guilty.'

It was at about this point that Baker complained to the Hornblower firm about the high cost of the detective agencies. 'So far, if my recollection serves me correctly,' Baker wrote, 'we have obtained very little benefit from the detective agencies.'[2]

Nevertheless, the Thiel operative staying with Mrs Francis continued his reports. Mrs Francis told him: 'Rice died on Sunday and Patrick was in my house all day and in the evening he asked me to go out with him for a walk ... If Mr. Patrick told me that he had killed Rice and forged the will, I would not believe him. He is no more guilty of what they say he is than you are.'

Mrs Francis told Patrick in the Tombs about her new boarder. 'I hope he is not a detective,' Patrick stated; 'you know they are very smooth.'

The operative established that there was a close relationship between Patrick and Mrs Francis. Patrick occupied the back parlor and she the front, without a bed in the front parlor, said one former roomer. Moreover, Mrs Francis and Patrick had occupied a cabin together in the seaside area of Bensonhurst in Brooklyn the previous summer. 'I don't care what people say about me,' Mrs Francis told the operative, 'I am not going to give them the satisfaction of knowing whether I am married to Patrick or not.'

# 32. The Wills

The 1896 will had been filed by the Hornblower firm in the Surrogate Court of New York in mid-October. The so-called Patrick will of 30 June 1900 had still not officially appeared for the contest that, as previously noted, the *Herald* had said 'promises to be one of the greatest legal battles that has ever taken place in the courts of this country.'[1]

Many thought that Patrick would now abandon his claim. Osborne told the press – with his characteristic certainty – that the will was 'the most remarkable instrument I have ever seen. Wetherbee gets $5,000 notwithstanding the fact that he is about the last man on earth to whom Rice would have left money. I believe Patrick to be a moral idiot. He thinks that every man has his price.'[2]

Baker and the Hornblower firm were preparing for a contest. 'We are busy everyday getting up testimony and preparing ourselves for the fight just as if we knew that the will is to be contested,' Baker wrote. 'I am no doubt running up a heavy expense,' Baker told Lovett, but expressed great confidence in the Hornblower firm: 'No one could have done more or better work.'[3] Lovett wrote back that 'the expense in the way of lawyers' fees ... we can regard with a considerable degree of complacency.'[4] With respect to the fees, Lovett thought that 'an equal division in this instance would certainly not be unfair.'[5] He suggested that Baker take up the issue before returning to Texas: 'if they are going to be unreasonable and unfair it is not too late to make some other arrangement, though of course that would be a last resort.'

One of the many issues that had to be dealt with was whether a special deal should be made to gain the support of some of Rice's heirs who would receive more under the Patrick will than under the 1896 will. Two of Rice's sisters from Massachusetts, for example, would each get $25,000 outright under the Patrick will, but only a life interest in $10,000 under the 1896 will. Baker wrote to his firm for advice:

If they contest the will of 1896, and they will no doubt be able to employ lawyers to make the contest upon a contingent fee, it might tie up the estate for twelve months, or longer, and in order to avoid this, would it not be better to try to make some settlement with them? We may be able to settle with them, if a settlement is deemed desirable, at less than the amount given them under the Patrick will. I think Byrne, and possibly Hornblower, are inclined to settle with these people, while I am rather against it.[6]

There was a split in the advice given by Baker's firm. Lovett was against any compromise: 'His wishes are expressed in the will, and it seems to me that it is your duty to carry them out.' Parker, in contrast, would have made a deal: 'This is not in my mind making a new will or revising the old one. It is simply protecting and preserving as far as possible under existing conditions the will as it exists.' As it turned out, no deal was made with the relatives at this stage. Captain William M. Rice, the testator's nephew, had made a special trip from Texas, at Baker's request and at the expense of the Rice Institute, to meet with this group of relatives. The Massachusetts relatives agreed to support the 1896 will, knowing that the law still allowed them twelve months after probate to contest the will if satisfactory arrangements were not made for them. No doubt some assurances were given by Captain Rice. Patrick's lawyers complained to the press that Baker was buying the support of the relatives.

After making a formal demand for the will from Patrick in the Tombs, the Hornblower firm asked the Surrogate Court for an order requiring Patrick to submit the 1900 will for examination. This motion was adjourned at Patrick's request, but only on condition that Patrick deposit the will with some third person or company. The will was therefore sealed and deposited in the safe of the law firm Guggenheimer, Untermeyer, and Marshall,[7] a firm that had offices in the same building as the Hornblower firm.

It was expected that Samuel Untermeyer would act for Patrick, but when the motion was heard, another law firm represented him. 'This is very fortunate for us, I think,' Baker wrote to Lovett, expressing an attitude typical of the period, 'as Mr. Untermeyer's firm, though composed of Hebrews, has the reputation of being quite strong and influential, Mr. Guggenheimer of that firm being the president of the City Council.'[8] In order to avoid any further connection with the case and consequent unfavorable publicity, Untermeyer arranged with Hornblower to turn the will over to the New York Security and Trust Company before the hearing.

Patrick was represented at the hearing, Baker told Lovett, by 'a young

Jewish lawyer by the name of Harby who I think formerly lived in Texas.' Harby was the junior partner in the three-man firm of Logan, Demond, and Harby. Baker's partner, Parker, was not impressed with Harby, stating in a letter to Baker: 'I know this young Harby. He is a Jew; has very black hair; wears glasses and used to write for the magazines. He was never regarded at the University as a man of any ability.'

# 33. December 1900

Far from withdrawing the will of 1900, in early December Patrick filed it for probate with the Surrogate Court and entered an appearance contesting the validity of the 1896 will. The opposition to the will of 1896 was on the basis – but without details – that the will was not properly signed or witnessed and was procured to be signed for a fraudulent and ulterior purpose. Some of Rice's relatives, who would profit through an intestacy if both wills were defeated, later joined in opposing the 1896 will on the basis that the William Marsh Rice Institute had no power to receive a bequest under the will because it had not commenced active operations within three years of incorporation as required under Texas law. Baker wrote to Lovett: 'we need not fear any attack under this provision of the Statute. Immediately after the charter was granted the corporation was organized and has been in active business ever since accumulating funds, etc., to be used in the erection and maintenance of the institution.'[1]

Handwriting experts now had access to the Patrick will. Baker wrote to Lovett:

In my letter to you of the 30th ult. I mentioned the fact that the Patrick will had been filed for probate, but had been examined by only one expert, Mr. Kingsley, who unhesitatingly pronounced it a forgery. Since then the signatures have been examined by Mr. Osborn, an expert from Rochester and an unusually bright and intelligent man; by Mr. Hagen, of Troy, by Mr. Tolman, of Chicago, Mr. Tyrell of Milwaukee, and Mr. Carvalho, of New York, and all of them unhesitatingly pronounce the signatures forgeries; in fact some of them say they are more palpable forgeries than the checks. The will is signed at the bottom of each page, and at the end, making four signatures in all. The measurements show some wonderful coincidences.[2]

Carvalho expressed his opinion this way:

They bear in and of themselves internal evidences of hesitation and method in
their general make up, and when compared with signatures made by Mr. Rice
... present so different an appearance in general pictorial effect, pen pressure
and relationship to a base line as to at once stamp them as having been made by
some one other than the person whose genuine signature they purport to represent. They are crude forgeries and I believe will be so determined.[3]

    Handwriting expert Albert Osborn wanted a random selection of
Rice's signatures for comparison: 'the selection should be made in some
arbitrary manner showing that they were not selected for the purpose
of showing a certain result. Perhaps the twenty signatures available nearest to the date of the will would be the best basis of selection.'[4] In fact,
seventy-nine check signatures were procured – all Rice's checks from
January to September 1900. Osborn concluded that the signatures on
the Patrick will 'must have been made from the same model.'[5]

    A detailed letter from Osborn to the Hornblower firm explained why
it was difficult to forge Rice's signature. Rice's handwriting, Osborn
pointed out, was in the early American style in general use before about
1840. Characteristic of this style of writing, which was similar to that
used in England and known as the English round hand, was 'a tendency
to shade in a pronounced manner all the capital letters and also all the
main downward strokes of the small letters.' For example, the curved
downward stroke of the capital 'W' is 'not found in modern types of
capital letters and is a difficult stroke to imitate, so much so that it would
not be likely to be followed accurately even in a tracing.' A forger would
likely choose a model that did not show this particular characteristic in
a pronounced manner. The absence of the characteristic shading or pen
pressure shows forgery: 'Pen pressure or shading is an unconscious habit
based upon the original style of writing learned. Shading or pen pressure
in a writer becomes a habit so fixed as to be almost uncontrollable and
it is not conceivable that [Rice] could have wholly departed from his
regular habit.'

    During the month of December, the Hornblower firm took extraor-
dinary steps to tie up virtually all the reputable handwriting experts in
the United States. Previously, they had approached only the leading experts. A young associate lawyer in the firm, William Wherry, went from
city to city seeking opinions based on photographs of the signatures
on the checks and the will. Wherry wrote to his firm from St Louis
on 15 December: 'Tonight I take the 9:05 p.m. train for Chicago and

will spend tomorrow there. If I am not to go to Minneapolis I shall leave Chicago for Pittsburgh at 8:00 p.m. arriving at 8:30 Monday morning. Tuesday night I will go to Syracuse, Wednesday night to Boston, Thursday night to Baltimore and Saturday morning will find me at the office.'[6] Plans to go to San Francisco were canceled because the experts who were to be seen there were then in New York.

Albert Osborn alerted the Hornblower firm about a Canadian handwriting expert whom Osborn had heard while giving evidence that a will had been forged in a Canadian murder case – the Sifton case in London, Ontario. The will in the Sifton case had also been dated 30 June 1900: 'a good day for bad wills,' Osborn wrote. Like himself, the Canadian expert was involved in a business school, the Shaw Business School, still in existence today: 'W.H. Shaw, corner Yonge and Gerrard Sts., Toronto, Ontario. He is a very competent gentleman, makes an excellent impression, and coming as he does from another country might add somewhat to the force of his testimony.'[7] There is nothing in the files to indicate that Shaw was contacted, but there is correspondence between Hornblower and one of the counsel in the case, the great Canadian advocate I.F. Hellmuth,[8] on the issue of whether the probate of a will must await the outcome of the murder case.[9]

The purpose in engaging the experts was, as previously mentioned, not just to get favorable evidence, but to 'kill' the witnesses and thus prevent Patrick from hiring them. Wherry wrote about one expert that he saw in Washington whose evidence was favorable to the Rice interests: 'I don't think we would want to use him as a witness but he could be coached in almost any way you suggested, though he would not *wittingly* falsify I believe. I think it is a good thing we killed him as he has been trying to get into the case and his solicitations might have seduced the other side.'[10]

Baker decided to return to Texas in early December to await being called back for the will hearing. His wife and children had returned to Texas in mid-November. 'Our baby [Jim] has not been well here,' Baker wrote Lovett: 'He suffered from a bronchial infection, and the doctor thought the climate here was not good for him.' Baker then moved from the San Remo Hotel to the Hotel Imperial at Broadway and 32nd Street. 'I am tired of the Normandie,' he wrote, 'and the others at which I would like to stop are crowded this week owing to the Horse Show.'[11] Baker returned to New York for a scheduled hearing on 20 December, but the hearing was again adjourned. The next day, Patrick, through a third party, asked Baker to see him in the Tombs to discuss a possible settlement of the will cases, but Baker replied that he did not care to see Patrick and certainly not that day as he was to leave for Houston that evening. Baker returned home for Christmas.

Patrick spent Christmas in the Tombs, Mrs Francis bringing him a special dinner on Christmas Day. He was encouraged by one recent development. District Attorney Gardiner had been removed from office a few days earlier by Governor Roosevelt for ignoring charges against gamblers and for not prosecuting Police Chief Devery, who had allegedly interfered with an election investigation. 'Patrick is very much pleased at the removal of District Attorney Gardiner,' Mrs Francis confided to the undercover operative: 'The change will be a benefit to him.'[12] Eugene Philbin, who many years later was appointed a justice of the Appellate Division of the New York Supreme Court, was chosen to replace Gardiner.[13] No doubt, Patrick was hoping that Philbin would not reappoint Osborne. But Osborne was kept on. 'This is particularly gratifying,' Baker wrote to the Hornblower firm from Texas, 'not only because Mr. Osborne no doubt desired to retain the place, but because of his ability and efficiency as a prosecuting officer.'[14]

The day after Christmas, Patrick's father arrived in New York from Austin to visit his son. He returned to Texas a few days later and called on Captain Baker in Houston. Baker reported the conversation to the Hornblower firm:

He exhibited to me a letter from Mr. Milliken, of St. Louis, his son-in-law, to the effect that he was satisfied of A.T. Patrick's innocence of any crime and of his ability to establish the will of June 30th, 1900, and that he, Milliken, stood ready to furnish the necessary money to defend against the criminal charge and to establish the so-called Patrick will. Mr. Patrick said that he shared Mr. Milliken's confidence and so did his son, A.T. Patrick, but that litigation was long, tedious and necessarily expensive, and he was in favor of a compromise, and had come of his own accord to see me with a view of determining what could be done in that direction; that if no settlement could be made, then he would, with Milliken's assistance, go to work in earnest to defend against the criminal charge and to establish the will of 1900.

Baker offered Mr Patrick, Sr, no hope for a compromise, telling the Hornblower firm:

I replied to him, in effect, that so far as I could see, the will of 1896 was either Mr. Rice's last will and testament and ought to be probated as such, or it was not, and in that event should be denied probate; that there was no compromising ground to stand upon, and I was satisfied no compromise could ever be reached and he should not lose any time in useless negotiations.

# 34. William Bacon

In early November, a letter was received by the Hornblower firm from a William Bacon in London, England, suggesting that the firm would find valuable information if it investigated an incident a year earlier in which Patrick, Potts, and Short – described by the writer as 'the triple alliance of crime' – helped in the 'cheating and defrauding of a poor woman's estate.'[1] Potts and Short, it will be recalled, shared space with Patrick and were sent by him to certify Rice's cheques. The woman, Bacon said, could not complain to the authorities because she was a married woman and had been found registered at a Jersey City hotel with a 'prosperous, handsome travelling man.' She would have been blackmailed into dropping any complaint she might have made.

The writer, identifying himself as a New Yorker with business interests in Europe and Siberia, had harsh things to say about the 'triple alliance.' Short, he said, was 'as black at heart as the holes of Calcutta' and Patrick, 'with his silk hat and with his slow, calculating talk,' was 'the most dangerous confidence man that the State Prison of New York State has ever had in its keeping.' Potts, he suggested, was the 'chief engineer' of the Rice affair. The three, Bacon said, 'have worked that case for nearly two years between themselves, conniving and planning how to complete the transaction.' Bacon claimed in his letter that he had personal knowledge of the matter: 'the compact was done, signed and sealed between the two [Potts and Patrick] last December. I cannot exactly tell the date, but it was on a Friday, in the Restaurant, at 150 Nassau Street, in the top floor.' By accident, he said, he had been in an adjoining office to Potts' and had overheard a private conversation between Potts and Patrick:

'We have got to get that fellow out of the road,' Patrick said.
'What will you do with Jones?' Potts asked.
'We have got to quieten him and you know I can do that.'

Later that day, he saw Patrick, Potts, and Short celebrating at the top-floor restaurant. It was not till he, Bacon, was in London and read about the death of Rice that he said he put two and two together.

After several letters back and forth to Bacon, Hornblower engaged a firm of London solicitors, Taylor Sons and Humbert, to interview him.

The solicitors established that Bacon's real name was in fact Grotty – Adolphus Waldorf Carl Grotty: 'six feet high, dark with a black moustache and all the manner and appearance of a more or less successful adventurer' – and that he was in fact the 'prosperous, handsome travelling man' described in the earlier letter. It was Short who had been the one to find him with the defrauded woman in the Jersey City hotel, and this had caused the breakup of Grotty's marriage. The London solicitors wrote:

Unless Grotty is a very good Actor this was and is a great blow to him and his great idea now is to revenge himself on these three men and he stated more than once that he had sworn to shoot them when he returned to New York.

We should think Grotty's statement as to what took place with reference to the Rice business is probably correct but his desire for revenge is so great it is impossible to say how far that has governed his recollection.

The Hornblower firm concluded that it would be difficult to use Grotty's evidence, but they called on one of the lawyers who had been involved in the transaction that Grotty complained of, a Mr Brown, to try to get him to obtain information from Short. Brown was questioned by a member of the Hornblower firm:

'Do you think it would be possible to influence Short?' Brown was asked.

'Could he at this time receive the moral assurance of this firm and of the District Attorney's office that he would not be criminally punished?' was Brown's reply.

'Well, I don't know about that; he certainly could rely upon our doing everything we could do for him.'

'That would not be sufficient,' Brown stated: 'He has been playing for large stakes and would not capitulate at this time without some assurance at least of perfect immunity. He is not a Jones, by any means, and no amount of coercion would induce him to reveal his hand.'[2]

Brown was willing to see Short and found a pretext to talk to him by offering to assist him in getting into the Masonic order. Brown subsequently told the Hornblower firm that Short 'very emphatically denied that there was any fraud or deception in the execution of the will and stated it was the free and voluntary act of Mr. Rice and resented any inference that the will might be a forgery.'

# 35. Morris Meyers

Morris Meyers was interviewed by District Attorney Osborne in mid-December. This was the first statement Meyers had been asked to make to the authorities. He had refused to talk to the press, except for one brief interview with a *Tribune* reporter on 27 September, when he was asked about an assignment of Rice's property to Patrick. His reply at the time was: 'I have not been a party to any assignment of any kind and I don't believe the police have what they say they have.'[1] To a *World* reporter several days later, he refused to comment, stating: 'I know all the circumstances, but I am not relating them for the benefit of the newspapers. If I am asked in court to tell what I know I will gladly do so.'[2]

The twenty-four-year-old lawyer lived with his parents at 168 Henry Street in the Lower East Side. One of six children, he had attended New York Law School, graduating in 1897. While attending and after graduating from law school he worked in Patrick's law office.[3]

Meyers told Osborne that he had witnessed Rice signing the will on 30 June 1900:

Q. I show you a photographic copy of what purports to be a will, June 30th, 1900, and I ask you if this is a photograph of the paper which you witnessed?
A. Yes, sir.
Q. Did you see Mr. Rice sign the original of this?
A. Yes, sir.
Q. Did you see him sign the four signatures written on this paper?
A. I did.
Q. And did you see Short also sign?
A. Yes, sir.

He had, he said, also witnessed an assignment by Rice to Patrick in September 1900. Osborne asked him why he had denied this to the *Herald* reporter. Meyers replied: 'The reporter has a part of it correct. He asked if I was a party to any assignment, and I said I was not.'

Osborne asked about the typing of the will:

Q. Do you know who made a copy of this will on the typewriter?
A. I did ... from memorandum handed to me by Mr. Patrick.
Q. How long before the 30th of June?
A. Three or four or five weeks. Several drafts had been made before that time. Mr. Patrick would ask me to draw parts of it, and finally the original draft was partly typewritten and partly written – from that I made a completed draft.

Osborne turned to the signing of the will:

Q. When you went into Mr. Rice's apartment was Jones in the room?
A. Yes. He was around the place. He let us in; he was somewhere about the place.
Q. Was he in the room at the time the will was executed?
A. I couldn't say. He may have peeped in.
Q. What did Mr. Rice say to you when you went into the room?
A. We said we came to see about the papers he had to execute, and we executed those papers. I filled in all that was necessary. They were properly witnessed. Then he said he wanted us to execute another paper – he took out papers – said it was his will.
Q. Did he read it?
A. I don't believe he read it all through. I think he took a glance at it – looked at a clause or two, and that is all.
Q. Did you read it?
A. I think I read a clause – the attestation clause. I didn't read the will.
Q. Do you recollect what kind of a pen it was?
A. My best impression is that it was a fountain pen.

The prosecution later noted in the file that in Short's interview with McCluskey three months earlier, Short had said that Rice took the pen, dipped it in the inkwell, and signed the will.

Meyers said that he knew that this was the will that he had copied and that Patrick was the residuary legatee of that will. Although he said that he had never seen Rice and Patrick together, he claimed that 'Rice spoke about Patrick a great deal.' Osborne pressed him on this:

Q. What did he say to you?
A. There were so many little things.
Q. Get right down to the point and tell me one thing he said about Patrick?
A. He would speak about Texas – the confidence he had in Patrick.

Q. Tell me one solitary thing he said about Patrick?

A. He would speak about Patrick as being a good lawyer, and a man who understood his business and that Patrick had handled his matters for him.

Q. What one matter?

A. His personal matters.

Q. Which one?

A. I can't think.

After further questioning on similar lines, Meyers mentioned the will fight:

Q. What will fight?

A. The Mrs. Rice's will fight. How the thing had been fought a long while and he didn't want to adjust it and so on, and also he spoke about Patrick as a man who is interested in various sociological schemes; that he was a deep thinker, and that he thought of religious topics, and was interested in all these things. He was a man of broad, liberal ideas, and Rice said he admired the man. I can't give you anything more in detail now.

The stenographer's transcript of the interview ends with a note: 'Meyers telephone address is 2876 Franklin.'

Exactly four weeks later, Meyers again appeared before Osborne for further questioning. Meyers expressed outrage that Osborne had not telephoned him to come, but instead had sent two officers with a subpoena. Osborne wanted to know all that had happened in Rice's apartment:

Meyers: I have given you that information.

Osborne: I would like to have it now, because I have not got it in your own way.

Meyers: You got the stenographer's minutes.

Osborne: I have not, I have a series of questions.

Meyers: You got the stenographer's minutes ... I don't think the conduct towards me is such as one member of the Bar should be to another.

Osborne: No conduct on my part has been in the slightest degree discourteous.

Meyers: Why did you send a subpoena for me?

Osborne: Because I wanted to see you.

Meyers: You could have telephoned to me, as you promised.

Osborne: I did telephone as soon as I got your number.

Meyers answered some further questions, but then declined to answer any other questions on the ground that he had already answered them

in the earlier interview. 'That is all I want from you at present, Mr.
Meyers,' Osborne said, concluding the interview.

# 36. Jones: More Statements

Charlie Jones' father had come to New York in November. According
to a letter Baker sent to his firm in Texas, Jones, Sr, after investigating
his son's confession, 'concluded that it was voluntarily made and that
it is to his son's interest to adhere to the same and try to corroborate
it in every particular, and thereby get the lowest penalty the prosecution
may be willing to concede.' Baker added his view that he is 'satisfied
the District Attorney's office will not prosecute him for murder, but
will be satisfied with a term of imprisonment for forgery, and they may
make greater concessions.'[1]

On 4 December Baker met with Jones at the House of Detention.
The only surviving record of this meeting, however, is a few lines in
a letter Baker sent to Lovett: 'I had a two hour interview with Jones
yesterday trying to reconcile some of his inconsistent statements, but
found him a hard customer to deal with. I sometimes think that he is
unable to tell the truth about anything.'[2]

Baker said that he was told by Jones' father that his son had received
chloroform sent to him by his brother, Lafayette Jones, living in Texas.
Baker wrote to Lafayette Jones in Cedar Bayou, Texas: 'Your father told
me while in New York that sometime during the summer your brother,
Charlie, wrote you for some chloroform and that you had sent it to
him. I want to know where you bought the chloroform and when, and
how much you got and by what express Company it was sent. I wish
you would let me have this information at your earliest convenience.'
Osborne was particularly anxious to find out from Baker what he had
found out about the chloroform. To Osborne, it seemed a more likely
cause of death than mercury. Osborne was being badgered by the press
about Professor Witthaus' report, which had still not been released. According to Osborne, Witthaus was still examining the viscera to see if
the mercury was present in quantities sufficient to cause death.

Max Harby, who was acting for Patrick in the will case, told the
press that he had written to Osborne to say that the defense could easily
disprove Jones' statement: 'We have three reputable witnesses by whom
we can prove conclusively that Patrick was not in Mr. Rice's apartment
at the time Jones says he looked into the old man's room and saw Patrick
stooping over Rice and holding a towel across his face.'[3]

In late January 1901 Battle met again with Jones. There is no record of their discussion. Nor is there any record of a discussion that Baker, who had recently arrived from Houston, had with Jones on 6 February.

The following day, Thursday, 7 February, Jones made another detailed statement to Osborne. The fifty-page transcript again outlined Jones' career and his relationship with Rice, but added new details. Mr Rice 'occasionally spoke of making another will and promised that if I stayed with him as long as he lived, I would never have to work after his death.'[4]

In late 1899, Jones said, Patrick came to Rice's apartment claiming he was a Mr Smith, a grain speculator from Texas, and asked to see Rice. Jones, however, did not let him see him. After several visits with Jones, Patrick told him who he was and what his interest was in Mrs Rice's will and, according to Jones, tried to get Jones to prepare documents showing that Rice's real domicile was Texas and not New York. Patrick, he said, could imitate other people's writing. 'I have seen Mr. Patrick sign my name, and he could write it so well that I couldn't tell that it was not my own handwriting,' Jones stated. Later, Patrick proposed making a new will for Rice.

According to Jones, Rice never knew Patrick, although Rice saw him talking to Jones at the apartment on many occasions: 'Patrick came in the room and said something to me in the presence of Mr. Rice, but Mr. Rice never knew who he was. Once Mr. Rice said, "who is the bald-headed man you were talking to last night?" I said it was a friend. But Mr. Rice saw him probably a dozen times or more at the house, but never talked to him, only that he might have said "good-evening."'

Jones then described the events surrounding Rice's death on Sunday, 23 September:

I got my dinner about five o'clock, and when I returned about half past five or a quarter to six, Mr. Rice was sleeping. He was lying quietly in the bed apparently asleep. I didn't hear him breathing. I went and wrote a telegram, – You know all about that Mr. Osborne, to a young lady friend of mine. She received the telegram. Capt. Baker has got the one that I wrote at the house and I went downstairs and telephoned Patrick. Johnny Houlihand took me down in the elevator, and I telephoned Mr. Patrick to meet me on 56th Street and 6th Avenue.

Jones told Osborne about sending the telegram to his girlfriend from the telegraph office at 56th Street and 6th Avenue, meeting Patrick at 7th Avenue, and walking back together as far as 55th Street and Madison Avenue:

On the way back, we were talking of Mr. Rice's condition and how we could best get him out of the way. He asked me how Mr. Rice was, and I told him he was resting quietly when I left. I thought he was asleep. Well, the substance of the conversation was that Mr. Rice must not be alive the next day. He asked me if he had taken the medicine, - the oxalic acid, - as he called it, and I told him he had taken a portion of it, and he seemed to be getting along pretty well. He told me that I knew that Mr. Rice must not be here to-morrow (Monday) as well as he did. He said, 'you know why,' and I think he told me that the drafts would have to be paid Monday. We talked about it in every conversation after the draft came.

Jones described how he had personally chloroformed Rice:

He then gave me a bottle of chloroform, and he told me that he was a married man and could not use it; that he had two little girls that were dependent upon him, and that all the property would fall into his hands and be in his name, and that in itself would be a conviction in itself. He also said if no motive could be shown for my using the chloroform that they could not convict me of any crime. He then told me to go to the house and fold a towel cone shape and to put a sponge in the small end of the cone, and saturate it with the chloroform and put it over Mr. Rice's face if he was sleeping and let it remain there about twenty or thirty minutes. When I left him on Madison Avenue and 54th Street, I went to the house and found Mr. Rice still sleeping; he was lying quietly in the bed, and I supposed he was sleeping, and I did just as I was told to by Mr. Patrick. I thought he was sleeping then, but he may have been dead.
Q. Do you recollect seeing any signs of animation?
A. No, sir; he was lying perfectly quiet, just as quiet as he could be.
     This towel remained over his face probably thirty minutes. I went back and removed it, and then I went to the ice-box and got his bottle of water and went to the room and lit gas and tried to arouse him, and I found that he was dead.

Jones continued describing the events that day:

I first burned the towel and sponge and broke the bottle in the kitchen on the range and threw it in the ashes. I then got James Scott, the back elevator man, to go for Dr. Curry. I telephoned Mr. Patrick that he had better come to the house at once that Mr. Rice was very sick. That was our previous agreement that I was to use those words. About nine o'clock Dr. Curry and Mr. Patrick came together, I opened the door and Dr. Curry asked how Mr. Rice was. I said he was dead. He said he was very much surprised. Mr. Patrick acted as though he was more than astonished. He said, 'Dead! Oh, my God!'; and he said, 'Doctor, this is the worst thing in the world that could have happened for me. Mr. Rice had promised to come downtown Monday or Tuesday and close a business transaction with me, which will now fall through, and it will be one of the worst things that ever happened for me.'

'The Will of June 30th,' Jones said, 'was gotten up before Mr. Rice's death, but not signed and executed until after Mr. Rice's death.' Even the earlier will of 26 May, Jones said, was not signed by Rice, but was witnessed by Short and Meyers in Patrick's office.

This statement by Jones was not released to the press.

# 37. A New Charge

John T. Milliken, Patrick's wealthy brother-in- law, was now financially supporting the defense. He was one of the richest businessmen in St Louis. When he died in 1919, the New York *Times* described him as 'probably the wealthiest citizen' of that city.[1] Mrs Francis told a Thiel Detective Agency undercover operative that 'he said he had enough money to buy up the court and the state's attorney's office and have something left.'[2] His wealth came from chemical products, banking, mining, and oil.

Milliken had met Patrick's sister, May, a beautiful widow, when he made a business trip to Austin, Texas, many years earlier. They had married and had built a magnificent house in St Louis costing half a million dollars. She had been urging her husband to support her brother.

The new funds permitted a member of Harby's law firm, F.C. Hanford, to travel to Texas to interview witnesses. There are no existing defense files on this stage of the proceedings, but there is a prosecution file on the various steps that the Rice interests and the McCane Detective Agency of Houston took to find out to whom Hanford had spoken and what was said. The detective agency, for example, reconstructed a conversation with the barber in the Rice Hotel in Houston, part of which is as follows:

Q. How often did you see Mr. Rice?
A. Every day, and sometimes twenty times a day.
Q. Did you observe any peculiarities about Mr. Rice in these visits?

A. I did.
Q. What were they?
A. His peculiarity and hobby was to make money.[3]

On Tuesday, 26 February 1901, Milliken and one of his lawyers, Charles Webster of Kansas City, deposited $10,000 in cash at the city chamberlain's office in Manhattan and took the bail form for the release of Patrick to Judge McMahon in the General Sessions court. The form had been endorsed as required by one of the assistant DA's with the words 'correct as to form.' Osborne was in Albany that day and knew nothing of the attempt to free Patrick. By chance, District Attorney Philbin heard about Patrick's imminent release and rushed to McMahon's court just as a 'highly elated' Patrick was about to leave the courtroom. Philbin asked that the matter be put over until Osborne returned the next day. McMahon acceded to the request and Patrick was returned to the Tombs.

The next morning, Osborne hurriedly obtained affidavits from Professor Witthaus and Jones and got a warrant for Patrick's arrest on a charge of murder from Judge Jerome of the Court of General Sessions, sitting as a magistrate.

'Patrick seemed calm and confident when he was taken before Judge McMahon during the afternoon,' the *Herald* reported: 'He was chewing gum and he glanced about the courtroom with an air of confidence.' 'His manner changed,' the *Herald* went on, 'after he had a brief consultation with his counsel and his hand trembled as he stroked his mustache.' His counsel, a lawyer associated with House, had obviously informed him that there was now a warrant for his arrest for murder and that if he was released he would immediately be rearrested. Under the circumstances, Patrick's counsel withdrew the application for bail and asked for permission to withdraw the $10,000 deposited with the city chamberlain.

Judge McMahon would not permit the murder warrant to be served on Patrick in the courtroom. Patrick was therefore returned to prison, the warrant was served, and he was returned to Judge Jerome's court. The clerk of the court read the two affidavits forming the basis of the new charge. In stilted legal language, Jones had sworn in his affidavit that:

On September 23, 1900, Patrick wilfully, feloniously and of his knowledge aforethought, did make an assault with a large quantity of a certain deadly poison called mercury and divers other deadly poisons (a more particular description of which is to the deponent unknown), and did then and there wilfully and feloniously give and cause to be given, administered to William M. Rice, and caused to be taken and swallowed by him down into his mouth, these poisons.[4]

There was no specific mention of chloroform in the affidavit. Similarly, Professor Witthaus' affidavit only mentioned the possibility of mercury poisoning:

I was present at an autopsy upon the body of W.M. Rice on September 23. I received the viscera as they were taken from the body. I thereafter made a chemical analysis of a portion of the viscera, and discovered therein the presence of mercury in the kidneys and intestines.

I have read the affidavit and information of Charles F. Jones and in view of the results of my analysis and in the absence of intercurrent causes of death, it is my opinion that if the said affidavit and information be true, the said W.M. Rice died of mercurial poisoning.[5]

A preliminary hearing into the charge of murder was adjourned until 10:30 on the morning of 14 March. The *Herald* noted that 'Patrick was still chewing gum when he was led back to the prison, held without bail on the charge of murder.'

On Thursday morning, 14 March, Patrick appeared with a new counsel, Robert M. Moore. The thirty-three-year-old Moore, who looked older than his age, had established a remarkable reputation as a criminal lawyer in upper New York State and had come to New York City about a year previously to join his law partner, William Cantwell. He gave the appearance of a country lawyer: the press described him as 'crude, plain and unvarnished,' but with 'unusual charm of magnetism' and with a 'cowlick on his high forehead.' Born in Canada, he came to upper New York with his parents and while a schoolboy worked in his father's blacksmith's shop. He later became a schoolteacher and the principal of the local high school, and still later studied law in a law office in Watertown, New York. He never went to university or to law school.[6]

Moore had already established a reputation in New York City as the defender of Dr Samuel Kennedy, a dentist charged with bludgeoning a woman to death in a hotel room.[7] The press also noted that he was a person of 'great optimism,' a trait that seemed to be required in the Patrick case.

Moore demanded that the preliminary hearing proceed, but Francis Garvan, the twenty-four-year-old deputy assistant district attorney who was representing Osborne, stated that the prosecution was still waiting for the report from Professor Witthaus as to the amount of mercury found in the dead man's organs. The prosecution obviously did not know whether to proceed on the basis of mercury poisoning or chloroform or both. Judge Jerome adjourned the hearing until 26 March.

# 38. The Preliminary Starts

The preliminary hearing on the murder charge against Patrick – Jones was not charged – began on Tuesday, 26 March 1901, before Justice William Travers Jerome, sitting as a magistrate, in the district attorney's library on the third floor of the Criminal Court Building. Although the conditions in the building had been improved by District Attorney Philbin over the past several months[1] – the stained glass dome in the building had been cleaned – the overall effect was still depressing. Jerome called the building an 'abortion.'[2]

Jerome had established a reputation as an anticrime, anticorruption crusader. The forty-one-year-old lawyer had graduated from Columbia Law School in 1884 and after a few years as an assistant district attorney had in 1894 become the assistant counsel to a legislative committee under Senator Clarence Lexow that had investigated and found corruption in the police and Tammany Hall politics. As a result, Jerome was appointed by the successful 'fusion' candidate for mayor, Mayor Strong, to be the head of the Court of Special Sessions in Manhattan. From 1895 on, he had led raids on gambling establishments throughout Manhattan. Indeed, the month before, he and Philbin led a secret raid – later well publicized – on a poolroom that fronted for a gambling house. Seventy-five patrons, including the president of the Board of Public Improvements, a 'well-known professor,' and several out-of-uniform police officers, were held in a rear room while Jerome opened court on a poker table and examined the found-ins.[3]

Jerome's obituary in the *Times* stressed that he was interested in 'good government and honesty in public office' and that he was not a 'typical reformer.' He was, the paper said, 'an inveterate cigarette smoker ... drank whatever he liked when he felt like it, played poker regularly, and used language at the head of his raiding parties that would have mantled [a reformer's] cheek with blushes.'[4]

Jerome's official biographer records that he had a very unhappy home life and that 'some time during his service as district attorney, he met and fell in love with a beautiful, cultivated and sympathetic blonde lady ... about twenty years younger than Jerome.' The biographer also notes that 'as a public man and more ironically as a standard-bearer of civic morality, he had to keep it a secret.' The secret relationship lasted until he died in 1934.[5]

Jerome was a favorite cousin of the former Jennie Jerome, the beautiful wife of Lord Randolph Churchill and the mother of Sir Winston. Jerome, like Sir Winston, had political ambitions. He had his eye on running for district attorney of New York at the next election in October.

For most of the first day of the hearing, David Short gave evidence of his dealings with Rice. He maintained – as he had in his earlier statements to Osborne and McCluskey – that he had properly witnessed Rice's will on 30 June.[6]

At seven o'clock that evening, Meyers appeared at the hearing dressed in tails, having just acted as the best man at a wedding. The next day the press reported on Meyers' 'remarkable lapses of memory.'[7] Byrne wired Baker: 'Meyers examined last evening; made most unfavourable impression; severely criticized by Judge: was manifestly untruthful, deliberately forgetful and evasive.'[8] A follow-up letter from Byrne stated: 'Both of the witnesses made very poor impressions. Neither was frank; both were forgetful, evasive and hesitating. No one, upon hearing their testimony, could think they were telling the truth, or that they were dealing with transactions which actually took place.'

Doctor Curry, the next witness, was too ill to give evidence in court and so the court went to his home. Propped up with pillows in a big armchair, he gave evidence that he had prescribed pills containing mercury for Jones when he had pneumonia, but had never prescribed mercury for Rice during the six months he treated him.[9] Osborne asked about Patrick's relations with Rice:

'Did Patrick tell you he was Rice's lawyer?'
'He did not.'
'Did you ever mention Patrick's name to Rice?'
'Jones requested that I should not.'
'Did you ask Jones why?'
'No.'

In cross-examination Moore asked:

'Do you still believe Rice died a natural death?'
'I do,' Curry replied.

On Friday afternoon, Short and Meyers were arrested in their offices
and charged with forging the 1900 will. They spent the night at police
headquarters and were brought before Justice Jerome on Saturday morning. Moore suggested bail of $2,500, but Osborne wanted $10,000 each,
stating:

'This is a conspiracy, one of the most widespread conspiracies that has ever been
brought to your Honor's attention. These men are not only guilty of forgery,
but of perjury as well.'
    'Conspiracy!' retorted Moore in his deep bass voice. 'Why, this conspiracy will
resolve itself into another one of Jones' stories, which are now so numerous that
even the D.A. can't keep track of them.'[10]

Jerome fixed bail at $5,000 each.

# 39. Mrs Francis

Mrs Addie M. Francis, described by the *Times* as 'the most intimate
woman friend of Albert T. Patrick,'[1] was the first witness called on Monday morning, 1 April. Osborne wanted to pin down her story at an
early stage of the proceedings. She had earlier declined to be interviewed
by Osborne. Dressed in black, with a fur collarette and a flower-trimmed
hat, she at first answered Osborne's question about her background:

I am a widow, the widow of Warren C. Francis. I have lived in the County of
New York for twenty years and have known Mr. Patrick since January, 1893. It
was about that time Mr. Patrick came to New York ... I met him first where I
boarded at 72 5th Avenue. At that time his wife was living; that was in January,
1893. When his wife died he was living at 145th Street and Convent Avenue. I
bought out his apartment there, just a short time before his wife died. His wife
went South for her health, and I boarded there when his wife went South, and
he roomed there. His wife died in December, 1897.[2]

Osborne asked further questions about her relationship with Patrick.
The *Times* noted that during the questioning Patrick 'appeared nervous
and ill at ease':

'What room did Patrick occupy at your house?' asked Osborne.

'The back room on the parlor floor.'

'What room did you occupy?'

'No stated room. Further than that I decline to answer.'

'When did Patrick first speak to you about Rice?'

'I refuse to answer on the advice of my counsel, Mr. Moore – on the ground that it would incriminate me,' she added.

'I make no charge against this witness,' Osborne insisted: 'I have no intention of making any.' Moore, however, stated that the arrests of Meyers and Short after their testimony justified her refusal to answer. He had warned her, he said, that if she said anything favorable to Patrick, Osborne would have her arrested.

'Why did you believe that I would have you arrested?' Osborne asked her.

'I saw in the papers yesterday that there would be more arrests.'

'And you believe, despite my declaration to the contrary in open court, that I would arrest you?' asked Osborne.

'I do.'

'Patrick is not a man, but a cur,' Osborne said in a stage whisper to his assistant, Francis Garvan. Justice Jerome called for an hour's adjournment and asked Mrs Francis to seek independent advice. If she persisted in her refusal to answer, he said, he could not see his way clear to compel her to reply. During the intermission Patrick told the press: 'Osborne has given out interviews indiscriminately which would tend to terrify witnesses and prevent them testifying on my behalf. The steps of every one who knew me have been dogged for weeks. Such has been the suspicion cast upon them.'

Mrs Francis returned to the witness box and withdrew her objection to testifying. Patrick, she said, was in her boarding house the day Rice died until he was called by Jones at eight o'clock and informed that Rice was dead or dying.

'Patrick was in various parts of the house during the day. In the morning he was in the back parlor, reading his papers; at noontime, about 1:30 he had his dinner; at 2 o'clock he was singing in the parlor; a lady was playing and he was singing. Then he went to the fourth floor of my house to do a little job for me, not a Sunday job, but putting locks on the linen closet, and while he was at this work the bell rang and I went down to the door and let in Mr. Potts and his daughter Edna Potts, about 4 o'clock. Then I put them in the parlor. I went up to the top floor, called Mr. Patrick down; he came down and visited with our friends in the parlor. Then we went up in their room, the suite they had engaged from me, and stayed there until the supper bell rang, I would say, to the best of my recollection, 6:30; that is my present suppertime and I believe it was then.

Then the people came down to supper and were brought in the parlor and were introduced to Mr. Potts and his daughter. We had a general conversation, and remarks. They went away.

We went down to the dining room for supper, and I would say stayed there until some time around 7 o'clock.'[3]

After seven o'clock, she went on, the others at the dining table went to church. She and Patrick, she said, stayed in the back parlor reading the Sunday papers.

'There was no other person, so far as you know?' Jerome asked.
'No other person so far as I know.'

Her evidence supported Patrick's claim that the checks were brought to him by Jones the day before Rice died: 'Patrick and I had a conversation about the envelope that Jones brought ... He told me that the envelope contained valuable checks for the settlement of this transaction of the contest over the Rice will.' As far as she was aware, she said, Patrick was Rice's lawyer with respect to his estate, although not for other matters.

In a private note, Patrick congratulated Mrs Francis on her testimony: 'Addie, you made a splendid witness; no better. Osborne could not shake you. I felt sorry for you, as it was I who put you in that awkward position and I felt that I am a damned dog, as Osborne called me, for drawing you into this case.'[4] Patrick then added: 'Your appearance on the stand was striking.'

# 40. Jones' Testimony

Dressed in a black suit and a black tie, Charlie Jones gave his evidence in a matter-of-fact monotone. The press had expected that he would stay with his story that Patrick had actually done the killing. The papers up till then had contained no reference to the latest statement Jones had made to Osborne, admitting that he himself had killed Rice.

In a calm and emotionless tone, Jones told Jerome that he had administered to Rice, at Patrick's order, oxalic acid, mercury, and other things to endeavor to break down Rice's health. Still, Rice kept getting stronger. Perhaps the baked and raw bananas Rice took might have finished him off, Jones said, but Patrick wanted the job down quickly:

I was afraid to do it. I refused. Then he persuaded me. He said all the property was in his name, and that would be adduced as a motive if murder was done. He told me to fold a towel in a cone shape, put a sponge saturated with chloroform in it, and hold it over Mr. Rice's face for half an hour. He would probably laugh, he said, but that would only be the effects of the chloroform.

I did just as he told me. I got the towel and sponge, made the towel into a cone shape, and saturated the sponge with chloroform. I tried it on my own face and got a strong effect. Then I put it over Mr. Rice's face and ran out. I walked up and down the hall and my room. Someone rang the bell. I didn't let them in, and they went away. In about half an hour I went back and raised the windows and threw the sponge and towel in the range. They burned as if they had oil on them. I poured the remaining acid out the window.

Then I telephoned to Patrick that Rice was very low. He came with Dr. Curry.[1]

Moore expressed confidence to the press that 'the confession of Jones would be torn to pieces,'[2] but, in the words of the *Times*, 'severe cross-examination failed to discredit his story or to confuse him.'

Patrick was on his feet during the cross-examination. At one point when Moore was having some difficulty reading to the court an earlier statement by Jones, Patrick took the statement, saying, 'Let me read it.' In what the *Times* described as a 'firm voice,' Patrick read a part of Jones' previous statement: 'Patrick felt Rice's pulse and listened to his heart. Then he told me to get a towel and a sponge ... Then he wrapped a towel around his hand in a conical shape and pinned it with a safety pin he took off the bureau. He placed the sponge in it, saturated with the liquid, and then placed the funnel end of the towel on Rice's face.' Jones said that he could not recall the false statements he had made, but he remembered vividly the truth. The general thrust of Moore's cross-examination was to show that Captain Baker was responsible for Jones' testimony. Jones admitted to Moore that he knew that Patrick would be sent to the electric chair if he was convicted of murder on his confession.

The case was adjourned until the following Tuesday as Moore had a trial in his hometown of Malone, New York. Jones would be subject to further cross-examination at that time.

Corroboration tending to connect Patrick with the crimes would be needed, Jerome had warned the DA. A conviction, he said, cannot be based on the uncorroborated evidence of an accomplice[3] (this is still the law in New York today)[4] and he would apply this rule to the committal proceedings. Osborne assured the press that there would be no difficulty in finding corroboration:

Patrick was the principal beneficiary under the will of 1900, so if I prove Jones killed Rice, as he says he did, it will certainly show that he was not conducting an eleemosynary [or charitable] institution for the purpose of getting people out of the way, but for some definite purpose. That purpose was to get the old man's money ... The best corroboration of all is the fact that Rice is dead and Patrick holds the deeds to 9/10 of his property.

Over the weekend, the press discovered that by order of the district attorney's office Jones had been allowed to leave the House of Detention and spend Friday evening, accompanied by Detective Brinley in plain clothes, in the Tenderloin[5] area of mid-town Manhattan, visiting saloons and other establishments. The *Sun* reported that Jones 'went to some of the theatres on Broadway and subsequently sampled imported beers in half a dozen saloons and restaurants between Thirty-fourth and Twenty-third streets.' Osborne admitted that this had indeed happened on a number of occasions, but explained:

In the first place you must remember that Jones, in the eyes of the law, is not a criminal. Whatever confession he may or may not have made, legally he is merely detained as a witness[6] ... There have been a number of witnesses we want to secure, and I wanted to get Jones' assistance in locating them. Again, Jones has been very despondent of late. We have had the greatest possible difficulty in preventing him from committing suicide.[7]

Patrick told the press that he had heard from various sources that Jones was plentifully supplied with money, was taken out 'buggy riding,' and was otherwise treated with great kindness and consideration. Rice died of heart failure, Patrick said, just as Rice's last surviving brother, Captain Frederick Rice, had the day before in Texas, at the age of seventy:

Jones never killed W.M. Rice. His fairy story is the result of a collaboration with Captain James A. Baker, Jones' lawyer, Battle, who is hired by Baker, Assistant District Attorney Osborne, who stops at nothing, and Professor Witthaus, the professional expert. The object of Jones' story is to have me held in prison pending the will litigation ... The stock in trade of the opposition to the 1900 will is their already demonstrated ability to control the District Attorney's office.

Osborne responded: 'I have read the statement made by Patrick, and have nothing to say. I cannot make myself popular with the criminal classes, and expect to be maligned at every chance.'

When the court convened again on Tuesday morning, Moore continued his cross-examination of Jones. Jones admitted that he couldn't say for sure whether Rice was alive when he administered the chloroform:

'Mr. Rice was lying perfectly still,' Jones said, 'He may have been dead.'

'Do you know whether Rice was dead or not when you came back?' Moore asked again, reinforcing the point.

'No. I don't know whether his eyes were closed or not. He was quiet. I placed the chloroform sponge and towel over his face and ran out. I don't remember whether he laughed or not.'[8]

On redirect examination, Osborne tried to counter the suggestion that Jones had concocted the story at Baker's instigation by bringing out testimony from Jones that he had first told the story to House:

'Jones, to whom did you tell the story about your giving Mr. Rice chloroform?'

'Mr. House.'[9]

The statement, the *Times* reported, caused 'a profound sensation,' and, again according to the *Times*, 'Patrick's pink bald head turned very white.' Moore immediately objected.

Moore: 'We move to strike it out, upon the ground that any communication to Mr. House, in the absence of Mr. Patrick, is a privileged communication and cannot be disclosed by any of the parties to it without the consent of the other. I think that is a well settled rule. Mr. House cannot go on the stand and contradict this witness.'

Jerome: 'Yes, he can.'

Moore: 'The privilege is the privilege that belongs to Mr. Patrick.'

Jerome (turning to Jones): 'You are not an attorney at law are you?'
Jones: 'No, I am not.'
Jerome: 'You never acted as Patrick's attorney did you?'
Jones: 'No, sir.'
Moore: 'There is no pretence of that ... '
Jerome: 'I shall allow it.'
Moore: 'I would like to have the matter delayed until I can submit some authorities to your Honor.'
Jerome: 'I do not think there is any use of submitting any authorities. The weight of authority is against you. Undoubtedly Mr. Patrick could keep Mr. House's mouth sealed if Mr. House is to be called, on the ground of privilege, but this witness does not plead any privilege.'[10]

Osborne continued his questioning of Jones:[11]

Q. When did you tell it for the first time?
A. The first time I told it to Mr. House.
Q. When and where?
A. I can't recall the exact time, Mr. Osborne, but it was in the Counsel Room of the Tombs, just before the Coroner's Inquest was set the first time.
Q. Who was present at the time?
A. Mr. Patrick, Mr. House and myself.
Q. State all that was said by Patrick and all you told too.
A. We went down that morning. We were called to the counsel room and when we got down Mr. House told us – asked us rather – if Mr. Rice had been murdered or put out of the way and I had first said he had not. Mr. Patrick asked me to excuse him a minute while he talked to Mr. House and I went to the opposite side of the room and waited while Mr. Patrick and Mr. House had a whispered conversation. Then Mr. Patrick called me in the other corner and told me that I had better tell Mr. House that I had murdered Mr. Rice; that he was very anxious to know the exact state of the case, but I must not connect him with it in any way. I said that I would not tell Mr. House unless I would tell the truth about it, but Mr. Patrick never did agree that I should mention him giving me the Oxalic Acid.

Jones said that he told House that he had given Mr Rice mercury on several occasions and that he had also administered chloroform. He told House, he went on, that he got the mercury from a place on 56th Street and the chloroform from his brother in Texas. Osborne continued his questioning:

Q. Did you tell him in the presence of Patrick?
A. I did.
Q. What did Mr. Patrick say then?
A. I do not remember just what Mr. Patrick said.
Q. Well, did he deny it?
A. No, I do not think he denied it, I think he acknowledged that he was con-
nected with it.

Moore on re-cross-examination established that Jones had talked to
Baker before any statement by Jones to House, assuming that Jones in
fact confessed to House.

The Thiel Detective Agency operative reported that Mrs Francis
speculated about Jones' testimony: 'Is it not possible that Captain Baker
is the one who got Jones to do away with Rice and not Patrick?'[12]

# 41. Committal for Trial

Other witnesses were called by Osborne. John Wallace testified about
the checks that Patrick tried to cash at the Swenson Bank the day after
Rice died. Walter Wetherbee, also from Swensons, gave similar evidence
and also told about the approach he claimed Jones had made to him
many months before Rice died to participate in creating a new will.
Wetherbee's evidence, Osborne stated, provided 'the strongest possible
corroboration of Jones' story' in that 'Wetherbee was approached by
Jones with this will proposition which he refused, and was then left
$5,000 in the new will when it was drawn in order to keep his mouth
shut.'[1]

Baker had arrived from Texas the previous week, while Jones was
giving his evidence. It was not certain that he would be called. Byrne
had written to him: 'it is, of course, desirable to make out a case from
the hostile witnesses, if possible.'[2] Osborne, however, did not want to
take any chances and called Baker. Baker testified that as far as he knew
Patrick never had any relations with Rice up to the date of his death.
He, Baker, was Rice's lawyer.

'Did the relations between you and Rice as counsel and client ever cease?' Osborne asked.

'No, I received a letter from him the day before his death regarding this very
will litigation.'[3]

In cross-examination, Moore tried to bring out that Rice was always changing his will:

'He had a mania for will making, didn't he?' Moore asked.
   'I don't know, sir.'
   'Haven't you heard that when Rice had litigation of importance on he under-took to influence it by making a will?'
   'I never heard it,' Baker replied.
   'Never heard that about the '96 will?'
   'Never.'
   'Didn't Rice tell you that now that his wife's heirs were trying to get part of his wife's estate, he would make another will, leaving largely to charity in order that it might be made public after the case got into court and thus influence public opinion?'
   'He never did.'
   'Was Mr. Rice a popular man in Houston?'
   'I don't know that he was a popular man in the ordinary sense of the word.'
   'Didn't you know that there were ugly rumours in Texas about the death of Rice's wife?'[4]

Moore was referring to rumors that Rice had poisoned his wife. Jerome rebuked Moore for the question and told him that he would not permit any such questions tending to reflect on the reputation of the dead man.

Immediately after Baker's testimony, Jerome increased Meyers' and Short's bail from $5,000 to $10,000. Meyers had been able to raise the earlier bail and had been free for a week. The increase came as a surprise to Meyers, who was in court chatting with Mrs Short at the time. The *Times* reported that 'his face became white in an instant and a court policeman took hold of his arm and hustled him off toward the Bridge of Sighs before he had time to realize what had happened.'

Drs Donlin and Williams and Professor Witthaus gave evidence of the autopsy. Witthaus' evidence with respect to mercury was not as strong as the prosecutor would have liked. Witthaus said that he found traces of mercury in the liver, kidneys, and intestines, probably taken about two weeks before death, but not, he said, in sufficient quantities to cause death. The prosecution would therefore have to rely mainly on Jones' chloroform story.

Moore tried to keep out the handwriting evidence on the ground that the experts had never seen the defendant write, but Judge Jerome properly brushed the objection aside and permitted experts Kinsley and Carvalho to testify.[5]

On Thursday afternoon, 11 April, the hearing ended. Jerome reserved his decision. He would take the transcript home with him, he said, and decide whether or not Jones' story had been sufficiently corroborated to warrant holding the prisoner for the action of the grand jury.

The next day, Meyers and Short appealed Jerome's bail decision to Judge Goff. Moore thought that $2,500 or $3,000 would be a proper amount to secure their presence for trial. Deputy Assistant District Attorney Garvan replied, however, that nine further charges would be added, including perjury and conspiracy to defraud. 'We hope to connect these two men with the murder,' Garvan said. Judge Goff fixed bail at $20,000 each. Mrs Short told the press that the high bail figure 'is for the obvious purpose of unduly influencing him through his love for me and the children, to perjure himself against Mr. Patrick.'[6]

The following Tuesday, Jerome announced that he was holding Patrick without bail for murder to await the action of the grand jury: 'An examination of the evidence satisfies me that the witness Jones is adequately corroborated within the meaning of the code by evidence tending to connect the defendant with the commission of the crime charged.'[7]

Osborne told the press: 'I believe I have enough evidence to convict Patrick before any jury.' Moore's partner, Cantwell, said that Patrick would be acquitted: 'We have enough evidence to clear our client both on the charge of murder and that of forgery. This is as true as the Gospel.' Moore, who was contacted while on a trial in upper New York, added: 'Jones' so-called confession is a pack of lies.'

# 42. The Grand Jury

The grand jury's task was – and still is – to satisfy themselves that there was enough evidence to warrant a trial with a twelve-man petit jury.[1] If they so found, they would find a 'true bill' and 'hand up' the indictment to the presiding judge. Each month there was a new grand jury consisting of twenty-three men drawn from a list of about a thousand respectable citizens.[2] The April grand jury also had the particularly important task of looking at indictments against at least five police captains and possibly also against Deputy Commissioner Devery.[3]

Colonel William C. Church, a sixty-five-year-old Civil War veteran, was appointed by the court[4] as the foreman of the April grand jury. He was the editor of the popular *Army and Navy Journal* and one of the founders and the first president of the National Rifle Association.[5]

The grand jury met on 22 April 1901 in the recently enlarged quarters next to the district attorney's office on the third floor of the Criminal Court Building. The accused and defense counsel were not present, having no right to take part in the proceedings. A murder indictment with ten counts drafted by Garvan was before them.[6] Patrick was charged with various permutations and combinations of murder[7] – murder with chloroform; murder with mercury; and murder with an unknown substance – as well as counts alleging the administration of poison that caused Rice to 'then and there die' and poison that caused him to die after being 'mortally sick and distempered in his body.' The prosecution was obviously unsure of its case and did not want to risk not being permitted to amend a single count.[8] Count number one alleging that chloroform caused Rice to 'then and there die' was under the circumstances the most important count. In addition, there were a number of forgery counts against Patrick, Short, and Meyers. Perjury charges against Short and Meyers would later be added.

After an hour's discussion, the grand jury invited Patrick, Short, and Meyers to appear before them:

You are hereby notified that the Grand Jury of the County of New York, now in session, is willing to hear any explanation you may think proper in relation to a certain charge against you, pending before that body, or any statement of facts which you may think will tend to your exculpation.

But you are to distinctly understand that you are not and cannot be, under any circumstances, required or compelled to appear before the Grand Jury ...[9]

They were brought from the Tombs to the antechamber of the grand jury room. Short appeared anxious to tell his story, but Patrick and a representative of Moore's firm talked him out of it.

Basically the same witnesses were called in private by the district attorney before the grand jury as were called at the committal proceedings. Jones was, of course, again the star witness. (Today, he would be given so-called transactional immunity,[10] but that was neither the law nor the practice then.) The grand jury quickly found a 'true bill,' which was 'handed up' to Judge Goff.

A motion by Moore to inspect the minutes of the grand jury was dismissed by Goff.[11] Although such inspection was common a few years earlier, a legislative change in 1897 had cut down the scope for inspection.[12] Moore immediately filed a so-called demurrer motion,[13] alleging that the counts 'do not state facts sufficient to constitute a crime.' This motion was dismissed on 7 June 1901.

No new charges were laid against Jones and the original forgery charge was dismissed. On 10 June, at the request of the prosecutor, all the cases were put over until 22 January 1902.

# 43. Approaching the Trial

After not eating for at least five days in early May, Jones was moved from the House of Detention to a 'first-class boarding house in an extremely good neighbourhood' at 200 West 44th Street, occupying three rooms on the second floor. He was under constant guard and was visited almost every other day by Dr Hamilton Williams, the coroner's physician. The district attorney's office was worried about whether Jones would live. Garvan told the press that, 'overcome with remorse, he sees no hope for the future. He really wants to die.' He reassured the public, however, that if Jones did die they would be able to use the stenographic report of his testimony in the criminal case.[1]

The Hornblower firm was concerned, however, that Jones had not yet given any evidence in the will case which could be used if he later died. The will proceedings had been adjourned pending the committal proceedings and then adjourned once again until mid-June. In the meantime, Hornblower and the other lawyers supporting the 1896 will attempted to take testimony from Jones at the boarding house but were unable to do so because of Jones' condition.[2] 'I should not be surprised,' his landlady said, 'if he were taken out a corpse any day.'[3]

In mid-June, Moore's partner, William Cantwell, argued for a postponement of the will hearing on the ground that his client's case would be prejudiced and his life jeopardized by the trial of the will controversy at this time. Should the case go on, Cantwell said, it would be necessary for Patrick to disclose his defense on the murder charge for the benefit of the district attorney's office. Byrne, on behalf of the Rice Institute, said that the institute was modeled after the Cooper Union in Manhattan; 'hence every time this case is postponed hundreds of citizens are deprived of a free education granted to them by the bounty of the testator.'[4] Judge Fitzgerald adjourned the hearing until November.

In September, Jones again tried to kill himself. Breaking a bottle on a radiator, he tried to cut his own throat, but one of the policemen guarding him was able to prevent it. Later, Jones inserted his head between the columns in the headboard of his bed and tried to break his neck by throwing himself off the bed. Again, he was prevented from doing so.

For six weeks in May and June, Osborne and Moore were busy squaring off against each other in the murder trial of Kennedy, the dentist accused of bludgeoning a woman to death. Moore had succeeded in obtaining a hung jury the previous December. This was Kennedy's third trial. Once again the result was a hung jury. Osborne, in his characteristic fashion, sounded off against the result: 'Meaning no reflection upon Mr. Moore as he did his best for his client I must say that the verdict seems to me a triumph for crime, fraud and chicanery ... I am not simply of the opinion that Kennedy murdered the woman. I know it.'[5] Such a comment would clearly be considered improper today.[6]

Over the summer, Short and Meyers had their bail reduced from $20,000 to $7,500, which Milliken put up in cash for them. Patrick remained in custody in the Tombs. In the fall, Molineux, whose appeal from his murder conviction had been allowed by the New York Court of Appeal,[7] returned from Sing Sing and was placed in the cell facing Patrick. They became good friends and were known as the 'aristocrats of the Tombs.' The decision in the Molineux case was thought to be very helpful to Patrick's case as it excluded some handwriting testimony. Former New York governor David B. Hill, who had argued the appeal for the State, said that on the basis of the decision 'I don't see how the State can get in the fact of the forgery of the Rice will on the trial of Patrick for murder.' Moore said that the importance of the decision to his client 'could not be overestimated.'[8]

The will proceedings were becoming increasingly complicated. Relatives who did not receive anything under either will wanted both the 1896 and the Patrick wills defeated – with a resulting intestacy – but were willing to settle with the Rice Institute for a share in the estate. Speculators were busy buying an interest in the litigation. Rice's relatives who were named in the 1896 will, but would have done better under the Patrick will, were willing to settle for the sum of just over $300,000. Moreover, there was serious movement to settle the litigation under Mrs Rice's will. Even J.T. Milliken, through a lawyer, approached the Hornblower firm suggesting that the will case could be settled if Milliken was given what he had expended so far, say $100,000, and if Patrick received perhaps $50,000. According to Byrne, Milliken's representative clearly understood that no settlement could affect the criminal case. Byrne wrote to Baker that he, Byrne, showed no interest in such a settlement, stating: 'I thought the best thing to do was to send a chill down his back by most positive expressions of confidence.'[9]

On the evening of 8 October 1901, William Travers Jerome, formally a Democrat, was nominated as the fusion candidate for district attorney of New York. Under the leadership of the mayoralty candidate, Seth Low, the president of Columbia University, the nonpartisan fusion coalition sought good honest government. Jerome stated in his acceptance speech: 'The real issue of the campaign [is] decency against indecency – honesty against grafters – law against anarchy. Where these are the issue all political lines vanish.'[10] 'They call me a crusader,' Jerome said the following week: 'If the man is a crusader who stands up for clean living and the purity of the home, then I am a crusader.'[11] During the six-week campaign Jerome gave eighty-six speeches, and he won the office of district attorney by more than fifteen thousand votes, running ahead of his ticket.[12]

Throughout the fall, Moore had been pressing the prosecutors to bring Patrick to trial. On 14 October, Judge Foster denied a defense motion to dismiss the indictment. The unusual delay is justified, the judge stated, because the case is one of 'unusual importance and is extremely complicated.'[13] A habeas corpus motion in early December was more successful. Judge Beach agreed with Moore that 'fifteen months is an unreasonable and outrageous time.' 'This prisoner,' Judge Beach said, 'has been deprived of his rights to a speedy trial'[14] and ordered that the trial commence between Christmas and New Year.[15] Counsel agreed, however, to wait until Jerome took office. Jerome was sworn in on 2 January 1902 and immediately swore in his assistants, including Osborne. Jerome said that it would be his aim to try every case within two weeks of indictment. 'Of course,' he added, 'there are exceptional cases like the Patrick case, which will not be tried so promptly because they will take longer to prepare properly.'[16]

Patrick's murder case was fixed to commence on Monday, 20 January, before Judge Goff.

# PART THREE
# The Prosecution

Judge John W. Goff, undated.

Criminal Law Courts, Centre Street, about 1900, since destroyed. The Bridge of Sighs on the left leads to the Tombs.

Assistant District Attorney James W.
Osborne: New York *Evening Journal*,
9 October 1900.

Defense Counsel Robert M. Moore:
New York *Journal*, 29 January 1902.

Davenport's impression of Albert T. Patrick: New York *Journal*, 28 January
1902.

Various versions of Charlie Jones. Clockwise from top left: New York *Journal*, 8 April 1901; New York *Evening World*, 19 February 1902; New York *Journal*, 3 April 1901; New York *Evening World*, 11 June 1901.

James A. Baker, Jr, in the witness box:
New York *Herald*, 29 January 1902.

Members of the jury: New York *Herald*, 23 January 1902.

# 44. The Trial Starts

On Monday morning, 20 January 1902, Judge John William Goff, the recorder of New York, entered Courtroom 2 of the Criminal Court Building for the trial of Albert Patrick on a charge of first-degree murder. The crowd at the courthouse was even greater than it had been for the Molineux case. Murder charges in New York City were then still relatively infrequent. In all of 1902, there were only eleven murder convictions there and only three in the first degree.[1]

The fifty-four-year-old white-haired and white-bearded Goff had been the recorder of New York since 1894 and would continue as the recorder and later a New York Supreme Court judge until he retired in 1919.[2] He had already handled many of New York's most famous cases, including the Molineux and Kennedy trials. Born in Ireland in 1848, Goff worked in England and Scotland as a telegraph operator until he came to New York at the age of fifteen, where he obtained a position as a telegraph operator, at the same time working as a clerk in a dry goods store.

He later graduated from Cooper Union, an institution that was very similar to the proposed Rice Institute, was called to the New York Bar in 1876, and practiced law until he became an assistant district attorney in 1888. He was defeated for the position of district attorney in 1890, but was appointed in 1894 as chief counsel – William Travers Jerome was his assistant – to the famous Lexow Committee which had been set up by the state Senate to investigate the police department of New York City. His work with that body made his name a household word, and when the committee had completed its work he was elected recorder of the city.

Throughout his life he was active in Irish affairs, at one point being the grand marshal of the St Patrick's Day parade in New York City. Many years earlier he had been one of the organizers of the expedition to Australia which had brought back some of the Irish agitators who had been transported there from the United Kingdom.

With his slender, erect bearing, piercing blue eyes, and soft, yet authoritative, Irish voice, he brought austere dignity to his courtroom. Those in his courtroom automatically stood when he entered. One great advocate, Lloyd Paul Stryker, was less charitable, referring to Goff as a 'despotic ... tyrant.'[3]

Shortly before noon, the clerk of the court called: 'The people against Albert T. Patrick, charged with murder in the first degree. Albert T.

Patrick to the bar.' The door leading to the prisoners' pen which connected through the Bridge of Sighs to the Tombs was opened and Patrick walked into court. The reporters noted that he had gained about twenty pounds since the preliminary hearing, and, according to the *World*, he looked 'the picture of health.' The *World* went on to describe Patrick's appearance:

> He carried a black square-topped derby hat in his right hand. He wore a long dark blue overcoat, the collar turned up. Pince-nez glasses rested on his nose. His frock coat was buttoned to the top. His trousers were well creased. His shoes were neatly polished. He wore a high standing collar and a white four-in-hand necktie. His beard was carefully trimmed and well pointed.

His appearance, the *Evening Journal* said, was 'that of a prosperous lawyer.' Patrick walked quickly to the inner inclosure and bowed low to the recorder. He removed his overcoat, folded it carefully, placing it over the railing, and shook hands with his counsel, Robert Moore, Frederick House, and a new counsel, Frank D. Turner. Turner, a member of the Illinois and Missouri bars, was Milliken's personal representative on the defense team. Described as a 'heavy set, stodgy, middle-aged man' continually wearing a 'tremendous expression of owl-like gravity,' he had retired from active practice after defending twenty-nine murder cases, and it was said winning all but one of them.[4] The press reported that Moore and House had received a telegram from Milliken, who had returned from New York to St Louis that weekend, stating, 'One Million dollars, if necessary, for Patrick's legitimate defense.'[5] Patrick sat beside Moore at the counsel table.

Assistant District Attorney James Osborne and Deputy Assistant District Attorney Francis Garvan were at the prosecutors' table. Osborne's back was deliberately turned to Patrick, and he did not even glance at him as Patrick entered the courtroom. Garvan twisted his head for a second to get a look at Patrick and then busied himself in looking over some papers. Jones' counsel, George Gordon Battle, occupied a seat near the clerk's desk. Jones, the spectators were disappointed to discover, was not in court, although he had spent several hours in Garvan's office that morning. James A. Baker sat in the body of the court, having arrived from Texas on Saturday.

A special jury panel had been arranged. Special jurors, like grand jurors, tended to be intellectually and socially a cut above regular jurors. The special-jury law was designed to speed up the selection of the jury.

All the special jurymen had been previously screened to ensure that they were not opposed to capital punishment.[6] The special jury law was controversial. Many thought it favored the prosecution. Prosecutors clearly found it desirable and were opposed to its abolition. A year earlier Osborne had gone to Albany and successfully argued for its retention.[7] The institution, later referred to as 'Blue Ribbon' juries, was not abolished in New York until 1945.[8]

The district attorney had applied for a special jury earlier in the month, Garvan stating in an affidavit:

That unnecessary delay and difficulty will be caused by an attempt to obtain an ordinary jury to try the issue raised by the People of the State of New York and the defendant in this case and that many days will be consumed in obtaining an ordinary jury owing to the great importance of the said case and the notoriety and publicity which has been given to it and to the fact that it has been widely commented upon.[9]

The defense had consented to the application and Judge Goff had granted an order to the commissioner of jurors to select two hundred special jurors from the three thousand special jurors in New York City.

# 45. Selecting the Jury

Out of the 200 special jurors summoned, only 170 appeared. Recorder Goff fined those not there $100 each. About sixty of the jurors that appeared sought to be excused from service. 'If any juror takes up the time of the court with social or business excuses,' the recorder said with great emphasis, 'I will fine him for contempt.' 'Citizens are becoming too well educated in finding excuses for the evasion of their duties,'[1] he added. A number of prospective jurors quickly withdrew their request to be excused. Several jurors who had served on recent lengthy cases were, however, exempted from service.

The first seven potential jurors were rejected, some peremptorily, that is, without the necessity of assigning a reason, and some for cause. In a capital case, each side had thirty peremptory challenges[2] and any number of challenges for cause.[3] It appeared as if the jury selection process would be a lengthy one. The Molineux jury selection had taken two weeks and the last Kennedy jury selection had taken a week.

Some jurors were excused because they expressed some doubt about whether they could render a fair and impartial verdict, uninfluenced by opinions previously held. Other jurors were excused because they expressed opposition to the death penalty. A Mr Chaffee, for example, was asked by Garvan:

Q. Have you any prejudice against the infliction of the death penalty in capital cases?
A. Yes, I have.[4]

The court took up the questioning:

Q. Mr. Chaffee, were you examined before the Commission of Jurors as to your qualifications to go on a special panel?
A. About five or six years ago, yes, sir.
Q. Do you remember your answers then?
A. Perfectly, your Honor.
Q. You remember that you then said you had no prejudice against the infliction of the death penalty in a proper case?
A. Yes, your Honor.
Q. Has anything occurred to change your opinion upon that question since?
A. Yes, your Honor.
Q. It has undergone a change?
A. Yes, sir.

He was then rejected as a juror.

Moore and House both took part in the examination of the jurors. Patrick, acting more like an associate counsel than a defendant, participated by suggesting questions and in deciding whether to accept or reject a juror.

The first juror chosen, James Machell, a diamond merchant, automatically became the foreman of the jury. Patrick, standing before the juryman, had looked him straight in the eye and indicated to his counsel that he was content to have him on the jury. 'No challenge, your Honor,' said Mr House.

The second juror selected was Frank Billmeyer, the secretary of a school furniture company. In the course of the examination Garvan had asked:

Q. Do you know of any reason why you could not be a fair and impartial juror to try the case?
A. There is no reason connected with the case at all. There is a fact that

should probably come to the knowledge of counsel on each side and to the court.

Q. What is the fact?

A. Prior to my coming to New York [almost ten years earlier] I was a practicing attorney and for two terms and a half District Attorney.

The juror was, understandably, acceptable to the prosecution. He was, surprisingly, also acceptable to the defense. House used the occasion to make a point to the press:

Q. I suppose when you were District Attorney out in Pennsylvania you realized something that is not well realized by District Attorneys in New York County, that defendants had some rights which the prosecuting attorney was bound to respect, is that so?

A. I don't know that I should be called upon to answer a question of that kind.

Goff was reluctant to exclude jurors. Moore tried to elicit the fact that one juror had a cold which affected his hearing. 'No,' said Goff, 'if a cold was a ground for excuse there would be an epidemic tomorrow on the jury panel.' Moore therefore had to use one of his peremptory challenges. In another case, Goff, again using the fear of an 'epidemic,' refused to excuse a juror simply on the ground that he knew the prosecutor: 'The trouble is,' said Goff, 'that an epidemic of knowledge would seize this courtroom.'

At the end of the first day, five jurors had been selected. Patrick expressed his pleasure with the selection thus far. He told the reporters as he was being led across the Bridge of Sighs to his cell: 'I like the jurymen. They seem to me to be excellent, representative businessmen. I am thoroughly satisfied with them. There are large money interests against us and for that reason it has been my aim to secure high-minded men who cannot be purchased.'[5]

By the end of the second day, four more jurors had been chosen. One potential juror, who owned a cigar store, told House that he talked repeatedly about the case with his customers:

Q. Now during the time that your customers were talking to you about the matter, did you not get an impression or opinion one way or the other regarding this case?

A. It was impossible; everyone had a different opinion.

Q. So you were not able to judge between the different opinions?

A. Naturally I did not have to judge. I had to side with my customers always.
Q. And the oftener you sided with your customers the more cigars they bought?
A. That is right.

The prosecution challenged the juror peremptorily.

The last three jurors were chosen on Wednesday morning. District Attorney Jerome made a personal token appearance in the courtroom and briefly took part in the examination of one of the jurors. When the jury box was filled, Goff asked Osborne and Moore to see him in his chambers. When they emerged ten minutes later, it was announced that the third juror chosen had been excused from the panel by consent. The press quickly investigated the juror's background and discovered that he had been indicted for forgery in New York City about fourteen years earlier, although the charges were withdrawn by the DA. After ten more potential jurors were examined without success, Gustav Schirmer, a music publisher, was selected. The jury was now complete.

Goff told the jurors that they would not be confined at night:[6] 'It is not the disposition of the court to confine you, to deprive you in any way of your home comforts. You shall therefore each day return to your home.' He then warned them not to discuss the case with others: 'You should be exceedingly careful of your conversation, and your association with people. Do not under any consideration speak to any person, or allow any person to speak to you regarding this case on trial ...' He did not tell them, however, as a judge would likely do today in such circumstances, not to read newspaper accounts of the case.

The jury, Moore told the press – no doubt hoping that the jurors would read his statement – 'is an exceptionally fine one ... keen, intelligent businessmen.'[7]

# 46. Osborne's Opening Address

'Is the prosecution ready to proceed?' Judge Goff asked. 'The prosecution is ready,' Osborne replied. Moore requested the court to order the district attorney to 'elect which of the counts in the indictment he desires to move upon.' Judge Goff summoned the counsel to the bench for a whispered conference. 'They ought certainly by this time, it seems to me, to know,' Moore stated, 'what they are going to charge us with and try us for.' 'At this stage of the case I will refuse your motion,' Goff replied, 'with leave to renew it at a subsequent stage of the prosecution.'[1] House had more success with his request that the Chicago lawyer, Turner, although not a member of the New York Bar, be permitted to appear as counsel.

Shortly after two o'clock on Wednesday, 22 January 1902, Osborne started his opening address to the jury, which would conclude Thursday morning. The case, he told the jury, will go down in history as one of the most remarkable murder trials on record. Like most prosecutors, he assured the jury that the accused was ably defended: 'There are no better criminal lawyers in this country than those who represent him at this trial. And you, gentlemen, are to be congratulated upon the fact that you may rest assured that everything that human nature and human power can do will be done for this defendant by his lawyers.'[2]

Jones's evidence, Osborne told the jury, is that of an accomplice and therefore corroboration would be required:

The mere fact that he admits that he commits an atrocious crime or is engaged in its commission shows right on the face of it that he is not as worthy a man as he ought to be, and, therefore, his testimony is to be accepted by the jury and weighed with great care, and it is not to be received unless it is corroborated by other evidence tending to connect the defendant with the commission of the crime.

He urged the jurors to accept Jones' story: 'I claim that it is not possible for any human being in the world, whose business is such as this accomplice's was, to invent such a story as this that he tells.' Nevertheless, Osborne went on, the case would be proved without having to rely on Jones:

Pay particular attention to what I am about to say, and that is this: that in this case we will make out this entire story, absolutely and in every detail almost, without any exception, almost without exception, without the testimony of the accomplice. We will be able here, as I will outline in my opening, to show you that this crime was complete. I will show the motive for it, the conspiracy between the two conspirators, its preparation, its consummation, murder, I believe, and all, without the aid of the accomplice.

Osborne went into the history of Jones and Rice, mentioning the William M. Rice Institute and its similarity to the Cooper Union in New York City, from which, it will be recalled, Judge Goff had graduated. Patrick's career as a struggling lawyer in New York City was set out:

And who is Patrick, again? We find from his history that he practised in Texas and made enough money to get away from Texas. I might describe his practice in New York City as a constantly shrinking practice. He was reduced to such an extent that but a few weeks before Mr. Rice died – I don't remember, but it was less than a few weeks, maybe ten days or less; wasn't it the 17th of September, he goes to his friend Potts and has to borrow from him $125; a man with no means; no practice to speak of, and as far as we have been able to gather, with never but one important case, and that was this case against Mr. Rice. This is the lawyer, now, that takes everything.

Throughout Osborne's address the defense counsel objected that the prosecutor was going beyond an opening address. The court agreed and repeatedly requested Osborne to 'confine yourself to a narration of such matters as you intend to prove before the jury.' Inferences, Goff said, can be drawn in the closing address.

Patrick's main blunder, Osborne told the jury, was in not knowing that it took at least twenty-four hours to heat up the retort in the crematory in order to burn the body:

Now, as I have said to you before, gentlemen, there is something wonderful about crime – that the criminal ship goes on safely apparently over well known reefs and well known shoals; all such have been accounted for; but, as a great writer says, sometimes, apparently in the smoothest sea and with the most favorable breeze it strikes the sunken rock and goes down.

Patrick was a lawyer and he knew all about assignments, he knew all about wills, knew all about checks; and I propose to show you that this crime, if crime you find it, and this scheme, if scheme you find it, was planned with a genuine and thorough knowledge of the criminal law; that it was planned with some knowledge of the great criminal cases.

You know the fatal blunders of Carlyle, Harris and Buchanan were that the bodies were not destroyed, and those fussy, musty things you call coroners, and an analytical chemist came in and analyzed the bodies. But no such blunders as those were going to be made by Patrick. That body was to be burned instantly. But Patrick, with all his knowledge of law, had failed to find out how long it took a crematory to get hot.

The consequence, he stated dramatically, was that the body was not burned until after an autopsy had been performed.

The 1896 will was compared by Osborne with the so-called Patrick will of 1900. Patrick wanted to keep the 1896 will in existence because the relatives would do better under the Patrick will and, in Patrick's view, would therefore support it: 'every human being who would be able to take the stand and swear that Patrick and Mr. Rice were never seen together, all of them get a legacy.' Nobody, Osborne told the jury, had ever seen Patrick with Mr Rice. Of course, they would do better if both wills were eliminated and there was an intestacy, so, Osborne went on, Patrick had to keep the 1896 will as the alternative to the Patrick will.

'Every man has his price is Patrick's theory,' Osborne told the jury:

Beautiful theory; beautiful theory, if you know just exactly what the price is of the man. But there are lots of people in the world that cannot be bought with money; and I am glad to say that in this case you will find that not a solitary soul that Patrick expected to be bought was bought ... none of them took it, not one, not even the elevator boy, not a soul.

Patrick and Jones acted as one, Osborne stated. A conviction for murder required motive and opportunity. Jones had the opportunity and Patrick the motive. 'We will show that Patrick had motive – motive to burn.'

'Why was it necessary for the old man to die on Sunday?' Osborne asked. It was, he went on to suggest, to prevent Rice from using the $250,000 in the New York banks to rebuild the mill in Texas:

You remember the historian's claim that Napoleon said that it would not do for a general to get too far away from his base of supplies, and that it was because of that fact that Charles the Twelfth lost the battle of Pultowa that changed the history of the world and made Russia a world power; but that is neither here nor there, Patrick wasn't going to make that mistake; that $250,000 was withdrawn from the bank in cash, and what was there left for Patrick, – a big fight, an absurd proposition to try to make this claim, under this will and these checks and some of those other things. With that money once gotten out of the bank it was all up with Patrick with only $125 that he borrowed from Potts. That was his base of supplies so far as we know for he borrowed that week from Potts his friend $125. Now he could not afford to get that far away from his base of supplies, and so we find that on Saturday the first draft comes from Texas, and is presented at 500 Madison Avenue in compliance with the old man's agreement to withdraw $250,000 out of the bank ... He finds out that Mr. Rice will be downtown probably by Monday, and certainly the next week, but that his condition was improving, and the presentation of that check and the knowledge of it brought to Patrick was that old gentleman's death warrant. You know what happened the next day. The old man died. He never got downtown on Monday, and he never paid that draft.

Patrick and Jones agreed, Osborne argued, that Rice would die by chloroform:

Patrick and Jones talk it over; Dr. Curry tells them that the old man will be able to come down next Monday, or certainly during the next week, and they agree to wait until Sunday. Sunday he is better still, and, in spite of the mercury that he has taken, very much better still, and Jones and Patrick on that day agree that the old man must die and die by chloroform on that day. They make that agreement. Then they provide themselves with chloroform ... Now, Patrick had agreed with Jones that when the final hour would come, he, Patrick, would not give the chloroform to Rice. You know he would not do it. No, that isn't his part. Wherever there has been a point of danger he has always sent somebody else to the front and so here he places Jones in the front and says, 'It is no sin to kill the old man; the old man poisoned his own wife; the old man was a miser and he is no good to anybody.' Then he goes on and tells Jones that he has two children, a family, and he cannot afford to do it; and, besides, that he is mentioned in the will and there would be an awful motive for him to do it, but there is no motive at all for Jones to do it. So on that Sunday afternoon Jones goes into the old man's room and gives him chloroform and the old man dies.

Leaning over the jury box and speaking slowly in low tones, Osborne concluded his address the following morning:

Now, gentlemen of the jury, you must take all these facts and circumstances, weigh them and measure them, you must take the old man, the lawyer and the valet, the money, the motive, and you must sift these circumstances, the one into the other, and then you will discover the plan. You will be the builders, and if you build according to the law of reason and the law of nature, it is not possible for you to make out of these circumstances but one structure and that structure must be a crime and that crime must be murder.

'While these accusations were being made,' the *Times* observed, 'Patrick sat a few feet from Mr. Osborne, watching him closely and listening intently. There was absolute silence in the court room except for the words of the Assistant District Attorney, and the only motion was the nervous rocking of Patrick in his chair ... He stroked his beard a thousand times during the day, took off his glasses and polished them, but always returned to the steady rocking of his chair.'[3]

Baker told the press that he was 'much impressed with the speech.' Moore, however, was not at all impressed, telling the press: 'When Mr. Osborne had completed his address I must confess I was jubilant. The prosecution is not possessed of one whit more alleged evidence than it had at the hearing before Mr. Jerome.'[4]

# 47. Prosecution Witnesses

On Friday morning, 24 January 1902, the prosecution called John Wallace, a clerk for twenty years with the banking firm of Swenson and Sons, as its first witness, and followed with other members of the Swenson firm. The defense told the press at an adjournment that the prosecutor was 'trying the case backwards.' 'If I were on the other side of this case,' Moore said, 'I should have begun the prosecution by putting Charles F. Jones, the valet, on the stand and asking him to repeat his alleged confession for the benefit of the jury.' 'No,' said a representative of the district attorney's office to the press, 'Jones will be the last important witness, and he may be the last of all.'[1]

Wallace, it will be recalled, was the teller at Swensons when, on the morning after Rice died, David Short brought in the $25,000 check, purportedly signed by W.M. Rice and payable to 'Abert' T. Patrick. Garvan questioned the witness:

Q. I show you a check dated New York, September 22nd, 1900, and payable to the order of Abert T. Patrick, signed by W.M. Rice, and I ask you when for the first time you ever saw that check?
A. On the 24th day of September, 1900, on a Monday in the counting room around 11 o'clock in the morning.
Q. And who presented that check to you?[2]

Moore objected to the question – the first of very many defense objections – 'on the ground that it is hearsay, incompetent and not admissible as against the defendant.' If the prosecutor seeks to rely on a conspiracy, Moore argued, he should first prove the conspiracy 'before he proves any act in furtherance of it.' 'We have to start somewhere,' Garvan replied. 'The order of proof must rest to a great extent ... in the discretion of the Court,' the judge said, allowing the line of questioning.

Wallace testified – with a trace of a lisp – how he and Wetherbee examined the check and discovered that it was erroneously made out to 'Abert T. Patrick' without the 'l.' He described Short leaving and returning with the endorsement 'Abert T. Patrick,' the subsequent telephone conversation with Jones, who told Swensons that Rice had died the previous evening, and the visit later that day by Patrick. Garvan continued: 'Now, I show you the signature on that check and I ask you if, in your opinion, or belief, that is the signature of W.M. Rice?' Moore objected on the ground that the question 'tends to establish a crime other than that charged in the indictment.' The recent Molineux case,[3] which today is still regularly cited in the New York courts, had established this important proposition. Without calling on the prosecution, Judge Goff overruled the objection. The question was repeated, and the answer given: 'In my opinion, it is not the signature of the late W.M. Rice.' Moore's cross-examination attempted to throw doubt on this conclusion, but Wallace stuck with his opinion, based on the general appearance of the check: 'I couldn't define it, but its general appearance was not satisfactory to me ... I have no doubts whatsoever.'

Walter O. Wetherbee, who also had worked for Swensons for about twenty years, was the next witness examined by Garvan. The prosecutor asked about Jones' visit to Wetherbee's home in Brooklyn, allegedly to get Wetherbee to take part in formalizing a new will for Mr Rice. Moore again objected to the evidence on the basis that no evidence of a conspiracy had yet been established, and this time Goff agreed with Moore: 'I cannot be called upon at this time, even in the exercise of a very wide discretion, to admit testimony where there is no foundation whatever to justify its admission.' Goff said that he would rule at the proper time whether the witness could be recalled to give this evidence.

Wetherbee gave evidence of the events that had been described by Wallace and, after much legal argument, was permitted to give evidence that the body of the check was in Jones' handwriting, but that the signature, 'based upon the general appearance of the writing itself,' was not that of W.M. Rice.

The final witness called from the Swenson firm was Eric P. Swenson, one of the partners in the firm, who, the *Times* stated, gave his evidence in a 'simple, straightforward manner.' Having known Rice for about twenty years, he stated, he 'became familiar with his signature' and expressed his opinion that it was not Rice's signature on the check. Swenson described his conversation with Patrick about Rice on the Monday afternoon after the checks were not paid.

Shortly after that he got up to go, and I asked him if Mr. Rice had been sick for some time and he said he had been ailing for several days. He said, 'You know Mrs. Van Alstyn.' I said 'Yes'; he said, 'Mrs. Van Alstyn induced him to or persuaded him to,' some such remark as that, 'to eat some bananas and that he ate nine' and he said that, in his opinion, was primarily the cause of his death, it brought on the – it was the reason for it. I then asked him when the funeral was to be, and he stated, 'To-morrow morning at 10 o'clock' ... I then asked him where the body was to be interred and he told me that it was to be cremated. I think I expressed some slight surprise at that, and Mr. Patrick stated that Mr. Rice was a crank on the subject of cremation. He said, 'You know he is a crank on the subject of cremation'; I told him that I had never heard of it; well, he said that he is to be cremated by an order that is in the hands of an undertaker over his own signature. I said that I had never heard of that. As far as I can recollect that was about all there was to the conversation.

Two further witnesses were called that day. Harold Acheson, at the time the New York correspondent of the *Houston Post*, testified that Patrick had told him over the telephone the night before the funeral that 'Mr. Rice was to be buried beside his wife in Milwaukee.' This story was printed in the *Houston Post*. No mention, however, was made of cremation. Acheson later confronted Patrick about why he had not told him about the proposed cremation:

I asked him why he led me into the error, and I thought it was rather mean of him, or something of that sort. He said he did not discriminate between remains or cremation or ashes, that they were the same in his mind, and I said they were not to most people's minds. He said it was the same to his mind; I said most people didn't think so, and that was the end of that part of it.

James Gerard, the lawyer for Swensons, who was contacted by the banking firm shortly after the checks were presented, was the last witness called before the weekend and he told about the various conversations he had had with Patrick. He testified that when he and Detective Vallely first called at Patrick's boarding house, he was told that 'Mr. and Mrs. Patrick' had gone out. As this might be considered a reflection on Patrick's character, Recorder Goff had it stricken from the record, although of course the jury had heard the evidence and it was fully reported by the press.

On Thursday of that week, Patrick's younger sister, Emma, had arrived in New York from Austin, Texas, with Patrick's younger daughter,

Lillian, a seven-year-old with curly brown hair and blue eyes. The elder daughter, ten-year-old Lucille, had remained in Texas. Emma told the press that Patrick 'was so religious and such a good brother and son that it was impossible that he could have committed the crime with which he is charged.' The Tombs officials would not permit Patrick to see his sister or daughter, who were staying with Mrs Francis, out of visiting hours. Patrick had a lengthy three-hour visit with Emma on Saturday morning and a visit with his daughter in the Tombs on Monday morning before coming to court. The meeting, the first between father and daughter in two years, took place in the warden's office so that the child would not see any prison bars. The *Evening Journal* published details of the touching meeting. The child, obviously unaware of Patrick's position, asked him why he didn't come home with her and Aunt Emma. Patrick said he would come later.[4]

# 48. The Second Week

It was not until the second week of the trial that the jury heard any evidence that Rice had been murdered.

Detective Vallely, looking 'neat and natty, in a white tie,' testified that he had identified the body in the morgue as being the same as the one he had seen at 500 Madison Avenue. He described the various conversations he had had with Patrick, saying that Patrick did not tell him that the body was to be cremated. But he had to admit that he had lost his book containing notes of the conversations. 'Rather an unusual thing for a detective officer to lose his memorandum book, is it not?' Goff interjected. Vallely, looking very uncomfortable, agreed that it was.[1]

Nor did the prosecutor score any points with the evidence of the undertaker and his assistant in furthering the theory that the embalming was Patrick's idea and was designed to cover up evidence of foul play. Plowright, the undertaker, giving his evidence, according to the *Sun*, in the 'hushed, whispering tones in which the undertaker gives directions at a family funeral,' admitted that he had himself advised the embalming:

It was I who said that the body was to be embalmed. Mr. Patrick said in regard to my suggestion, 'go ahead and do it.' I suggested that the body ought to be embalmed because it is what we always do. It was in order that the body might be preserved until it could be taken over to Fresh Pond and cremated, if such disposition was to be made of it.

Dr Hamilton Williams, the Irish-trained coroner's physician, gave important evidence for the prosecution. He was present when the autopsy was performed. 'I examined the vitals of Mr. Rice. I did so with great care ... What struck me most forcibly was the condition of the lung ... There was an intense congestion of the lungs co-extensive with the lungs themselves.' And most importantly, he had an opinion as to the cause of death.

Q. Did you form an opinion, and have you now an opinion as to the cause of
    death of Mr. Rice?
A. I have. In my opinion, the cause of death was the congestion of the lung,
    brought about by the inhalation of some gaseous irritant.
Q. Doctor, do you know such a substance as chloroform?
A. I do, sir. Chloroform is a liquid: it has a decidedly sweetish taste; it is hot also
    when tasted, and it has what would strike me as being an aromatic smell, a
    rather pleasant smell, not unpleasant.

Williams explained how inhaled chloroform acts as an irritant in the lungs which causes an increased supply of blood to rush in and which in turn causes congestion of the lung. If the condition continues, then oxygen cannot get into the blood and the person dies. Only a gaseous irritant, he stated, could have caused the condition:

The fact that the congestion was co-extensive with the lungs affected my judgment in this way: I had before me two facts. One is the intensity of the congestion; the other is the fact of its being co-extensive with the lungs. Having these two facts before me, I find myself unable to conclude that anything else, other than a gaseous irritant, could have brought about that congestion.

Pneumonia, he went on to say, which 'carries you off in three or four or five or six days,' does not invade the lungs as a whole.

The doctor had performed over one hundred experiments on dogs and cats, designed to show that the lungs of those killed by chloroform differed from those killed in other ways, such as by passing a needle or a knife into the brains or by a blow on the back of the head or by injecting air into the veins.

Dr Williams proposed to show the court the microscopic slides of the lungs of the animals he had prepared in these experiments. Two men came into court with a huge box containing Williams' equipment. Moore objected to the evidence because 'the experiments were made under cir-

cumstances that are not identical with the circumstances in this case.'
Goff sustained the objection and excluded the evidence of the experiments. But again, the jury had already heard the gist of the evidence.

Moore's vigorous cross-examination did not cause Williams to retreat
from his position that death was caused by chloroform. Moore referred
to medical authorities who did not mention congestion of the lungs in
connection with chloroform poisoning. 'That shows you,' Williams replied, 'how much you can think of authorities who neglect that most
important factor, because it is one of the most important of all the factors.'
Moore cleverly asked him about an earlier report to the Royal Medical
Society of London. Williams replied:

A. I have never read the report of a committee appointed by the Royal Medical
Society of London to investigate the effects of death by chloroform poisoning. If I had to read all the reports made upon chloroform poisoning I would
have to be as old as Methuselah.

Q. You never read that where an investigation was made upon six different
deaths induced by chloroform poisoning, and in every one of them there was
no inflammation of the lungs?

A. You ask me have I read that report?

Q. Have you?

A. Thank God, I have not.

# 49. Baker et al.

James A. Baker was called by the prosecutor, Osborne. The *Times* noted
that 'for hours the jurymen, the prisoner, and the spectators listened with
breathless attention. ... Patrick sat up close to the edge of the counsel
table staring straight at Captain Baker.'[1] The real contest, everyone knew,
was between these two lawyers.

The *Herald* described Baker as being 'stalwart and broad chested, suggesting mental and physical vigor, a good fighter, possessing the power
of self restraint.' Baker told the jury about his long association with Rice:
'I have known William M. Rice since about 1877. I knew him very
well. I was his personal counsel. My relations with him were just such
relations as naturally follow from a professional association of fifteen
to twenty years.'[2] Baker had known Patrick in the early 1890s when
Patrick was practicing law in Houston. Later, he had dealings with him
in the fall of 1899 when Baker was in New York taking testimony in the
so-called Holt litigation over Mrs Rice's will. Osborne questioned Baker:

Q. Were you ever informed, in any way, by Mr. Patrick that he was either the counsel or an acquaintance of Mr. Rice during the year before his death, up to the time of Mr. Rice's death?

A. If I remember correctly, Mr. Patrick told me that he knew Mr. Rice many years before in Texas; but not that he ever sustained any professional relations with Mr. Rice.

Captain Baker testified that he next saw Patrick when he arrived in New York on Thursday morning, 27 September, four days after Rice's death. He met privately with Patrick in the back room of Rice's apartment. Baker testified:

Mr. Patrick told me that after I left New York in the fall of 1899 that he thought he would take up the matter of settlement with Mr. Rice direct, if he could do so; that he knew Mr. Rice well enough to know that if he went to his apartments in the ordinary way and sent in his card that Mr. Rice would not receive him; that then he resorted to a ruse by putting an advertisement in some New York paper calling for the heirs of Elizabeth B. Rice, and signed the name 'Justice,' as I remember.

That this advertisement came under the eye of Mr. Rice, who answered it, and he then called on Mr. Rice and made himself known, and that he and Mr. Rice became very well acquainted, so much so that Mr. Rice retained him in all of his legal matters, except in the 'Holt suit'; that is, the suit of William M. Rice vs. O.T. Holt, about which I have already spoken ...

He said, in effect, that he made a very profound impression on Mr. Rice, and that Mr. Rice became thoroughly imbued with the idea that he, Patrick, was an able lawyer, counsellor and adviser, and had expressed the regret that he did not know him earlier in the litigation of Rice vs. Holt.

That, if he had, he certainly would have employed Patrick to assist my firm in that litigation. He said that it might be of interest to me to know that Mr. Rice gave him as one of the reasons why he had employed him, Patrick, was that Mr. Rice had lost confidence in me and my firm, and I asked him why, and he said, Mr. Rice told me that on one occasion, while testimony was being taken here in his apartments, that when the Commissioner adjourned the hearing until the afternoon, that I had invited Mr. Holt, my opponent, to lunch, and had done so in a rather cordial way; that Mr. Rice could not understand how attorneys that were opposed to each other in litigation as embittered as this was, could be so cordial as to take lunch with each other and a suspicion was aroused in Mr. Rice's mind by that incident, and from that time on he had lost confidence in me and in my firm.

Their conversation turned to Rice's new will:

He said that Mr. Rice had made a will in June, 1900, in which he was named as residuary legatee for a great part of Mr. Rice's estate ... I asked him how it happened that Mr. Rice named him as residuary legatee of all his estate, since he sustained no relation to Mr. Rice and was fighting him in this litigation. He said, in reply, 'As I explained to you, Mr. Rice and I were friends in all matters except in that litigation, and to be frank with you, the old man became, as it were, stuck on me; he thought I was the most wonderful man in the world.' He said that he was residuary legatee for about nine-tenths or fifteen-sixteenths, I don't remember which, of his estate, and that it passed to him without any conditions or limitations whatsoever. He said that he and Mr. Rice had discussed the matter of his being residuary legatee in the will in great detail, and that while he was residuary legatee without any limitations or qualifications, yet he knew that Mr. Rice wanted his estate distributed in a great measure to charity, and that it was his purpose, although there was no legal obligation on him to do so, to distribute it in a great measure to charities and to exploit the name of William M. Rice throughout the world as a philanthropist.

Patrick, he said, assured him that he, Baker, would 'bountifully be compensated' for his services as an executor. Moreover, Patrick told him that he would contribute to the Rice Institute:

A. So far as the William M. Rice Institute is concerned, Patrick told me 'Mr. Rice thought a great deal of that institution.' And he said, 'I will give whatever you think is right, say three or four or five million dollars,' I think he said.
Q. Patrick said that he would?
A. Yes. He said after that that he would like to become a director in the institute, if he gave this money.

In a later conversation the following week, while the safety deposit box was being opened, Baker said he asked Patrick why he had not had more objective persons witness the will and the assignment:

I said to Mr. Patrick, 'In view of your antagonistic and hostile relations to Mr. Rice, if you expected this will and this assignment to hold in any court in Christendom, why did you not have some friend of Mr. Rice, the Swensons, for instance, who had known him for thirty years, or some other good people in New

York who knew you and Mr. Rice, go with you to Mr. Rice's apartments, and in their presence offer this will and this assignment and tell these witnesses in the presence of Mr. Rice that this was Mr. Rice's act; that it was his last will and it was his assignment. Why didn't you do that?'

He said, 'I expect I ought to have done that. But,' he said, 'Mr. Rice, as you know, was peculiar, and he insisted always that our relations should be secret, and as far as I know, no one, no living man ever saw me in the presence of Mr. Rice, unless it was C.F. Jones, and I don't know that he ever saw me with him.'

The questioning turned to Rice's handwriting. 'I have been familiar with his handwriting for fifteen or twenty years,' Baker testified: 'I have seen him write frequently; innumerable times, almost.' He was shown the allegedly forged Swenson checks:

Q. I ask you whether or not the signatures to those are in Mr. Rice's hand-writing?

A. In my judgment they are not ... Mr. Rice's genuine signature, as reflected in the mental picture that I have of it, was written with a good deal of expression, so to speak. He shaded the downward strokes, which I find absent in the signatures now before me. To my eye the signatures appear studied and cramped, and lack that expression of a flowing, full execution that I remember in Mr. Rice's genuine signature.

In cross-examination, Moore attempted to show that the Rice Institute, incorporated in 1891, was a sham. No buildings had yet been put up to further its objects:

Q. Captain Baker, of all this large sum of money that the William M. Rice Institute of Texas has acquired, has any of it been expended for the purposes for which it was incorporated?

A. Most of it is real property; a very small portion of it is personal property; but to answer your question, none of it has been expended.

During a break in the proceedings, Patrick told a reporter for the *Evening Journal*: 'Do you suppose a keen, acute, old man like Mr. Rice would leave his hard-earned gold to a Mythical Institution? No; Mr. Rice and I entered into a secret trust, evidence of which I will produce in court at the proper time, to divide the estate charitably.'[3]

On the same day Baker was on the stand, the press observed an old black man talking frequently and warmly with the prosecutor, James Osborne. They wondered what evidence he would be giving. It turned out that he was a former slave of the Osbornes' in North Carolina who had been freed during the Civil War and had gone to live in Liberia. The seventy-year-old Peter Osborne – he had taken the Osborne name – told the curious reporters: 'I helped bring up Master James and I've come six thousand miles from Liberia just to see him and his family once more before I die.'[4]

Norman Meldrum, the banker who had intervened on Baker's behalf before Baker arrived from Texas, gave evidence similar to Baker's about conversations with Patrick after Rice had died. He claimed also to be familiar with Rice's handwriting and testified that the signatures on the checks were 'not in the handwriting of Mr. Rice.'

A number of witnesses who voluntarily came from Texas to give evidence also testified that they were familiar with Rice's handwriting and that the checks were forgeries. Emmanuel Raphael, a prominent member of Houston's Jewish community,[5] was the manager of the Houston banking clearing house and the secretary and a director of the Rice Institute.[6] He had had frequent financial dealings with Rice over more than twenty years and testified that he 'never knew Mr. Patrick to do any business for Mr. Rice' and that he 'never heard of him in any way in relation to Mr. Rice.'

Raphael's brother-in-law, Arthur Cohn, had been an employee of Rice's in Houston, handling many of Rice's financial matters. Raphael had arranged for him to come to Houston from Little Rock, Arkansas, about ten years earlier. Like Raphael, Cohn testified that he knew Rice's handwriting and that the checks and the will were 'not in Mr. Rice's handwriting.' Moreover, he was in almost weekly correspondence with Rice and stated: 'I did not know the defendant, Albert T. Patrick; I did not ever know him in any way to transact any business for Mr. Rice at any place.'

Another witness from Houston, Judge Thomas W. Ford, testified that he had visited Rice shortly before he died and Rice seemed friendly with Baker. Ford also said that he had met Patrick, by accident, in late August 1900 on the streets of New York City and that although they talked about Rice, Patrick said nothing about being Rice's lawyer.

Similarly, William Marsh Rice, Jr, Rice's nephew, testified that the documents were forgeries and that Patrick was not his uncle's lawyer:

'My relations with my uncle were intimate. I knew this defendant, Albert T. Patrick. I know who were the lawyers for my uncle; this defendant was not one of them. I never knew this defendant to have any business relations with my uncle.'

Other witnesses in the second week of the trial included the night watchman of the Broadway Chambers, where Patrick had his office. He testified that between one and two o'clock in the morning of Tuesday, 25 September, he let Patrick into the building. At about five o'clock in the morning he discovered that the toilet on Patrick's floor had over-flowed. Patrick came out of his office, he testified, and said: 'Watchman, excuse me, it is me done it, by using some coarse paper, and I overflowed the toilet.' He was not cross-examined.

# 50. The Third Week: Medical Evidence

At the start of the third week, because of the crowds awaiting admission, the trial was shifted from Courtroom 2 to the larger Courtroom 4.

Three doctors gave damaging evidence against Patrick on Monday, 3 February 1902, supporting Dr Hamilton Williams' testimony that the condition of Rice's lungs had been caused by a gas such as chloroform.

Dr Edward Donlin, the coroner's physician who had performed the autopsy on Rice and had performed over a thousand other autopsies, told Osborne:[1]

I found the lungs congested extensively, with a slight area of consolidated lung tissue in the lower lobe of the right lung ... I do not know anything else in the world which will cause an irritation of the lungs co-extensive with the lungs themselves except the inflammation of an irritating gas. I know of no disease that will do it. The vapor of chloroform is an irritant, and its liquid is an irritant. Chloroform is such an irritating gas.

He was asked by Osborne whether he had ever performed autopsies on persons who had inhaled gas:

A. I have performed autopsies on the body of human beings who died from the inhalation of some kind of an irritating gas, quite a number of them, in the morgue and at different hospitals.
Q. In all cases of death from the inhalation of irritating gas, did you find a con-gestion of the lungs themselves in cases of that kind?

A. Yes; coextensive over both lungs.

Moore brought out in cross-examination that in his autopsy report Donlin had simply said that there was 'congestion of both lungs' and had not said that the congestion was 'intense' or that that congestion was 'coextensive' with the lungs. Moore asked him what he had said to the reporters after the autopsy:

Q. And did you not say that he died from old age?
A. I don't recall that. I don't recall any such thing.

For the first time in the trial, during the re-cross-examination of Donlin, the suggestion was made by Moore that the embalming fluid might have affected the lungs, but, surprisingly, this important question was not allowed by the judge.

Q. Now, would the embalming fluid, assuming that it was used after death, the arterial process, would that have any effect upon the lungs?
By the Court: This is opening up a new line altogether. The Court proposes to limit the extraordinary dimensions which this case threatens to assume.

Dr Henry P. Loomis, who for ten years had been professor of pathology at New York University and was now professor at Cornell University Medical School, had examined Rice's lungs at Dr Witthaus' request. He also had had extensive experience in performing autopsies – about two thousand of them as the visiting physician at Bellevue Hospital. His evidence was similar to Donlin's:

I do not know any disease of the human body which will produce congestion of the lungs, which is coextensive with the lungs themselves – that is, all over the lungs ... I know of nothing outside or beyond an irritant vapor or gas that will produce congestion, co-extensive with the lungs. I know no disease that would do that. Chloroform would be an irritant vapor which, inhaled in excessive quantities, would produce congestion of the lungs.

The less atmospheric air that is mixed with the chloroform, he explained, the more intense is the congestion: 'chloroform kills,' he went on to explain, 'by getting down into these minute air sacs and being taken up by the blood and carried up into the lungs in the blood and paralyzing the cells of the brain that have to do with the two vital processes of life, namely with breathing and with heart action.'

Osborne was obviously worried that Judge Goff had cut off the questioning of Dr Donlin about the effect of the embalming fluid and so asked Dr Loomis if the embalming fluid could have affected the lungs. Loomis denied that it could have any effect:

Embalming fluid injected through the brachial artery could never reach the lungs. It might reach the heart, and it could not go through the heart, I don't believe, but it might just reach the valves of the heart. If it did get into the heart, there is nothing to carry it from the heart into the lungs. I don't believe, in my opinion, it is possible for embalming fluid, injected into the brachial artery, to go through the heart and so on into the lungs. In my opinion the lungs would retain, after death, their condition, in spite of the embalming fluid.

The *Times* reported that Patrick listened attentively, nervously stroking his short beard.

In cross-examination, however, Loomis admitted that he had 'never performed an autopsy on a person who died from chloroform poisoning.' But, he said, he had had someone gather reports from the literature and found that in eight out of nine reported cases of chloroform poisoning in the last ten years there was intense congestion of the lungs.

Dr Rudolph Witthaus, the distinguished professor of chemistry in the Cornell Medical School, who was present at the inquest and subsequently analyzed a number of Rice's organs, also stated that the embalming fluid would not affect the appearance of the lungs:

I don't know that formaldehyde would have any particular effect on the appearance of the lungs any more that it would in any other part of the body, and less on the lungs than on any other part of the body. Its effects upon the body would be to bleach it. Any embalming fluid would do that. It would affect the lung less than any other part of the body. It would affect the lung some.

Witthaus then described the analysis for poisons of the various organs: 'I made an analysis of these several parts. I made two analyses, in fact, of the intestines, and two of the liver, one of the stomach and one of the kidney.' He found, he said, mercury in the body: 'over half a grain in the intestines; over a quarter of a grain in the kidney' – more than three-quarters of a grain in all. Other testimony showed that the embalming fluid used on Rice contained no mercury.

In cross-examination, Witthaus admitted to Moore that the mercury taken by Rice was not the cause of death: 'The amount of mercury procured which I found was hardly sufficient to cause the death of a person if administered.' Death by chloroform, therefore, would have to be the theory of the prosecution's case.

While this scientific evidence was being given, juror number 6, John J. Campbell, was shivering in his seat with his overcoat on. The recorder therefore adjourned the trial early. 'I am well satisfied with the progress of the case,' Osborne told the *Evening Journal*. Moore also expressed optimism: 'I don't know of a criminal case of this magnitude where the position of the defence was in a better position than it is today.'[2]

The following morning, the juror was still too ill to proceed. There was, his doctor said, a risk of pneumonia. Osborne warned that if the juror did not recover in a reasonable time, they may have to select a new jury.[3] There was – and still is today in New York – no right to proceed with only eleven jurors and the technique of having alternate jurors hear the case had not yet been devised.[4] Juror Campbell was not ready to return to the jury until the beginning of the following week.

# 51. The Fourth Week

The twelve members of the jury assembled again on Monday, 10 February, the start of the fourth week of the case. Jones, the key prosecution witness, had still not been heard.

Towards the end of the day, John R. Potts was called to testify for the prosecution. It will be recalled that the district attorney's office had privately been told that Potts, a lawyer, was one of the masterminds behind the scheme to get Rice's money. As a witness, however, he was presented as a minor player, a friend of Patrick's from the time that they were children growing up in Navasota, Texas. In the spring of 1900 he had rented office space from Patrick and had his office adjoining Patrick's. He claimed that the first time he heard Patrick mention Rice's name was on 17 September 1900. Potts testified that he had loaned Patrick $150 and that Patrick had taken him to a safety deposit box and showed him a will signed by Rice, making Patrick the residuary legatee of the estate, along with a document settling the will contest and several blank cheques purportedly signed by Rice.

Potts claimed that he had been engaged as Patrick's lawyer several days before Patrick was arrested and so refused to answer questions about that period. Indeed, the *World* did not think much of his entire testimony,

stating that 'Potts forgot with unswerving regularity every point that
seemed likely to hurt the accused.' The *World* described how Potts
'wriggled and twisted in the witness chair' and gave his evidence 'speaking with exaggerated emphasis and superabundant gestures.'[1] At one
point, Mr House interrupted him, stating: 'don't make any speeches here,
Mr. Potts. Answer the question.' The court, recalling that Potts was
also a court stenographer, added: 'I suppose, Mr. House, that it is so
rare for a stenographer to get an opportunity to talk that he is taking
advantage of it.'[2]

The defense barely cross-examined Potts. Moore tried, with some success, to get Potts to admit that Patrick had taken the property in trust:

Q. Did you in that conversation – did Mr. Patrick tell you that the estate was
given to him in trust, or words to that effect?
A. Did he tell me those words?
Q. Or words to that effect?
A. No, sir.
Q. Didn't he tell you that while the estate was his apparently, as residuary lega-
tee, it was in fact a trust to be administered largely in his discretion?
A. He said –
Q. Or words to that effect?
A. He said this –
Q. Did he say that or words to that effect?
A. Well, part of it, yes, sir ...
Q. What was said?
A. I do not remember that Mr. Patrick used the word trust; I think, though, that
he said something about that he had an arrangement with Mr. Rice that he
could dispose of this as he pleased.

The following day, James Byrne, from the Hornblower law firm, wrote
to Baker: 'Yesterday Potts was on the stand and I think it may be considered the very best day the prosecution has had.' Baker had left New
York a few days earlier to be with his pneumonia-stricken eldest child,
Graham, an eighteen-year-old student attending the private Hill School
in Pottstown, Pennsylvania. Byrne assured Mr and Mrs Baker that 'with
good care and former good health on the part of the patient, pneumonia
is not a dangerous disease.'[3]

Another witness, John Whittlesey, clearly harmed Patrick. Whittlesey
had been friendly with Rice for many years and he had visited him every
few weeks over the last few years of Rice's life. He also knew Patrick,

who had done legal work for him on one occasion. Whittlesey testified that Patrick had asked him to speak to Rice about compromising the Holt litigation relating to Mrs Rice's will. Rice, Patrick said, refused to compromise. Whittlesey claimed that this conversation took place in March or April 1900. The date is important, Osborne told the press, because Potts had said that the settlement he had seen relating to Mrs Rice's will was dated 6 March 1900. If the settlement was genuine, why was Patrick trying to get Whittlesey to intervene? Moreover, Whittlesey testified, Patrick had told him that he, Patrick, did not know Rice well: 'I asked him why he did not speak to Mr. Rice, or if he had spoken to Mr. Rice, to the best of my recollection, and he either said he was not well enough acquainted with Mr. Rice, or was not acquainted with him, something like that; I am not positive in regard to the words he used.'

Moore's cross-examination was designed to show that Patrick's conversation with Whittlesey was in 1899, the year before the date Whittlesey had stated. The difference in dates was obviously important. Whittlesey would not budge: 'I am just as positive as I am sitting here and that it snows out of doors.' (New York City was at the time experiencing a severe February blizzard.)

Osborne now concentrated on the handwriting experts. Each juror was handed a card three feet long and a foot wide, with various signatures on it. The enlargements had been prepared by Dr E.J. Lederle, a chemist who later became the New York health commissioner and who subsequently founded the well-known Lederle Laboratories.[4] Various witnesses familiar with Rice's handwriting testified that the disputed documents did not bear Rice's genuine signature. One of the Swenson bookkeepers, W.F. Harman, had confidently given such evidence. In cross-examination, House had shown the witnesses five sealed envelopes with a slit in the front of each, showing only a 'W.M. Rice' signature on a slip of paper inside. The witness was asked in each case whether the signature was genuine. He was shown the third envelope:

Q. I ask you to look at what purports to be the signature of William M. Rice, and I ask you whether, in your opinion, that is the genuine signature of the late William M. Rice?
A. In my opinion it is Mr. Rice's signature.
Mr. House: I now offer it in evidence. The witness has stated that in his opinion it is the genuine signature of William M. Rice.
Mr. Osborne: I cannot see any relevancy in this to this case. It is a mere blank piece of paper with a signature on it.

Of course, that is exactly what House wanted the jury to see. House triumphantly told the press after the session: 'That shows what all their handwriting testimony is worth.' Osborne had his reply ready: 'It suits us either way,' he said: 'If the signatures are genuine, what is Patrick doing with them? If they are not, how is it that he can so well imitate Rice's signature as to be able to fool these people familiar with his writing for years.'[5]

Experts unfamiliar with Rice's handwriting were also permitted to give an opinion on genuineness based on a comparison with signatures proved genuine. A statute in 1880 had changed the common law rule which had excluded such evidence.[6] As previously noted, the prosecution and those upholding the 1896 will had virtually cornered the market on experts. The press speculated that the defense would have to import some of the experts from France who had taken part in the Dreyfus case.

The principal prosecution expert was Albert Osborn. The then more famous David Carvalho was in court and was prepared to give evidence for the prosecutor, but he was not called. The press speculated that this was because he was to be a defense witness in the pending Molineux retrial and the prosecution did not want to give him added prestige and credibility by relying on him in the Patrick case.

The expert Osborn brought with him a blackboard covered in white paper. With his black chalk, he gave the jury a lecture on disputed documents. The prosecutor would periodically ask in a loud voice, 'Are you sure of that?' – designed to wake up the jury. 'The relevant documents,' the witness said, 'are all forgeries: I have studied them all with great care and have been able to form an opinion as to whether or not the papers called the Swenson checks, the will of June 30, the assignment and revocation and the cremation letter, are or are not in the handwriting of Mr. Rice. I think they are not.'

He outlined to the jury the difference between Rice's English round-hand style of writing taught in the United States before 1850 and the style then being used. Osborn continued:

One who writes an entirely different style of writing finds it much more difficult to simulate or imitate or forge the handwriting of one who writes an entirely different type of handwriting, because the problem that is presented to him is a double one, that of eliminating his own characteristics ... and the second, of incorporating the characteristics of the hand that he is seeking to imitate.[7]

'The genuine signatures of W.M. Rice,' he told the jury, 'do not show deliberation.' The dotting of the 'i' in the word Rice, for example, shows 'no particular care' and is not done neatly over the letter. In contrast, a forged signature is too perfect, too carefully done. The four disputed checks 'were undoubtedly made from the same model.' The same is true, he stated, of the will of 1900: 'The four signatures on that will are mathematical reproductions one of the other, so far as the four points of beginning are concerned, and many other points.' The very act of forging a will causes the forger to be too careful:

It is more difficult to forge a million dollar will than it is a ten dollar check, because the conditions affect the writer. It is more difficult to produce a fraudulent signature in imitation of a genuine one, than to produce a signature simply to show the skill of the writer, on account of the mental condition that is involved in a realization of a criminal act being performed and the necessity of its being done well, and, like any piece of acting, it is overdone, so much so that it is one of the almost inevitable evidences of forgery that the forged signature is too well done – that is, that attention is given to it throughout, and I think that is particularly the case in connection with these signatures. It is undoubtedly so in connection with the will signature.

In cross-examination, Osborn, the handwriting expert, did not qualify his opinion in any way. Moore wanted the witness to admit that Rice would give great care and deliberation in signing his will, but even here the expert's evidence did not assist the defense:

Q. Now, I ask you, would not, in your judgment, a person use greater deliberation and greater care in writing his signature to his will than he would in writing his signature to ordinary business papers? ...
A. A person might or might not use greater deliberation in writing his signature to his will than he would in writing his signature to a letter. For instance, a letter might be a very formal document. Generally speaking, in the case of all writers, it depends upon the circumstances.

After over a day devoted to the examination-in-chief and over a day to cross-examination, Judge Goff warned that he would be limiting the use of handwriting experts:

The Court wishes to state to counsel on both sides that it has afforded every latitude to both the prosecution and the defense for examination and cross-examination of Mr. Osborn, as an expert in handwriting. Each side has taken more than a day – I mean more than a day to examine and cross-examine respectively. Now, the court proposes to limit the number of experts in handwriting, and also to limit the extent of the examination and cross-examination.

A number of cashiers from Houston then gave evidence that the disputed signatures were not Rice's. While Moore was cross-examining one of the witnesses, the judge stopped the questioning: 'Stop. I decline to permit you to question any further as to those checks. It is manifest that the cross-examination is degenerating into levity.'

John F. Tyrell, an expert penman with Mutual Life of Milwaukee – described by the *Evening Journal* as 'the famous handwriting wizard of the Northwest' – gave similar evidence to Osborn's. All of the disputed documents, he testified, were forgeries. The cremation letter, for example, showed that there were 'seven pen-lifts to accomplish what Mr. Rice did in three.' The will of 1900, he said, contained 'the most remarkable collection of signatures I have ever seen. They are peculiar – peculiarly alike, peculiarly unlike Mr. Rice.'

Baker was absent throughout the handwriting testimony. His son had died in Pennsylvania of pneumonia and the Bakers had returned to Texas with the body. Baker wrote to Byrne that although willing to return to New York he would 'prefer to remain here as long as possible. Mrs. Baker, while not confined to her bed, is far from well, and I want to be with her as long as I can.'[8] Byrne replied: 'we are all glad to have you here but there is no reason why you should be worried about the case. It has gone wonderfully well.'[9]

# 52. Jones Takes the Stand

Late Tuesday afternoon, Charlie Jones was called by Osborne to give his evidence. This was the testimony that the press and the public had been waiting for. The press had been keeping careful track of Jones' movements. A reporter for Hearst's *Evening Journal* had accompanied 'Valet Jones' and Detective Sergeant Brindley on a tour of the Tenderloin district the previous evening and to the courthouse the next morning. No detail was too small to report. 'Before going to the Criminal Court,' the *Evening Journal* reported, 'the two men made a visit to Foo Ching's laundry in West Forty-Second street, where Valet Jones left his laundry.' 'My name is Charles F. McKay Jones,' the star witness told the reporter, 'not Valet Jones.'[1]

Wearing a close-fitting dark suit and dark-colored bow tie, Jones entered the witness box. The press reported that Patrick watched Jones closely, but that Jones did not even glance at Patrick. For the first time in several weeks, there was a large crowd in the courtroom. Supreme Court Justice Woodward sat on the bench with Recorder Goff, and among the interested spectators spotted by the press was a former postmaster general of the United States, the premier of Nova Scotia, a rear admiral, a judge from Massachusetts, and the Reverend Lyman Abbott, the father of juror Abbott.

The press noted the many 'handsome women stylishly dressed' who had come to hear Jones' testimony. 'They craned their necks curiously,' the *Times* reported, 'as Jones, followed by an officer, walked with firm tread to the witness stand.' 'Twenty members of the Women's League for Political Education went to the morning session of the trial,' the *Sun* reported in a tone typical of the attitude of the time, 'and tried to improve their minds by gazing at the back of Patrick's head through open glasses and lorgnettes.' The *Evening Journal* noted the absence of Maude Mortimer, the woman who was to have seen Jones the night Rice died. Now married, she was tracked down by the *Evening Journal* in Harlem. The *Journal* did not reveal her married name, but reported in detail her story: that it was her cousin Mabel Whitney who had been engaged to Jones and had visited him in the Tombs. She, herself, had not visited him in the Tombs or gone to court to see him: 'I never saw the inside of a courtroom and do not intend to,' she said.[2]

The press was still concerned about the image of hypnotism. 'Jones looked at Mr. Osborne,' the *Evening Journal* reported, 'like one under a hypnotic spell.' The next day, however, according to the *Evening Journal*, it was Patrick who was trying to cast the spell over Jones: 'Patrick's hypnotic eye has seemingly failed to influence the man who swears that the lawyer instigated the murder.' Not to be outdone, Pulitzer's *World* (which had from the beginning talked about Jones being the hypnotist) wrote that Patrick 'stared unwinkingly at Jones in an absorbed dreamy way as if the man in the witness chair had hypnotised him.'

Jones' evidence-in-chief, which was essentially the same as he had told Jerome at the preliminary hearing, apparently made a favorable impression on those who heard it. The *World* reported that Jones was in 'perfect command of every detail,' and the *Evening Journal* stated that Jones told a 'strong and convincing story.' Byrne wrote to Captain Baker, who was still in Texas: 'It is to my mind extraordinary in what good shape the case has gone in so far. Jones' testimony has had the same effect

upon the newspapers and people generally that it always has had. Everyone seems to believe it.'[3]

Osborne took Jones through his evidence in great detail, outlining
Patrick's various activities:

Q. Did Patrick ever say anything to you about playing chess?
A. Yes. He said he intended to manage the affair just as he played chess.
Q. When was the last time you heard him say anything about playing chess?
A. In the Tombs. Mr. House was present. Mr. Patrick said he worked the scheme
   just as he played chess.
Q. What did Mr. House say?
A. That he was a very poor chess player.[4]

On the third day of his testimony, Jones, giving his evidence in a 'clear
firm tone,' described how it was that Patrick had suggested chloroform:

Q. Did Patrick ever ask about Rice's health?
A. Patrick asked how Mr. Rice's health was early in August.
Q. Tell the conversation.
A. Patrick asked me in August, 1900, how Rice's health was. I said he seemed to
   improve every day. Patrick then asked if I didn't think he was living entirely
   too long for our plans. He asked if there was not some way we could put him
   out of the way. I replied, laughingly, only with a Gatling gun. He said to let
   him know some night when Rice slept and he would come over and put him
   out of the way. I told him he could not do that, as Rice slept too lightly. I said
   if there was anything of this sort to be done it ought to be left to Dr. Curry.
   Patrick said no, that Dr. Curry would have nothing to do with such a thing:
   that he would do anything that was right, but nothing in the least way wrong;
   that I was not ever to mention the matter to Dr. Curry.[5]

Osborne asked if there was any discussion of chloroform before this:

A. Yes. In June or July an article appeared in The Omega Magazine about chloroform and its use by dentists in their profession. Mr. Rice read it and called
   my attention to it. Rice said something ought to be done to prevent its use. I
   said there was a doubt in my mind if chloroform could be discovered after
   death as the cause of demise. Rice said, ask Dr. Curry and settle it. I told Patrick of this conversation and showed him the article, and told him I doubted if
   chloroform could be discovered as a cause of death. He read the article.
Q. State all you said to Patrick about this article.

A. Patrick said he would ask Dr. Curry about the effects of chloroform himself, and asked me to also ask him. I did. Dr. Curry said it would be very difficult to detect the effects of chloroform if the deceased had heart disease as very little chloroform would kill. He said the chloroform acted on the brain. Patrick told me Dr. Curry told him the same thing, only that he said it acted on the nervous system.

Q. Was there any talk that dentists laid the blame for any death from chloroform to weak hearts?

A. Either he told me that or I told him Rice said so.

Q. After reading the article what else did you do to familiarize yourselves with chloroform?

A. I read and showed to Patrick and he read an article in the encyclopedia in Rice's apartments about chloroform: how it was made, how administered and its effect.

Q. Any talk about symptoms or post-mortem effect?

A. I don't remember.

Q. You say the talk about getting the chloroform was in August?

A. Yes. He asked me then if I couldn't get him some. He said he wanted it for a toothache, that it was hard to get here on account of the strictness of the laws. He said there was no reason why I should not get it. I said I might get some from a nurse at the Presbyterian Hospital. However, I wrote my brother in Hyatt, Texas, to send me some. I sent him $5 Patrick gave me. He sent me by express a four-ounce bottle. I gave it to Patrick. Subsequent to the first inquiry as to Rice's health. Patrick again asked me how he was getting along. I said he still improved. He asked if he still slept lightly. I said he did. He suggested giving him laudanum to make him sleep. He told me of a place in Coney Island where I could get laudanum without a prescription. I said I would get some there, but didn't.

   I let the matter stand until he again asked me subsequently how Rice was. I said he was the same. He suggested that I feed him sapollo in his food to break him down. I said this was impossible: that he prepared his own food, and was very careful what he ate. He then said give him baking powder. I said this was equally impossible. He then asked me to get him some more chloroform at the same place I got the first. I sent to my brother in Texas again and received from him a two-ounce bottle of chloroform and a two-ounce bottle of laudanum. I gave these to Patrick also. From time to time he asked how Rice was. I said he seemed to grow better as the weather grew colder. He said, give him mercury to break down his system, and asked if I had any. I said I had some mercurial pills Dr. Curry prescribed for me.[6]

On the Sunday of Rice's death, Jones testified, Patrick insisted that as 'a man of family,' he, Patrick, should not be the one to kill Rice. Jones went on:

He said, 'If Mr. Rice had poisoned his wife or caused her to be poisoned, it would be no sin to put him out of the way'; and gave me a bottle of chloroform and told me to take it to the house and administer it to Mr. Rice. I refused, of course, saying that I had not promised to do anything of that kind and did not expect to, and would not do it. He said that, if I did not, that the check would become due the next day, and would draw out all the money, and Captain Baker would be on very shortly, and probably all the scheme would be revealed and we would lose everything. After considerable persuasion I said that I would take the chloroform, and do as he had instructed me to do; and I took the chloroform and went home.

Jones then testified about the administration of the chloroform.

After looking some time for a sponge, I found one that Mr. Rice had used for cleaning his clothes, and I made a cone of a towel, placed the sponge in the small end, and took it and saturated it with chloroform and placed it over my own face. I got a very strong effect from it. I then added a little more and went into Mr. Rice's room. I found he was still sleeping and placed it over his face and ran out of the room.

Mr. Patrick had given me these instructions and I followed them out as near as I could. He told me also to leave the chloroform on his face about thirty minutes. I stayed out of the room thirty minutes, stayed in my room part of the time, part of the time in the hall, and part of the time in front, in the dining room, part of the time. At the expiration of the thirty minutes, someone kept ringing the bell very frequently. Of course, I was very much excited that they should be ringing the bell at this moment, so that I went to the door and looked through and I could see some one, but didn't know who they were. It looked like a lady, but I wouldn't say whether it was a lady or not, but my impression was it was two ladies at the door.

After the thirty minutes had expired I went back to Mr. Rice's room, and found him in the same position that I had left him, with that cone shape over his face. I removed that and put it in the range in the kitchen, and lit a match to it, and burned it, and returned to Mr. Rice's rooms, and opened all the windows, straightened everything around to its usual appearance, and telephoned to Mr. Patrick that Mr. Rice was very ill.[7]

Recorder Goff wanted more details:

Q. I wish you would describe accurately how you placed the towel and sponge on Mr. Rice's face.

A. I held the towel this way, Your Honor, and wrapped it round and round this way. Then I took my hand out and put the dry sponge in the small end of the cone and wet it with chloroform. The defendant was lying on his back – oh, I beg your pardon: I mean the deceased was lying on his back, with a very small pillow under his head.

The mistaken reference to Patrick caused those in the courtroom, including Patrick, to laugh nervously. The recorder continued his questioning:

How did you put the chloroform on the sponge?

A. I held the cone in my left hand with the small end down and poured in the chloroform.

Q. Did any go through the sponge onto the towel?

A. Yes. Then I held the cone over my own face.

Q. Did any of it touch your face?

A. No, Your Honor. Then I placed the cone over Mr. Rice's face.

Q. Did not the sponge touch Mr. Rice's face?

A. I think not, Your Honor. May I give you the reason? I put the sponge in dry and pressed it tight in the small end of the cone, then I poured on the chloroform.

Q. Did you devise this method yourself?

A. No, sir. The defendant gave me the instructions. He told me to make the cone with a towel and pin it, and place the sponge in the small end, pour on the chloroform, then leave it thirty minutes on the face of Mr. Rice. He said Mr. Rice would be apt to laugh, but I was not to be alarmed, for that would only be a sign that the chloroform was taking effect.

Q. Did you hear any sounds from the room in which Mr. Rice lay?

A. My impression is that I heard a laughing – a sound of some kind in the room. I expected to hear it, Your Honor, for Patrick had told me I might hear it, but I was so excited that I was not sure.

The *World* reported that Jones 'stuck to his testimony.' It was now the defense's turn to cross-examine Jones.

# 53. Cross-examination

Over the weekend the press speculated that either Meyers or Short, the witnesses to the Patrick will, was 'practically secured' to give evidence for the prosecution. 'Witness to Will to Turn upon Patrick,' headlined the *Evening Journal*. The stories were reprinted in the Texas papers and Baker immediately wired Byrne: 'Morning papers report that Short or Meyers will turn States evidence. Is this true?'[1] Byrne wired his reply: 'Doubtful,' and then expanded in a letter:

I did not think it wise to telegraph at any greater length. So far as I know, very little has developed with reference to confession on the part of either of these men. I have never had any hope Short would confess, because I consider that he is more or less steeped in crime; and Meyers, I fear, is too stupid to confess. Still, there will always be a possibility of Meyers' confessing up to the time the case of the people is closed.

Moore commenced his cross-examination of Jones late on Tuesday, 25 February. It lasted into Friday. (There was no hearing on Monday because House's father-in-law had died.) Moore had told the press over the weekend that 'before we conclude our defense the entire onus of the murder of the old man will fall directly on Charles F. Jones.' Moreover, Moore said, 'if Jones did put chloroform over the nostrils of the old miser, as he confessed, he was trying to kill a dead man' because 'it is next to an impossibility to chloroform a sleeping man without waking him.'

The cross-examination began with Moore showing that Jones had been well treated by the prosecutor and that Jones had had many discussions with the prosecution:

Q. During the time you've been at the boarding house you've frequently visited theatres and various portions of the city?
A. Yes. I've been to the theatre several times.
Q. How frequently have you visited the District Attorney's office?
A. Up to two months ago about a dozen times – since, nearly every day.
Q. Did you talk over this case when you came?
A. Yes.[2]

The following day, Moore went through the various different statements Jones had made:

Q. How many different statements?
A. What do you mean, verbal or written?
Q. Both.
A. I have made a statement to Mr. Osborne –
Q. I say how many different versions – I will put it that way, not repetitions of the same statement, but how many different stories have you told?
A. Well, that is different.
Q. Yes?
A. I will tell you in just a moment. (After reflection) Four.[3]

Moore went through each statement in detail. Why had Jones said nothing about chloroform in the earlier confessions? Was he promised immunity if he cooperated with the prosecutor?

Q. You said nothing about chloroform in that statement?
A. No.
Q. Didn't you in your letter to the press written the day before you cut your throat say you were innocent of wrongdoing?
A. Yes.
Q. Didn't Mr. Osborne tell you your statement that Patrick killed Rice was untrue, as it could not be corroborated?
A. Yes.
Q. Didn't he tell you that if you wanted to do yourself any good you had better tell the truth?
A. He told me the truth was consistent, and could always be corroborated.
Q. Weren't you promised immunity by the District Attorney?
A. No.
Q. By an Assistant District Attorney?
A. No.
Q. Didn't you say before Justice Jerome you had not been promised absolute immunity, but had been promised some?
A. I don't remember.
Q. You've never been indicted for murder or forgery?
A. I have never received official notice if I have.
Q. Didn't Mr. Osborne tell you if you wanted any consideration at the hands of the District Attorney you must tell the truth?
A. Words to that effect.
Q. Who brought Mr. Battle, your attorney, to see you in hospital?
A. Captain Baker.
Q. Didn't you swear before Justice Jerome that Mr. Battle told you he had had a

talk with Mr. Osborne, and that if you told the truth about this matter you
would receive some immunity?
A. In substance, yes.[4]

The cross-examination turned to the day Rice died. Jones said he had
gone out for dinner at about five o'clock:

Q. You never saw him again awake?
A. No; when I came back from dinner he was lying in the same position that he
was when I left.
Q. So far as you know, Mr. Rice may have been dead, then, when you returned?
A. So far as I know, yes. I think he was sleeping. I didn't speak to him.

Moore asked Jones how he burned the chloroformed sponge and the
towel enclosing it. He said he threw it into the range and threw a match
in after it; that it burned up quickly, as there were papers in the range.

Q. Have you ever said before that there were papers in the range!
A. I don't remember.
Q. Have you been told since you testified before Justice Jerome that chloroform
was not easily combustible?
A. No.

Moore then read Jones's testimony on this point given before Justice
Jerome. Jones said then that the sponge and towel 'burned as if they
had oil on them.'
    In redirect examination, Osborne asked Jones about the promise of
immunity:

Q. Jones, was one word said to you about immunity in that conversation from
beginning to end?
A. No, sir.
Q. Was anything said to you about anything you were to receive in any respect,
in that conversation?
A. No.[5]

Assistant District Attorney Garvan then took up a line of questioning
to show that Jones had told House about the chloroform shortly after
he and Patrick were arrested:

A. Mr. House was the first person I told about the chloroform.
Q. And when did you tell Mr. House that you had chloroformed Mr. Rice?

Moore's objection to the admission of the evidence was overruled by Goff.

A. On the 26th of October of 1900, as near as I can tell you.
Q. Who was present?
A. Mr. House, Mr. Patrick and myself.
Q. Had you any conversation with the defendant on the same day prior to your making that statement to Mr. House?
Mr. Moore: I object to that on the ground that it is reopening the case.
The Court: Objection overruled. Exception.
A. I had.
Q. Will you tell all your conversation with Mr. House at that interview?
Objected to. Objection sustained.

Garvan ignored the substance of the ruling and asked Jones essentially the same question again.

Q. Did you at that interview with Mr. House tell substantially the same story that you have told here upon your direct examination?
A. I did.
The Court: Strike out the answer.
Mr. Moore: I object to that upon the ground ...
The Court: Objection sustained.
Mr. Garvan: May I be heard upon the –
The Court: No.

Although, for reasons that are not entirely clear, some of the evidence was excluded, the jury had, of course, heard it.

The press felt that Jones had successfully withstood Moore's intense cross-examination. The *Evening Journal* reported: 'Jones stood the ordeal well ... There was no attempt at concealment.' The *Herald* stated that Jones was 'undaunted and preserved a remarkable equanimity.'

# 54. More Evidence for the Prosecution

Forty-two more witnesses were called by the prosecutor before the case was finally closed. One testified that he had presented a draft for $24,000 at Rice's residence on Saturday, 22 September, the day before Rice died. The money was to be used by the Merchant and Planters Oil Company to rebuild the Texas mill that had burned down. The evidence therefore supported Jones' story that Patrick wanted Rice killed before Rice's available cash was used up. Four telephone operators were called to confirm various telephone calls that were made between Rice's apartment and Patrick's residence. Their account also tended to support Jones' evidence.

A lady gave evidence that she and a friend got no answer from Rice's apartment when they called to visit him on Sunday, 23 September, about the time that Jones said he was murdering Rice. She said that they had waited downstairs and that the elevator operator had gone to the apartment. Jones had claimed, however, that it was his impression that two ladies had been at the apartment door.

A stenographer who took sixty days of testimony in 1899 in the litigation over Mrs Rice's will, much of it at 500 Madison Avenue, testified that 'during those sixty days, to my knowledge, William M. Rice and Albert T. Patrick never met.'[1]

The prosecutor also called further handwriting experts. After a lengthy examination and cross-examination of John Truesdale, an expert from Syracuse who had been involved in disputed handwriting controversies since the 1850s, the prosecutor called William Kinsley, the expert who had been involved in the case from the early stages. Recorder Goff said that he had heard enough: 'I think this is the proper time to draw the line. I think the proper limit has been reached.' Osborne said that he merely wanted to ask Kinsley's opinion. 'That would open the way to a lengthy cross-examination,' Goff replied, and said that if Osborne examined Kinsley he could not examine any more bank tellers. Kinsley was therefore dismissed and a series of bank tellers were called. When the sixth paying teller was about to be called, the court again said that it had heard enough:

The Court: I think, Mr. District Attorney, that you have reached the limit on this line – what I consider to be the limit.
Mr. Osborne: You don't want me to call any more bank tellers?
The Court: No.

Patrick's Houston associate, J.M. Coleman, gave evidence for the prosecution. Osborne had been anxious to have Holt and Coleman come to New York to give evidence about letters Patrick was said to have written several weeks before Rice died. Baker had heard about these letters from Coleman himself shortly after Rice died. According to Coleman, Patrick had written Holt in mid-September 1900 asking him to confirm the settlement of the Holt litigation, stating: 'Mr. Rice, as you know, is a very old man, and is likely to die at any time. He has been very much upset by the Galveston storm. It has affected his heart, and he is sinking fast.'[2] The prosecutor wanted to use these letters to show that Patrick was planning Rice's death.

Coleman had been very ambivalent about testifying. He was an old friend of Patrick's, having graduated a year before him at law school. He told Lovett in a conversation in Houston at the beginning of the trial that he was undecided about going to New York. His wife, he said, did not want him 'to have anything to do with the case,' but he thought it was his duty to go. Solicitor-client privilege, however, would prevent him from testifying about Patrick's letters:

The contents of those letters, I gave to Captain Baker in the strictest confidence. My purpose was only to indicate to him that there was such evidence and where it could be found. Holt imparted the information contained in those letters to me as his attorney, and I of course cannot testify or mention it, but Patrick's murder of old man Rice was such a bold and outrageous thing that I could not remain contented to know of such evidence and not tell Captain Baker about it.

Holt declined to go to New York. He had become a candidate for the mayor of Houston (and won) and did not want to be more closely associated with the Patrick case than he already was. Assistant District Attorney Osborne wrote flatteringly to him, urging him to come:[3]

My dear Mr. Holt:
I take the liberty of addressing you in this familiar way because I feel as though I know you. I have heard so many people from your City talk about you that I know your reputation and personality quite well. I have heard you spoken about by every one as a man of character and force. I am a Southerner as you are. I wish to say that we have quite a good deal of soiled Southern linen to wash and I wish you to help me. You know a great many facts about this case which will help either the People or Patrick. No matter who will be helped, your testi-

mony, I think, ought to be given. I am of the opinion that you will always regret not coming here as I am now hearing your absence commented on.

But Holt still refused.

When Baker returned to Texas during the trial to bury his son he was able to persuade Coleman to testify. He wrote to Byrne on 19 February:

We have been working upon J.M. Coleman, an attorney here, with a view of getting him to go to New York to testify in the Patrick case and he has finally consented to leave tomorrow night. Coleman in conversation with me says that on one occasion Patrick told him that Mr. Rice wished his body to be cremated after death. This, of course, we do not wish to draw out. Coleman is smart, but I am afraid wholly unscrupulous and I think it would be best for Osborne to talk to him very fully in the presence of Garvin or some one else so as to have him fully committed before putting him on the stand.[4]

Byrne later wrote to Baker: 'Osborne and Garvin have seen him and are well satisfied with what he has to say.'[5]

Coleman testified at the trial that he had been in New York City with his family for ten days in August 1900 and had met Patrick every day. 'When I was here in New York,' he told the jury, 'he did not tell me anything about whether he did or did not know Mr. Rice. The question of his acquaintance with Mr. Rice was never mentioned to me by him.' Rice's name did come up a few times in conversation, he said. One reference was to the Rice Institute, Coleman testified:

'I suppose the people in Houston' – the defendant stated, 'I suppose the people in Houston expect to get that institute when old man Rice dies?' I said, 'I suppose so,' or 'They certainly do.' His reply was, in a general way – I can't give the language, that if the people expected to build an institute with old man Rice's money, they would wait a long time, or it would be a cold day, or some such remark.[6]

Another reference was to cremation:

Mr. Patrick and I were together on the steamer on Saturday evening – afternoon, I should say – going out to see the fireworks at Manhattan Beach, preparatory to my going away next morning.

When we came in sight of the Greenwood Cemetery, I pointed it out and said, 'There is the farfamed Greenwood Cemetery.' He replied, 'Yes.' And I made some general remark, that I wondered if a man would be any happier in the next world for having been buried there. His remark was that Mr. Rice – 'Old man Rice wants to be cremated when he dies.'

The main reason why the prosecutor wanted Coleman's evidence was to have him testify about the letters Patrick had sent a few weeks before Rice died. The prosecutor had laid the foundation for secondary evidence of their contents by showing that they were not able to obtain the originals from Holt in Texas. Coleman testified:

As to the contents of those letters, I will take the first letter, which was dated 15th of September, 1900; I cannot state the entire contents, though I read them three or four times. I can give the substance of the contents – give those portions that particularly occupied my attention. The first letter was of about this import – it was addressed to Mr. Holt, as the Executor of Mrs. Rice, and I cannot state, Gentlemen of the jury, the order in which the letter came; but the substance of it was that he had arranged, through a party by which he had secured a written agreement from Mr. Rice to settle his controversy between him and Mrs. Rice – Mrs. Rice's estate. He stated – I can't remember what was contained in the first or second letters on this point, but I think in the second letter, and am reasonably sure it was in both. 'That Mr. Rice is quite sick,' or 'is growing very weak, the Galveston storm having destroyed or injured his property' – I can't give the exact language – 'was a great blow to Mr. Rice, and it was evident that he would not live very long,' or 'he did not think he could live very long,' or that 'he could not live very long.' I can't give the language.

On the following day or night, a letter dated next day was received. The substance of it was that he thought it well to write him again, after having written the letter of the day before, urging either an immediate reply or immediate action – I forget now which – 'as Mr. Rice is growing worse; his heart action is growing very weak'; and I think this expression was in the letter, 'The doctors say his heart action is getting very weak, and it is evident that he cannot hold out very long,' or language to that effect.

I cannot remember anything else now.

The defense did not cross-examine Coleman.

The prosecution was pleased. Coleman showed, Osborne told the press, that shortly before Rice's death, Patrick was not claiming that he represented him and that Patrick had predicted in writing Rice's speedy death.

But Patrick's lawyers were also publicly 'jubilant' because, they said, the evidence tended to show that Patrick really was bargaining with Rice to settle the Holt litigation over Mrs Rice's will and that he knew that Rice was failing fast.[7]

# 55. The People's Case Is Closed

Charlie Jones' brother, William Lafayette Jones, came from Texas to give evidence that on two occasions he had purchased chloroform from a drugstore in Galveston in the summer of 1900 and sent it to his brother in New York. The prosecution had hoped to get drugstore records of the sale, but records were not kept of cash purchases. Moreover, W.L. Jones was not able to identify who had sold him the chloroform.[1] In cross-examination, Moore tried to get him to admit that he was giving this evidence simply to help his brother. He denied that he had told his brother's friend, Alex Stanbery, that he had never sent any chloroform. It is clear, however, that some glass bottles were sent by someone from Galveston to Charlie Jones in New York. Osborne called two American Express employees to confirm such a shipment.

Another witness for the prosecution was Joseph Mayer, who had been the office boy in Patrick's law office. Mayer had left New York for Europe in the fall of 1901 and the prosecution had tracked him down, with the assistance of Pinkertons, at his uncle's home just outside Berlin. George Hamlin, a member of the Hornblower firm, had already left for Europe to interview potential witnesses for the case. The Hornblower firm had cabled Hamlin in London: 'Jewish office boy eighteen years old, curly black hair, bright black eyes, alert looking, arrives Liverpool Steamship Bohemian today or tomorrow as passenger or employee. Real name Joseph Mayer. May be under assumed name. Shadow him until further instructions.'[2] Hamlin managed to get a hundred-page affidavit from Mayer, sworn to before the US consul in Berlin, and then paid to bring Mayer voluntarily back to New York with him. The press had been tipped off and were there to greet them. The *Times* headlined: 'Runaway Office Boy Makes a Confession against Albert T. Patrick.'[3]

At the trial, Mayer told Garvan, the assistant prosecutor, that he never heard Patrick mention Rice's name until after Rice died:

Q. What were your duties in Patrick's office?

A. I copied, mailed, and filed letters; ran errands, attended the telephone; made myself generally useful.

Q. Where are you employed now?

A. In Col. R.G. Monroe's office. Mr. Garvan got me the position.

Q. Did you ever see Jones in Patrick's office?

A. Yes. First in June, 1900. After that about three times a week.

Q. Did you have any instruction from Patrick regarding Jones's visits?

A. Yes. To let no one into Patrick's office while Jones was there. If any one called, to telephone Patrick from the outer office.

Q. What instruction regarding the mail?

A. He said I was to drop his mail into the slot in his desk: that he got mail from both sides (in the Holt case) and didn't want anybody to get at this mail. I never filed any letters from Rice to Patrick. I saw one envelope with Rice's card thereon. I never took any messages from Patrick to Rice's house. I never heard Patrick mention Rice's name until after the latter's death. Dr. Curry I saw in Patrick's office about ten times during the Summer of 1900. I went to the safe deposit vault with Patrick. He told me to tell no one not even my mother, that he had rented a box there.

Q. Did you have any talk with Patrick after his arrest about any statement?

A. Yes. I made a statement to Mr. Campbell in Cantwell & Moore's office.

Q. Did you ever see any writing in Patrick's office with Rice's name on it?

A. Yes. I saw a small slip of paper with 'W.M. Rice' written on it on his desk. There was nothing else on it. I told Patrick. He said it was of no importance; not to mention it unless asked about it at the examination, as there was no use putting things in the District Attorney's mouth.

Q. Did he tell you the more questions you answered 'I don't remember,' the better it would be for all concerned?

A. Something like that.

Q. Did you ever copy any letters directed to Rice?

A. No.[4]

Garvan tried to establish that Patrick had asked him to purchase mercury tablets for him. Mayer had given such evidence in his affidavit in Berlin, but at the trial he stated: 'I never had any conversation with him about mercury tablets exactly.' When Garvan asked him, 'Was your memory better when you appeared before the United States Consul in Berlin than it is now?' Mayer admitted 'I may have had the conversation.'[5]

In cross-examination, Moore attempted to show that the evidence Mayer had given in Berlin was because money had been promised to his mother:

Q. Were you promised any money for testifying before you went?
A. No.
Q. Afterward were you promised $500?
A. My mother was.
Q. Was part of that arrangement that you were to go to Berlin and return in a spectacular manner?
A. There was no talk of $500 until after I got to Berlin.
Q. Didn't you write your sister and say (reading) 'I have heard nothing from Osborne and I don't believe he will send me the $500'?
A. Yes after my mother had written me from home that my cousin had approached the District Attorney and that $500 would be given her if I came back.
Q. Isn't it a fact you were to go away and then come back and testify against your employer?
A. It is not.
Q. You expected to receive $500 when you made your statement in Berlin?
A. Yes.[6]

Walter Wetherbee, the Swenson employee who was one of the first witnesses called by the State, was recalled and testified that Jones had come to see him in early January 1900 to get him to become an executor to a new will. Moore objected to its admission, but Goff ruled that there was 'sufficient prima facie proof in this case to justify the admission of the declaration of one co-conspirator against another in pursuance of the alleged conspiracy.'

That ended the case for the prosecution. Judge Goff, however, wanted Dr Donlin recalled. In his examination, Moore had asked: 'Now, would the embalming fluid, assuming that it was used after death, the arterial process, would that have any effect upon the lungs?' Goff had not permitted the question, although Osborne had no objection, 'on the ground that it would widen the field of inquiry.' The judge was now prepared to permit the question. He did not want to give the defense a possible ground of appeal if there was a conviction. Donlin replied, supporting the prosecution's case:

It could not reach the lungs if injected through the brachial artery. Of course it would affect the lungs if it touched the lungs; but in my opinion, the fluid injected through the brachial artery could not reach the lungs. I have not investigated as to the authorities upon that subject, but I know the anatomy of the person, and know what channel it has to go through before it reaches the heart.

There are two stoppages before it reaches the heart, I mean to say it could not reach the lungs.[7]

Goff also reconsidered another crucial ruling that he had made when Jones was discussing his conversation with House. Jones had testified that he had told House that he had killed Rice. Goff's ruling on the questioning seemed to permit Jones to say that he had first told House about the murder, although the ruling had excluded some of the details. Goff, perhaps thinking of a later appeal if Patrick was convicted, now excluded the question entirely: 'I want to give the defendant the benefit of every possible doubt on the subject. I consider that the objection should be sustained and the answer to the question stricken out, and the jury directed to disregard it.'

The Court: Is there anything else?
Mr. Osborne: That is all that I know of.
The Court: Gentlemen of the defense, the case is with you.[8]

The defense would start its case the next morning, Thursday, 6 March.

# PART FOUR
# The Defense

Patrick whispering to his counsel, Robert M. Moore: New York *Journal*, 24 January 1902.

Assistant District Attorney Osborne and Patrick: New York *World*, 23 January 1902.

## SENSATIONAL PATRICK
## TRIAL, ON TO-MORROW

Mrs Addie Francis: New York *Journal*, 19 January 1902.

Mr. Moore insists upon "details! details, sir!"

Defense Counsel Moore: New York *Evening Journal*, 25 January 1902. Patrick is
in the middle.

Assistant District Attorney Osborne
cross-examines Dr Walker Curry:
New York *Herald*, 8 March 1902.

Experts experiment with the burning
of chloroform: New York *Journal*, 13
March 1902.

Assistant District Attorney Osborne addressing the jury: New York *Herald*, 24
January 1902.

Patrick listening to the verdict: New York *World*, 27 March 1902.

Patrick and the electric chair: *Brooklyn Citizen*, 16 January 1906.

# 56. The Defense Opens

The following morning, 6 March 1902, House asked Judge Goff to instruct the jury to acquit without calling on the defense on the basis that the evidence for the People was insufficient to warrant a conviction. 'Not one single man,' House said, 'has been called here to testify that there is any truth as to the combination between Jones and this defendant to kill outside of the testimony of Jones himself.'[1] Even conceding that Patrick forged the checks and the 1900 will to get 'old man Rice's' money, House went on, 'there is no evidence in this case establishing the fact that this defendant ever did enter into a combination with Jones, as Jones has testified, to kill old man Rice.'

The existence of a criminal conspiracy cannot be established by the testimony of a co-conspirator, House argued: there must be corroboration of the testimony. House read the relevant section of the New York statute: 'A conviction cannot be had upon the testimony of an accomplice, unless he be corroborated by such other evidence as tends to connect the defendant with the commission of the crime.'[2] The section – still essentially the same today – is based on the danger that an accomplice may lie to shift the blame to the accused or to curry favor with the prosecutor.[3]

Osborne conceded that House had properly stated the law: 'I want to say at the outset that I think that Mr. House has made a very beautiful and a very clear argument, and so far as the law is concerned, I entirely agree with him, absolutely in every respect.' But he disagreed that the People's case was weak. 'I think I can claim with all sincerity,' he told Goff, 'that never in the history of criminal law, from the time of William the Conqueror down to the present time, has ever such a case been established in a court of justice, without a single exception.' Osborne repeated the assertion with his usual self-confidence: 'I call attention to every criminal trial that has ever been held in America, and there never has been such a case established.'

Osborne briefly went over the evidence and ended by stating: 'Jones is Patrick's opportunity. Patrick is Jones's motive, and your crime is complete – preparation, motive, opportunity, murder, the possession of the fruits of the crime.'

The Court: Mr. House, I deny your motion and give you an exception. Are you
ready to proceed?
Mr. House: I take an exception to your Honor's ruling.

The Court: I have already directed that.
Mr. House: Thank you.

The jury was then brought back in and House gave his opening address to them. He reminded them of the importance of their task and the consequences of making a mistake:

Human life, once taken by an act of ours, so far as this defendant is concerned, is taken for good and all. And, if it shall subsequently turn out that we made a mistake, when we set in motion the majesty of the law and took from a citizen his life, no matter how much we may regret that act, no matter how much we may be bowed down by the weight of the mistake that we have made, that life is gone beyond our power to recall or give back. And that is the situation with you twelve men to-day.

Just as Osborne had done, House stressed the skill of his opposing counsel and downplayed his own talents:

When the great Creator put me here on earth, he did not give me the power of speech that he has given to my brother, Osborne ... He will try and lead you from where you are into the realms of speculation. He will seduce your minds if he can by the force of his argument, and I therefore at this stage of the case, on the part of the defense, desire to warn you against his power and his skill in that direction.

House then flattered the jury: 'I want to say this, not by any means intending to flatter, I never have appeared in a case where I was as well suited with the class of men that make up the jury as I am with you.'

Members of the jury, he stated, would have no difficulty in concluding that Patrick had nothing to do with the killing of Rice – 'if he was killed':

But, permit me, gentlemen, to say, without intending to interfere with the right and prerogative which you have to determine this question of guilt or innocence, that you will never be able to reach a verdict of that kind, because the answer which we shall make to the charge against us on the part of the People will be so clear, so distinct and so conclusive, there will be no trouble upon your part in arriving at the conclusion that, so far as this defendant himself is concerned, he had nothing to do, nor was he directly or indirectly concerned, in the killing of William M. Rice, if he was killed.

In fact, House argued, Rice died a natural death:

> But I say to you now, gentlemen, that we of the defense are firm in our belief and steadfast in our opinion that, when you shall have heard the testimony which we will introduce upon the subject of the death of this lonely old man, that you will arrive at the conclusion that his hour had come and his death was caused by the act of One Who, sooner or later, will cause the same disposition of each and every one of us.
>
> William M. Rice did not die a foul and criminal death; and we shall show beyond peradventure, through those who are competent to tell you, because of their great experience regarding these things, that nothing was revealed when that autopsy was performed, that justifies Dr. Donlin, that justifies Dr. Williams, that justifies Dr. Loomis in coming into this court and saying under their oaths that, in their opinion, his death was caused because he had taken into his lungs a gas or a vapor of chloroform; that that caused old man Rice's death.
>
> If Jones now, for the sake of the argument, tells the truth, he killed Rice. If Jones, for the sake of the argument, tells the truth, Patrick was concerned with him in killing, and together, jointly, they caused that death, and if from the mouth of Jones have fallen words of truth, that was a foul murder; but if our theory is correct; if we will be able to establish to the satisfaction of you twelve men beyond a reasonable doubt, and through agents that you cannot help believing, the correctness of our theory, then I say to you – and, as God Almighty is my Judge, I never spoke with more firmness and emphasis and determination than I do now – then I say a fouler murder is being attempted in this case.

Note that House took on the burden of proving Patrick innocent – and proving it beyond a reasonable doubt. This would seem to have been a serious – although perhaps inadvertent – tactical error, even though Judge Goff would later properly place the burden on the prosecution to prove the case beyond a reasonable doubt.

The autopsy, House said, was not carefully performed:

> It was not a complete and careful autopsy, not made with that degree of care and consideration with which it should have been made; but that all Donlin wanted and all Williams wanted was enough of the portions of that body to allow a chemical analysis to be made as to whether there was or was not metallic poison sufficient to kill in that body, and that, so far as Williams is concerned, so far as Donlin is concerned, so far as Loomis is concerned, I charge here in this court now, and before this jury that the theory of chloroform poisoning was an afterthought upon their part, and not true, and they know it.

Gentlemen, we will make good that statement, bold and emphatic though it is.

The conspiracy, he said, was by individuals:

... banded together in the State of Texas for the purpose of getting down there these millions of old man Rice, in order that they may employ them in any way they please, though they would have us believe that they are to make use of these millions simply to carry out his intention as to the William M. Rice Institute, which has about 6 1/2 acres in the City of Houston, Texas, or in that locality, but just where, the president of the Institute does not tell you, gentlemen, though it was stated that they had planted a few trees there and have got a shanty, which they call the caretaker's shanty, where the caretaker lives, to keep the boys, I suppose, from playing hockey on the ground!

House outlined the evidence he would call. There would be witnesses who would show that Rice and Patrick had been seen together:

We shall be able to show you the manner in which this defendant did come in contact with Mr. Rice. We shall be able to show you, notwithstanding the story that Jones has told here upon the stand, that so far as he knew, no living person ever saw Rice and this defendant together – Mr. Osborne has said to you in his opening, and has contended to you all the way through when he was putting in the People's case, that so far as he knew, and so far as his witnesses knew, no human being, no living person upon the face of God Almighty's green earth, to use his expression, ever saw this defendant and Rice together; and yet, we believe that we shall produce in this court, in this chair, under the solemnity of their oaths, witnesses as to whose credibility and truthfulness there can be no question, witnesses who have no object in coming into this court and telling a story that is not true, witnesses who will come here with the truth in their mouths and the truth in their hearts, and they will locate this defendant and Rice together, and upon several occasions.

Rice was not chloroformed, he told the jury:

Then, again, gentlemen, if his Honor will permit, we will make several experiments here in this Court. We will attack this man Jones' story upon the manner in which he administered the chloroform on the night when he said he did, and we believe, we shall prove to your satisfaction, by the very best experts that can be brought from any part of God Almighty's green earth, the fact that it is utterly impossible to have chloroformed Mr. Rice, if he was chloroformed, in the manner in which Jones says that he did it. We shall call the greatest expert in this country, regarding the administration of chloroform, who is conceded by the entire medical world to be an expert upon that proposition, and he will tell you that, in the presence of many physicians in public institutions in this city and elsewhere, he has made 26 attempts to transform a person from a natural sleep into a chloroformed sleep and he has failed in every one of them. ... We will produce physician after physician of eminence and standing in this community and elsewhere, who will tell you, gentlemen, that it is a physical and it is a scientific impossibility to chloroform a person in the manner in which Jones says that he did chloroform Mr. Rice; that when they do attempt to bring a person from a natural into a chloroformed sleep that there has to be some force and some power used in keeping them quiet.

'Old man Rice,' he went on, 'died a natural death':

Now, you want to know what that natural death is? We will show to you, gentlemen, beyond peradventure that Rice died from nothing else but an oedema of the lungs, what was known and is known to the lay mind as dropsy of the lungs. Now, what does that mean? We will show, to your satisfaction, that the blood in old man Rice's system was turning to water, and it had been turning to water for some considerable time; that from his knees to his feet, the blood had been changing through the tissues until it had got into the shape of water and puffed his limb up for many months; but as long as the watery condition remained in the lower extremities there was no danger; it was only when the water got up into his lungs and drowned him in the water of his own blood, the same as he would have been drowned had he fallen overboard in mid-ocean and taken up in through the nostrils and down into his breathing apparatus where the air ought to have been, that he died. That is what killed old man Rice.

The defense would conduct a crucial experiment, House said, that will show that Jones is a liar:

If his Honor will permit, we will make an open demonstration here in this Court. I make this declaration now, without conference with either one of my learned associates, and if you can take a towel and saturate it with chloroform, place it on this table in front of you, allow it to remain here for thirty minutes and then burn that towel, I will concede that the prosecution have made out this case, and I will advise this defendant to enter a plea of guilty. Jones lied when he said that he burned that chloroform in that way, because chloroform will not burn. Whoever put up Jones' story made the great mistake of confounding chloroform with ether, because you may have ether and be six feet away from it and strike a match, and there will be an explosion. The person who fixed up the story of Jones, whether it was Baker from Texas, or from some of the other Texas contingent, I do not know, but they were very poor chemists; they thought that chloroform would burn the same as ether, and that is where they made a fatal mistake in this case.

The opening concluded with the statement: 'We ask you to ask the great Almighty, in his wisdom, to guide and direct you in your deliberations, and, with His help, and what little we can give you, we feel that we can satisfy you that the only just and proper verdict that you can render in this case is one of not guilty.'

# 57. Doctor Curry

The first defense witness called by Moore was Doctor Walker Curry, who had treated Rice and had signed the death certificate. Curry had been stricken with pneumonia a year earlier and was now very infirm. The court waited for over thirty minutes while he came from a hotel where he was waiting across from the courthouse and 'climbed with difficulty to the witness stand.' The *World* described the sixty-six-year-old doctor as a 'pathetic spectacle'; the *Sun* called him a 'pathetic figure.'

Rice, he testified, died a natural death. In part, this was because of indigestion and diarrhoea caused by eating bananas:[1]

Mr. Rice ate those bananas on the 15th or 16th of September; there was a lady in from Fifth Avenue in his apartment, and said to him that she was taking them for digestion, and they had been of great service to her, and so he sent Mr. Jones, and he brought him nine. He ate four, cooked, or five cooked, and the other four – about half and half – one half cooked, and the other half raw, and that caused indigestion and diarrhoea. ... He was then quite weak, though the discharges had ceased for more than an hour when I returned there, and so I did not give him any medicine, because he was just simply in a weak state from this diarrhoea.

Dr Curry saw him the day before he died. There was, he said, 'nothing the matter with his lungs,' although there was 'a difficulty in his breathing. He was very weak. On the morning of the next day, his condition was about the same.' When Curry saw him on Sunday, shortly after he died, he concluded, he testified, that he had died a natural death: 'His features were calm and placid; I saw nothing to indicate that there had been any violent struggles or anything of the kind; they were perfectly normal, had a perfectly natural appearance, what you would expect a person dying of his age and without a struggle, almost.'

Moore established that Curry had performed a great many operations in his career and was very familiar with chloroform:

Q. What anaesthetic was used?
A. We generally gave chloroform in the Southern army, so that I have had a very large experience in the use of chloroform. I would be able to detect chloroform after it has been given to a patient; by the smell.
Q. Within how long a period may that be detected?
A. Well, I – I can safely say four or five hours; though I think I could detect it a longer time than that – but I can safely say four or five hours. Upon the occasion of my examining Mr. Rice, that Sunday evening after death, I did not detect any evidence of chloroform. I state, in my opinion, that if chloroform had been administered to Mr. Rice within a half an hour or three-quarters of an hour of the time I came into the room, in a quantity sufficient to have caused death, I would have been able to detect from the smell, the odor of chloroform upon the occasion of my visit. Undoubtedly.[2]

Curry denied ever talking with Jones about chloroform: 'At no time did I have any conversation with Charles F. Jones, with reference to the effect that chloroform is revealed by an autopsy. I never had any talk with Charles F. Jones as to the effect of chloroform when inhaled into the body. I never had any talk with Charles F. Jones with reference to the effect of chloroform, and about chloroform.' Moreover, during the time he treated Rice, he said, he discovered no evidence of mercurial poisoning.

In the middle of September, he testified, he told Patrick that Rice was 'an old and weak man, and in his condition, with his heart as it was, that he was liable to die at any time.' Coleman, it will be recalled, had testified that in mid-September Patrick had written to Holt to this effect.

Osborne cross-examined Curry for five hours. Why had Dr Curry not previously mentioned the conversation with Patrick in mid-September about Rice being liable to die at any time? Was not Curry's experience with chloroform derived from operations where chloroform was administered over a long period and thus saturated the room? What right did Dr Curry have to discuss Rice's condition with Patrick? Was it not improper to do so?

A. I did not think of anything improper in it, because I considered Mr. Patrick a gentleman. I had been introduced to him as such.

Q. Do you think that you have a right, knowing that a lawyer is on the opposite side of the case from your patient, that you have a right to disclose to that lawyer the condition of your patient's health, and the state of his mind?

A. It depends upon the lawyer. If I consider him an honourable man, I would think it was nothing more than proper or right – if he was an honorable man.

Q. And you think it was entirely honorable and right for you to tell Albert T. Patrick, this defendant, the condition of Mr. Rice's health?

A. I did.

The impression made on the spectators by Dr Curry, the *Times* reported, 'was that of a guileless old Southern gentleman of the ante-bellum school.' His testimony set the stage for the expert medical evidence that Moore was to call.

# 58. Expert Medical Evidence

The seventh week of the trial began on Monday, 10 March. The defense had lined up a number of highly respected medical experts. The *Evening Journal* predicted that this would be the 'greatest battle of medical experts waged in New York courts in years.'[1]

The first witness called was Robert H. Aurich, who was in charge of the autopsy department at the city morgue, where Rice's autopsy was performed. Aurich had been present at the autopsy and claimed to have heard Dr Donlin make a statement concerning the result of the autopsy. Moore asked him: 'Did Mr. Donlin in that statement made there say that "The old man's time had come, and he died from old age and that is all you can make out of it," or words to that effect?'[2] Osborne objected to the question, and the judge sustained the objection on the ground that Donlin had not been asked with sufficient particularity about the remark when he had given his evidence and thus his evidence could not be contradicted. He had, however, been asked whether he had told the reporters after the autopsy that Rice had died of old age and had said he could not recall saying that.

Doctor Edward Wallace Lee, a well-known surgeon who had assisted in the operation on President McKinley after he had been shot in Buffalo, testified that he had administered chloroform as an anaesthetic perhaps four or five thousand times. His evidence was similar to Dr Curry's:

I say that the ability to detect the odor of chloroform after it has been administered to the patient in a room where the chloroform was administered is very great. It is easily detected. The length of a period after an operation in which it can be detected in the room of course depends upon circumstances, the condition of the room, and so forth; but chloroform's vapor has a tendency to remain a long time; several hours.

Moreover, Lee stated, the fact that 'the patient to whom the chloroform is administered has a mustache and a full beard (as Rice had) would tend in itself to cause the odor of the chloroform to be detected for a longer period upon the patient.'

Moore put a hypothetical question to Lee – just as a lawyer in New York would do today:[3]

Q. Now, Doctor, assume that two ounces of chloroform – that a sponge had been saturated with two ounces of chloroform, that the sponge was wrapped inside of a towel in a cone shape, and then placed over the mouth of the patient, and left there for thirty minutes, the patient lying in bed and having a full beard and mustache: State whether in your judgment the odor of chloroform could be detected very well upon the patient and in the room within a half or three quarters of an hour after the cone had been removed.

A. I think it could.

Lee was asked 'whether a sponge saturated with chloroform, two ounces, and placed in a towel, arranged in cone shape, could be placed over a sleeping patient and left there without being held.' Lee answered, 'I don't think it could,' but Goff struck out the question on the ground that 'the jury are just as good judges of that as the witness.' Osborne said he had no objection to the question and the judge let it stand. Moore asked Lee why it would be so. Lee replied: 'The natural tendency would be, if the patient moved, for the cone to fall off. When chloroform is first administered, the natural tendency of a patient is to excitement and that excitement would naturally produce more or less muscular action, and consequently the cone would fall off.'

Moore then framed a detailed hypothetical question as to the cause of death. Lee replied:

A. My opinion is that the cause of death was due to congestion of the lungs and diseased kidneys.

Q. Now, Doctor, what in your opinion would cause the patch of consolidated lung tissue, assuming the conditions to be as revealed by the autopsy?

A. That may be due to a commencing pneumonia, or it may be due to a passing congestion that has been going on for some little time.

Finally, he was asked whether chloroform is combustible:

A. I have performed experiments involving an attempt to burn chloroform after it had been used in a cone with a towel, and upon a sponge.

Q. What do you say, Doctor, as to the ability to burn?

A. Chloroform is not combustible.

In cross-examination, Osborne asked whether the towel would burn if you waited half an hour. Lee replied: 'I don't know.' He admitted to Osborne that the only disease that could produce a congestion of the lungs, coextensive with the lungs, is pneumonia. Tuberculosis could also produce it, but it is easily discovered in a post-mortem.

Dr James Ewing, professor of pathology at Cornell Medical School, also testified that the cause of death was pneumonia. The thirty-three-year-old doctor had performed over two thousand autopsies and assisted in perhaps five thousand others. (He would later become well known as the director of Memorial Hospital, the predecessor to the famous Memorial Sloan-Kettering Hospital, and as one of the founders of the American Cancer Society.)[4] Moore asked him through a hypothetical question about the cause of death:

A. I should say that the cause of death was fully accounted for in the presence of the area of pneumonia, and the congestion and oedema of the lungs; in view of the clinical symptoms, and in view of the other conditions found in the viscera.

Q. Now, doctor, with such a condition as I have described in this last question, in your opinion, was the death due to chloroform poisoning – the question I have just put to you?

A. There is no indication whatever, in the findings which you have read, to indicate that death was due to chloroform poisoning. The patch of consolidated lung tissue that has been described in the lower lobe of the right lung could not, in my opinion, have been produced by the inhalation of chloroform vapor.

Osborne's cross-examination put to the witness various statements contained in some of the two dozen medical texts Osborne had with him in court.

Other experts who gave similar evidence that the cause of death was not chloroform were Dr Alexander H.P. Leuf of Philadelphia, who was an expert on lung diseases and had performed over three thousand autopsies, Dr Isaac Newton Love, the resident physician of the City Hospital of Saint Louis, and Dr Austin Flint, the distinguished professor of physiology at Cornell Medical School and one of the founders of Bellevue Hospital.[5] The witnesses testified that a sleeping patient would throw off a cone containing chloroform left on his face.

Dr John Girdner testified that he had published numerous articles on chloroform and had conducted a number of experiments with chloroform and its effect upon the human system. One experiment, published in 1883, involved using chloroform on sleeping patients in order to transfer them from a natural sleep into a chloroform sleep. In thirty-two such experiments upon sleeping patients he was not able to transfer any of them without waking.

Q. Now, Doctor, in your opinion, is it possible to take two ounces of chloroform, saturate a sponge with it, arrange a towel into a cone shape, put the sponge saturated with chloroform inside the cone, place that upon the face of a sleeping patient, and leave it there for thirty minutes, without awaking the patient, or his struggling to throw it off?

A. I do not think it could. In order to transfer a patient from a natural to a chloroformed sleep, it would require that a very small portion of chloroform be mixed with the air that the person inhaled – if it were accomplished at all, and the cone very slowly – a cone such as you describe placed over the face, would produce such a shock and sense of smothering that it would certainly awake the person that was asleep.

I don't think that there is a man on earth that would not resent it if he had an ounce of energy left in him. Nature revolts at choking more than anything else. That is what the process is, it is one of choking.

He then testified that chloroform is not combustible: it puts out fire. Osborne conceded that this was so; but the question was whether it would burn if left for half an hour. Girdner had recently conducted some experiments to test this issue. Moore questioned him:

Q. Doctor, if a towel were saturated – if a sponge were saturated with two ounces of chloroform, and the sponge was put inside of a towel, arranged in cone shape and permitted to remain there for thirty minutes and then put in a range, where there is no fire, and a match is applied to it, in your opinion would it burn up quickly?

A. It will not.

Q. Now, Doctor, in your opinion, can you burn a towel or sponge so saturated with chloroform until after the fumes of the chloroform have disappeared?

A. It is my opinion that you cannot burn a towel saturated with chloroform, until such time has elapsed as the chloroform shall have evaporated, then the towel will burn naturally, after the fumes of the chloroform, after evaporation has taken place.

Q. Now, Doctor, state whether or not, in your opinion, a person with a full beard and mustache would retain the odor of chloroform longer after the administration of it to him than a person with a smooth face?

A. I should think likely; yes, sir.

Girdner's evidence concluded:

Q. Now, Doctor, assuming the state of facts that I have narrated in your opinion, did the patient die from chloroform poisoning?

A. There is no evidence of it in anything you have said.

An actual experiment was then worked out between Moore and Osborne, with the approval of Recorder Goff. For several days each side had invited the other to make such a test. Doctor Girdner and a doctor chosen by the prosecution, Dr O.H. Schultze, would buy chloroform, towels, and sponges. They would then make a cone, pour two ounces of chloroform onto the sponge, wait thirty minutes, and then light a match to it. This would be repeated using a different type of toweling. Osborne had wanted the test done in the courtroom, but Goff directed that it be done in an anteroom in the presence of Osborne and Moore. Patrick waived his right to be present, but requested that the cone be placed on its bell-shaped end, while waiting thirty minutes: 'I think, your Honor, that while the cone is left standing thirty minutes it should be covered at the bottom.'

Would the towel 'blaze' quickly, as if saturated with oil? Jones had said it did so at the preliminary inquiry and at the trial. Moore had told the press before the experiment: 'It will put the match out before it gets within three inches of the towel. It smothers flame just like a fire extinguisher, instead of blazing up like a torch.'[6]

The experiment was conducted over the noon recess. When the trial recommenced, Dr Girdner returned to the witness stand carrying a tray with two piles of black ashes. He described the experiments. In the first case, the towel continued to blaze for nine minutes, then the blaze went out, and the towel smoldered for fifty-one minutes, leaving a pile of ashes. In the second case, the blaze lasted six minutes and it smoldered for fifty-four minutes, again leaving a pile of ashes. The jury examined the ashes. Girdner described the blaze: 'The blaze that came from the two cones during the time that they did blaze, burned slowly with just a small blaze, which circled around the cone a little, as it went along, spreading slowly; it was not a swift blaze, but slowly. I should call it a slow burning blaze.'

The test was therefore ambivalent. Moore, however, appeared jubilant, telling the press: 'They took a long time to burn; there was no blazing up.' The *Sun* reported that the result of the experiment 'was rather in favour of Patrick,' but the *World* said that the towels had, as Jones had said, 'burned right up.'

Osborne offered to participate in another experiment: chloroform would be poured on a towel or a beard of human hair and left for half an hour by an open window. The judge said that he had had enough experiments. The press reported, however, that at a recess Osborne poured chloroform on a handkerchief and that after nine minutes only a slight odor of chloroform was detected.

The associate editor of the *New York Medical Journal*, Dr Kenneth Millican – no relation to Patrick's wealthy brother-in-law – was called to the stand by Moore. A graduate of Cambridge University and member of the Royal College of Surgeons and Physicians, he had studied the literature on death from chloroform poisoning and over three hundred reports of autopsies contained in various British, French, Italian, and American journals. The court would not permit Moore to ask the number of such autopsies in which there was a congestion of the lungs, but he was permitted to state that in none of the nineteen principal medical texts he examined was there 'any indication that chloroform is an irritant to the respiratory passages, while there are many that distinctly say that it is not.'

In cross-examination, Osborne brought out the fact that for two or three months during 1898, before coming to New York, he had been the corresponding secretary in St Louis for John T. Milliken's bacteriological laboratory. 'I am personally on good terms with Mr. Milliken, the brother-in-law of the defendant,' the doctor admitted to Osborne.

Surprisingly, what neither side brought out was that Dr Millican had originally been engaged almost a year earlier by the prosecution through Dr Hamilton Williams. Millican claimed that he did not know why Dr Williams wanted the information about chloroform until he was told to submit a bill for $100 to the district attorney. Doctor Millican had apparently not revealed to the defense the fact that he had studied the literature for the prosecution until the defense had come to him seeking his help. In a confidential document prepared by Dr Millican the week before he testified for the defense, he set out the above facts and concluded: 'The circumstances above detailed, as I look back on them, convince me that the whole story of attempted murder by chloroform was an afterthought, and that so late as August 9th, 1901, the prosecution was in doubt whether it would "*hold water*" or not.'[7]

# 59. More Defense Witnesses

The defense called a number of witnesses to show that, contrary to the prosecutor's contention, Rice and Patrick had in fact been seen to have dealings with each other.

Maria Scott, Rice's black housekeeper, gave evidence that she had let Patrick into Rice's apartment several times. For the first time in the trial, Patrick's Chicago counsel, Frank Turner, took part in examining a witness. Maria Scott testified:[1]

I opened the door for him – the front door – after coming up on the elevator, and asked him into the writing room, the dining room. No one was in the dining room at that time. Then I went to Mr. Rice's room. After that I continued my cleaning. Mr. Rice dressed himself and went into the dining room. That was the same room I had asked Mr. Patrick in. I do not know how long he stayed on that occasion. Once after that I asked him down to Mr. Rice's bedroom. I opened the front door for him. He went in. Nobody but Mr. Rice was in the room at the time.

She also assisted the defense by testifying that she saw Rice writing cheques on the day before he died. Further, she testified that the trash she had put in the range that day was still there unburned when she returned on Monday, the day after Rice died. Jones, it will be recalled, had said that there was a fire in the range on Sunday.

In cross-examination, Osborne questioned her about statements she had made to him at an earlier time:

Q. Now, did you not say, 'I never saw any checks. The papers he had in his hands were white. That is all I recollect of saying'?
A. I told you they looked like checks. I do not know whether I said what you read to me or not. You hollered at me and I was so scared that I do not know hardly what took place. I said it to you, but I never said it to no lawyer but you. You hollered at me and got me so scared.

Finally she admitted: 'Well I might have said it; I do not remember positively that I did.'

Mrs Carpenter, a beneficiary under Patrick's will, but not under Rice's 1896 will, testified that she and her late husband had known Mr Rice for almost twenty years. She visited Rice almost every week. She testified that she saw Patrick and Rice together in May 1900:

Q. Did you at any time ever see Patrick and Rice together?
A. I did. There is no doubt in my mind as to that, none. In May, 1900, I think, I went up to Mr. Rice's house nearly every week. Nearly everything he ate for a year I cooked for him. On this occasion I took him some delicacies, and he was in the sitting room writing. Mr. Patrick was there. Mr. Rice said he was very busy. He gave me a newspaper and I went into the parlor and stayed until after Patrick left. I could hear Mr. Rice's voice and Patrick's, but I could not hear what was said.[2]

She also assisted the defense by testifying that every time Rice read something about cremation in the newspapers (he took the New York *Times*, the *Times* was happy to report) he discussed cremation with her. She also testified that he was 'dreadfully worried' about what he had lost in the Galveston hurricane and that his condition began deteriorating:

I did notice a change in the condition of Mr. Rice after the Galveston Flood; he cried; he was dreadfully worried; he said he had lost about a million dollars. I noticed a great change; he had diarrhoea, that was caused by this worriment; I haven't a doubt in my mind, that caused his trouble.

While I was there on this Saturday afternoon before the death of Mr. Rice, I noticed his condition then. He tried to speak to me, he put both his hands out for me to take, and he cried. I tried to help him to his bed; I put my arm around the old gentleman, and it seemed to affect him very much; when he got on the bed, instead of lying down, he put his hands up like this (indicating), and I noticed he was crying terribly. He wouldn't lie down; he seemed to feel ashamed of his own weakness.[3]

Osborne put to Mrs Carpenter in cross-examination that her late husband had signed a twelve-page statement prepared by her son that he, Mr Carpenter, had never heard of Patrick being in Rice's apartment. Mrs Carpenter said that she could not read the statement as she had forgotten her reading glasses at home. 'This is a terrible ordeal,' she told Osborne.

Q. Is it a terrible ordeal to say a twelve-page statement is in your son's handwriting? Will you read it?
A. I'm sorry but I can't use these glasses for reading. I have a pair at home I use for reading and sewing. To tell you the honest truth I can't make out one of these words.[4]

The witness returned to her home in New Jersey and disregarded Osborne's subpoena to give further evidence.

Another witness, Christian Schepflin, a seventy-five-year-old friend of Rice's, testified that he had also seen Patrick in Rice's apartment and that Rice had mentioned Patrick's name to him. Osborne conceded that Rice would have mentioned Patrick's name – 'with considerable hostility.' Schepflin was prepared to say that Rice told him that he intended to change his will and leave his property to a young lawyer he had met in New York, but this important evidence was excluded as hearsay.

About a week earlier, the defense had received a letter from a Charles T. Adams, a lawyer friend of Rice's, saying: 'I deem it my duty to inform you as counsel for Mr. Albert T. Patrick that Mr. William M. Rice stated to me ... in the summer of 1900 ... that he was in favor of cremation and that after death he was to be cremated. I inform you of this as I understand that the fact of cremation of Mr. Rice's body is to be used against your client.'[5] Adams was called by the defense to give this evidence. He also testified that Rice had written to him in 1897 that he wanted his will changed:

Dr. Mr. Adams:

I wish to make a change in my will, taking from some and giving to others, but I wish to make no mistake. Will you kindly instruct me in the matter?[6]

No change in the will was in fact made by Adams, although a codicil to the will had been drafted by him.

Osborne's cross-examination was very brief. He simply asked Adams if he was familiar with Rice's handwriting and whether the Patrick will was genuine. Adams replied: 'I know Mr. Rice's handwriting. I have seen him write. The so-called will of June 30, 1900, shown to me, in my opinion is not in Mr. Rice's handwriting.'

Three witnesses were called to show that Patrick had not left his boarding house on the day that Rice died. Jones had said in his evidence that Patrick had met him in the morning, again at noon, and then in the late afternoon, when Patrick allegedly gave him the chloroform. Mrs Elliott and her daughter, Mabel, were boarders at the time. Mabel, who was now studying at a Bible institute in Chicago, and her mother said that they saw Patrick at breakfast, at lunch, and in the afternoon, when Mabel played hymns on the piano and Patrick sang. Later, they saw Patrick at supper from about 6:30 until they left for a Christian Endeavour meeting after seven. Mrs Edna Potts, accompanied by her father, lawyer John Potts, said that they called on Patrick at the boarding house in the afternoon and did not leave until about 6:30:

It was about half-past six, from the time that I first saw this defendant on that Sunday afternoon on which I and my father left the house, the defendant was never out of my sight at any time, not a minute, and from the time that I first saw this defendant on this Sunday afternoon, the 23rd day of September, 1900, until I and my father left the house, no strange person, man or woman that I had ever seen before came in there and saw him.[7]

Osborne's cross-examination of the witnesses was designed to show that Patrick could easily have slipped out for five minutes without them noticing it. He asked Mrs Elliott: 'Now, do you mean to tell this jury that ... you kept your eye glued on Patrick to such an extent that you are prepared to swear that he did not go out of the room, even for five minutes?' She claimed that she had.

# 60. The Defense Closes Its Case

Morris Meyers and David Short both gave evidence supporting Patrick. 'It was supposed until very recently,' the *Sun* told its readers, 'that one or both of these witnesses would follow the example of Jones, the valet, and turn State's evidence against their former employer.'[1] This did not happen, however. They both told essentially the same story that they had given previously: that they were at Rice's apartment on 30 June 1900, witnessing some documents, when Rice asked them to witness his will. Meyers testified: 'We executed two or three papers, Mr. Short taking acknowledgments, when Mr. Rice says, "While you gentlemen are here I want you to witness the signing of my last will and testament." He brought People's Exhibit E – the will – from a depository that he had there. He brought this paper out, looked it over and said that he wanted us to witness it.'[2]

Throughout Meyers's cross-examination, Moore interjected so often that Judge Goff threatened to have him ejected from the courtroom:

The Court: I will direct you to be put out of the courtroom for disorderly conduct.

Mr. Moore: I can't help that.

The Court: I wish it put on the record here the number of times that Mr. Moore has persistently interrupted the Court, and persistently spoken after the Court has made its ruling and continued to argue, and if he continues to further do so, the Court will take measures and will prevent it and will secure order in the Court.

Mr. Moore: I except to the remarks of the Court.

The Court: Yes, give him an exception.

David Short gave similar evidence and said that Rice wanted them to keep the matter secret: 'Before he handed it to him he had the paper in his hand, and he says, "I want you gentlemen to promise me one thing, not to say a word to a soul on earth about this until after I am dead and gone." That is the words that he used, as near as I remember it. We said that we would not.'

In cross-examination, Osborne tried to bring out that Short had been discharged from a shoe store in Chicago for larceny and had been involved in the phony US Health Reports. Goff, however, sustained objections to these questions. The jury perhaps knew of the Health Reports because the press had reported at the start of the trial that Short was involved in the scheme – described by the *Saturday Standard* as 'one of the greatest swindles ever perpetrated in New York.' The *Standard* even said that Patrick was known as 'the backer of the schemes.'[3] Osborne did establish that Short and Meyers were on bail on forgery charges and that the bail had been put up by John T. Milliken, Patrick's brother-in-law.

Osborne continued to fight the case with vigor both inside and outside the courtroom. 'I never prosecute a defendant if I think he is innocent,' he told the New York *Daily News* during a break in the proceedings. 'In fact,' he went on to say, 'I never appear against a defendant if I entertain any doubts in my mind at all of his guilt.'[4] Such a statement by a prosecutor to the press today would probably result in a mistrial if it reached the attention of a juror,[5] as Osborne no doubt hoped it would. In any event, it probably could be the basis for a professional reprimand.[6]

The defense had a number of handwriting experts lined up to testify. The first expert was Charles French, described by the *World* as a 'tiny man, white-haired and white-bearded and seventy-six years old.' For fifty years, French testified, he was the head of a commercial school in Boston. For the last year he had been an examiner of questioned documents. He had, he told Moore, examined Rice's acknowledged signatures and the disputed documents:

Q. State whether or not, as a result of that comparison – state whether or not in your opinion, the same hand penned all of those signatures?
A. I think it did, sir.
Q. Now, Mr. French, give your reasons for that conclusion?
A. When I first examined these signatures, the first point that attracted my attention was in the four will signatures as compared with the four standard signatures, which, I believe, were written on the same day; and the point between them was the difference in shading; the absence of shading in the four questioned signatures, and the heavy lines or shading in the four standards. If on further examination, I had found that the questioned signatures were lacking in many characteristics, other than the shading which I found in those standards, I should say, that with that absence of shading, it would have been, in my opinion, a very strong point as evidence that these will signatures were forgeries; but, if, on the other hand, on further examination, I found that there are a great many characteristics –
The Court: Strike out all of Mr. French's testimony from the time he used the first 'if.'
Mr. Osborne: I ask that it be allowed to stand.

The Court: I will not permit it to remain.

Mr. Osborne: I think it helps the prosecution.

The Court: That is not my concern.

Mr. Osborne: If the defense does not object, I do not object, I beg your Honor's pardon –

The Court: That does not bind the Court. The Court will control this testimony of expert witnesses. Mr. French's statement was based upon the preposition 'if,' and that is not testimony.[7]

Moore, taking tactical advantage of Judge Goff's very technical ruling, then asked to have the witness withdrawn:

Mr. Moore: Now, if your Honor pleases, we ask for the privilege of withdrawing Mr. French now, as his evidence has been stricken from the record in the case.

Mr. Osborne: I see no objection to that.

Mr. Moore: The defendant rests.

At precisely 2:52 p.m. on Wednesday, 19 March 1902, the defense unexpectedly closed its case.

Defense lawyer Turner told the press: 'We have six handwriting experts ready to be called. They have been here five weeks, but it is useless to put them on and have them treated in this way ... The bench is a partisan. What's the use of going on under those conditions? We have won the case, anyway.'[8]

'The Recorder's rulings to-day were outrageous and will not stand,' House added.

"Oh, no; don't say that,' broke in Moore, 'we are not going to have to take the case up higher. We are going to get an acquittal.'[9]

'Abraham Lincoln used to say,' Osborne commented, 'that when a lawyer had a good case on the facts he should go to the jury; when he had a good case on the law he should appeal to the Judge, and when he had neither he might blackguard the court and the lawyers on the other side. That's what these lawyers are doing.'[10]

Lawyers contacted by the *World* thought that Goff's action might help the defense 'by the spread of a theory among the jurors that they could have proved the genuineness of the will, the cheques and the assignments produced by Patrick but for their clash with the Court.'

The tactic may also have provided a convenient subterfuge to help paper over the fact that Patrick had not testified. Although no inference could then – or now – legally be drawn on the failure of the accused to testify,[11] many jurors would understandably take the accused's failure to testify into account. Today, many, if not most, criminal lawyers would say that an accused who did not testify in a case such as this would have a hard time obtaining an acquittal.

It is not clear why Patrick did not testify. He did not have a criminal record which could be put to him in cross-examination, which is sometimes the reason why an accused stays out of the box. And he would clearly have been an articulate witness. Perhaps his lawyers felt that to put him in the witness box would mean that the entire focus of the trial would shift to the accused's believability.[12] If he went into the box, Osborne could question him in depth about the circumstances of the checks and the 1900 will. If he was not believed on these matters, there would be a good chance that he would be convicted on the murder charge. Moreover, there was probably less pressure then than today for an accused to testify; many persons at the time could still remember the time when an accused was not *permitted* to testify.[13]

The prosecutor now had the opportunity to rebut the defense evidence.

# 61. Rebuttal Evidence

Osborne called in rebuttal the noted handwriting expert David Carvalho. His evidence was confined to the type of inks and pens used in signing and witnessing the Patrick will. He clearly showed that the ink used for Rice's signatures on the 30 June 1900 will was different from that used for the other documents signed by Rice that day. The will ink was a product of coal tar, whereas the other signatures were in an iron ink. When David Short and Morris Meyers were recalled by Osborne, neither could say whether Rice had used the same ink for all the documents. The ink purportedly used by Rice in signing the will was also different from that used by Meyers and Short, who, Carvalho said, used a fountain pen in witnessing the will. The differing inks were suggestive of wrongdoing, but inconclusive.

The prosecution had more success with the medical evidence. Dr Hobart Hare, professor of therapeutics at the Jefferson Medical College in Philadelphia, said that he had studied chloroform for over eighteen years.

Ten years earlier he had gone out to India to conduct a study for the government of India on death by chloroform. Chloroform is sufficiently powerful, he said, that it killed elephants in India. A hypothetical question was put to him by Osborne, ending as follows: 'And assuming that a cone is made of a towel wrapped around the hand, that a sponge is put in the end of the cone, and an ounce and a half of chloroform is placed upon the sponge, and that that cone is placed upon the face of the old gentleman while he is sleeping and is left there. In your opinion, what would be the effect?'[1] His answer was 'Death.' He was asked to state the grounds for his opinion and replied:

My reasons are, the testimony indicated that the old gentleman was in fairly good health for a man of his years, and the description of his symptoms does not lead me to believe that he would have died of natural causes. Secondly, that the chloroform is a powerful depressant poison, which kills all living things with which it comes in contact in concentrated form; and because an ounce and a half of chloroform poured on a towel, which is placed upon the face in the shape of a cone, is more than adequate to produce death, because when chloroform is used for medical or surgical purposes, you never put more than a teaspoonful on at a time, which would be one-twelfth part of that which was put on the sponge ... It kills everything with which it is brought in contact, if it can be brought in contact with it; but when inhaled it comes in contact with the lungs, and immediately after with the heart. It is a depressant to all the tissues of the body, to the heart and the circulatory system in general.

Dr Hare also testified that he had 'made a study of chloroform in regard to its odors':

I have frequently administered to my classes a common test for chloroform with the object of impressing upon their minds the fact that they must be careful not to use impure chloroform. I have shown them that if chloroform is poured on a plate or over the hand so that it runs off the plate or hand in this position (indicating) that a very few minutes after that is done there would be no odor of chloroform left upon the hand or any oily odor, or anything to show that it had been there at all.

Osborne continued with a further hypothetical question, outlining facts as stated by Jones and concluded: 'Now, in your judgment, would the odor of chloroform be detectable in the room by a human being at the end of an hour?' Dr Hare replied: 'Most emphatically, no.'

Assuming, Osborne went on, that after half an hour the sponge were placed in a range and set on fire:

Q. What would be the effect of the then remaining chloroform on the combustion of the towel and the sponge?

A. There would not be any chloroform there. It could not have any effect upon it. It would not be there. It would be gone. Whether it would be burned, would depend upon whether the fire was hot enough to burn the towel.

Q. Then it would be a question between the towel and the flame and not a question between chloroform and failure?

A. Yes, sir.

During Moore's cross-examination, juror Lawrence Abbott interjected with a question about whether Rice could have thrown off the cone:

Q. In your experience with chloroform, is it possible to place a cone such as has been described here over the face of such a patient as has been described, and to produce his death without his struggling to throw the cone off?

A. Entirely possible.

Dr Hare had expressed a similar opinion in a text he had written. Moore attempted in cross-examination to soften the effect of the evidence:

Q. Now, isn't it a fact, doctor, that where that has been successfully done, extreme care was used by the operator in bringing the patient under the effects of the anaesthesia; that is, by that I mean that he gave it to him gradually and let him gather in the odor of the chloroform by degrees?

A. On general principles I would say yes, but I can't testify that it always has been so.

Q. And coming stealthily upon the patient?

A. Yes, sir.

Q. Now, if you came upon the patient with abruptness and put the whole force of the pungent odor upon the face, its immediate effect is to strangle or suffocate, is it not?

A. No, not to strangle or to suffocate; it is not so severe as that.

Q. It is enough to produce discomfort and make the patient probably turn his head from it, in this manner (indicating) and if he turns his head he would throw it off, wouldn't he?

A. Yes, provided that the man was in a healthy condition when it was put over his face.

Q. If he was healthy enough to turn his head, it would be thrown off, wouldn't it?
A. No, not necessarily.
Q. Isn't it difficult to keep that on his head there?
A. No, not at all.

Other doctors gave similar evidence supporting the prosecution's case. A telegram in the file indicates that the prosecution tried to contact the great Sir William Osler from Johns Hopkins, but he was in Canada at the time. Dr Robert Coleman Kemp, an associate professor of internal medicine at the New York Clinical School of Medicine, who had for the past five years engaged in special experimental researches on the effect of chloroform in organisms, also replied 'death' to Osborne's hypothetical question involving the effect of chloroform on Rice. He went on to state:

Chloroform has killed on inspiration, on the fourth or fifth inspiration, when only twenty to twenty-five drops have been administered at this inhalation. Now, the whole method of the scientific application of chloroform as an anaesthesia is to give it with the greatest degree of safety, and the greater degree of concentration of your chloroform the greater danger to the patient; consequently if chloroform is administered in the concentration vapor form, death will be practically instantaneous within two or three inspirations. That is the reason.

Further, in answer to a hypothetical question as to whether the chloroform would be detectable if the windows were open for half an hour after the towel was burned, Dr Kemp replied: 'Absolutely not one iota of odor, not one speck.' If the doors and windows were closed, however, he admitted to Moore in cross-examination, 'there would be an odor of chloroform in the room certainly.'

Doctor Alfred E. Thayer, an instructor in pathology at Cornell Medical School – the same institution that Dr Ewing, who gave evidence for Patrick, worked at – also supported the death by chloroform theory, as did Dr Otto H. Schultze.

A doctor who had been at the autopsy, Dr John Downs McAllister, was called by Osborne as a rebuttal witness. He had been teaching pathology and operative surgery, spending most of his time at the morgue. He had, he testified, seen almost every post-mortem in the County of New York for the past five years. He was present when the autopsy on Rice was performed. Contrary to what Dr Curry had said, he did not see any dropsy in the limbs from the knees down.

Finally, two witnesses were called to dispute the fact that Patrick could not have slipped out to see Jones on the day that Rice died. Lucy Galvin, who worked as a waitress at the boarding house for two weeks in September 1900, stated: 'I rang the tea bell in Mrs. Francis' house on September 23, 1900 between half past five and six o'clock.' The cook, Elizabeth Costello, supported this evidence. The defense evidence had been designed to show that dinner was later than this.

At that point, at 11:15 in the morning of Friday, 21 March 1902, at the end of the eighth week of the trial, Osborne declared: 'the prosecution rests.' And Moore added: 'The defendant also rests, your Honor.'

# 62. Moore's Jury Address

Moore immediately renewed his argument that the prosecutor should be forced to elect on which of the ten counts in the indictment he wanted to proceed. Without hearing argument, Goff denied the motion. A further perfunctory motion to have the court direct an acquittal was also dismissed without argument. Moore was successful, however, in having the case put over for final argument until after the weekend. The price for the adjournment, the press hinted, may have been a public apology to the court by Moore:

Now, if your Honor please, this has been a long trial, necessarily made so by the volume of testimony and the intricacy of the evidence introduced, and counsel, as your Honor knows, in cases of this duration, have upon them a great strain, which does, at times, become severe, and, that being so, counsel sometimes forget themselves in addressing the Court. Accordingly, on the part of the defense – at least for myself – I think it is due to the Court in this case to say that the defense has no complaint to make, and that your Honor has exercised much indulgence to our side in the trial of the case. That being so, if your Honor please, we would ask at this time a further indulgence of the Court. We would ask your Honor to forget past offences and to let the argument in the case go over until Monday.[1]

The recorder granted the request, stating: 'I appreciate your statement, Mr. Moore, and consider it worthy of you and worthy of the occasion.' Counsel agreed with the judge that Moore would address the jury on Monday, Osborne on Tuesday, and the judge's charge would be on Wednesday. The practice in New York was, and still is, for the prosecution to address the jury last.[2] Goff said that as far as he could control it, he wanted the jury to be finished with the case before Good Friday. Patrick's sister Emma was quoted by the press as saying that by Friday 'I think Albert will be out of that horrid prison and eat his Easter eggs with father and myself.'

On Monday morning, the start of the ninth week of the trial, there was a great rush of spectators trying to get into the court. Patrick's sister Emma and their father, Captain Henry Patrick, were there, as was Mrs Francis. Captain Baker had returned from Texas and was seated in the body of the court, just back of the lawyers' enclosure. Charlie Jones was not in court.

Patrick entered the courtroom, under guard, wearing a black frock coat and a red cravat. He marched with 'a quick nervous step,' according to the *World*, and a 'jaunty swing,' according to the *Sun*.

Moore started his jury address shortly before eleven o'clock. Excluding a break for lunch, he spoke to the jury for five and a half hours. He started in an easy, conversational, almost inaudible tone, warning the jury of the danger of a wrongful conviction:

It is with something of a feeling of pleasure, and yet with a feeling of a great deal of regret that I come before you this morning to make the last argument I shall make on behalf of the defendant here. It is with pleasure that a long and arduous duty is nearly ended. It is with regret that I feel and appreciate the inability of any man, myself, or any other, to adequately plead for another when that other's life is the forfeit ...

And therefore I say it is a solemn duty devolving upon you. If, by your verdict, you say this man shall be condemned to die, and that verdict should subsequently prove to be erroneous, not through fault of yours, but through fault of circumstances or fault of evidence, you could never right the wrong, because the law has stepped in, your judgment has been carried into execution, and the defendant is no more.

'A human life is at stake,' Moore emphasized, looking directly at Patrick: 'if you err in judging this man and send him to the electric chair, you can never right the wrong.' (The special jury, it will be recalled, was specially drawn from a group that had no objection to capital punishment.)

Patrick, Moore argued, had no motive to kill Rice. The defendant, he said, took under the will as a trustee for benevolent purposes:

Much has been said to you, gentlemen of the jury, about motive, and much has been said to you that this defendant's motive for killing the deceased was to acquire millions of his property, and yet I am going to make the bold assertion here now, gentlemen of the jury, and I challenge its contradiction, that absolutely no motive existed in this defendant to murder old man Rice, absolutely no motive.

Why? Because the defendant, by reason of the circumstances that have been presented to you in this case, could not acquire one dollar of old man Rice's property; and it was because, gentlemen of the jury, that we knew questions of law in this case of importance would come up that the defendant's counsel were willing to have upon the jury a man who is trained in law, and were willing to have him sit, even though he had for six years acted as a prosecutor in a neighbouring State.

Now I say to you – and I repeat it – absolutely no motive existed in Albert T. Patrick to murder old man Rice; and I am going to prove that out of the lips of the People's witnesses themselves.

Why? Is there any doubt in your minds, gentlemen of the jury, from the evidence but that Albert T. Patrick took the residuary estate under the 1900 will, so-called, as a trustee for benevolent purposes? If he did, then Albert T. Patrick could not, under the laws of the State of New York, spend one dollar of that property for his own purposes.

Although, Moore admitted, nothing was said in the will about a trust, Patrick had acknowledged its existence to John Potts, to Detective Sergeant Vallely, and to James A. Baker.

Moore then began a vicious attack on Baker, accusing him of conspiring with Jones against Patrick:

Mr. Osborne has said to you repeatedly this: Jones was Patrick's opportunity; Patrick was Jones' motive for killing old man Rice.

Gentlemen of the jury, I want to reverse that coined expression, and I want to say to you that Captain Baker was Jones' motive and Jones was Captain Baker's opportunity.

Captain Baker's objective, Moore said, was to have Patrick electrocuted so that Captain Baker and his 'contingent' could get the estate:

Captain Baker comes on here after the death and he finds, as is often the case, that the best laid schemes of mice and men often gang aglee. Baker, with a few others in Houston, Texas, arranges a plan to acquire old man Rice's property, and old man Rice had reason to believe that that was the purpose of this coterie of people in Houston, Texas. Captain Baker did not know that the old man had become aware of that, and he comes in here and finds another will, and that their plans have gone astray. Captain Baker is ready to do anything and everything to defeat the 1900 will, and acquire this property.

Now, the best way in the world, when somebody has an unsatisfactory job to do, is to let the accounter of your estate do it for you, if he can be induced. It would have been an enormous expense upon Captain Baker and his contingent to have tried out this will contest before a civil court; but if a charge of murder or a charge of forgery could be put up to this defendant, and he is electrocuted, there would be help in the will contest, the 1900 will would vanish into thin air and the plan of the 1896 will be restored.

This Texas crowd were bound to defeat the 1900 will in any way that they could; and therefore I say that Jones became Baker's opportunity and Baker was Jones' motive for telling this story which he has told here upon the witness stand.

Referring to the Rice Institute, Moore, shaking his finger at the jury, thundered: 'Why, gentlemen, the secretary of that wonderful Rice Institute hardly knows where the office is. But Baker knows where the money would go.'[3]

Baker, Moore said, was behind each of Jones' statements:

Now, it is not for me, gentlemen, to stand before a jury and malign anybody. If the facts in this case did not warrant what I am about to say, I could not state it to this jury; I assure you that my lips would be sealed, even though I knew my client would suffer for it; but I say that the story as finally told upon the witness stand as the story of Charles F. Jones follows the story of Captain James A. Baker, and is told with a motive, that of getting these six millions or seven millions of dollars; and I say that that was not the first story put together by Captain James A. Baker in this case, but was the final outcome, because the others would not stand muster, as I shall point out to you.

Now, why do I say that – and I do say just that? What do we find? We find Patrick and Jones both arrested. We find them both put into the Tombs. We find a short time after that a communication from Captain James A. Baker to Jones to go and see him, a written communication. We find, in pursuance of that, that one afternoon about four or half past four o'clock, Jones is led from the Tombs – where?

Over to the District Attorney's office; not to see the District Attorney, but to see whom? Captain James A. Baker. And where? Behind four closed walls.

And what? I don't know; you don't know, but we do know this: that after a two or three hours' conference with Captain James A. Baker, when the doctors reported that the autopsy had failed, when Witthaus reported that the findings of poison had failed, we do know that after Jones and Baker had their private and secret confab there for several hours, that the next day Jones starts in with his confessing again!

Why? Can you tell? Is there anything in that? Can it be theorized from that fact alone that the motive that prompted Jones to make this story was the argument of the wily, astute and crafty lawyer with the weak individual Jones? Can it be said that behind those walls there was a conversation running along the line with this? – 'This will is a forgery; these checks are forgeries; this assignment is a forgery; you were so closely associated with Albert T. Patrick in those papers that we are going to convict you both, and the punishment therefor is sufficient to keep you in Sing Sing prison for the balance of your natural life!'

An argument of that kind would be a mighty potent factor with Jones, innocent or guilty – I don't care which way you put it – if he believed that himself and Patrick were going by the might and power of this strong gentleman, were going to be railroaded to Sing Sing prison, and I want to assure you, gentlemen, that it would not be the first time that men have gone there who were innocent; if that were the purpose, then I say that it would be the strongest argument that could have been brought to bear by Captain James A. Baker upon that occasion.

Jones' six statements were then examined at great length, showing their various differences and inconsistencies. Jones, Moore argued, was 'the pliant and willing tool of Baker'; he was 'Baker's man Friday,' changing his evidence to try to ensure a conviction for murder. Moore went on:

Gentlemen, you are not mind readers. I am not a mind reader; and we cannot go into the realm of speculation, but must stay with the evidence, and if those stories of Jones' are so inconsistent each with the other as to make them improbable, then it is not for you to say and it is not for me to say which one of the stories is true, the one told to Captain McCluskey, the one told to Mr. Osborne, the one told to Mr. Battle, the one in writing, sworn to before the magistrate, or the long detailed examination before Judge Jerome, or six, the vastly different one he has told here upon the witness stand? It is not for you to say, it is not for me to say, and when you are placed in that position it seems to me there is but one thing for you to do, and that one thing is for you to absolutely throw out the evidence of Jones.

Even Jones' attempt to commit suicide and young Mayer's going abroad, Moore argued, were concocted by Baker:

Now, I say, Gentlemen, I have not had a great deal of experience in throat cutting, but I think that, with that little knife, with a blade perfectly clean in it, and perfectly free and fairly sharp, two inches long, that I could cut the jugular vein of my throat without a great deal of trouble, if I undertook it. Jones made a hack at it, and failed, and I say that he was mighty careful to make a failure of it, and that it was part of a pre-arranged and deliberately concocted scheme; the same as Mayer going abroad was a part of the scheme upon the part of this same man.

Now, I want to exonerate Mr. Osborne from any part or parcel in the going abroad of Mayer, but I do say that somebody – and that somebody was Captain Baker, or his tool – induced Mayer to go abroad, the same as they induced Jones to testify as he did, so that Mayer could be brought back in that spectacular way, and so that Mayer could give his evidence, of course, as though the defendant had spirited him away, and that embracing Justice and embracing Law and Order, while at the same time assisting the District Attorney with true hearted generosity, these Texas people bring Mayer back!

Assuming, however, that Jones was telling the truth about placing chloroform on Rice, was the jury sure that Rice was alive at the time? Moore went on:

Jones says that on the next day, in the afternoon, around about five o'clock, the old man was so weak that he had to carry him into his bed, and that when he laid the old man down upon the bed, he looked up into his face and he says, 'Jones, you have got a pretty big baby.' Now, then, the point I want to make is this: Jones says that he laid the old man on the bed and that he left him there for some time and when he came back he was still lying in the same position. He was a weak old man; that he then went out and got his dinner, and while he was gone he gets this chloroform and is gone about forty minutes; when he comes back, the old man is lying in the same position that he was in when he laid him on the bed, nearly an hour and a half before, and he did not know whether the old man was living or dead. That is the proposition, gentlemen, that I put up to you.

Now, I put this to you: Is there enough in that condition of this old man as described, so that you have a right to infer that in that hour and a half a different condition was brought about, and that the old man could have died? Have you, in other words, a right to speculate that he was alive? Can you say, from the evidence in this case, beyond a reasonable doubt, that old man Rice was living on that fatal night when Jones returned with the chloroform? Assume, I say now, that he did return with the chloroform, can you say, from anything in this case, that old man Rice had not gone before his Maker, before the murderer placed the cone, saturated with chloroform, over the mouth and nose of that old man?

Moore downplayed the handwriting testimony:

Now, you heard the evidence of the handwriting experts in this case. One of them says that this is a forgery, because there is a tremble in it. Yet, when he sees that same tremulous movement in the genuine writing, why, it is indicative of old age. When you see it in the disputed writing, it is indicative of nervousness. When you see a peculiar kind of shading in the genuine writing, that is because the pen was of a peculiar style; when you see it in the disputed writing, there it comes from the habit of the writer. And, then, horror of horrors, the serious thing in this whole business is that the thing itself looks real, the thing itself looks genuine, there are all the characteristics of the old man's writing there, but these four will signatures are so nearly alike in measurement that it would be impossible to reproduce them. I don't want to say but little on that, because I don't think it is worthy of much discussion. We are not here charging Mr. Patrick with the crime of forgery.

The handwriting experts are not objective, he said. They have a motive for testifying in the way they do:

The same motive that actuated the Texas contingent in declaring these signatures forgeries; the same motive actuates a handwriting expert, like a lawyer or like a doctor. They take up a case and it may be a hopeless one, but they will do the best they can for their patients. You take a lawyer into a case, it may be a hopeless one, but he will do the best he can for his client. You take a handwriting expert into a case, it may be a hopeless one, but he will do the best he can for his client, – and they will do the best they can for the District Attorney.

Moore, saying nothing about Patrick's failure to testify, analyzed the evidence of the various witnesses in great detail. He concluded his address close to six o'clock, asking the jury to find, not just that there was a reasonable doubt of Patrick's guilt, but that there was no reasonable doubt of his innocence:

Now, I do not ask you, at the close of this case, is there a reasonable doubt as to this man's guilt, but I do put to you the reverse of that: Is there a reasonable doubt but that he is innocent? Is there a possible doubt but that Jones is a liar?
Is there a possible doubt but that chloroform was not administered?

Is there a possible doubt but that old man Rice's death was natural and due to natural causes, not the reverse of that? And, it was for that reason that our case was so strong, and the facts so clear and convincing, that I said to you, in my opening, that we do not want favor, we do not want sympathy, we want justice at the hands of this tribunal and, gentlemen of the jury, we believe we will receive it at your hands.

I thank you.

# 63. Osborne's Address

Starting just before eleven o'clock on Tuesday, 25 March, James Osborne spoke for over six hours, walking back and forth in front of the jury box and looking squarely into the eyes of the jurors. Like Moore, he started his address in a quiet tone. The *World* noted that his address was 'so fascinating that the twelve men in the jury box listened with unabated interest.' The *Evening Journal* said that it was like 'a play with Osborne in the role of Matinee idol.'

Osborne opened his address by defending Baker's character:

I heard yesterday an assault made on the character of a man here in open Court that I do not think is possible in any jurisdiction or in any courts, except in the courts of New York. If any of you gentlemen can find in this record one solitary thing against Baker, I want it known now. If there has anything been sworn to on that stand against Baker I want to hear it; I want it known now; and I want Mr. Moore to call my attention to the record before I go on.

Mr. Moore: I did that yesterday, Mr. Osborne.

Mr. Osborne: You did not. And not in one single, solitary sentence you said from the beginning to the end of your speech was there reference made to any record – not one. I have never in my life had my intelligence so insulted, and neither has any jury ever been treated with the contempt that Mr. Moore treated you gentlemen; because not one solitary sentence is there in that record against the character or conduct of Baker.

Now, I am not here as an advocate of Baker. I don't care that (snapping fingers) for Baker, except as I do for any other witness, but when Mr. Moore was before the Jerome hearing he said that it was I that put up the job on Patrick. I just want to tell you that so that you will understand how much truth there is in the matter to be relied on.

Mr. Moore: It seems to me, your Honour, that this is improper.

The Court: Yes, Mr. Osborne –

Mr. Osborne: Your Honour should have said to him yesterday; 'Mr. Moore, there is not one word in this record against the character of Mr. Baker.'

The Court: Mr. Moore based his argument upon the testimony in the case.

Mr. Osborne: No sir. He said: 'That is what I believe.' I say there is nothing in the record about it.

The Court: Mr. Osborne, I will take care of all that when I come to instruct the jury.

Mr. Osborne: Yes, sir, I thought I would take care of it right now, your Honor. Now, gentlemen, I thought I would refer to these things in passing. I do not care anything more about Captain Baker than I do about any other witness in this case. There is no fight between Patrick and Baker, and there is no fight between Mr. Moore and myself. I think Mr. Moore did the best he possibly could do for a desperate case. When Mr. Moore was speaking he was the mouthpiece and advocate for his client. He could say nothing except what the situation suggested to him, and like other people in desperate situations the only thing that suggested itself to him was abuse.[1]

The strategy of the prosecution's jury address was to appear to focus on evidence of witnesses other than Jones:

Now, let us begin and get down to the case. Mr. Moore asked you at the outset yesterday to disregard the testimony of Jones. Let us see! I am so glad that Mr. Moore and myself can find a common ground. We will meet him. Out of the door goes Jones! Let us disregard him and see where we are. Let us regard Jones and Patrick as together. Leave Jones out of consideration. I won't refer to his testimony for the main argument in my speech at all; and I base this entirely upon evidence outside of Jones.

If he could not show that Patrick is guilty, he said, the jury should acquit. But if he does prove Patrick to be guilty, he told them:

Then, I want you to have enough of that original manhood in you, enough of the stern virtues of our ancestors, to come into this Court and to justify law and order. I want you to add your mite to the preservation of law and decency.

I think the criminal classes have gone far enough toward owning the country. I think crime has become rampant enough in this country. I think we are nearing the point of anarchy; and I think you have seen more anarchy in this Court room during this trial than you have ever seen before in your life.

I myself have seen scenes in this courtroom during this trial that startled me, that made me feel that the very foundations of society were being attacked by the criminal classes; and for reasons that I will point out to you as I go on. The attitude of counsel towards the Court, for one thing. Then putting those men Meyers and Short on the stand, and they deliberately committing perjury right here in the face of twelve men.

Why, it seemed to me that I would see the walls go open, and see them struck down dead, like Ananias and Sapphira. It was as much as I could do to sit still and see it quietly. There was not a man in that jury that did not know that those young men put their hands on the Bible and swore deliberate lies; and both their lawyers knew it, too.

Patrick, Osborne went on, was like a southern turkey buzzard scenting its prey and settling down to its deathwatch.

Rice, for his part, had only one great interest, Osborne argued, the Rice Institute:

He had but one design, and that was to build an institution for the benefit of mankind. And some people have said that he picked out the best place in the world to build it, where they needed it most. He was going to build it in Houston, Texas. Now, that was the one design of his life, concentrated upon one idea, to build a great institution.

He then examined Patrick's legal practice and his relationship to Rice. Patrick, he said, had a 'shrinking practice':

Now, how do we know that he did not have any great amount of practice? In the first place, he never kept a diary. Now, there is not an active lawyer on earth who can do business in New York City without having a diary to put down what he is doing. He never kept a register to record the events he was doing. He never kept a cash book to charge up accounts; never had any of the books or paraphernalia which are absolutely necessary to keep accounts among lawyers in New York City.

You can't go into a tu'penny, ha'penny, half-rate lawyer in New York that you don't find those books there. You can't do any business without taking and keeping accounts of the things you do. It would be impossible to remember all the motions and adjournments and other steps in cases. You couldn't do it for a minute.

Now, according to the testimony in this case, Patrick did not have any of those things that were necessary. He had envelopes I believe, on the back of which

he noted things. I merely call attention to that to show the kind of a lawyer he
was.

Where, Osborne asked, is the evidence of a solicitor and client relationship between Patrick and Rice?: 'Where is the witness who swore
that at that time Patrick knew Rice? Where is the witness who at that
time swore Rice knew Patrick? Where is the human being in the world
brought here to testify or to show that at that time Rice knew Patrick?'
Patrick interrupted: 'Mrs. Carpenter so testified.'

Mr. Osborne: When?
Mr. Moore: May 25th.
Mr. Osborne: This was going on, gentlemen of the jury, was going on anterior
to that time. Can you show us one at the time of the preparation of this will?
Can you produce one who will swear to the month of January, 1900? I like
these interruptions. I crave them.

Osborne invited counsel and the jury to interrupt him whenever they
wished.

Why has Patrick not produced any documentary evidence of his relationship with Rice? Osborne asked.

We lawyers have got to live, and before we can make a living we have got to
make a bill. You have got to have a bill. Now, in order to have a bill, you have
got to have a charge. In order to make a charge you have got to make a memorandum, consequently we have got to keep books of account.

If Patrick was Rice's lawyer, he could establish that fact in just two minutes.
He could establish that fact in just two seconds. Where are those books, where
are Patrick's books? Where are his charges against Rice? Where is one letter he
wrote to any one individual on the face of this earth about Rice's business?
Where is that one man that he ever went to and talked to on behalf of Mr. Rice?
Have you seen him go on the stand here?

There are some things in this world that you can't establish. You can't establish the track of a serpent across the rock, and you can't establish the passage of a
ship into the mist. But there is one thing that you can prove without any doubt,
and that is a client's relations with his lawyer, from the necessity of the situation.

Osborne could not legally comment on Patrick's failure to testify,[2]
but he left the jury in no doubt that Patrick could have personally shed
light on the issues. He went on:

Do you think that Patrick is on trial for disorderly conduct, gentlemen of the jury? Do you think he is on trial for riding a bicycle too rapidly? Is he on trial for driving too fast in the park, or for playing baseball on Sunday?

Great God! Gentlemen of the jury, this man is on trial for murder; murder; murder in the first degree; and he has got it in his power to prove that he is Mr. Rice's lawyer and he has not done it. And he has not done it!

Why hasn't he done it? You know why he has not done it, do you not? I pray you remember that he has got more at stake here than any man on earth could have except one that had his life at stake. On the one side is life and death, infamy, disgrace and dishonour; and yet not a scrap of paper has been produced here tending to show that Mr. Rice ever wrote to Patrick!

The press noted that for much of the address Patrick was rocking gently on the back legs of his chair.

Osborne referred to the contract of settlement, dated 6 March 1900, signed by Rice. Why has it not been produced? he demanded. If it were produced and contained Rice's signature, Osborne said dramatically, he would drop the prosecution:

Now, all that the defendant has got to do is to hand up the original to this paper, in the handwriting of Mr. Rice, to the view of the District Attorney. That is all that has got to be done. All of these learned lawyers, who have been talking about everything in the world except this case, all they have to do now is to hand up that original contract signed by Mr. Rice, and out of court I go, with a bowed head, having made a great mistake, having made a false charge, having earnestly worked for six weeks in order to bring about a verdict of guilty against this man. I will go out in humiliation and despair, for there will be nothing to show for all my exertion and everything else. If that original document is produced in court, and is signed by Mr. Rice, I am willing to abandon this case. Where is it? Why is it not produced? And the law is that, if evidence is substantially traced to the possession of the defendant accused of crime, and he fails to produce it, it is a strong presumption of guilt. I charge him with having made up a bogus contract.

Osborne stressed that Whittlesey went to see Rice about a settlement of the Holt litigation, as he had testified, after 6 March 1900, not in 1899 as the defense argued:

If you decide that Whittlesey visited Mr. Rice in the Spring of 1900, I tell you now that you are bound to find this defendant guilty of murder in the first degree. Now, this is an awfully solemn moment in this trial. If Whittlesey visited Rice in the Spring of 1900, there is no question about it, Patrick is guilty of murder in the first degree, and the consequences just follow each other as naturally as that two and two make four, and add three to that and it makes seven, and add two to that and it makes nine.

Why did Rice write to Baker in mid-September 1900 about preparing for further testimony in the Holt litigation if the matter was settled? The letter, otherwise inadmissible as hearsay, had been introduced by the defense:

On the 15th of September, having in mind his own business, and knowing that he has got to go on the stand in that Holt litigation again, he writes the letter asking his lawyer to send him the deposition, which would have been absolutely impossible if there had been any agreement of settlement in the case.

A voice from the dead, gentlemen! A voice from the dead! And that was heard in this court by the inadvertence of the counsel for the defense. I would never have been allowed to read you that letter if Mr. Moore had not read it. I did not stop him when he did it.

The whole scheme was fraudulent, Osborne asserted. Why did he choose Meyers and Short as witnesses? 'I want you to register that right now, that if Patrick had an honest will, making him residuary legatee of the estate, the last two people in the world that he would have gotten would have been two witnesses that were as close to him as were Meyers and Short.'

Why would Rice give Patrick all his money, he asked?

I have been listening to Mr. Moore's conversation here, and you have, and I want you to remember that this is not a case of a man against whom suspicion has arisen, that suspicion hastened into an accusation, that accusation, that of murder, into an indictment, and the man dragged into a court of justice and hurried on to a conviction.

Oh, no! This man has had two years practically to prepare his defense. He has had the assistance of the most astute counsel that can be found at the criminal Bar. They had had the advantage of every book, paper, scrap of writing that the District Attorney could give them. I have handed to them here before you everything in my power. We have made all the investigation and obtained all the light that was to be had, and not one solitary reason has been assigned why Mr. Rice should give Patrick all his money.

Now, what has been any reason assigned for Mr. Rice to give this Patrick all his money, the residue of his estate? Not one iota of reason. The statement on the face of it is so absurd and ridiculous that I hardly feel like standing before a jury and arguing.

Where is the evidence of a secret trust? he asked the jury, again suggesting that Patrick could and should have testified. 'Mr. Moore, I think, said something about a secret trust? Where is that secret trust? Why wasn't it produced? Where is the writing of the trust? Why, it is the easiest thing in the world to produce a trust. Just hand it up to the Judge. Not so! Absolutely nothing of the kind. His money left out and out to Patrick.'

Why wasn't Mrs Francis called as a witness? he asked. 'Now, why wasn't Mrs. Francis called here as a witness? There she sits (pointing to Mrs. Francis in the body of the court). There she is – Mrs. Francis and Patrick were together on the door step and he had plenty of time to go over and have that talk with Jones.' Mrs Francis, described by the New York *American* as 'a tall woman in black, wearing a black hat with a large ostrich feather,' rose defiantly, but was told to sit down by the attendants.

Osborne referred to the alleged statement that Jones had made to House:

He tells Mr. House that he killed the old man with chloroform; that is undisputed, uncontradicted and undenied on the record of this Court, and there is a living, truthful witness of high character that could take the stand and deny it, if Jones was not telling the truth. It is the law, that where it is in the power of the defendant to call a witness and he does not call that witness that could contradict a statement, that the jury are to consider that fact as a strong presumption of the truth of the statement. Will any jury say that Mr. Rice was not chloroformed, as long as there is a witness to deny that Jones told him that, and that witness would not take the stand and deny it?

Mr. Turner: I object to that statement before the jury. The law prohibits Mr. House from taking the stand, unless with the consent of both parties.

The Court: I cannot sustain your contention upon that point, Mr. Turner.

Mr. Turner: Without the consent of both defendants, your Honor.

Mr. Osborne: When Jones went on the stand he opened the door so that they could no longer talk about the privilege at all. The only person that could forbid him from going on the stand would be the defendant himself.

Mr. Turner: I say that if Mr. House had taken the stand in this case, you would
have had the privilege of cross-examining him upon any matter you pleased,
and Mr. House would be derelict in his duty if he did –
Mr. Osborne: Right you are, and that is the truth. What objection has innocence
to being cross-examined? What objection has innocence to have this lawyer
cross-examined? What fact is there that Moore knows, that House knows,
that occurred between Patrick and themselves that they would object to having come out before this jury? Right, Mr. Turner is, and there is no question
about it; absolutely right. Mr. House, under cross-examination, would have
been compelled to reveal this whole scheme of murder and fraud.

Jones, Osborne said, told the truth: 'Jones, though he is a murderer,
I admit he is a murderer, and a sneaking, low murderer, still, at the
same time, he is capable of telling the truth. There is no man living,
that you ever saw, that could tell that story of his unless it was the
truth, and answer as he did – not a man on earth could do it.'

The all-day address concluded shortly after 6 p.m. with a plea to the
jurors to do their duty:

I leave this case with you, gentlemen, with a feeling of absolute certainty and assurance that your verdict will be a just and an honest verdict; that your verdict is
going to tend to preserve law and order in this community; I don't believe that
any one of you is going to allow that natural timidity, that natural shrinking
from an unpleasant thing, to interfere with your doing your duty.

This man has an advantage in this respect. The People of the State of New
York is but a corporation, a soulless corporation, with no flesh, no blood, no
feeling. The defendant is real in presence, real in flesh, and real in blood. This
jury look on him and they see his quivering, they see his suffering, and naturally
that appeals to their sympathy; but if, in a plain case like this, you permit feelings of humanity, or a shrinking from doing your duty, to overstep your reason
and your common sense, as long as you live, and as you go down the corridors of
time, your conscience will be whispering to you the words: 'Coward! coward!
coward!'

# 64. Goff's Charge

For almost three hours, starting just before eleven o'clock, Recorder Goff
– 'looking like a silver bust of himself' – charged the jury. Patrick listened
intently. Captain Baker, occupying a seat near the reporters' table, pressed
the silver end of his cane to his lips as he listened to the charge.

Goff told the jury about the presumption of innocence and reasonable doubt:

A presumption of innocence remains with the defendant throughout the case until his guilt be proven beyond a reasonable doubt. When his guilt is so proved the presumption of innocence is overthrown.

The defendant is not called upon to establish his innocence. The burden of proving his guilt rests upon the prosecution throughout the case.

He is entitled to the benefit of a reasonable doubt upon the whole case, and if there be a reasonable doubt upon any material question in the case it must be resolved in his favour.[1]

The failure of the accused to go into the witness box, he said, should not be taken into account by the jury: 'The defendant may take the witness stand in his own behalf, but his failure to avail himself of that privilege must not be taken to his prejudice.'[2] Of course, the very mention that they should not be prejudiced would highlight the fact to the jury that Patrick did not testify. He stressed that 'the jury are the exclusive judges of all questions of fact': 'The weight and value of all testimony and the credibility of every witness are matters for your exclusive determination.'

The case could be one of first-degree or second-degree murder, he said. It could not be any other form of homicide. Goff defined murder:[3]

Murder in the first degree, that degree of crime with which the defendant is charged, is the killing of a human being when committed from a deliberate and premeditated design to effect the death of the person killed.

Murder in the second degree is the killing of a human being when committed with a design to effect the death of the person killed, but without deliberation and premeditation.

There are three main propositions, he said, that the jury must find before they convict:

The case of the prosecution rests upon three principal propositions which must be established as facts to warrant a verdict of guilty of murder in the first degree, and unless they are established as facts to your entire satisfaction the defendant is entitled to a verdict of acquittal.

These propositions are:

First: That on the 23rd day of September, 1900, Charles F. Jones, with intent

to kill, placed a towel wrapped in the form of a cone containing a sponge saturated with chloroform, upon the face of William M. Rice.

Secondly: That William M. Rice died from the effects of chloroform, and
from no other cause.

Thirdly: That the defendant, with intent to procure the death of William M.
Rice, aided, abetted, counselled, advised, or induced Jones to kill him.

If these three propositions be established to your satisfaction, and beyond a
reasonable doubt, you should render a verdict of guilty; if they are not so established, you should render a verdict of not guilty.

Patrick would be guilty, even if he did not personally kill Rice. Goff
read to the jury section 29 of the New York Penal Code: 'A person
concerned in the commission of a crime, whether he directly commits
the act constituting the offense or aids and abets in its commission, and
whether present or absent, and a person who directly or indirectly coun-
sels, commands, induces or procures another to commit a crime, is a
principal.'[4]

Jones is an accomplice, he warned, and the evidence must therefore
be received with caution:

The law receives his testimony, though he be an accomplice in the crime. Indeed,
it is one of the perils attendant upon the commission of crime, that those who
engage in it are liable to betrayal by their associates. Where crime is conceived
and planned and executed in secret, it frequently happens that justice would be
thwarted, were the testimony of an accomplice to be excluded. It, therefore, in
many cases of crime becomes necessary to the ends of justice that the secret
workings of a criminal plot be laid bare by one of the participants.

But such testimony should be received with great caution and be very carefully considered, and the law, ever watchful of the interests of the accused, provides that he cannot be convicted unless such testimony be corroborated.

The section of our Criminal Code declaring this rule is as follows: 'A conviction cannot be had upon the testimony of an accomplice, unless he be corroborated by such other evidence as tends to connect the defendant with the commission of the crime.'

Goff quoted some New York Court of Appeal cases[5] to the jury and
went on:

You will observe, gentlemen, that in the last case the Court says that it is not necessary that the corroborative evidence of itself should be sufficient to show the commission of the crime, but that it is sufficient if it tends to connect the defendant with the commission of the crime. And the learned judge who wrote the opinion says, – his literal language being slightly modified and altered by me to be adaptive to the case on trial – 'Though each circumstance taken by itself may be quite inconclusive, it is sufficient if, when considered together, they furnish some corroborative evidence.'

Although the recorder stressed that the facts were for the jury to determine, he outlined in skeleton form the facts alleged by Jones:

Many weeks have elapsed since Jones testified; many witnesses have been examined before you, and it would be beyond the capacity of human memory to have distinct and clear recollection of all the particulars and details which he narrated. For the purpose of aiding you in calling up to your recollection some of the points in his testimony, I will read a few extracts, without expressing any opinion whatever relating to them, and reduce those extracts to the merest skeleton, so that you will be enabled by reference to remember the whole context of his testimony in relation to these transactions.

For the next thirty or forty minutes, the recorder recited portions of Jones' testimony. Unlike an English or Canadian trial judge, a New York judge will express no opinion on the facts.

Goff then told the jury that Patrick's failure to produce documents could indeed be held against him: 'The rule is that, if a defendant has it peculiarly within his power to produce articles or documents which would explain or elucidate the transaction, the fact that he does not do it creates the presumption that the instruments, if produced, would be unfavorable to him.'

The jury were told that they could consider Jones' various statements in judging his credibility:

You have a right, on the question of Jones's credibility, to consider the fact that he has made various statements and confessions differing with each other and differing from his own testimony on the stand; and on the question of his motive in testifying, whether it was to acknowledge a murder for the purpose of securing immunity for the commission of that crime or for the purpose of escaping prosecution for forgery, conspiracy or other crime of which he might be accused in connection with the Rice estate.

The fact that Patrick has also been charged with forgery should not affect the jury's judgment upon the question of guilt or innocence, Goff said. But the testimony of forgery was admissible 'upon the question of the defendant's motive.'

That completed the substance of Goff's charge. He then dealt with fifty requests by the defense for specific charges on particular points. Goff accepted thirty-seven of these and rejected thirteen. Many of them were simply alternative ways of looking at such concepts as reasonable doubt. For example, request no. 3, which Goff accepted, stated: 'In order to find the defendant guilty of the murder of William M. Rice you must be satisfied that the evidence in this case to a moral certainty, or beyond a reasonable doubt, excludes or removes every other hypothesis with regard to the death of William M. Rice, than that of the defendant's guilt as charged in the indictment.'[6]

Request no. 4, which was also accepted, told the jury that they should acquit if they believed the evidence that Rice died a natural death, 'even though you may believe that the defendant intended to cause the death of William M. Rice.'

Request no. 16, similarly accepted by Goff, required the jury to find that the will of 1900 was a forgery. Goff charged the jury:

If you believe the will of 1900 to have been forged as claimed by the prosecution, you have the right to consider that fact as evidence establishing the motive of the crime charged. If, however, you believe from the evidence that the will of 1900 was not forged and was a genuine document, then the claim of the prosecution as to motive fails, and your verdict must be not guilty.

He refused to charge the jury on some of the other requested charges. For example, he refused to charge the jury that: 'The corroboration of the evidence of an alleged accomplice must tend to prove *each* of the facts constituting the crime, for otherwise a person might be convicted of an offence as to one of whose elements there existed no proof except that of the accomplice.'

Goff ended his address with some further observations on reasonable doubt, telling the jury that 'in human affairs absolute certainty is not always attainable' and that: 'If the evidence establishes the proof of guilt to a reasonable and moral certainty, a certainty that convinces and directs the understanding and satisfies the judgment beyond a reasonable doubt, then it becomes your duty to render a verdict of guilty against the defendant of the crime charged against him.' Do not be nervous of making a mistake, he told them, or be concerned about what will happen to Patrick:

Bear in mind, in coming to your conclusion, that the importance of it, while necessitating great caution and care on your part, must not excite in your minds such dread and apprehension as may tend to weaken your judgment.

If any such matters should tend to arouse in your minds a dread or an apprehension of making a mistake, then be careful that your judgment become not enervated; that you become not nervous in the performance of a duty; that the dread or apprehension of something possible to occur hereafter should not stay your lips from pronouncing the words which you believe to be true in your verdict.

Whatever your verdict may be, I am sure, gentlemen, carefully selected as you have been by both the prosecution and the defense, agreed upon as the judges of the fact in this case, selected from a panel of gentlemen in this city that is assumed to possess certain qualifications of intelligence and other matters – whatever your verdict will be, it will carry with it the impress of loyalty to yourselves, loyalty to your oaths, and loyalty to the law; and I submit the case to you.

The jury retired at 1:50 p.m. to consider their verdict.

# 65. The Verdict

The jury went immediately into the juryroom. Patrick was taken to the holding cell in the basement of the court. House and Moore went to Moore's nearby law office. Everyone settled in for the inevitable long wait for the verdict.

Just before three o'clock, the jury emerged to go for lunch at Holtz's Restaurant at the corner of Broadway and Franklin. The press reported that they had spent the first hour deciding whether they would go for lunch. They returned at four o'clock.

At 5:55, they told the clerk that they had arrived at a verdict. Goff's attendant, Thomas Kearney, came into the courtroom and announced: 'The ladies in the court room will please retire so that the room will be ventilated.'[1] All the women left, including Emma Patrick and Mrs Francis. The great doors of the courtroom were then closed behind them. The New York *American* reported that 'this is the rule in all capital cases' and then added, 'Justice abhors scenes.'

At 5:58, the jury filed into court. Patrick was brought from the cells, but because his counsel had not yet arrived, he was taken into the juryroom to wait. Whether he could detect his fate from any scraps of paper in the room is not known.

At 6:08, Moore and House arrived. The clerk announced: 'Order in the court. His Honor, the Recorder of New York.' Goff ascended the bench. Patrick was brought into court and attempted to take his seat beside his counsel, but was motioned to stand at the bar of the court behind the railing. None of the jurors looked at Patrick. The clerk asked:

Clerk Brophy: 'Gentlemen of the jury, have you agreed upon a verdict?'
Foreman Machell: 'We have.'
Recorder Goff: 'There will be silence in the courtroom.'
Clerk Brophy: 'Jurors, please rise and look upon the prisoner; prisoner look
    upon the jurors. How say you, gentlemen of the jury? What is your verdict?'
Foreman Machell: 'Guilty.'
Clerk Brophy: 'Do you find the defendant guilty of murder in the first degree, as
    charged in the indictment?'
Foreman Machell: 'Guilty of murder.'

The *World* reported the next day that when the jury had returned 'those practised in reading jurors faces at once agreed that their verdict meant death to the prisoner.' House asked that the jury be polled[2] and each juror in turn answered: 'That is my verdict.' As the last juror, John Burgraff, replied 'my verdict,' Patrick turned and looked affectionately at his father.

House requested time to prepare a motion to Goff for a retrial and the recorder set Monday, 7 April, as the date for formal sentencing. The clerk of the court asked Patrick a series of standard questions:

Q. Your name?
A. Albert T. Patrick, New York City.
Q. Age?
A. Thirty-six.
Q. Business?
A. Lawyer.
Q. Married or single?
A. Single.
Q. Read and write?
A. Yes.
Q. Habits?
A. Temperate.

Q. Ever arrested?
A. Never before.

'Remove the man,' Recorder Goff ordered.[3]

Patrick reached over the rail for his square-topped derby hat and brushed a speck of dust off of it. He caught his father's eye and motioned to him to meet him at the door leading to the Bridge of Sighs, but Captain Patrick was unable to get to it before Patrick disappeared. The press reported that all the sympathy in the courtroom was for Patrick's white-haired father, Captain Henry Patrick.

Emma Patrick and Mrs Francis, waiting in a room outside the court, were aware from the reporters' activity that something serious had happened. The press reported their reactions, whether actual or supposed, when they were told of the verdict. The New York *Times* stated:

Miss Patrick burst into tears and sank into her friend's arms. Mrs. Francis without a word fell to the floor in a faint. Court officers brought her water and fanned her, but for ten or fifteen minutes she remained unconscious. She was carried into the courtroom, still unconscious. Miss Patrick followed and threw herself hysterically against the railing where her brother had stood, sobbing bitterly and declaring his innocence. 'Oh the devil! The devil!' she sobbed accusingly. Women friends comforted her and tried to revive Mrs. Francis. All but the intimate friends of the weeping women turned away from the sight of their grief.[4]

The jurors refused to discuss what had gone on in the juryroom. Foreman Machell stated: 'I cannot discuss what took place in the juryroom as we agreed not to talk of it. This was not because anything took place that cannot be published to the world, but because we wish to avoid unpleasant notoriety.' Nevertheless, the press was able to piece together that there were only two ballots. The first took place shortly after they returned from lunch and was 7 or 8 in favor of conviction and 4 or 5 blank ballots. After further discussion, a second ballot was taken, which was unanimously in favor of a conviction. 'I expected a speedy verdict. It was no surprise,' Foreman Machell told the press. He added: 'What evidence did the defense submit?'[5]

Patrick was taken back to the Tombs and told the deputy warden: 'No one in the courtroom was more surprised than I, as a lawyer, at the result of my trial.' 'They convicted me,' he said, 'mostly on my neglect to show evidence, and never before has it been known that the defense must show evidence.' The deputy warden agreed, saying: 'I thought it sure it would be a disagreement.'[6] This was apparently the general reaction. In an editorial, the New York *Times* referred to the 'universal surprise' at the verdict. Patrick was lodged in his same cell, cell no. 50 on Murderers' Row, although the usual practice, as a further safety precaution, was to move a convicted murderer down to the cells on the ground floor.

Both Moore and House told the press that they were 'shocked by the verdict' and that they would begin work on an appeal immediately. House said: 'We hope to get it before the Court of Appeals in September. We are confident the verdict will not be sustained.' Patrick, House said, was 'convicted on the summing up of Mr. Osborne and by the charge of the Recorder and not by the evidence.' House elaborated:

I hold that we have a good case on the facts and that our claim that the verdict was against the weight of evidence will be sustained by the Appellate Court. Eight doctors of the highest reputation swore that the death of Mr. Rice was not due to chloroform and that other conditions developed by the autopsy were sufficient to account for the death. It seems to me, and I am sure the higher court will see it in the same light; that such evidence is sufficient to create that doubt of which the law says the accused shall have the benefit.[7]

Moore met the jurors by accident as he was leaving the courthouse. Each juror insisted on shaking hands with him, and they collectively expressed regret that their finding had been against him, but that the verdict was in accordance with the evidence. 'Well, I think you would have found otherwise had Mr. Schepflin's testimony been admitted,' Moore stated. Schepflin, it will be recalled, was prepared to testify that Rice had intended changing his will and that Rice had told him that he proposed leaving all his estate to a young lawyer whom he had met in New York, who could be trusted to fulfill his schemes for the employment of his fortune. The evidence was, however, excluded as hearsay. Patrick also stressed the importance of Schepflin's evidence, stating: 'How can the declarations and determinations of a dead man be otherwise arrived at than through the testimony of a third person? This is done every day in the Surrogate's Court.'[8]

Baker, who spent the evening at Byrne's home, refused to make any statement for publication, and Osborne simply said that 'It was a triumph for justice,' adding: 'We shall put Meyers and Short on trial at once and expect to convict them for perjury.' The press wanted to know what would happen to Jones. 'We are not ready for Jones yet,' he replied.

District Attorney Jerome agreed that after a rest they would prosecute Short and Meyers, and said that he, Jerome, had not yet had an opportunity to discuss with Osborne what would happen to Jones. 'But unless immunity is promised in cases of this kind,' he added, 'it is sometimes very difficult to get a conviction. For this reason, it is often necessary to turn a bad man loose.'[9] Patrick told the press that Jones would never be tried: 'They wouldn't dare put Jones on trial for anything. If they did, he would let out the truth.' The veteran lawyer William F. Howe, of the notorious firm of Howe and Hummel,[10] who had heard the addresses of counsel and the judge's charge, predicted: 'What I anticipate next is another confession from Jones that he lied in his latest version of the murder.'[11]

Patrick gave a number of interviews to the press. He told the *Evening Journal* that 'it was impossible for me, as it is impossible for any one, to obtain a fair trial before Recorder Goff, in combination with District-Attorney Osborne.' He was asked why he did not go into the witness box. He replied: 'What do you think would have happened to me if I had taken the stand? An atmosphere of murder, perjury and forgery would have been thrown about me; all the little frailties of my life raked over and enlarged and my testimony, however important to myself, would have been rendered valueless as far as the jury was concerned.'[12]

Patrick was asked by the New York *American* what he thought of the handwriting experts – 'Did they convict you?' He replied, referring to the recent Dreyfus case in France:

They did very largely, but all evidence founded upon their opinions is unsafe where the popular feeling is against a defendant. This was clearly shown recently in France. All the handwriting experts and paying tellers in France pronounced the papers in the Dreyfus case to be forgeries by Dreyfus – because France was against him. In America, where sympathy was with Dreyfus the experts decided otherwise. After they had convicted the man, publicly degraded him and sent him to Devil's Island to die, Esterhazy confessed that he wrote the bordereau, became a fugitive from the country and his coadjutor blew out his brains. The truth disproved the best expert testimony in all France. The truth in my case will disprove the experts. Man for man, we had just as many bank tellers and experts ready to swear that the Rice signatures on the checks and the will were genuine as the prosecution had produced to pronounce them forgeries.[13]

Jones told Hearst's *Evening Journal* the following day: 'I heard the news last night and am happy over the result. Patrick deserves all he got.' The same enterprising paper contacted Mrs Francis, who said: 'Mr. Patrick is as innocent today as he ever has been in his life, and nothing can change my belief in him ... All I can say is that he is innocent, innocent, innocent.'

# PART FIVE
# Appeal

New York State Capitol, Albany, 1915: New York State Library, Albany.

New York Court of Appeals in the Capitol Building, Albany, prior to 1916: Albany Institute of History and Art, McKinney Library Photograph Collection.

Edgar M. Cullen, chief judge, New York Court of Appeals, 1904–13: *National Cyclopaedia of American Biography.*

David B. Hill, undated; probably about 1900.

Above: Albert T. Patrick: New York
*Evening Journal*, 15 January 1906.

Right: Patrick's brother-in-law John
T. Milliken: New York *World*,
5 December 1912.

Milliken's home, 35 Portland Place, St Louis, purchased in 1916 and still
standing.

# CHILD SLEEPS IN PATRICK'S ARMS;
# HILL PLEADS FOR PRISONER'S LIFE.

Patrick and his two daughters: New York *American*, 15 March 1905.

# 66. Leaving the Tombs

The trial had been the longest on record in New York City.[1] The result, stated the *Times* in an editorial, was a surprise to the general public. Some letters to the editor supported that sentiment. The *Times* editorial, said one writer, 'voices the sentiment of nine out of ten citizens of the city.' Why not prosecute Jones? the letter went on to state: 'The man testified on the stand that he had been promised nothing. If that is true what excuse can the District Attorney offer for his monstrous proposition [that Jones be given immunity] ... If the man's testimony to the jury that he had been promised nothing was false, then ... the rest of his testimony was equally incredible.'[2]

Another letter-writer to the *Times* pointed out that Patrick was being sent to the death chamber and then asked: 'Where is this miserable Jones? While walking up Eighth Avenue, near Fifty-fourth Street ... the writer saw the villain leisurely sauntering down the street, evidently having a fine walk and enjoying God's free air. His companion may have been a private detective to look after this modern Münchausen; in other words, the State is providing this Jones with a valet to take him around the Tenderloin and other places of enjoyment.'[3]

Other letters, however, disagreed with the *Times* assessment. One writer, who signed his letter 'A Lawyer' and claimed to have 'some first-hand knowledge' of the case, said that the reason that the public was surprised was because of poor reporting by the press. Rather than stating, as the *Times* did, that the result 'does not confirm general confidence' in the courts, it would be more accurate to state, the writer went on, that the result 'does not confirm general confidence' in the press.[4]

On Good Friday, two days after the verdict, Patrick announced to the press that he and Mrs Francis were engaged. He refused to elaborate, stating simply, 'I feel that it would be rather indelicate for me to go into details ... I have known Mrs. Francis intimately for eight years and no one could have been more devoted and assiduous to me in my troubles than she has been.'

The press quite rightly pointed out that if Mrs Francis was not married to Patrick, she could not visit him in Sing Sing. Only spouses and other 'members of his family'[5] could do so. Marriages in Sing Sing were not permitted.

Flynn, the warden of the Tombs, and Hynes, the New York commissioner of corrections, refused to permit a ceremony in the Tombs. 'We don't want any such sensationalism in the Tombs,' said the commissioner. 'If Patrick is so anxious to be married, let him be married on the train on the way to Sing Sing – that is, if the Sheriff will permit it.'

On Sunday, 30 March 1902, the couple were secretly married in the Tombs. Their friend, Samuel Bell Thomas, a lawyer who, like Patrick, was a Texan and a graduate of the University of Texas, was able to take advantage of a new law that had come into effect in New York at the beginning of 1902. That legislation recognized marriages by contract when properly entered into and registered.[6] They had been engaged since 1898, Thomas told the press, and had planned to be married on the day of his acquittal.

Under the pretext of signing some documents, the forty-three-year-old Mrs Francis, dressed in black with a black hat and black plumes, and accompanied by Patrick's father, sister, and younger daughter, Lillian, met with the thirty-six-year-old Patrick in the matron's room in the Tombs. The marriage contract was signed and witnessed. The form stated that the two named persons 'have agreed to unite in bonds of matrimony and become husband and wife from henceforth.' Patrick personally added the words 'until death do us part.' The 'ceremony' was sealed with a clasp of hands.[7]

The next day, lawyer Thomas took the document to be registered. City Clerk Scully had his doubts. The statute required that the document state the 'place of marriage,' and the document that was submitted said that it had been entered into at the 'corner of Centre and Leonard Streets.' The clerk wanted it to state 'The Tombs.' Thomas pointed out, however, that the address of the Tombs in the telephone book simply stated 'Centre and Leonard' and so the document was eventually accepted. The contract is 'perfectly valid,' A.H. Hummel of the Howe and Hummel law firm told the press, but 'when sentence is pronounced on Patrick next Monday, to all intents and so far as the State is concerned, he will be as one dead' and so she will be free to marry again.

Patrick's father, his sister Emma, and his daughter returned to Texas. His new wife, Patrick said, would help him gain his freedom. He told the *World*:

'A man in jail can't help himself. A lawyer is just as helpless as anybody else. Other people must be hands and feet for him. It reminds me of what they call boggy cattle in Texas. There the country in some places is thick with marshes into which cattle will wade to drink. They sink deeper and deeper, and the more they struggle the less their chances of escape become.

'Ranchmen hire people to go around and pull these cattle out of the bog. Well, that's the way with a man in jail. Unless he has somebody on the outside who will work to pull him out he hasn't much chance to get away from the people who are after him.'[8]

Jones' testimony, he said, was false. Under his own byline, Patrick wrote in the New York *Journal* that Jones had confessed because of the 'third degree.' On the night of 30 October, he said, Jones was made to stand for nine hours while Captain Baker, Police Captain McCluskey, and District Attorney Osborne grilled him. Patrick went on:

Then, on a signal, he was suddenly escorted into a darkened room. It was as still as death, and the nerve-racked, trembling man was left standing there alone for a full five minutes. Fully cowed, he didn't dare move. While he must have been thinking what new torture was in store for him a strong, white light suddenly flashed across his eyes, and as he started back in terror he saw at arm's length from him a figure of Mr. Rice. He fell shrieking to the floor in a dead faint. Half an hour later he recovered consciousness, to find himself surrounded by his tormentors, who read to him an alleged story of his ravings, which he signed as his confession to escape further persecution.[9]

On Monday, 7 April, Patrick appeared for sentencing before Judge Goff. His three counsel were there, as was District Attorney Jerome and Assistant District Attorney Garvan. Osborne had left with his wife for a month's holiday in Europe. Goff entered the court. Patrick stood in an enclosure behind the bar of the court with his hands loosely clasped behind his back.

Jerome moved for the imposition of sentence: 'The defendant, Albert T. Patrick, was convicted this term of Court by a jury, of murder in its first degree. On behalf of the People, we now move for judgment on that conviction and the imposition of sentence.'[10] House objected and brought a perfunctory motion for a new trial. The eight specified grounds dealt with generalities, the first part being, for example, that 'the verdict is contrary to law.'

Without calling on Jerome, Goff stated: 'I deny your motion on the several grounds mentioned.' Four further boiler-plate objections were made by House on a motion in arrest of judgment and again the motion was denied.

Goff then pronounced the sentence of the court. Patrick held his head up and looked straight at Recorder Goff:

Albert T. Patrick, the judgment of the Court is that you, Albert T. Patrick, for the murder in the first degree of William Marsh Rice, whereof you are convicted, be, and you are hereby, sentenced to the punishment of death.

Executions were required to take place 'not less than four weeks and not more than eight weeks after the sentence.'[11]

And it is ordered that, within ten days after this day's session of the Court, the Sheriff of the City and County of New York deliver you, together with the warrant of this Court, to the agent and warden of the State Prison of the State of New York, at Sing-Sing, where you shall be kept in solitary confinement until the week beginning Monday, the 5th day of May, 1902, and upon some day within the week so appointed the said agent and warden of the State Prison of the State of New York at Sing-Sing is commanded to do execution upon you, Albert T. Patrick, in the mode and manner prescribed by the laws of the State of New York.

# 67. To Ossining

Shortly after twelve noon that same day, Patrick was in a closed carriage pulled by two black horses on his way to the train that would take him to Sing Sing Prison. His clothing and books had been packed in a small trunk. His right wrist was handcuffed to the deputy sheriff's left wrist.

The carriage arrived at Grand Central Station in time for the 1:05 p.m. train that would take Patrick the forty miles 'up the river' – that is, the Hudson River – to Sing Sing Prison. Mrs Patrick was waiting for him at Grand Central Station and affectionately kissed him good-bye.

Handcuffed to Deputy Sheriff Bell, he entered the smoking car. A crowd drew around him in the car as he told why he would be shown to be innocent and drafted a document with his shackled hand addressed to the warden of Sing Sing demanding that he not be placed in solitary confinement in the death house pending his appeal to the Court of Appeals. Notice of appeal had already been filed by Moore and House. They had also attempted to block the transfer to Sing Sing, but without success.

At the town of Ossining, a carriage took him to the south gate of Sing Sing Prison, the gate that was closest to the death house. At 2:30 p.m. he entered the massive prison.

Sing Sing Prison[1] was selected as a site for a new prison in 1825 because of the extensive quarry of white stone resembling marble that was found there. Indeed, the words 'Sing Sing' are said to come from an Indian phrase 'Rock on Rock.' Construction was started on the banks of the Hudson River in 1826, using one hundred prisoners from the older Auburn prison, and was completed three years later. They used the rocks found at Sing Sing, the same rocks that would later be used to build the State Capitol in Albany.

The six-story buildings covered fifteen acres and contained twelve hundred cells. (Some of these structures are still in use within the prison today, although not to house prisoners.) Over the years, the prison was periodically condemned. A report the previous year from the New York Prison Association concluded that Sing Sing had outlived its usefulness and should be replaced.[2] Originally known as Mount Pleasant State Prison, its name was later changed to Sing Sing. The town of Sing Sing, however, disliked the resulting notoriety and had that same year changed its own name to Ossining.

The notoriety of Sing Sing had been heightened by the death house that was constructed there after electrocutions were introduced by law in 1888.[3] Formerly, executions were conducted in the county where the trial had been held. In New York State, they now took place at Auburn, at Sing Sing, and at a prison in Dannemora, construction of which had been authorized in 1844. The world's first electrocution took place at Auburn in 1890, and thereafter all the executions in New York would take place in one of the three state prisons.[4]

Electrocution replaced hanging in New York as the result of a state legislative commission that was established in the 1880s. At that time, there was great rivalry between Edison's direct current system and Westinghouse's alternating current. Edison's strategy for gaining the upper hand was to show how dangerous Westinghouse's alternating current was. It could kill. The legislative commission then seized upon this fact, watched some demonstrations of its lethal quality, and recommended that hanging be replaced by electrocution in the state prisons. Hanging was officially replaced by electrocutions in New York State in 1888.

As soon as he entered the prison, Patrick handed his written demand not to be placed in solitary confinement to Warden Addison Johnson. The warden was sympathetic. He himself had recommended in his last annual report that he have discretion to place prisoners facing execution but under appeal in the main part of the prison. 'It is a terrible thing,' he wrote, 'to keep a man in solitary for a year or two when his conviction may be reversed and he may walk out a free man.' A bill had subsequently been presented to the legislature but had not passed. He had no choice, he told Patrick, but to place him in solitary in the death house.[5]

There were three other prisoners then in the death house and two guards who constantly watched the prisoners. Security in the death house had been tight for the past ten years – ever since two condemned prisoners had escaped in 1892.

Executions were not particularly frequent at the turn of the century. There were then perhaps two or three a year in Sing Sing. In all of New York State from 1890 to 1907 there were 112 executions out of over 1,300 persons condemned to die: about 900 had their sentences commuted (normally to life imprisonment) and about 350 had been pardoned.[6]

Patrick was placed in a cell at the extreme end of the easterly side of the structure – a cell which had a direct view of the door, the so-called 'little door,'[7] leading into the execution chamber. This was a constant reminder of his possible fate – day and night. During the day, the glass skylights flooded the death house with light, and at night, gas and electric lights steadily burned. The eyes of the guards were constantly on the prisoners as the guards moved noiselessly about the corridor in their felt slippers. When an execution was to take place, a curtain was pulled in front of each cell.

Patrick was given a bath and a shave and was given a somber black 'death' suit and felt slippers. His furniture consisted of a cot, a small table, and a washstand. Condemned prisoners were given only a half-hour of exercise once a week.

On Friday, his wife, who was allowed two visits a week, came for the first time. The curtains were drawn before the other cells. A guard sat in front of Patrick's cell. His wife, who spent an hour with him, sat behind a wire screen placed about six feet from the cell door. They could not touch. She returned to New York City. 'Every hour of my life from today until he is a free man,' she said, 'will be spent in proving him innocent.'[8]

# 68. Probate

The day after Patrick was transferred to Sing Sing, the contest of the two wills was again brought before Surrogate Judge Fitzgerald in the New York County Court House. William B. Hornblower and a large array of legal talent sought to uphold the 1896 will.

Cantwell and Moore, representing Patrick and the 1900 will, announced that they were not ready to proceed and that it was likely that
they would be substituted by other counsel. Baker reported the proceedings in a letter to Lovett, adding: 'After the Court adjourned, Cantwell and Moore said that they had advised Patrick to abandon the contest
of the will, and that unless he did so they would retire from the criminal
case. It is now reported that Wellman and Tomlinson will represent
Patrick in the will contest.'[1]

Virtually every North American lawyer today knows the name Frances L. Wellman.[2] He is undoubtedly the best-known criminal lawyer
from that period, in part because of his widely used classic, *The Art
of Cross-Examination*,[3] in part because of the many books he wrote about
his famous cases, and in part because of his remarkable success as an
advocate. A graduate of Harvard Law School, where he was valedictorian
in 1878, he taught briefly at Boston Law School and at Harvard before
moving to New York in 1883. He represented the city in civil cases
for a number of years, and from 1891 until he went into private practice
in 1894 he prosecuted murder cases, particularly those involving poisoning, as the first assistant district attorney. One of his best-known cases
was that of Carlyle Harris in the early 1890s, in which the key issue
was the effect of embalming fluid on the identification of poison. Jerome,
it was well known, had been the losing defense counsel in the case.[4]
In his period as a district attorney, the *Times* obituary later said, 'Wellman
was accredited with more verdicts of murder in the first degree than
had been obtained by any other prosecutor up to that time in the United
States.' The *World* reported that Wellman and Tomlinson had also been
retained to handle the appeal from the murder conviction. Baker and
Hornblower knew that Wellman would be a formidable opponent in the
will contest and on the criminal appeal.

When the will case was resumed the following week, however, only
Tomlinson appeared for Patrick. John T. Milliken had made an arrangement with Tomlinson to handle the case on a day-to-day basis for a
contingent fee. Wellman's role would be principally as an adviser.

John C. Tomlinson had practiced law in New York for twenty-five
years, but did not have a particularly strong reputation. He is one of
the few lawyers in the Rice case who did not later rate an obituary in
the *Times*. Coincidentally, his office was in the Drexel Building on Wall
Street, the same building that contained the Swenson Bank and Baker's
temporary New York office. Again coincidentally, he had acted for Baker

several years earlier in the pending litigation involving Mrs Rice's will. For reasons that were never made clear, he had a strong hostility to Baker. On 16 April 1902, Surrogate Fitzgerald commenced the trial of the wills. Tomlinson had sought an adjournment on the basis that Short and Meyers were about to be tried and so could not be compelled to testify and also because Patrick's appeal had not yet been heard. 'I have no doubt that Patrick's conviction will be reversed on appeal,' Tomlinson argued, 'so that if Your Honor should proceed with this case and admit the will of 1896, and Patrick should subsequently establish the 1900 will, what would become of the property to which he would be entitled?'[5]

Fitzgerald, however, ordered the trial to proceed. It had already been adjourned over twenty times, he said. David Short was the first witness called by Hornblower, but on the advice of his counsel, Samuel Bell Thomas, the lawyer who had arranged Patrick's marriage, he refused to testify on the ground that it might incriminate him. Meyers also refused to testify, but took the opportunity to complain to the press outside the courtroom that he was being hounded by the district attorney's office:

A man named Connelly, a detective attached to the District Attorney's office, so far as I am able to learn, has been shadowing me since the commencement of the Patrick trial. He reaches No. 302 Broadway, where I have my office, every morning about the time I arrive. He remains in the hall, lets everyone in the building know his business and that he is shadowing me ... He follows me from place to place, even going so far as to follow me to court, and remains there throughout the entire period while I am attending to my regular busi- ness ... The result of this persecution has been that my landlords refuse to renew my lease and I am having considerable difficulty in securing a law office.[6]

Jerome told the press that Meyers could try to seek an injunction if he wanted.

The first witness to testify was Walter Wetherbee from the Swenson Bank, who went over his earlier contacts with Jones and the attempt to certify the check the day after Rice died. Many of the other witnesses at the murder trial were called by Hornblower, including the handwriting expert Albert S. Osborn. He was cross-examined by Tomlinson:

'Could anything change your opinion as to the signature to the will of 1900?'
'Nothing.'
'If two very reliable witnesses were produced and testified that they saw Mr.

Rice sign that will, what would you say?'
'I would say that they were either lying or that they were mistaken.'
'What if Archbishop Corrigan and Bishop Potter so testified?'[7]

The last question was not allowed.

Baker complained to Lovett that Fitzgerald was only devoting two days a week to the hearing and that Tomlinson was taking up too much time: 'Tomlinson, Patrick's new counsel, like a new broom, sweeps clean, and consumes most of the time in re-threshing old straw.'[8]

Midway through the proceedings, Wellman and Tomlinson brought a writ of prohibition to prevent Fitzgerald from continuing with the case. 'There is no substantial merit in the petition,' Baker wrote Lovett; 'it is but one of the many efforts that have been made here to block the proceedings to probate the Will – another instance of so-called reputable lawyers trying to establish a "nuisance value." '

Justice Bischoff of the Supreme Court denied the writ, and his decision was upheld by a five-member panel of the Appellate Division of the Supreme Court. Patrick's remedy, the court said, is to appeal from the surrogate's final decision, not to bring prohibition.

The case continued before the surrogate. Tomlinson called a number of handwriting experts. Charles French from Boston, whose testimony had been struck out by Judge Goff at the criminal trial, testified. The defense experts – Cantwell from Albany, Drake from Chicago, and Wood from Pittsburgh – gave evidence upholding the will of 1900. Collectively, however, they would not come close to matching Hornblower's experts in stature or authority.

'I never was quite so tired of anything,' Baker complained in a letter to Lovett, 'as I am of my stay in New York. I don't have enough to do to keep me busy, and consequently time hangs heavily on my hands.' Moreover, he said, Mrs Baker, who was in New York with him, was ill: 'she has not been well since January when she got a severe cold ... and she has coughed constantly for the last two or three months.'

On 18 June 1902 at 6:30 in the evening, directly after hearing argument, Fitzgerald admitted the 1896 will to probate:

The judgment of the Court is that the 1900 will be rejected, upon the ground, firstly, that the proponents of that will have not made out a case which is provided for by the Statute as to the execution and publication of a will by a decedent.

I make the further finding that on the evidence adduced, that the signatures to the paper of 1900 are not the genuine signatures of William M. Rice.[9]

Two days later, Assistant District Attorney Osborne appeared before Judge Goff and applied to have Jones, who had not been called as a witness at the will trial, admitted to bail. He was still being held as a material witness on the forgery and perjury charges. Thomas Devine, a horse dealer in New York and no doubt a professional bondsman, furnished $1,000 cash bail. Jones' brother, William, told the recorder that he would take his brother back to Texas and would see that he was returned to New York if he was needed.

Tomlinson gave notice of his intention to appeal from Fitzgerald's judgment. The appeal would operate as a stay, although the surrogate had the discretion to grant letters testamentary in spite of the stay. 'Thus, things move along, but oh! so slowly,' Baker wrote Lovett, adding that there has been some hint of a compromise: 'Some intimations have been thrown out to us that Patrick's counsel would abandon the case and not take an appeal – upon the payment of $25,000 to $50,000. If such a proposition should materialize what do you think should be done with it?'[10] Baker said that he personally was 'very much inclined to settle if it can be done within the figures mentioned.' Why settle? he asked rhetorically. 'The reply is: simply for business reasons; take no chances, and clinch the matter while you can ...' Hornblower's firm agreed, but were worried that the DA would be disappointed, thinking that this 'would be a bargain with a criminal, prejudicial to the prosecution.' Lovett immediately wired back his advice that 'it would be very unwise to entertain the proposition made under any circumstances.'

Baker waited in New York for the surrogate's decision on whether letters of administration would be granted in spite of the appeal. He again complained to Lovett: 'It seems to be contrary to the dignity of the Courts here to intimate to counsel or to suggest to them any particular time when the matters they have under consideration will be passed upon and the decisions handed down.' On 18 July, after more than five months in New York, Baker left, writing to one of the members of the Hornblower firm: 'Justice moves with such slow pace in New York that my stock of patience – which I thought was abundant – has been exhausted, and I am off for Texas, where we do things in a hurry.'[11]

Two months later, Surrogate Fitzgerald issued letters of administration to Baker and others for the 1896 will. A bond of $7 million had to

be put up – according to the clerks of the surrogate office, the largest
bond ever given in such a case in New York County's history.[12]

# 69. Motion for a New Trial

On Monday, 4 August 1902, the first execution since Patrick arrived
in Sing Sing took place. Aaron Hall had been convicted three years earlier
of killing his girlfriend. After a bitterly contested case, his final appeal
to the Supreme Court of the United States had been turned down. In
mid-June he had been resentenced to die in the week of 4 August. The
*Times* reported that at the resentencing he turned to his counsel and
'said good-bye to him, adding that everything had been done for him,
and that he was prepared to die.'[1] The night before the execution, Hall
went to bed at 10:30, awaking at 4:00. He then ate an entire watermelon
he had requested before lying down. Principal Keeper Connaughton said
he had never seen a man go so 'eagerly' to his death.

The current was applied at 6:03 a.m. and sixteen minutes later Hall
was pronounced dead. Three shocks were necessary at 1,700 volts each.
One of the witnesses, a doctor, fainted when the third shock was applied.
The curtains of the cells of the other inmates of the death house, including
Patrick, had been drawn, but the inmates throughout the penitentiary
were aware of each application of electricity as the lights throughout
Sing Sing dimmed as each shock was applied.[2]

Patrick's own series of appeals was about to commence. He must have
given much thought as to whether his fate would be the same as Hall's.

On 6 October 1902, the junior counsel assisting Tomlinson, Edgar
Kohler, appeared before the Court of Appeals in Albany to clarify how
much time Patrick had to perfect his appeal. On 1 September 1902,
a statute had come into effect allowing only six months.[3] Did the six-
month rule apply to Patrick? The Court of Appeals held that the six-
month rule commenced in Patrick's case on 1 September and therefore
he had until 1 March 1903 before the appeal had to be heard.

The twenty-seven-year-old Edgar Kohler, like his older brother, Max,
had graduated with honors from Columbia Law School. Edgar had
topped his class. Their father, Rabbi Kaufmann Kohler, was perhaps
the most important figure in Reform Judaism at the time. He was then
the chief rabbi of the important Temple Beth-El on 5th Avenue opposite
Central Park and was about to become the president of the Reform Movement's Hebrew Union College in Cincinnati.[4]

Edgar Kohler worked closely with Tomlinson on the next stage of the case, an application to Judge Goff for a new trial. Frances Wellman did not publicly take part in these proceedings, although the press continued to treat him as one of Patrick's lawyers. During this period, Patrick's wealthy brother-in-law, Milliken, was trying to find another eminent counsel to take the appeal.

In mid-November, Tomlinson and Kohler filed an application for a new trial before Judge Goff. In the United States, unlike the practice in England and Canada where such motions are not permitted, a motion for a new trial can be made to the trial judge. In the case of a capital offense in New York, it could be made at any time before execution.[5] A lengthy affidavit by Tomlinson accompanied the application, along with affidavits by others detailing what was claimed to be 'newly discovered evidence.'

The hearing started on Friday, 5 December, before Goff in the Criminal Court Building where the original trial had taken place. The People were represented by two young prosecutors, twenty-seven-year-old Francis Garvan, who had assisted Osborne at the trial, and twenty-six-year-old Henry G. Gray.[6] Gray, who had graduated from the Harvard Law School two and one-half years earlier, was the son of John C. Gray, a judge of the New York Court of Appeals since 1888.

Garvan argued that the motion was not made in good faith, but for the purpose of getting a lot of irrelevant material before the Court of Appeals that would be considering the case in March.[7] Such was no doubt Tomlinson's objective, although to the defense, of course, the new evidence was not considered irrelevant. However, they probably had no realistic hope of having Goff actually order a new trial.

Evidence was introduced by the defense to show that Jones had never been indicted for his actions. This complete immunity, Tomlinson argued, was 'in the nature of an illegal bargain between the District Attorney and Jones and constituted in law a bribe to the witness at the hands of the prosecuting officers of this county which would ... have destroyed his entire credibility as a witness before the jury in this case, had they been informed of the real facts.'[8] The action of the district attorney, Tomlinson said, was 'a fraud upon the court.'[9]

Garvan countered by calling George Gordon Battle, Jones' counsel, to show that there was in fact no direct promise of immunity by the district attorney. Battle said he personally believed that Jones would be given immunity, but Osborne 'would not make any promise of immunity.' Tomlinson harshly criticized Battle's conduct, stating: 'Mr. Battle served three masters and he served them well. He succeeded in getting Patrick convicted, the will declared a forgery, and he also freed Jones. I think he made himself guilty of unprofessional conduct in this case.'[10] 'I say that that statement is unfounded,' Battle replied, 'and I cannot express that too strongly.' Tomlinson softened his stance and conceded that Battle had acted 'unwittingly.'[11]

Meanwhile, as part of the war to influence public opinion, if not the Court of Appeals, news reports were emanating from Texas that Jones was telling people that Rice died of natural causes. A Houston detective, J.L. Mott, Jr, hired by Milliken, said that he had such affidavits from people Jones had spoken to, but refused to say who they were. Osborne told the press that 'it would be natural for some persons interested in Patrick to try to get a recantation from Jones.' And Garvan said that they had not kept track of Jones but he had 'no doubt that Jones would repeat his former testimony if called as a witness.'[12]

House was called by Garvan, but claimed attorney-client privilege. 'Now, what do you say to that, Mr. District Attorney?' Goff asked, playing directly into the prosecutor's hand. Garvan said that the prosecutors are being accused of improper conduct by in effect offering Jones a bribe to make him testify falsely. Garvan wanted to ask House whether Jones had made a similar confession to him before confessing to Osborne. 'I simply want to show,' Garvan went on, 'that the allegation made by defendant's counsel against public officials of this county that they had invented this crime, and had taken part in railroading Patrick to the electric chair, was not made honestly.'[13]

A three-hour confused legal argument ensued. Could Battle waive the privilege on Jones' behalf? Had Jones waived the solicitor-client privilege at the trial? If Patrick was present at the interview, did he also have to waive the privilege? Could Tomlinson do it for him? In the end, House refused to testify as to any conversations with Jones stating: 'as I see the duty of counsel, no one can waive the privilege, and there is nothing that would persuade me to violate the confidence of a client.' Goff hesitatingly upheld the claim of privilege. But Garvan had made his point to Judge Goff and to the public.

The majority of Tomlinson's affidavits related to the medical evidence at the autopsy. It will be recalled that Dr Donlin, who performed the autopsy, and Dr Williams, who was present, had testified at the trial that the condition of the lungs was abnormal. Donlin and Williams, Tomlinson argued, were not 'disinterested public officials,' but were 'heavily interested in furnishing evidence designed to please the prosecution.' Although Dr Williams was receiving a salary of $3,000 a year from the city as a coroner's physician, he had charged $7,500 for his services in the prosecution of Patrick. The sum had been certified as reasonable and proper by District Attorney Osborne, although in the end Williams was actually paid $5,200.

An affidavit was filed by the morgue attendant, Robert Aurich, whose evidence for the defense had been excluded at the trial. After the autopsy, Aurich said, Donlin turned to Williams and remarked: 'Considering the evidence of the autopsy finding, I should say the man died of old age, wouldn't you?' Williams, Aurich said, replied 'Yes.' Donlin, according to Aurich, then told the waiting press: 'It's all up, boys, there is nothing in it. The man died of old age.' Donlin filed an affidavit denying that he had ever made those statements. Dr Williams was in Europe and was unavailable.

Another witness, John Fane, the keeper of the morgue, swore that after the autopsy Dr Williams asked him for a light for his cigarette. 'What is in it, Doctor?' Fane asked and Williams allegedly answered: 'That old fellow died of old age.' Edward Hart, the coroner who had ordered the autopsy and was present during its performance, swore that Donlin had 'found no violent cause of death' or 'anything suspicious'; if Donlin had, he, the coroner, would have been told. Indeed, he said, after the autopsy, Donlin directed that the body be disposed of on Dr Curry's original certificate.

Dr Albert T. Weston, an experienced coroner's physician who had performed over twenty-five hundred autopsies in his career and had been prepared to testify for the prosecution at the trial but was not then called, now gave evidence for Patrick. He had not been present at the inquest, but stated that 'the absolute failure of Dr. Donlin and Dr. Williams to notify Coroner Hart of any suspicious cause of death found by them is ... absolutely inexplicable, if in point of fact a suspicious cause of death had been discovered.' Weston denied Garvan's suggestion that he would receive a contingency fee of $12,500 if Patrick was awarded a new trial.

The defense attempted to place on the record the evidence of the handwriting experts that they had called at the will trial, but were unsuccessful. Goff said: 'The prospect of the proportions of this motion is becoming simply appalling ... I will exclude all matters relating to the Surrogate's record.'

Tomlinson's closing argument took five hours. He reserved his strongest criticism for the district attorney's office: 'I tell you this act of the

District Attorney is the most shocking act I ever came in contact with. It is a sign of barbarity ... Jones was allowed to lie on the stand. The trial was a judicial farce, a travesty on justice. It was a fraud upon the court and a fraud upon the administration of justice.'[14]

Garvan did not present any oral closing argument, but submitted a sixty-page printed brief outlining why a new trial should not be granted.[15] The evidence, he argued, was not 'newly discovered':[16] it was available at the time of the trial. He ended by referring to the failure of House to give evidence about what Jones had said to him: 'Mr. House sits silent with the knowledge that if he, a respected member of the bar, took the stand and denied Jones's statement, his client must go free.' Patrick, he said, has never given House permission to testify: 'Is this position of the defendant and his counsel one calculated to attract the exercise of the discretionary powers of this Court to grant a new trial on the grounds he states?' Moreover, Patrick himself did not present an affidavit. The brief concludes: 'This defendant has failed to show any reason why the solemn verdict of the jury, rendered in no delayed or uncertain voice, should be upset.'

Goff reserved his decision.

# 70. Preparing for the Appeal

The motion for a new trial concluded late Tuesday, 16 December 1902. On Thursday, Mrs Patrick visited her husband in Sing Sing to relay what had occurred. Prisoners were not officially allowed to read newspapers. Mrs Patrick told a *Journal* reporter that she had been spending all her time trying to prove Patrick innocent: 'If I have to go through fire and water to save him I will do it.' 'Twice a week I go to Sing Sing to see Mr. Patrick,' she told the female reporter: 'I consult with him through bars. I tell him what I have done; he racks his memory for dates and facts that will help me. I return to this little room.' The 'little room' referred to a small front room of an uptown apartment to which she had moved. The reporter noted that she was wearing black, which 'accentuated the gray pallor of her face,' and was now 'careworn and weary, excessively thin.'[1]

There were now six persons in the death house. Patrick had been unanimously elected the 'Mayor' of the death house by the other inmates. The position was to be for a year, unless, as the press liked to put it, he was 'sooner removed.'[2] As mayor, he would solve disputes between inmates and control unnecessary talking during the frequent chess and checker games which were played by calling out moves and using pieces molded from dough. Patrick was the champion chess player and was said to be able to play simultaneously with all the other inmates.

Patrick's wealthy brother-in-law, John T. Milliken, and Patrick's sister, May, visited him in February. Mrs Milliken told the Press: 'I know that the Rice millions will buy up anything that may be discovered to my brother's advantage, so I shall be very careful in talking about new evidence in his favor ... I think I may say that we are constantly getting new evidence, and more especially in regard to the wretched valet, C.F. Jones.'[3] 'My brother', she said, 'awaits Recorder Goff's decision with impatience.'

On Monday, 2 March 1903, Goff delivered his judgment, denying a new trial: 'In view of the fact that the case is now in the Court of Appeals,' he wrote, 'and that in due time the material questions of law and fact involved will be examined, I believe that to write an opinion would not be consonant with judicial proprieties.' He then briefly stated his conclusions:

That there is not legal proof that any evidence of a material character has been newly discovered since the trial; that substantially all of the matters and conditions now claimed to have been newly discovered were within the knowledge of one or all of the counsel who represented the defendant from the inception of the criminal charge until after judgment was pronounced; that the exhaustive cross-examination of the witnesses for the People by the learned counsel for the defense clearly indicates a knowledge of, and familiarity with, such matters and conditions, and if such knowledge were not possessed in the minute detail set forth in the moving affidavits, it could have been acquired – if considered of sufficient importance – by diligent use of the means and opportunities then available.[4]

The new evidence, therefore, was not in his opinion 'newly discovered,' and errors at the trial could be dealt with by the Court of Appeals.

Tomlinson and Edgar Kohler had gone before the Court of Appeals in Albany a few weeks earlier and had obtained an extension of time for the appeal. The extension was granted, with the consent of the prosecutor, until forty days after the settlement of the case by the recorder. The two sides negotiated for many months over what should be included in the appeal papers. The process was not completed until over a year later. In May 1904, Judge Goff finally settled the record and seventeen copies of the documents were sent to Albany. The record consisted of over four thousand pages in five volumes and was said to be the largest ever filed with the New York Court of Appeals.[5]

Following Goff's refusal to grant a new trial to Patrick, the DA's office took active steps to have Meyers and Short tried for forgery and perjury. In May 1903, L.P. Sharp, one of the detectives who had charge of Jones in New York, was sent to Texas to bring him back. Sharp called on Baker, who immediately wired Hornblower: 'L.P. Sharp claiming to represent District Attorneys office is here looking for Jones but has no papers showing who he is. Does he represent District Attorney?' Hornblower replied with the single word 'Yes.'[6] Still, Jones was not located. It may be that Baker had no interest in helping to have Meyers and Short tried at that time. If they were acquitted, it would reopen the question of the validity of the Patrick will of 1900. The Hornblower firm had written Baker earlier to get Jones' address and Baker had apparently not responded to the request.

Baker obviously knew where Jones was. In the summer of that year, a story appeared in the press that Jones had disappeared. 'Disappearance of Jones a Blow to Jerome,' headlined the New York *American*.[7] George Gordon Battle, who had acted for Jones in New York, told the *Times* that he believed Jones was dead: he had corresponded with him until about five months ago, when the letters suddenly ceased. Baker wrote to the Hornblower firm in response to these reports: 'this is simply a sensational report without foundation, as we believe we could locate Jones with comparatively little difficulty.' Hornblower then replied that proceedings against Meyers and Short had been put off and that the assistant DA 'says that for the present at least he does not think it worth while for you to trouble yourself about Jones's whereabouts.' Tomlinson had been asking the DA's office for a delay until Patrick's appeal had been concluded. 'It's highly desirable,' one of Patrick's counsel wrote, 'that the trial of those indictments should not be pressed until after the Patrick appeal is disposed of. If perchance a conviction of Meyers and Short should be had upon the eve of the hearing of the Patrick appeal the moral effect would of course be very unfavourable to Patrick's interest.'[8] So neither Patrick nor Baker wanted Meyers and Short to be tried at that time.

Much of the work in settling the record for the appeal was done by Max Kohler, Edgar's older brother, who had been an assistant US district attorney in the 1890s and was now in private practice.[9] Max Kohler became involved in the case because of the illness of his brother Edgar, perhaps brought on by a disciplinary charge against him made by Jerome to the New York Bar Association. On 8 April 1903, a charge of attempted bribery against Edgar was made public by the district attorney's office.[10] The press gave the charges enormous coverage.

The charges arose out of a meeting in January 1903 between a female friend of Mrs Patrick and Sergeant Nicholas Brindley of the New York Police. Brindley had been in charge of Jones while he was in custody. The woman, a detective who had been assisting the defense, apparently wanted Brindley to say that Jones had been offered immunity by the DA and that Jones admitted being untruthful in his testimony. Brindley reported the conversation to Assistant District Attorney Garvan, who asked him to continue the discussions and allow others to overhear what took place. This was done in an uptown restaurant. Jerome alleged that the woman, on behalf of Edgar Kohler, had offered $7,000 for the evidence, a figure that Brindley said he himself had suggested.

Kohler vigorously denied the allegation: 'The accusation is as false as it is unfortunate,' he told the press.[11] Assistant District Attorney Rand acknowledged that the offers were not made by Kohler personally. 'No overt act was committed by Mr. Kohler,' he said, 'and therefore charges were made to the Bar Association instead of the grand jury ... The charges are of such a serious character that we couldn't do anything else but bring them before the grievance committee.'[12]

A hearing was scheduled on 20 April before the nine-member Grievance Committee of the bar. Kohler was represented by former US district attorney Wallace Macfarlane. But Kohler himself did not appear and the hearing was adjourned. He was ill. Over the next year and a half, undoubtedly as a result of this charge, Kohler was in hospital and for health reasons on extended trips to Europe.

In December 1904, the hearing before the Grievance Committee commenced, and it was heard from time to time over the next two months. Many leaders of the bar, such as Paul Cravath and Louis Marshall, gave evidence of Kohler's good character. In early February 1905, at the close of the testimony and without adjourning to deliberate further, the committee unanimously decided in Kohler's favor.[13]

# 71. Upholding the 1896 Will

In March 1903, Patrick's lawyers argued the appeal from Surrogate Fitzgerald's ruling upholding the 1896 will. A former judge of the Court of Appeals, Charles F. Brown, was brought in to argue the appeal,[1] assisted by Tomlinson and Edgar Kohler. This was just before the charges against Kohler had been made public. Francis Wellman was no longer involved in the case. The Rice interests were again represented by Hornblower, assisted by four other lawyers.

Two weeks later, Fitzgerald's judgment was upheld by Judge Chester McLaughlin for the Appellate Division of the New York Supreme Court, sitting in Manhattan.[2] Hornblower immediately wired Baker in Texas: 'Opinion of Appellate Division satisfactory on every point.'[3] The substance of the judgment was then set out. McLaughlin had stated:

The name of William M. Rice appears four times upon the alleged will of 1900, and upon a critical examination of these four signatures it will be found that they correspond almost exactly – a coincidence which could not possibly happen in the case of four genuine signatures of a person upwards of eighty years of age, and for this reason it does not need the testimony of experts to demonstrate that these signatures were not genuine, but tracings.[4]

Baker immediately wired back to Hornblower: 'Accept our heartiest congratulations. Opinion of the Court could hardly have been more satisfactory.'

A further appeal to the Court of Appeals in Albany was taken by Tomlinson in October 1903. The court dismissed the appeal without even giving reasons.[5]

Hornblower and Baker were, however, worried that because of the particular wording of the New York Probate Code, Patrick could challenge the will at any time within two years after he ceased to be imprisoned. Imprisonment, like being underage or mentally unsound, was considered a 'disability,' and the statute permitted an action 'two years after such disability has been removed.'[6] Hornblower's firm recommended that they bring a suit in equity now to preclude a later suit by Patrick. 'There never can be a certainty,' Byrne wrote, 'until two years have elapsed after Patrick gets out of prison, or is executed, that some such suit will not be brought. There is nothing in the past history of this litigation to justify the belief that Patrick, or those representing him, will be discouraged by successive defeats from bringing new suits.' Moreover, Byrne argued, if the executors bring a suit in equity it would be heard by a judge alone, whereas a suit by Patrick would be a suit 'in law' with a jury, thus bringing a measure of uncertainty to the outcome.[7]

Baker agreed with this assessment. If Patrick was executed, that would effectively end the threat of a lawsuit. 'But if the judgment of conviction is reversed,' Baker wrote, 'and Patrick is finally acquitted, he would no doubt give us trouble in the matter ... We see no reason why the executors should not take the offensive.' Nevertheless, for reasons that were never made clear, such a suit was not brought. Perhaps it was because of concern about the cost of the proceedings.

Lawyers' fees were mounting rapidly. Baker had discreetly asked Hornblower what fee he proposed charging: 'the Executors believe it is their duty to have some understanding in reference to the fee, now, rather than leave it open and undetermined.' The executors' concern, Baker assured Hornblower diplomatically, is 'not prompted by any feeling that you will overcharge them if no fee is agreed upon.'[8]

No fee was, in fact, agreed upon at the time. A year later, however, after the will appeals had been heard, but the criminal appeal had not, Hornblower submitted a bill to the estate for $275,000 for the 'balance in full for services rendered in litigation in connection with Rice will contest.'[9] There is no indication in the materials how much was claimed by the Hornblower firm for previous work done in the case, particularly with respect to the criminal proceedings. One of the Rice executors, John Bartine, expressed his anger to Baker at the size of this latest Hornblower bill and the fact that Hornblower knew that the executors did not want a controversy just before the criminal appeal was to be heard:

I cannot regard it in any other light than extortion ... They knew that they were in possession of all the papers, the data and facts which would be necessary in case of further trouble, and, therefore, they made use of their information in that regard. They knew that it would be injudicious for us *at this time* to have a controversy with our lawyers, and they have profited by it. They will never have another case like it while they live.[10]

Baker and Botts received $100,000 from the probate court in Texas for their legal work in New York on the will case.[11] The firm also received a $100,000 fee for its work on the case involving Mrs Rice's will.[12] It is not clear what additional fees were charged. Baker himself would presumably have received a substantial sum as an executor.

These sums, when put in the perspective of lawyer's earnings at the time, were enormous. An excellent recent book, *Baker and Botts in the Development of Modern Houston*, by Lipartito and Pratt, shows that the total yearly *gross* income of the entire Baker and Botts firm in 1900 was apparently only $48,000 and in 1905 only $112,000.[13]

Patrick's lawyers did not do as well. Tomlinson was paid $5,000 and subsequently sued Milliken in the US District Court in St Louis for an additional $20,000, but after a week's trial the jury held against Tomlinson.[14] John Bartine wrote to Baker, enclosing a clipping from a New York paper on Tomlinson's lawsuit and fee, and remarked: 'There is quite a difference between what Tomlinson gets and what our counsel have been paid.'[15] There is no record of what Moore or House received for their work on the case, although it is known that Milliken also resisted their fees and the matter had to be renegotiated by Milliken's lawyer, Frank Turner. Even Turner eventually had to bring a suit against Milliken for his own fee.

Not only did Baker and his firm receive enormous fees from the estate, but as chairman of the Rice Institute board he also had a large measure of control over an important source of capital. As Lipartito and Pratt state: 'The Rice trust was probably the largest local source of capital available to developers in early twentieth-century Houston.' Money could be loaned for projects that Baker favored. Lipartito and Pratt discreetly state that 'a man as active as Captain Baker could not eliminate all potential conflicts of interest.'[16] In any event, Baker and the Rice Institute board were very successful in making the endowment grow from $4.8 million in 1904 to $9.8 million in 1912.[17]

When the Court of Appeals in Albany upheld the will in the fall of 1903, the Houston press made the point that although it had been known for some time that 'a princely sum has been in litigation, few Houstonians have taken the time to think what the Rice Institute really means to the city.' 'This gives to Houston,' the *Houston Post* stated, 'the largest educational institution in the South – in fact, excepting the [Rockefeller-endowed] Chicago University, probably the most richly endowed educational institution in the country.'[18]

The *Post* added that 'the laws of New York, however, are peculiar, as, under them, Albert T. Patrick can now bring suit to set aside the will.'

# 72. David B. Hill

It was obvious to Milliken that Tomlinson was not the right person to handle the appeal from the murder conviction. Milliken may have had his eye on Francis Wellman, but for reasons that never appeared in any of the files, Wellman had dropped out of the picture and he does not mention the Patrick case in any of his many books.

Moore and his partner, William Cantwell, had wanted former governor David B. Hill – who was known for his brilliant oratorical powers – to take the case. Shortly after Moore and House had been replaced by Tomlinson, they had gone to Albany to see if Hill was willing to handle the appeal, but nothing came from those discussions. Whether Milliken was involved at this time is not known.

Milliken's friend and legal adviser from Denver, John M. Waldron, had discussed the situation with John G. Milburn, described by the New York *Times* as 'one of the foremost lawyers in this State,'[1] who was then in the process of moving his law practice from Buffalo to New York City. Milburn had practiced law in Denver many years earlier and probably for that reason was known to Waldron. Milburn was probably asked and declined to take the criminal appeal himself, but he recommended that David B. Hill be engaged as counsel. In a subsequent letter to Hill, Milburn stated: 'the record presents serious and interesting questions on which there should be a reversal.'[2] Waldron subsequently saw Hill in Albany in mid-December 1903 and a contract was concluded whereby Hill would take the appeal for the sum of $7,000, with $2,000 payable at that time and the remaining $5,000 by way of a certified cheque payable 'immediately after the conclusion of the oral argument upon said final hearing.'[3]

Patrick's sister, Mrs May Milliken, was delighted that Hill would be taking the case. Milliken wrote to Hill:

It is needless for me to say that my wife is overjoyed because you are going to plead her brother's case before the court of last resort. Neither she or I believe that Mr. Rice died by foul means, but on the other hand it is quite evident to my mind that after you have read the record you will find more evidence of a conspiracy to commit a judicial murder than you will of Mr. Rice having been murdered.

The financial arrangement was confirmed by Milliken. Indeed, he arranged for the whole $7,000 to be payable in advance because if he forwarded a certified check he would have to leave the funds to cover it in the bank: 'You might as well have the money as the bank,' the ever-practical Milliken said. He also wanted Hill to send a copy of all the material to Waldron in Denver, who would then be in a position to argue the appeal if anything happened to Hill. 'Some insane mugwump might take a fatal shot at the world's best democrat,' Milliken wrote, 'and if he did Mr. Waldron would be prepared to continue the fight.'[4]

David B. Hill, who, indeed, may well have been the world's best Democrat, had ruled the Democratic party in New York State for many years. At the time he was engaged by Milliken he continued to be the head of the party. Politics was his life. As the New York *Times* obituary stated: 'Hill, alone among the great bosses in the era of great bosses, was singleheartedly devoted to the pursuit of politics and had no other mistress.'[5] He never married, did not smoke, and rarely took a drink. The *Times* described him as 'a cold, silent, domineering man of great personal force and passionate will.' He lived alone in a thirty-six-room mansion in Albany with his library of three thousand books.[6]

Coming from a rather humble background, the sixty-year-old lawyer, who learned his law in a law office in Elmira, had worked his way up the political hierarchy. He had been the mayor of Elmira, a state assemblyman, lieutenant-governor of the state, acting governor, and then for two consecutive three-year terms, from 1886 to 1891, the governor. Among the many laws he brought in as governor was the one that required execution by electrocution. From 1891 to 1897 he was one of New York's two senators in Washington, then elected directly by the Democratic-controlled state legislature. It was in that capacity that he had successfully blocked the confirmation of William B. Hornblower to the Supreme Court of the United States.

Hill had one great ambition in life and that was to become president of the United States. In 1892 he and Grover Cleveland had battled for the Democratic nomination. Cleveland won and again became the president. Hill, however, continued in his quest for the office. An article in the *Albany Times Union* which appeared in 1902 on the day Judge Goff was charging the jury – no doubt planted by Hill's supporters – stated that 'seven out of every ten Democrats of note here in Washington favor David B. Hill as the next Democratic candidate for president' in 1904.[7] Hill's prospects faded, however, when his candidate for governor of New York in the 1902 off-year election was defeated by the Republican.

Within a week of Hill's engagement for the criminal appeal, Milliken wrote to him about reopening the will case:

Would you be willing to undertake to set aside the probate of the will of the late Wm. M. Rice of 1896 and establish his will of 1900, provided I can procure the interest of one of the heirs of Mr. Rice? ... Mr. Rice was worth 8 million dollars when he died and the Texas people have not stopped at anything to acquire his wealth. I believe in the validity of the 1900 will.[8]

'If after investigation,' Milliken went on, 'you are satisfied that you have an even chance to defeat the probate of the will of 1896, we will then discuss the question of fee and enter into a contract accordingly.' Hill, however, advised against purchasing the claim of one of the heirs and challenging the will.[9]

Every few weeks and often more frequently, Patrick would write to Hill discussing some aspect of the appeal. 'In view of the voluminous record,' Patrick wrote courteously after Hill was engaged, 'it may be that I can call some things to your attention which otherwise might pass unnoticed.' Patrick made it clear that he did not want to give up his claim to the validity of the 1900 will. 'I do not wish it conceded for the purposes of this appeal,' he wrote Hill, 'that any of the disputed signatures were forged. I should like that proposition to be combatted vigorously.'[10]

On 20 May 1904 the Court of Appeals, with the consent of counsel, postponed the hearing until the October term of the court. Patrick wrote a polite letter to Hill expressing his hope that the case would be heard in the fall: 'I have your letter of the 20th inst. I have no doubt you have done the most advisable thing, and I prefer a well considered preparation to a hasty one. However, I feel that I am justified in expecting that the case will be ready for argument at the first session of the Court in the Fall.'[11]

Patrick, still the mayor of the death house, had now been in solitary confinement in Sing Sing for twenty-six months. Once a week he was permitted half an hour of exercise outside his cell. And twice a week a barber would come and shave him: his beard and long mustache were now gone. There were then thirteen persons on death row and the executions were becoming more frequent. William Ennis had been executed in December, Thomas Tobin in March, and a mentally ill inmate, Oscar Bergstrom, was scheduled to be electrocuted on 14 June and two others on 22 June. Later in the summer, Patrick was able to stop the execution of Michael Brusch, who had been convicted of killing a policeman. The firm of Howe and Hummel, who had acted for Brusch, thought that an appeal was useless, but Patrick dictated a notice of appeal which acted as a stay. The electrocution eventually took place, however. What effect these conditions and the executions had on Patrick is not clear, although

Principal Keeper Connaughton told a reporter at the time that Patrick was 'almost invariably cheerful and hopeful.'[12]

Patrick, however, wanted Hill to bring proceedings to have him taken out of solitary. The warden and Superintendent Collins, he said, would support, and the district attorney would not object to, an application to the Court of Appeals to modify the terms of the confinement, or to the governor to exercise his pardoning power to the same effect. No such application, however, appears to have been made by Hill.

The conditions in the death house slowly improved. Patrick was reported to be a frequent contributor to the prison paper, *Star of Hope*.[13] No doubt as a result of his agitation, Superintendent Collins issued new rules permitting each condemned person to exercise in the prison yard for half an hour a day. Patrick was also able to have the chaplain, the Rev. George Sanderson, fired for cruelty to his own daughter. The Society for Prevention of Cruelty to Children of Ossining made the formal complaint. There had been personal animosity between the chaplain and Patrick when Patrick had refused to return a book he had borrowed and the chaplain sent a keeper to get it.[14]

Further, a sum of money was set aside by the state to improve the death house. Patrick, who had training as an engineer as well as a lawyer, sent in elaborate plans for a new structure that contained greater privacy for each cell and an exercise yard around the outside. Superintendent Collins, however, labeled the plans 'impracticable.'[15]

Patrick had now been in Sing Sing for over two and one-half years. The press speculated that the appeal would not be heard in October, 'as Mr. Hill will at that time be vitally interested in the Presidential campaign.'[16] This proved to be correct, and the case was put over until March 1905.

Hill had given up on the idea of becoming president, but instead had arranged for his friend, Alton B. Parker, to receive the nomination. Parker had run Hill's gubernatorial campaign many years earlier and Hill had rewarded him with an appointment to the Court of Appeals. He was now the chief judge of the court, a fact that may well have influenced Milliken in selecting Hill to argue the appeal. Hill, however, persuaded Parker to give up his judicial appointment and seek the Democratic nomination against William Randolph Hearst at the convention in St Louis in July 1904. By this time, Hill and Milliken had become friends, and Hill stayed in Milliken's mansion while at the convention.[17] Parker won the nomination through the skillful management of Hill, his campaign chairman,[18] but soundly lost the presidential campaign to the Republican, Theodore Roosevelt.

Even before the election, Hill announced that whatever the result of the campaign he would withdraw from active politics and devote 'more time to his personal affairs and professional duties than he has in the past.'[19] This he did, and at the end of 1904 he ceased to be 'the boss' of the Democratic Party of New York. But as leader of the party until then, he was involved in making decisions about two important positions: who would run for governor of New York in the 1906 election and who would replace Parker as chief judge of the Court of Appeals.

In mid-September 1904, Hill went to New York City to meet with District Attorney Jerome to discuss Jerome's possible candidacy for governor. They met for an hour and a half in Jerome's third-floor office in the Criminal Court Building. Whether they also talked about the Patrick case is not known. After the meeting, Hill was noncommittal when asked if he offered Jerome the governorship.

'I cannot talk about the conference, but isn't this a fine day.'

'Did you discuss politics with Mr. Jerome, or was your call in reference to private business?'

'It is a fine day.'

'Do you think Mr. Jerome could make a good candidate for Governor?'

'It is a fine day.'[20]

Jerome was equally noncommittal. The press reported that he sang a then popular tune: 'I don't care for Wurtzburger beer; I would rather have gasoline.' In fact, Hill found Jerome too independent and refused to support him. Jerome would make no promises: 'if the Albany leader and the forces he controls wanted to give it to [me] without any strings, all right; if they didn't, all well and good anyway.'[21] Hill backed someone else and the convention chose Hearst for governor over Jerome.

Judge Edgar M. Cullen, a Democrat, was nominated by the Republican governor, Benjamin B. Odell, Jr, for chief judge. Hill opposed him, preferring another candidate.[22] The press reported that Hill wanted to punish Cullen for his decision in an election case many years earlier in which he had branded Hill and his associates as criminal conspirators.[23] Cullen was, however, selected as chief judge and would chair the seven-member panel of judges who would hear the Patrick appeal several months later.

# 73. The Medico-Legal Society

Sometime during October 1904, while Patrick was preparing an analysis of the medical evidence to send to Hill, he began to argue obsessively that the embalming process may have caused the congestion of Rice's lungs, assuming there was any congestion. Up until this point, his analysis had been that Dr Williams and the other doctors were lying or at least mistaken when they said they saw congestion. This had been the approach Tomlinson had taken a year earlier on the application for a new trial.

On 20 October Patrick wrote to Hill about his idea. 'The embalmer,' he wrote, 'could have reasonably produced, by the method of embalming employed by him, a post mortem artificial congestion of the lungs, simulating and easily mistaken for the "active, coextensive congestion of both lungs."'[1]

Milliken asked Hill to look into the new theory for the sake of his wife, Patrick's sister, and write back to him:

My wife is familiar with Mr. Patrick's latest theory, and this ex-bachelor has discovered that it is a pretty hard matter to satisfy a woman's demands when her brother is in Mr. Patrick's position. It won't take you very long to write a letter, but it will take me the balance of my natural existence to try to explain to my wife why her brother's latest theory could not be used in his defense.[2]

A 'waste of money' was Hill's response. The theory, he said, was the 'first thing that would occur to a first class physician.' Patrick's reply was that 'it would no more occur to a first class physician than the theory of gravitation occurred to scientists prior to Newton.' Even if the new evidence will not be admitted before the Court of Appeals, Patrick went on, 'much can be done by making the public know that the blood would be so forced to the lungs.' 'I am taking steps,' Patrick told Hill, 'to let the world understand and accept the proposition, that every embalmer knows of and practices the driving of blood into the lungs and taps the lungs and draws it off.'

Patrick had also written to Dr Kenneth Millican, who discussed the theory with some of his colleagues and concluded that Patrick was 'dead right.' Patrick then arranged for his friend, Samuel Bell Thomas, a graduate of the University of Texas and the Southwestern University Law School in Georgetown, Texas, to come to Sing Sing to discuss the matter. The thirty-five-year-old Thomas, who, it will be recalled, had arranged Patrick's wedding in the Tombs, was the secretary of the Medico-Legal

Society of New York.[3] On 15 November, Thomas saw Patrick and two days later the issue was made public at a regular meeting of the Medico-Legal Society at the Waldorf Astoria. 'The embalming of a body before rigor mortis sets in, without the withdrawal of any blood,' Thomas told the society, 'produces the same effect of congestion of the lungs as that produced on the lungs by vapor poisoning.'[4]

The president of the society, Clark Bell, appointed a committee to investigate the issue and report back to the group. The seventy-two-year-old Bell was a distinguished lawyer who had been the editor of the *Medico-Legal Journal* since 1883 and over the course of his career would serve as president of the society for sixteen years. He was the author of numerous books on medicolegal subjects.[5]

A meeting was arranged between Hill and Thomas in New York. Hill suggested that Thomas conduct some experiments, and Milliken authorized the expenditure of $1,000 for medical evidence.

In mid-December, Clark Bell appointed Dr Ashbel P. Grinnell, a specialist in medicolegal cases, as the chairman of the Special Committee. Thomas sought out the other members of the seven-member committee. Milliken refused to offer any direct compensation to the committee, writing to Thomas: 'I think it would be very unwise to have anything coming from the Medico-Legal Society to be tainted in any manner with partisanship ... it must come from them without any compensation from me and must be of their own free will and good faith.' The hypothetical questions submitted by Thomas to the committee were in fact prepared by Patrick.

Professor Howard S. Eckels from the School of Embalming of Philadelphia was the only embalmer on the committee. He claimed to have performed over ten thousand embalmings. The only other non-medical person on the committee was W.H. Francis, a former judge of the Federal District Court in New Jersey. Eckels wrote to Grinnell, the chairman, that as he had in his classroom 'several comparatively fresh cadavers,' he embalmed them through the brachial artery and he and his students observed the effect on the lungs and heart which he had exposed.[6] The experiment confirmed Patrick's theory.

The Medico-Legal Society met at the Waldorf-Astoria on Wednesday evening, 15 February 1905. District Attorney Jerome declined Clark Bell's invitation to attend. Professor Eckels read a paper to the effect that embalming by the Falcon process would produce the same conditions that were allegedly found in Rice at the autopsy. The committee adopted Patrick's theory and released a tentative report to the press: 'The committee is satisfied, after a review of all the evidence, that Rice died from old age, weak heart, etc., or, in other words, from the conditions embraced in Dr. Walker Curry's certificate of death, and on which the authorities allowed the body to be cremated.'[7] The next day, the headlines were strongly in favor of Patrick: 'Doctors Uphold Patrick Defense,' said the *World*; 'Patrick Is Innocent, Say Medico-legal Men,' stated the *New York Press*. 'I don't see how any doctor could have reached any other logical conclusion,' Patrick told the press, and Mrs Patrick said that 'it is the first step in the right direction' for her 'honest, good and brilliant' husband. Patrick, she added, was permitted to hold her hand through the bars.

Jerome was not impressed. He told the New York *American*: 'That committee report has no more bearing in the present status of the Patrick case than would the opinion of any sandwich man in the street. I haven't read it and do not propose to.'[8]

The following Monday morning, two more inmates of the death house were electrocuted: Frank Rimieri and Adolph Koenig. Governor Higgins had turned down their pleas for commutation the previous Friday. Rimieri, carrying a crucifix through the 'little door' leading to the death chamber, was declared dead at 5:50 a.m. Seventeen minutes later, Koenig, who had strangled a woman in Manhattan, was pronounced dead. Each was given two shocks of 1,820 volts at 8 amperes for 30 seconds.

Patrick requested that their bodies be embalmed and autopsies made to determine the effect of the embalming fluid on the lungs. The authorities turned down the request.[9]

# 74. The Court of Appeals

In December 1904, Hill completed his brief for the Court of Appeals. Patrick was pleased and wrote to him: 'I have received your brief. It is a strong document and insures a reversal.'[1]

The People's brief had been prepared by thirty-four-year-old Howard Gans, the deputy district attorney in charge of the appeals bureau.[2] A Harvard and New York Law School graduate, from a wealthy New York Jewish family, Gans was highly regarded by Jerome and in later years, when they had both left the district attorney's office, Gans often acted for Jerome. Gans was assisted by Judson S. Landon,[3] the author of *The Constitutional History and Government of the United States*.[4] A resident of Schenectady, the seventy-five-year-old lawyer had been a trial judge since 1873 and then in 1899 was appointed by the Republican governor of New York, Theodore Roosevelt, to the Court of Appeals. He served for two years on the court. All seven members of the Court of Appeals who would hear the Patrick appeal were colleagues of Landon when he served on the court. It was generally not – and apparently in the United States is still not – considered improper for an ex-judge to appear before his former colleagues.[5]

Patrick received a copy of the brief. The People's brief, Patrick wrote to Hill, is 'far stronger than the case [against me].'[6] Patrick also wrote an eleven-page letter to District Attorney Jerome, outlining the new medical evidence and telling Jerome that it was his duty to tell the Court of Appeals that he should be discharged:

Now I am asking no favors of you when I say that it is your official duty to go to the Court of Appeals and formally submit to them that what I have here set down is true; that you did not upon the trial produce sufficient evidence of wrongful death to warrant the submission of the case to the jury or to justify the conviction; that you have no such evidence now and under the circumstances cannot hope to have it; that under the law my motions to instruct the jury to acquit should have been granted, and that you now consent that the judgment of conviction be reversed and the defendant discharged. I think I am warranted in saying that if you do less you fail in your duty as an officer and as a man.

In February 1905, the disciplinary charges against Edgar Kohler were dismissed by the Bar Association and he immediately offered his services to Hill to assist with the appeal: 'command me in any way you think.' Patrick wanted the Kohler brothers and Tomlinson to participate in the appeal hearing and Tomlinson to share the oral argument with Hill. Indeed, Patrick had already written to Chief Judge Cullen to say that Tomlinson would be there. Milliken wrote Hill that their participation was up to him, 'provided they do not render me any bills for their services.' He clearly did not want Tomlinson, whom he described as a 'slippery citizen' and a 'windbag,' to take part in the appeal. It will be recalled that Tomlinson was at the time pursuing a suit against Milliken for his fee. In the end, neither Kohler nor Tomlinson went to Albany for the appeal.

The hearing was set for Tuesday, 14 March 1905. Patrick had written to Chief Judge Cullen, requesting that he be permitted personally to attend the hearing. On Saturday, 11 March, permission was granted, the first time it had ever been granted in a capital case in New York.[7] Hill, who had not previously known about the request, arranged for Tom-

linson to go to Sing Sing and try to talk Patrick out of attending. Patrick
at first agreed to remain in Sing Sing, but later changed his mind.

Early Tuesday morning, handcuffed to State Officer Jackson, Patrick
went to New York City and caught the New York Central's Empire
State Express, which arrived in Albany at 11:10 that morning. Apparently, nobody recognized the now beardless Patrick. He and Officer Jackson walked the quarter-mile to Superintendent Collins' office in the Capitol Building.

There, he met his mother, whom he had not seen in seven years,
his sister, May Milliken, and his two daughters, thirteen-year-old Lucille
and ten-year-old Lillian. His father had died a year earlier. The family
had traveled from St Louis the previous day, and had planned to visit
Patrick in Sing Sing, after seeing the governor of New York and getting
his permission for the children to see their father in the reception room
of the prison rather than in the death house. The family had not expected
that Patrick would be in Albany.[8]

When Hill found out that Patrick was in Albany, he dispatched
Thomas to instruct Patrick to return immediately to Sing Sing, but Patrick refused to leave. After lunch with his family at the Ten Eyck Hotel
(now the site of the Albany Hilton Hotel), where they were staying,
he was escorted back to the Capitol Building to hear Hill's opening
argument.

The seven black-robed judges entered the courtroom on the third floor
of the State Capitol Building at two o'clock. (The Court of Appeals
remained in the Capitol Building until 1916, when the paneling and
other furnishings of the courtroom were moved to the present structure,
the State Hall, originally erected in 1842.)[9] Patrick, 'neatly dressed in
a well-fitting coat of dark blue with a white vest,' sat at the rear of
the lawyers' enclosure with his sister and mother on each side of him
and his daughter Lillian on his knee. His wife did not arrive in Albany
until the evening. The courtroom was full; indeed, many senators, as-
semblymen, and government servants who had come to hear a famous
advocate in a famous case were turned away.

As a major political figure in New York for decades, Hill had some
involvement with each member of the panel of seven judges. In some
cases, he had initially appointed them to the bench to fill a vacancy
or supported their election; in other cases, he had opposed their selection.
We have already seen that several months earlier he had opposed the
selection of Chief Judge Edgar Cullen as the chief judge to replace Parker

who was running for president. The sixty-two-year-old Cullen,[10] who had been a colonel in the Civil War, had been a Supreme Court justice in Brooklyn from 1880 and was appointed to the Court of Appeals in 1900. Would he hold a grudge against Hill for opposing his appointment as chief judge? What role would be played by Denis O'Brien, a fellow Democrat and a very close friend of Hill,[11] who had been the attorney-general of New York from 1884 to 1888 while Hill was governor and was elected a judge of the Court of Appeals in 1890 with Hill's support?[12] Or John Clinton Gray, also a Democrat, who had been appointed by Hill to the Court of Appeals in 1888?[13] The private papers of the members of the court who sat on the appeal have never been made public; and so there is no way of knowing whether their prior relationship with Hill affected the hearing.

Hill argued that there was no reliable evidence that a murder had been committed. Rice, he said, died a natural death and Jones' testimony was 'unworthy of belief.' The congestion of the lungs, he went on, was not caused by chloroform, but, as the Medical-Legal Society had shown, by the embalming fluid. The coroner's physicians were not 'disinterested public officials,' as they appeared to the jury to be. Further, the trial judge should have granted a new trial on the basis of newly discovered evidence. Finally, 'the conduct of the court below was such that a fair and impartial trial was not given the defendant.'[14]

At the end of the day's hearing, Patrick tried to approach Hill, whom he had never in fact met, to congratulate him on his presentation. Before Patrick could speak to him, Hill had left the courtroom, in what was probably accurately reported by the press the next day as a 'direct snub.'

Patrick wanted to stay with his guard in the Ten Eyck Hotel that evening, but Chief Judge Cullen ordered that he be taken to the Albany Jail on the outskirts of the city. Perhaps the fact that many of the judges of the Court of Appeals resided in the Ten Eyck influenced Cullen's decision.

The following day, Hill concluded his argument and Howard Gans commenced his presentation of the case for the People. Patrick's two children were taken out of the courtroom during this part of the proceedings. The press reported that they played with the revolving door at the State Street entrance to the Capitol Building. 'We're playing merry-go-round,' the younger daughter told the reporters.

The hearing concluded with a submission by Judge Landon on Thursday afternoon. Patrick finally had the chance to meet and congratulate

Hill. He then said good-bye to his family – the shackles were taken off for the last embrace – and returned to Sing Sing on the 7:45 train that evening.

He told Warden Johnson, who met him at the railway station at Ossining, that he was pleased with the appeal. The New York *American* reported from Albany: 'there is hardly a lawyer here tonight who has heard the arguments who does not believe Patrick will have a new trial.'[15]

# 75. Judgment of the Court of Appeals

On 9 June 1905, three months after the hearing concluded, the Court of Appeals announced that the murder conviction had been upheld by a vote of four to three. The majority judgment was written by Judge John Gray and the dissenting judgment by Judge Denis O'Brien. A recent historian of the New York Court of Appeals remarked on the 'extraordinary length' of the judgments,[1] which occupy ninety-one pages of the New York law reports.[2]

Judge Gray, who was joined by Judges Edward Bartlett, Albert Haight, and William Werner, stated that the jury reached a 'just conclusion': 'A careful reading of this record and a grave consideration of the matters of proof have convinced me that the jury reached a just conclusion, and that there is no warrant for, nor do the interests of justice demand, our interference with the judgment.'[3] After a long recitation of the evidence, Judge Gray concluded that there was ample evidence to corroborate Jones' testimony. 'Corroborative evidence is sufficient,' he ruled, 'if it tends to connect the defendant with the commission of the crime.'[4]

Goff's charge to the jury was 'absolutely fair in its statement of facts and in its instructions as to the rules of law,' and, he went on, the jury properly brought in a verdict of guilty: 'The jury rendered a verdict of guilty as charged, and, in my opinion, no other verdict could have been reached, upon a dispassionate and intelligent consideration of the evidence.'[5] Further, it was not improper for Jones to testify that he told his counsel, House, when Patrick was present, the same story about chloroform that he later told the district attorney: 'the privilege is the client's.'[6] Gray conceded that 'some of the rulings of the recorder were erroneous,' but none, he said, 'was of sufficient gravity to justify us in reversing the judgment of conviction. The evidence conclusively established the defendant's guilt, and led to the verdict rendered,' and thus under the 'harmless error' provision of the New York Code of Criminal Procedure[7] the errors did not justify a new trial. Finally, the evidence on the application for a new trial was not 'newly discovered evidence': it was either in the knowledge of counsel or 'could have been acquired by use of the opportunities afforded.'[8]

O'Brien's strong dissent argued that there was no proof that murder had been committed: 'The fact, if it is a fact, that the defendant hoped he would die, and was prepared to seize his vast estate by forgery and fraud if he should die, has no bearing upon the question which over-reaches all others – whether he actually died a violent death.'[9] Did Jones kill Rice? No one can ever know, O'Brien stated, even assuming Jones was telling the truth:

Jones was gone about 40 minutes, and on his return Mr. Rice was lying in the same position as before. He had not moved a muscle, so far as Jones observed. Jones believed he was alive, but he could not swear that he was alive. He saw no sign of life. He did not see him move or breathe, and did not know but what he was then dead. Believing that he was alive, he tried to kill him. With murder in his heart, he did all he could to compass his death; but he did not know, and no one ever can know, whether he acted upon a living man or upon a corpse.

But, he went on, is Jones to be believed? After reciting the evidence connected with chloroform, O'Brien stated: 'The use of that drug as the agency of death occurred to no one until Jones had made his fourth and last confession, after he had recanted three others as they were successively demonstrated to be false.'[10] The autopsy was criticized as being 'careless' and the coroner's physicians' testimony was 'in the expectation of receiving extravagant compensation.'

'The case,' O'Brien said, 'was tried in an atmosphere charged with necessity of making the defendant a victim in order to defeat his claim to an estate worth millions upon millions.' Jones testified under a promise of immunity: 'No fair mind can reach any conclusion from these facts except that this accomplice and author of the crime testified under a promise of immunity.'[11] O'Brien concluded his analysis of this aspect of the case by stating:

So we have a case where the three principal witnesses for the people – clearly the witnesses that produced the conviction – were testifying at the trial for great prizes and great rewards. The reward which Jones expected and received was nothing else than his life, and what will not a man give for that? The two physicians testified with the expectation of receiving large rewards in money, and they were not disappointed.

Further, O'Brien held, Patrick did not have 'a fair and impartial trial ... the rules of evidence in criminal cases were ignored or violated at the trial to the prejudice of the accused.'[12] Evidence of Jones' 'feigned or unsuccessful attempt at suicide' should have been excluded as unduly prejudicial to the accused; one of the medical experts for the defense, Dr Lee, should have been permitted to answer a hypothetical question as framed; the morgue attendant, Aurich, should have been permitted to say that the coroner's physicians said after the autopsy that Rice died a natural death; Dr Kenneth Millican should have been permitted to testify about his search of the medical literature concerning chloroform; Jones' statement to House should have been excluded; and so on. Errors, he said, are conceded. They are not 'harmless' within the meaning of the statute:

We are deciding cases at almost every term and reversing convictions for errors of law that do not compare in importance with those that I have attempted to point out. Indeed, it can be safely asserted that in all the records of this court no case can be found where a conviction for a capital offense has been sustained in the face of such objections as this case presents.[13]

A new trial, he concluded, dissenting, should therefore be granted. Irving Vann concurred, and Chief Judge Cullen agreed that a number of serious errors had been made by Goff at the trial which warranted a new trial. But the majority of the court held otherwise.

Warden Addison Johnson came to Patrick's cell the next morning with the news. Patrick was eating breakfast:

'Well, Warden, any news from Albany?'
'No official news, but the newspapers print the news this morning.'
'How is it?'
'It is against you.'
'Impossible.'[14]

That afternoon Mrs Patrick and Edgar Kohler traveled up to Sing Sing to discuss the judgment with Patrick.

The Court of Appeals had resentenced Patrick to die during the week beginning 7 August. 'I shall never go to the electric chair,' Patrick told the press; 'I shall carry the case to the United States Supreme Court.'

Patrick, however, was worried that the governor would commute his sentence to life imprisonment. 'Any application to you to lessen the penalty adjudged me will be without my authority,' Patrick wrote to Governor Higgins: 'I will accept no compromise.' A number of possible options open to Patrick were spelled out in his letter to the governor: a petition for reargument to the Court of Appeals; an appeal to the federal courts; a motion for a new trial; the appointment of a medical commission to examine new evidence; and an application for 'full pardon on proof of innocence.' A commutation was not one of the options mentioned.[15]

That summer, three more inmates on death row were put to death. James Breen and Charles Jackson were executed one after the other on Monday, 17 July. Breen had requested that his body be embalmed and then an autopsy performed to help Patrick. The authorities, however, again refused the request.

# 76. Reargument

Immediately after receiving word of the judgment of the Court of Appeals, Hill announced that he would seek a reargument from the court. That weekend, Milliken and Thomas went to Albany to discuss strategy with Hill.

Patrick felt excluded from the deliberations. He wrote to Hill that he had ideas for the reargument, noting that Justice O'Brien clearly indicated that he had been denied 'due process of law.' 'The motion for rehearing,' he told Hill, 'ought to raise all these Federal questions as a basis for an appeal to the U.S. Supreme Court.' Could Hill come to Sing Sing? 'I think we ought to have a conference,' Patrick wrote; 'I cannot come to you, so you should come to see me.'[1]

'I shall be unable to visit you at Sing Sing for consultation,' Hill replied: 'I do not see that any consultation is necessary at the present time. Everything is being done for the protection of your rights permitted by the law.' Patrick was not satisfied with the arrangement. 'It is not satisfactory,' he replied; 'I would like to see your petition for rehearing before you file it.' Any counsel representing him would, Patrick wrote, 'have to respect *my direction and control*,' underlining the words 'my direction and control.' 'If you ignore me,' he warned Hill, 'I shall likewise ignore you ... and shall proceed with my campaign independently of you, in person and with such attorneys as I can secure and such means as I can command.'

'My decision,' Patrick wrote, 'is unalterable.' Nevertheless, several days later, after Thomas had visited Sing Sing to warn Patrick that Hill might leave the case, Patrick wrote to Hill expressing confidence in him: 'I believe you can retrieve the situation and I want you to do it.' But Patrick still wanted to be consulted. He did not hear further from Hill and wrote to him again at the end of June: 'you are instructed not to appear on my personal behalf in any criminal case or proceedings, without express authority from me.' Milliken and other members of the family chastised Patrick, saying that they would not pay for any counsel except Hill. 'Keep your mouth shut and your pen still,' Milliken wrote him.

The execution date of 7 August was fast approaching. Milliken wrote to Hill that something had to be done: 'My wife is very anxious to have you get a stay of execution; she is worrying considerable about that.'[2]

On 20 July, Hill filed a motion for reargument, returnable on 2 October 1905, the day the Court of Appeals would recommence sitting. On Saturday, 22 July, Hill and Edgar Kohler went to Watertown, New York, and obtained a stay of execution pending the reargument from the dissenting judge, Denis O'Brien. Kohler had been engaged to assist Hill, with a retainer from Milliken of $1,000.

The brief for the reargument raised basically the same legal points dealt with on the appeal, but added a new dimension. Judge Gray, who wrote the majority judgment, should not have participated in the appeal, the brief argued, because his son, Henry Gray, had participated as an assistant DA in the earlier motion for a new trial before Judge Goff. Hill had heard rumors that a month before the judgment of the Court of Appeals was released, the DA's office in New York was aware that Judge Gray was writing an opinion against Patrick. The attack on Judge Gray was a strong one. Kohler tried to get Hill to modify the brief: 'I note three or four places which I would like to call to your attention as perhaps unduly strong in the tone of criticism of Judge Gray and for that reason maladroit and impolitic.'

Howard Gans took the unusual step of writing to Chief Judge Cullen (with a copy to Hill) warning the court about Hill's brief, which 'attempts to reflect invidiously upon the judicial conduct of a member of the Court of Appeals.' Gans warned that when the briefs are made public 'it will afford an opportunity for sensational newspaper writers to indulge in a fling at the court or its members with impunity,' without the dangers of being held in contempt of court. 'My purpose in writing,' Gans said, 'is, therefore, that you should be apprized of the facts in advance in order that you may determine whether any action on the part of the Court is advisable.'

There is nothing in any of the files to indicate that Chief Judge Cullen attempted to contact Hill. On 2 October, the briefs were made public and the attack on Judge Gray was given great prominence by the press. 'The new pleading,' the *Times* stated, 'was as remarkable as any of the phases which hitherto have made this case the most extraordinary in the criminal history of this State.'[3]

The People's brief was filed by Howard Gans. The seventy-five-year-old ex-judge Landon, who had been associated with Gans on the appeal and had worked on the People's brief against a reargument, had died in early September. The People's brief stated that 'the suggestion that Judge Gray violated the proprieties in taking part in this case is as contemptible as it is impudent.'

On 27 October, without hearing oral argument, the Court of Appeals denied the motion for a reargument. Chief Judge Cullen gave the judgment for all the members of the panel except Judge O'Brien, who was said to be absent. Cullen held that the propriety of Judge Gray sitting on the case was for him alone to decide, adding:

The objection is now presented not to Judge Gray alone, but to the whole court, and it is only just to our associate that we should express our views on the subject. Many and great judges have allowed their relatives to practice before them; others have declined to hear cases in which near relatives appeared as counsel; but we have never heard of a judge refusing to sit in any case because at some earlier period his relative had taken part in the legal proceedings in the cause ... Mr. Gray in no way appeared in the preparation or in the argument of the appeal.[4]

Whether a similar result would be reached today is not clear. The American Bar Association's 1990 Model Code of Judicial Conduct provides that 'a judge shall disqualify himself or herself in a proceeding in which the judge's impartiality might reasonably be questioned,' including 'instances where ... a person within the third degree of relationship ... is acting as a lawyer in the proceeding.'[5] Would Justice Gray's son's involvement come within the present rule? Probably, yes.

Hill was censured by the court for waiting until the Court of Appeals had decided the case before objecting to Judge Gray sitting and added that 'there must at some point be an end of the litigation.'

Hill, however, was unrepentant and told the press: 'With all due respect to the learned Court of Appeals I still insist that Judge Gray was disqualified from sitting in the Patrick case ... These and numerous Federal questions involved in this remarkable case the defence hopes to present to the Supreme Court of the United States for final decision.'

# 77. Further Steps

Both Hill and Kohler were pleased with one aspect of the Court of Appeals' reasons for disallowing a reargument: the language of the judgment made it easier to appeal to the federal courts. The Court of Appeals had stated: 'We have examined with care the elaborate brief filed by appellant's counsel and find no objection discussed therein that was not considered by the court before it decided the appeal.'[1] The 164-page 'elaborate brief' had deliberately included a number of 'due process' and other federal issues. The federal courts, then and now, would only intervene in a state prosecution if there was a violation of federal law or the federal constitution, particularly in this case the 'due process' provision of the Fourteenth Amendment.

Hill wrote to Kohler: 'they must have considered all our Federal points contained in our motion for reargument which were not contained in our original brief. For this much thanks.'[2] In a letter to Hill that crossed with Hill's letter to him, Kohler took the same approach: 'In view of Judge Cullen's sweeping statement that every objection urged by us on the re-argument had been considered by the Court prior to its decision, I am inclined to believe that the record even in its present form will permit of the suing out of a writ of error to the Supreme Court.' In early November, Milliken had authorized Kohler to go ahead with an appeal to the US Supreme Court and sent him an additional $1,000 fee. Kohler brought a further application to the New York Court of Appeals to amend the formal documents (the remittitur) so that the federal 'due process' issue would be more clearly on the record, but the court refused the motion. Justice O'Brien, however, again dissented.

Ever since the Court of Appeals decision in June, Milliken and Hill had been active in paving the way for new proceedings or for a pardon. In July, Milliken, with Hill's approval, had five thousand copies of Judge O'Brien's dissent printed and mailed from New York City to every lawyer in the state. Milliken also ensured that Patrick's Masonic Lodge dues had been paid. A few weeks later, a Mason from Houston wrote to Hill claiming that he had evidence that the prosecution had 'bought' one of the jurymen. 'If you are a Mason,' he wrote, 'you will more fully understand why I should take any interest in Mr. Patrick's case.'[3]

Milliken did not want to leave any stone unturned. 'We must not lose any opportunity that presents itself,' Milliken wrote, 'to do all we can to try and avoid the electrocution of Albert. It will be a disgrace that none of us want handed down to our children.'[4] This was stated in a letter to a friend of Milliken's in New York, B. Brooks, who was the general superintendent of Western Union. In the letter – a copy of which was sent to Hill – Milliken wanted Brooks to arrange to have a lawyer friend of Brooks' privately speak to one of the judges of the Court of Appeals to tell him that the district attorney's office knew that Judge Gray was going to write the opinion against Patrick. The copy of the letter contains blanks for some of the names and does not specifically refer to the judge, although later correspondence shows that the intended recipient was Justice Werner, who had voted with the majority. The letter states in part:

During our brief stay in Albany we had a very interesting interview with Sen. Hill. He is extremely anxious for you to have Mr. _____ see his friend, the Judge, as soon as possible ... We think it should be shown that the District Attorney's office was expecting Judge Gray to write that opinion long before it came out. If we could furnish this proof to other members of the Bench, it might do some good.

As it turned out, Brooks refused to participate in the scheme. He was a distant relative of Patrick's and did not want anyone to know this.

Hill's files also contain a number of letters indicating that newspaper articles were probably being planted in order to influence the courts. Just prior to the Court of Appeals hearing, for example, Milliken sent Hill a favorable editorial from the *Salt Lake Telegram* and suggested that Hill 'get this reproduced in one of your Albany papers, which doubtless would reach the eyes of the Judges of the Court of Appeals.'[5] And after the Court of Appeals judgment, Milliken's Denver lawyer, Waldron, sent Milliken a letter which was passed on to Hill, stating: 'If you or Hill would like to have any article he may write published in the *Denver Republican* as coming from a western lawyer send me the copy and I will see that it is published without delay.'[6] The article would then be reproduced in one of the Albany papers. It is not known whether these two suggestions were acted upon. The lack of protest by Hill suggests that these tactics were not uncommon.

Just as Milliken and Hill attempted to stir up favorable opinion in legal circles, they attempted to do so in the medical field. Shortly after the Court of Appeals' original decision, Dr Kenneth Millican, the editor of the *St. Louis Medical Review*, and Clark Bell, the president of the Medico-Legal Society, met with Hill in Albany. J.T. Milliken wrote to Hill: 'I want Dr. Millican to interest some of his medical friends in New York City, where he formerly lived, to start an agitation in medical circles down there as to the unjust and unscientific testimony of Williams and Donlin.'[7] Shortly after this meeting, Dr Millican published an article on the case in the *St. Louis Medical Review* and Clark Bell published a lengthy analysis in the *Medico-Legal Journal*.[8] The 'agitation in medical circles' had begun.

A number of medical experiments were conducted. Former coroner's physician Albert Weston, for example, conducted embalming experiments at Hill's request and concluded that 'beyond question' embalming fluid enters the lungs.[9] This issue had been ignored by the Court of Appeals. Even O'Brien did not discuss it – to Patrick's great disappointment.

Other experts were retained by Hill, such as Dr Grinnell, the chairman of the earlier special Medico-Legal committee, Professor Howard Eckels from Philadelphia, who had conducted experiments for the committee on whether the embalming fluid could have entered the lungs, and Dr Joseph Bryant, the president of the Medical Society of the State of New York. Hill obtained other experts not formerly connected with the case: Dr Carl Barnes, the head of Barnes School of Anatomy, Sanitary Science and Embalming in Chicago; Dr George Biggs, a pathologist at New York Hospital; and many more. Dr Biggs wrote to Hill that 'Falcon embalming fluid injected as described does most emphatically reach the lungs.'[10]

Dr Donlin, who had given evidence for the prosecution at the trial that the embalming fluid could not reach the lungs, was now having second thoughts. He went to see Robert Moore, Patrick's counsel at trial, to ask 'if there would be any ethical impropriety in him holding an autopsy, and if he found ... the same conditions that were found by the Medico-Legal Society's experts, for him to make an affidavit setting forth what he had discovered and giving an opinion that would reverse his testimony in the Patrick trial.' Moore told him that not only would there be no impropriety, but 'it was his duty to do it.'[11]

# 78. The Texas Trail

Milliken attempted to follow Jones' trail in Texas. Leonidas E. Hill from Denver, who had married another of Patrick's sisters, spent June and July 1905 in Texas trying to locate Jones. He reported his progress to Milliken, who passed the letters on to Senator Hill.

Leonidas Hill first visited some distant relatives of Rice's in Waco, Texas, to get what information he could 'out of the enemy's camp.'[1] This proved useless. He then picked up Jones' trail through a lawyer acquaintance in Houston, Judge J.A. Gillette, who 'is the old friend, playmate and attorney of Jones' brother and knows the whole family.' Gillette, who was promised '$10 per day for his time and a bonus ... if he gets anything good in the way of affidavits,' tried to locate Jones in Goose Creek, where he had been living. Leonidas Hill reported that they were unsuccessful:

Came to Houston to get Gillett's report of what he did and saw and heard down about Goose Creek. It amounts to little so far – except that Jones seduced the maiden daughter of one William Wright. He was ostracised by society around his home, and only went to two houses besides his father's and sister's – those two families were Geo and Bill Wright's. Jones' own brother-in-law told Gillett about Jones seducing the girl and hiding out since to avoid parental ire – as they claim. The girl is to bear her young Jones bastard in 30 or 60 days, if this report is to be credited and I suppose it is as it came from Jones' own father and mother to the son-in-law.[2]

Milliken was warned by Leonidas Hill not to say anything about the seduction because 'we could never prove the truth of this matter and if we gave the circumstances publicity ... there are plenty who would call on you to prove or pay.' Moreover, he went on, the seduced girl's father is trying to get Jones to marry the girl and is unlikely to be cooperative.

Another person that Leonidas Hill contacted in Houston was a lawyer, Norman G. Kittrell, Jr. At one point, Leonidas Hill went to see Kittrell's father and found him with Captain James A. Baker. Leonidas Hill reported the occurrence to Milliken:

I went up to the Dist. Court yesterday to see Judge Kittrell, father of the one I'm seeing, and found him and Baker engaged in a long confidential talk. I mentioned this to young Kittrell and he said, 'Yes, Mr. Baker took dinner at our house today.'

Of course this may be only a coincidence but it is also possible that some one tipped it off to Baker ... Possibly a trap is being laid for you to catch you buying testimony. That is what I'm afraid of all the time – you know what they did to Kohler! They would be pleased to find an indictment against you!

In the end, Leonidas Hill returned from Texas empty-handed. 'He is a quitter,' Milliken wrote Senator Hill: 'I could have done much better myself.'[3] Milliken was convinced that Baker had spirited Jones away and wrote to Hill: 'Baker is afraid for Jones to be seen around his haunts at the present time. If Baker is hiding him out, there is a strong presumption that perhaps he has been talking and that Baker was afraid that he would talk more, hence, he gets him away until after Patrick will have been electrocuted.'

Milliken had more success with another approach he took regarding the Texas evidence. He got Charles Tinsley, a businessman from Texas who had been a friend of Rice's, now living in St Louis, to locate persons to whom Jones had talked about the case. Tinsley had first contacted Milliken to say that back in 1892, when he was the manager of the Houston Cemetery Company, Rice told him that he wanted to be cremated. Tinsley had also seen Rice in New York in 1900, and Rice had told him about 'a young lawyer there in New York from Texas' who was trying to settle the Holt litigation for $250,000.[4] This, of course, supported Patrick's story.

Tinsley went to Texas in June 1905 to see what he could find out. Leonidas Hill, who was there at the same time, was apparently not told of this second front. Contact was made with a Houston lawyer, Judge Railley, who had formerly been a justice of the peace in Houston. Milliken reported to Senator Hill:

Tinsley met Judge Railley here along about the first of this month, and he told Tinsley that if I would give him a fee of $1,000 that he would either get me an affidavit from Jones denying the murder of Mr. Rice, or that he would get Jones to admit in the presence of Railley and two other persons that he swore falsely against Patrick. I told Tinsley that I would not give a cent to Jones to make such an affidavit, but that if Railley wished to enter my employ as an attorney and could deliver to me such documents either from Jones, or three reliable trustworthy people, that I would give Railley a $1,000 fee for his services provided the three parties to whom Jones made the statement were reputable and would appear in Court in New York if necessary and testify that Jones made the statement.[5]

Again, Jones could not be found. Railley wrote to Tinsley that he and others had spent a week looking for him: 'I have searched every nook and corner. My helpers have done the same. He must have heard something and is in retirement for the present ... I think I know where he is but it will be impossible without a search warrant to enter the place.' But, Railley went on to say, 'I can however get you satisfactory affidavits from (3) three unimpeachable witnesses that Jones confessed perjury to clear himself and was promised immunity for so doing.' Another $1,500 on top of the $1,000 initially offered by Milliken was demanded: 'This I consider dirt cheap for what I get you.'

Tinsley advised Milliken either to come to Texas himself or instruct his bank to arrange for the money to be given to him. Tinsley would personally examine the witnesses and, he told Milliken, 'if I have found that his witnesses are "first class" I shall give it [the money] to them.'

Three affidavits were sworn by persons who claimed that Jones had told them that he had lied on the witness stand to save himself. The witnesses, Fayette Lee, James Riordon, and Joe Jordan, were prepared to come to New York to give evidence to this effect. Joe Jordan, a fisherman, for example, swore that he met Jones at Morgan's Point, near Galveston, a few months earlier and in conversation Jones had told him: 'I made a statement to them in New York stating that Patrick was the one to blame for all the trouble. Patrick had nothing to do with the death of William M. Rice and did not advise me to do anything or to injure old man Rice in any way and I hope Mr. Patrick will come out all O.K. of his trouble as he does not deserve to be punished.' Jones told Jordan why he put the blame on Patrick: 'They threatened to electrocute me and I thought if they did not do that they would send me to the penitentiary for life; consequently the blame was laid on A.T. Patrick by me in order to save my own life.' We will hear more of Joe Jordan later.

Judge Railley and Tinsley personally brought the affidavits to Milliken in St Louis. He immediately arranged for them to see Senator Hill in Albany, wiring Hill: 'Railley and Tinsley be at your office early Monday morning with important papers. Please make it convenient to see them so they can return west same day.' Hill saw them and took possession of their affidavits. Hill appeared impressed. A month later, four more affidavits were brought to Hill in Albany by Judge Railley. Another motion for a new trial now appeared to be a strong possibility.

For some time, Milliken had been trying to get information from Alexander Stanbery, the Texan who was a friend of Jones and had been Rice's valet before Jones took the job. Milliken had met him in New York prior to Patrick's trial, but at the time Stanbery was unhelpful. A lawyer representing some of Rice's relatives who would profit if the 1896 will was defeated alerted Patrick's lawyers that Stanbery had important information about Jones, obtained when they roomed together after Jones had returned to Texas from New York. 'I know Stanbery,' Milliken wrote Hill, 'and I understand he is in the army at San Francisco; I am going out west on my vacation, and if Stanbery is at Frisco I will find him, and if he knows anything I will get it out of him.'

Milliken found Stanbery stationed at Alcatraz Island and reported the meeting to Hill:

He swears that Jones came to see him at the Spindle Top oil fields in August 1902 and told him that ... the reason he told so many lies was 1st to save himself and 2nd to prevent any one from believing him but that the d__m fool jury believed him notwithstanding the manner in which he perjured himself, that Baker put him up to sticking Albert for the murder of Rice notwithstanding that Rice died a natural death.

Milliken went on to say that Jones told Stanbery that 'if he was sure that he would get off with a light sentence for perjury that he would go back to New York and tell the truth.' Stanbery claimed that Jones showed him 'a roll of money.' 'This fellow Stanbery,' Milliken wrote, 'strikes me as a man who is telling the truth for the truth's sake.'

In typical Milliken fashion, arrangements were made to have Hearst's San Francisco *Examiner* 'discover' Stanbery in San Francisco and 'wire a long account of his testimony to Hearst's N.Y. paper.' Milliken reminded Hill that 'Hearst hated Jerome.' Stanbery sailed for the Philippines on 5 October.

# 79. Resentencing

Addison Johnson, the warden of Sing Sing, swore an affidavit that he knew of no legal reason why Patrick should not now be executed, and in mid-November 1905, Jerome gave notice that he was applying to the

Supreme Court of New York to have Patrick resentenced.[1] Why a resentencing was required is not clear. Perhaps the Court of Appeal had
inadvertently forgotten to set a new date for the execution when it rejected the motion for reargument.

A few weeks earlier, Jerome had been reelected as district attorney
of New York City. When it was announced over the summer that he
was going to seek reelection as an independent candidate, Milliken wrote
to Hill offering to contribute to the campaign of anyone opposing Jerome:
'I see that Jerome is going to run "Independent"; that fellow is a fool;
he will be the worst beat man that ever ran on an independent ticket.
He is willing to sacrifice everybody else's interest so he can step up
on their dead bodies and reputation to office and his own aggrandize-
ment.'[2] Milliken went on to say: 'I am willing to contribute to the campaign fund (any campaign fund) that will transport Jerome "up Salt
River," the further the better.' Unfortunately for Patrick's interests, the
Republican candidate, Charles Flammer, was a nonentity and the Democratic Tammany Hall candidate was none other than James Osborne,
the vigorous prosecutor of Patrick at the trial, who was now in private
practice. Jerome accused his friend Osborne of being 'a house-broken
pup feeding out of the hands of the Tammany leaders,' but Osborne
replied that if he was a 'pup,' 'why did he reappoint me in 1901? Why
did he entrust me with the complete charge and control of the most
important cases in his office?'[3] On 8 November, the results showed that
Jerome had received 107,718 votes and Osborne 104,193.[4]

The resentencing motion came on for hearing before Judge Stover
in the Manhattan County Court House on Wednesday, 6 December.
Jerome, Garvan, and three other assistants appeared for the People. Edgar
Kohler and Thomas represented Patrick. David Hill had become ill several weeks earlier and could not appear. This illness would effectively
end his legal career.

Word spread that Patrick would be appearing in person, an unusual
procedure in such a case. The press carefully covered his movements.
Leaving Ossining on the 12:07 train, he arrived at Grand Central Station,
wearing a new black overcoat, a black bow tie, and a black derby hat,
shortly after 1:00. A large crowd of curious onlookers were at the station
when he arrived, shackled to Detective Jackson and accompanied by
Warden Johnson. Many went with him into the subway entrance at 42nd
Street and Madison Avenue for the trip to the County Court House
beside the City Hall. It was Patrick's first trip on the newly constructed
subway. The press reported that there were 'several thousand' waiting

at the City Hall and at the Court House to catch a glimpse of the famous prisoner.[5]

Judge Stover ruled that the resentencing should be done at the Criminal Court Building, and arrangements were made to have Judge Rogers hear the case later that afternoon.

Jerome opened the proceedings before Judge Rogers with a history of the case and asked that Patrick be again resentenced to death. Kohler replied that only the Court of Appeals or the trial judge had this power. Rogers was about to rule on the question when Patrick intervened: 'Before your Honor rules, I have some legal reasons to present to show why proofs should be admitted to show that sentence should not be passed at this time.' 'If your Honor please, I should like a few minutes to consult with my client,' the surprised Kohler said.

After a brief conversation with his lawyer, Patrick addressed the court:

The judgment, I know, is not reviewable – but it may be set aside if it be proved to have been procured fraudulently. That proof I am ready to furnish. Will your Honor please consider one proposition: Men have been convicted of murder and executed, and then the person supposed to have been murdered turned up alive. A case of this very kind occurred in Tennessee only two years ago. Suppose the man said to have been murdered in this case were to be produced in court here, would you hesitate to disregard the decision of the Court of Appeals?[6]

The thought that Rice might appear in court in person caused a stir in the courtroom.

I am not going to claim that Rice is not dead. The question is, Was he ever killed? I have proof positive that he was not. That proof was in the hands of the District Attorney who first sought my conviction. The evidence proffered to the effect that Rice was killed was, in fact, false, fraudulent, and known to be so by the then District Attorney. I am ready to produce witnesses here to prove this. If you act on this, your action will not be a review of the higher court's decision – it will be the entertainment of an independent suit brought in a court of original jurisdiction.

'The scene,' the *World* reported, 'was the most dramatic ever witnessed in the court.' The argument was, however, to no avail and Judge Rogers sentenced Patrick to be executed 'during the week beginning January 22, 1906, according to the manner prescribed by law.' 'To which,' Patrick added calmly, 'the defendant excepts on the ground that the action of the Court is contrary to the Fourteenth Amendment of the Constitution of the United States, providing that no citizen shall be deprived of his life or liberty without due process of law.'[7]

Patrick returned to Sing Sing at 7:30 that evening, telling the press: 'If the worst comes to the worst – I will make no trouble. But the worst has not yet come. My limbs are not yet shackled to the death chair. All that I ask is a square deal, and, by George, I'm going to have it. I will be back.'[8]

# PART SIX
# Further Steps

Governor's Room, Capitol Building, Albany: Albany Institute of History and Art, McKinney Library Photograph Collection.

Frank Higgins, undated, but probably while New York governor, 1905-6: New York State Library, Albany.

Charles Evans Hughes, later chief justice of the United States, undated, but probably while New York governor, 1907-10: New York State Library, Albany.

The United States Supreme Court, 1907: Chief Justice Fuller in center; Justice Day far left rear. Collection of the Supreme Court of the United States.

Federal Building in Manhattan at Broadway and Park Row, about 1900, since destroyed, containing the post office and the US District and Circuit Courts.

Above: Judge John W. Goff as
Davenport saw him: New York
*Journal*, 28 January 1902.

Right: Dr Hamilton Williams,
coroner's physician: New York
*World*, 28 January 1902.

Defense Counsel William Olcott and some Texas witnesses: New York *Herald*,
20 February 1906.

William Travers Jerome, district attorney, New York City, 1902–9, undated.

Ernest W. Huffcut, dean of the Cornell Law School, about 1905: Rare and Manuscript Collections, Carl A. Kroch Library, Cornell University.

# 80. Another Stay

Public opinion was slowly moving in favor of Patrick. The New York *Times*, for example, published an editorial entitled 'Sympathy for a Fighter,' stating that 'when brought here on Wednesday for the resentence that may or may not be his last, Patrick so carried himself when before his Judge as to wake something of admiration and sympathy from all who saw the remarkable scene.'[1] The *Houston Post* reported: 'public sentiment here in New York has to a large extent, undergone a change in regard to Patrick.'[2] And Justice Michael Hirschberg of the Appellate Division of the New York Supreme Court gave a speech, stating: '[We have] seen sentiment change from irritable impatience at the failure to execute him to a grave doubt as to whether he should be executed at all.'[3]

Patrick sent a petition to Governor Higgins in early December 1905 asking for a stay of execution and for an order taking him out of solitary confinement and allowing him to leave prison under escort during business hours 'to enable him personally to prepare and bring further proceedings.' 'The present petition is denied,' the governor stated, 'but without prejudice to an application for Executive clemency.'[4]

An application for a stay of execution to Justice Rogers of the New York Supreme Court was then brought by Edgar Kohler later in December. This was also turned down. In the course of an exchange between Kohler and Jerome, the district attorney stated: 'Look here, Kohler, I had you once where I could have had you disbarred. I let up on you because your friends promised to place you in a sanatorium.' Kohler broke in protesting and beating the table with his fist. The judge ordered him to sit down.

'No', cried Kohler, 'I am an officer of this court, and I demand to be heard.'

'Well, I am Justice of this court,' the Judge said, 'and you must obey my order.'

Kohler continued to object and the judge stated: 'sit down or I'll put you in charge of a court officer.' The lawyer grabbed his hat and coat and walked noisily out of the courtroom.[5]

Kohler wrote to Hill that evening that he would 'take steps to protect my reputation ... and to force Mr. Jerome to apologize.' 'The incident confirms the fact,' he went on to say, 'that some one older and other than myself ought to appear in Court, to argue whatever applications, however unimportant, are, in future, to be made in the case.'[6] Kohler wrote to the Grievance Committee of the Bar Association of New York City, complaining about Jerome's conduct. Several months later, the Bar Association sent Kohler a letter acknowledging that he had earlier been personally cleared of the charge that Jerome had brought against him, but said nothing in the way of censure against Jerome. On the advice of his brother and his friends, Kohler did not pursue the case any further. The well-known lawyer Louis Marshall, who had been assisting him in the matter, wrote to him that it was 'all we could possibly have expected.'[7]

Because of his illness, Hill's doctors ordered that he go south for the winter. Patrick therefore needed new counsel. Hill suggested to Milliken that John Milburn should take his place: 'there is no better man in the State to employ.'[8] It will be recalled that Milliken had first approached Milburn to take the appeal and that he had declined and recommended Hill. Once again, Milburn reluctantly declined and recommended ex-senator William Lindsay of Kentucky. Milliken met with and was impressed with Lindsay, with whom his brother had served in the Confederate Army in the Civil War.

Patrick's preference, however, was for another former governor of New York, Frank S. Black.[9] The fifty-two-year-old lawyer had been the Republican governor in 1897-9 and had successfully defended Molineux at his new trial. Mrs Patrick went to see him. Black was noted for his high fees and asked for a $5,000 retainer, which Milliken was apparently unwilling to provide.

Arrangements were, however, made to engage Black's forty-three-year-old law partner, William M.K. Olcott,[10] to replace Hill. A graduate of Columbia Law School and, like Black, a Republican, he had served as district attorney of New York for two years and then as judge of the New York City Court for a further two years. Since 1899 he had been in private practice as a member of the firm of Black, Olcott, and Gruber; today he is perhaps best known as counsel for Henry Thaw, accused in June 1906 of murdering Stanford White, a then well-known architect.[11]

Judge Olcott, as he was often known, would handle any application for a new trial or for clemency to the Republican governor, Higgins; and Senator Lindsay would take care of proceedings in the federal courts. The seventy-year-old William Lindsay had been elected to the Kentucky Court of Appeals in 1870, serving as chief justice from 1876 to 1878.

From 1893 to 1901 he was a senator from Kentucky in Washington. He then came to New York, entering the law firm renamed Lindsay, Kremer, Kalish, and Palmer.[12]

Lindsay was to be assisted by Archibald Shenstone, a New York lawyer whom, coincidentally, Wetherbee had consulted in early 1900 after Jones had allegedly suggested that he fraudulently take part in preparing a new will for Rice. Edgar Kohler would have been happy to stay on, but, according to Milliken, he demanded too high a fee. Milliken wrote to Hill: 'he modestly struck me for $2,000 down for him to consult and explain the situation to Senator Lindsay, $1,000 more for him to go to Washington to obtain a writ of error and $5,000 more if a new trial was secured.' Milliken told Hill that he wanted to get rid of 'this dirty little insulting Jew.'[13]

'Counsel have decided upon writ of error as best and safest. Sen. Lindsay will prepare it,' Milliken wired Patrick. Patrick telegraphed Hill that he did not want a writ of error: 'I forbid writ of error until habeas corpus fails, then both consolidated in Federal Supreme Court.' By doing this, Patrick wrote Hill, he would get 'the record and the new facts before the court as well as the choice of remedies.' Today, habeas corpus would clearly be the appropriate and, indeed, the only remedy in the federal courts.[14] The writ of error was abolished in the federal system in 1928.[15] But in 1905 the choice of remedy was obviously less clear.

Patrick was also unhappy that Milliken had 'hired two strange lawyers over my protest.' 'If I am not able to secure counsel who will confer with me and carry out my instructions,' he wrote Hill, 'I shall personally sue out my writ of habeas corpus or ask the court to assign me a leader of the bar to assist me to do so.'[16]

At the end of December 1905, Dr Allan McLane Hamilton,[17] visiting physician at the Manhattan State Hospital and president of the Psychiatrical Society, took a renewed interest in the case. He had sworn an affidavit a year earlier that 'the so-called confession of one Jones was the testimony of a mentally unbalanced and irresponsible man.'[18] Hamilton was the author of a number of books on medical jurisprudence and had appeared in a great number of murder cases, including the trials of the two presidential assassins. He wrote to the *Times*, stating: 'It appears to me and to many medical men that Patrick has never had a chance, and that he was convicted upon the flimsiest imaginable testimony.'[19] And in an article by him published in the *Herald*, he stated that 'in the thirty-five years during which I have appeared in court I know of no case, either in our own or any other civilized country, where a man has been so mercilessly railroaded to death as the unfortunate occupant of the death chamber in the State prison at Sing Sing.'[20]

A petition was circulated by Dr Hamilton asking the governor for clemency, stating in part:

The undersigned, believing that the conviction of Albert T. Patrick for murder in the first degree is unwarranted by the evidence presented at his trial, respectfully ask you to exercise clemency, believing in time that the mystery of the case, like that of others, will be explained.

An inspection of the evidence given in his trial convinces us that there is certainly reasonable doubt of his guilt.[21]

Leading members of the bar, such as Joseph H. Choate and former district attorney DeLancey Nicoll, and influential doctors, such as the president and a former president of the New York State Medical Society, signed the petition. Important public figures such as ex-president Grover Cleveland and Samuel Clemens, better known as Mark Twain, also signed.[22]

Jerome telephoned a number of the doctors who had signed, questioning their knowledge of the case. Dr Hamilton sent a note to the doctors who had signed the petition saying it was none of Jerome's business: 'I do not know that it is any of Mr. Jerome's business as to how or where you obtained your knowledge upon which you formed your opinion, and I regard his importunity and meddling in this matter as a piece of impertinence.' The New York *Times* expressed the view that the public 'will be inclined to resent Mr. Jerome's latest activity in the case.'[23]

Momentum was gathering. 'I have examined a great number of criminals,' Dr Hamilton told the press, 'and never before was I so much impressed with a man's innocence as I have been in this case.'[24] Over one hundred other petitions, representing some two thousand names, were gathered in Texas and forwarded to the governor.

Governor Higgins was unsure what to do. 'How can I go against the courts?' the *Times* reported him as stating. He decided to hold a public hearing in the executive chamber in Albany.[25]

On 15 January, the week before the execution was to take place, Olcott appeared with Hill, who, following a personal appeal from May Milliken, got out of his sickbed to attend. The press reported that Hill 'plainly showed the effects' of his illness. Dr Hamilton was unable to be there. Jerome attended with Garvan and Gans. It was to be Gans' last appearance in the case as he had a few weeks earlier announced his intention to enter private practice. Counsel came prepared to argue whether the governor should appoint a commissioner to take testimony under an 1887 New York statute,[26] but the governor wanted the petition limited to the question of executive clemency. Patrick's counsel did not put forward an application for a commutation, and counsel for both sides agreed that a temporary stay was in order to enable Patrick to seek another remedy.

After an hour's adjournment, Governor Higgins ordered that a reprieve be granted until 19 March 1906, stating:

It appeared that Patrick was not at this time an applicant for Executive clemency, but that he desired to present newly discovered evidence ... Patrick should exhaust his legal remedies before asking the Governor to intervene ... The importance and notoriety of this case should not lead the Governor to establish a precedent for setting up an extraconstitutional court of last resort to retry the issues raised on the trial.[27]

Because of the case, a bill was introduced by Assemblyman Eagleton in the New York Assembly the following week to substitute life imprisonment for capital punishment.[28] Patrick told Warden Johnson: 'I want freedom, not a life sentence. If I cannot prove my innocence then I want to die in the chair.'[29]

Jerome had told the governor that his office would not make any flimsy technical objections before a court on a motion for a new trial. Would this include permitting a judge other than Goff to hear the motion?

'I should like to make a motion to a court that has not prejudiced the case,' Hill remarked, implicitly referring to Judge Goff: 'It is now the custom that the District Attorney shall select the Judge.'

'We will meet you lawyer-like and as gentlemen,' Jerome remarked.

'Then it's all right,' Hill said.[30]

# 81. Another New Trial Motion

At the end of January 1906, the district attorney was served with papers seeking a new trial. 'We will pit science against perjury,' Olcott told the press.[1] As previously mentioned, the procedure in New York – as in other parts of the United States – was, and still is, to permit an application for a new trial to be made to the trial judge.[2]

The defense feared, however, that they could not possibly get a fair hearing from Judge Goff, who had already turned down two earlier motions for a new trial. Goff would not grant a new trial, Milliken wrote Hill, 'if Old Man Rice himself would appear in Court.'[3] Hill, who was leaving that week for South Carolina, said: Goff is 'an honest man,' but in this case 'he naturally sides with the prosecution. He cannot help it.'

Hill, therefore, wrote to Olcott: 'We are not required to make the motion before him. I advise that the application be made to Judge O'Sullivan. He is a new man, a fair man, and I believe he has the courage of his convictions. He is under no obligations to Mr. Jerome and can afford to do us justice.' This application was crucial, Hill went on to say, because he personally had 'little confidence in an appeal to the United States Court' and this would leave 'only the slender thread of Executive clemency to rely upon.'

No doubt because of Milliken's expressed preference, the application was brought before Sessions Judge Martin McMahon. The judge agreed with Jerome, however, that the hearing 'according to law as well as practice must go to the Trial Judge,' in spite of Olcott's complaint that the recorder was 'unintentionally prejudiced.' Olcott was given a 'bill of exceptions' by McMahon for possible use in later federal proceedings.[4]

Goff claimed that he did not want to hear the case, stating: 'I have expressed my views on this case to you, Mr. Jerome, and to the counsel for the other side, and I see no reason why I should not say publicly that I would be glad to be relieved. I think the matter ought to be heard by an open mind that is strange to the case.' Jerome, however, insisted, on the ground that it would take another judge at least two weeks to read the evidence of the former trial. 'I'll hear the motion,' Goff ruled: 'I do not wish to escape any duty.'

More than thirty affidavits had been filed by Olcott. About half related to new medical evidence and half to witnesses from Texas who had contact with Jones after his return there. One particularly important affidavit related to a postcard Mrs Patrick had accidentally come across, sent by John Whittlesey to Patrick in 1899, which showed that Patrick had indeed met with him in 1899 and not in the year 1900 as Whittlesey had testified at the trial. The prosecutor, it will be recalled, had relied on Whittlesey at the trial to show that Patrick did not have personal dealings with Rice in the months before he died.

The district attorney had the right to cross-examine the witnesses on their affidavits in the order he wished. He chose Joe Jordan as the first witness.

Joe Jordan was one of a group of seven colorful Texans who had arrived in New York over the weekend. Dressed in flannel shirts and wide-brimmed hats, 'their rough-and-ready costumes,' said the *Evening Sun*, 'lent a cow-punching atmosphere to the proceedings and suggested a round-up rather than a court hearing.'[5] 'Their statements,' Olcott told the press, 'are emphatic and as clear as a bell.'

'Scrawny and weather-beaten,' Jordan limped to the witness box, wearing a blue-flannel shirt and clutching his wide-brimmed felt hat. Jordan said that he had known Jones for many years and had talked to him about a year earlier, near Galveston – at Morgan's Point – and that Jones had said that Rice had died a natural death. He, Jones, lied to save himself.

Jerome asked Jordan if he had ever been convicted of a crime? He said he had not, apart from many convictions for drunkenness. Also, he added, 'once I was arrested on a charge of assaulting a policeman with the intent of killing him, but they could not make it stick.'

'Were you not in prison in Texas from 1877 until 1882?' Jerome asked.

'No; that was a cousin of mine. He was convicted of horse stealing; was sentenced for twelve years; this was cut down to five.'

'Could you describe your cousin?'[6]

Jordan described the amazing similarity between his cousin and himself. They were the same age and they looked alike. Their names were the same, both had a cross and the initials 'J.J.' tattooed on their arms, and both were crippled in the left leg. His cousin, he said, was now dead.

Unfortunately for Jordan, the district attorney called John Frame, a Houston police officer who identified Jordan (alias 'Skinny' Martin) as the person whom he had seen in the Huntsville Penitentiary in 1881 or 1882. Jerome also called William Murray, who had been a guard at the penitentiary in the 1880s and 1890s and had been in charge of a woodchopping crew of thirty persons, which included Joe Jordan. 'I could identify his skin in a tannery,' he told Jerome.[7]

Many of the other witnesses were equally unsavory. One had served two years in the penitentiary for uttering a forged check, and another had been arrested just before he came to New York but managed to give the jailer the slip. 'Of course,' Olcott told the press, 'the District-Attorney picks out the most vulnerable among the witnesses and puts them on the stand first.'[8]

Police Officer Frame described the Texans as 'a gang of loafers' hanging out at Big Annie's saloon in Houston. Joe Jordan had described Big Annie's to Jerome: 'Oh, it's a beer joint, a whisky joint, a place where you play high five and poker – a joint, you know.' Judge Railley, who had collected the affidavit, testified that he was not aware of the witnesses' previous records. The voluble sixty-one-year-old former judge had good things to say, however, about Big Annie: 'Annie's heart was as big as her body and her place as good as any in the City of Houston.' The *Times* described his 'uncommonly poor memory' in response to Jerome's questions. 'You see,' Railley explained with his Texas drawl, 'I have heard so much Jones in the last year – really, I have almost been Jonesed to death.'[9]

The enterprising New York *World* took the Texans out on the town. 'We didn't discuss the case. We were out for a good time,' the paper stated: 'we wanted to show our Texas friends the Great White Way, the brilliant scintillating Tenderloin, beautiful, bright Broadway!' The reporters claimed they liked Joe Jordan best of all, although after his court experience they noted that he seemed depressed. To add to his depression, the reporter noted that the Hotel Roland, where the Texans were staying, was nonalcoholic. The *World* reported Jordan's comments about a similar hotel in Houston:

He told us of seeking lodgings for a belated and extremely intoxicated friend in Houston once. Mr. Jordan said he bore the overcome friend into the office of a big hotel like carrying in a side of bacon. It was 3:00 a.m.

'Don't bring that man in here; this is a temperance house!' said the night clerk.

'It is all right,' said Mr. Jordan; 'he's too drunk to know it.'[10]

The following week, Jordan was arrested for perjury, pleaded guilty before Judge McMahon, and was remanded for sentence. He was later sentenced to a year and a half in Sing Sing. Whether Patrick ever met him there is not known. In the meantime, Jordan was brought back into Goff's courtroom and admitted that it was really he and not his cousin who had been in the penitentiary. Olcott tried to repair the damage:

'Why did you lie on the stand when you were asked about your prison record?' Olcott asked.

'I was ashamed to acknowledge the disgrace.'

'You have lived a right life since, for twenty-five years?'

'Yes, sir. No one can dig up anything else against me except arrests for drinking.'

'Were all the other things you have testified to here true?'

'Yes, sir, every one of them.'[11]

# 82. More Witnesses

Judge Railley had also brought to New York a Texas teacher, Miss Minnie Gaillard, who taught in a school at the large Santario sugar plantation in Texas. The press, as usual whenever a woman appeared, described how she was dressed. 'Wearing a large white hat decorated with a green bow and a tilted feather,' said the *Evening Telegram*, she testified that she had known Jones for many years and had met him perhaps eight times since 1903. Jones, she said in her affidavit, told her: 'Well, I lied to beat the band on Patrick. He, Patrick, didn't have anything to do with Rice's death and neither did I ... I was advised to make the statement I did and to make it as hard for Patrick as I could. That if I turned State's evidence, it would secure my own freedom.'[1]

She also claimed in her affidavit that she was thirty-nine years old. For fully five minutes, Jerome and Goff questioned her about her age:

'How old are you now?' Jerome asked.

'That's got nothing to do with the case,' she replied.

'I direct you to answer, Madam,' Goff interjected.

'I think a lady has the right to give one answer and then to be done with it.'

'I give you one more chance. If you do not obey, I shall reluctantly have to use compulsion, but I don't want to resort to extreme means.'

'My age has no relevance to this matter.'

'You were not asked as to that. Will your reply tend to incriminate or degrade you?'

'Oh no, not at all.'

'Then I shall be forced to hold you guilty of contempt of court if you don't answer, and confine you to jail until you do answer.'

'Oh, I didn't know it was a criminal offense. I beg your pardon.'

'All right', said the Recorder, 'How old are you?'

'From 39 to 50.'[2]

After another round of questioning by Jerome, it was established that she was probably forty-five years old.

When the examination was almost concluded, she mentioned an incident that had not been included in her affidavit – described by the *American* as 'startling' and by the *World* as 'sensational' – about a conversation she heard on a streetcar in Houston:

'I was on a street car, an open car, in the summer of 1904. In front of me sat Mayor Rice and Charles F. Jones.'

'Do you mean Mayor Baldwin Rice, of Houston, a nephew of the late William Marsh Rice?' asked Mr. Jerome.

'I mean him and Jones,' replied the witness. 'Mr. Rice patted Jones on the back and said to him: "Well, old fellow, you certainly studied those instructions well," and Jones replied "You bet I did."'

'What did Mr. Rice say to that?'

'He said: "How are your coffers?" I thought they were trying to use words that could not be understood generally. Then he added "How are you supplied?"'

'And did Jones say anything to that?' demanded Mr. Jerome.

'Jones answered "Not so well." Then I heard Mr. Rice say, "Well, they will be supplied whenever it is necessary." Jones nodded his head.'[3]

The district attorney questioned her about the fact that this evidence had not been included in her affidavit. Under Olcott's gentle questioning, she testified that she had in fact told the story to him but he decided not to include it in her affidavit: 'You told me that the whole truth would not do, and that the story was too steep.'[4]

Mayor Rice, a nephew of William Marsh Rice and a possible Democratic candidate for governor of Texas in the next election, left immediately from Texas, saying that Miss Gaillard's evidence was 'absolutely and unequivocally false.'[5] When he reached New York, he was immediately called to testify by Jerome. He admitted that he had known Miss Gaillard and her family for many years, but, he said, 'I never saw Charles F. Jones in my life.' He went on to say: 'I never sat next to Jones in a street car and I never slapped him on the back. William M. Rice's nephews in Texas don't pat criminals on the back and they don't give money to them.'[6] He admitted to Olcott that he believed Patrick to be guilty and would like to see him executed. Olcott later told the press that he had been informed that he could get forty witnesses from Texas to prove that Mayor Rice had frequently been seen with Jones.

The hearing was then adjourned for a month to allow both sides to prepare for the medical testimony. On 12 March 1906, at Olcott and Jerome's request, the governor extended the reprieve, which was about to run out, until 18 May.

As the hearing concluded, Jerome turned to Olcott and said: 'In the meantime will you see your client and ask him if he is willing to waive his privilege so that Mr. House may be allowed to tell what happened between him and Mr. Patrick in the Tombs.'[7] Olcott remained silent. Jerome addressed the court: 'The defendant has an excellent chance to clear himself and he does not avail himself of it. No innocent man ever stood in such a position, refusing to unseal the lips of counsel.'[8]

Earlier in the new trial hearing, Jerome had called House as a witness, stating that when he, Jerome, was sitting as a magistrate he heard Jones say that both he and Patrick had confessed to House. Goff said that he would only take a personal waiver from Patrick. The district attorney then offered a provocative challenge to Olcott: 'if Patrick would waive his rights and permit his former counsel to go on the stand and deny having received such a confession, the case would be dropped at once and no objection be made to Patrick's getting a pardon.' It was not made clear whether Jerome was referring to a confession by Jones or by Patrick. Jerome's subsequent question to House related only to what Jones had allegedly said: 'Did Jones tell you, in substance, that he had killed Rice with chloroform in the presence of Patrick?' Goff refused to permit the question.[9]

House told the press, as he had at the trial itself, that he could not divulge what was said: 'It would be highly unprofessional, as well as illegal, for me to do so. The language of the statute ["shall not be allowed to disclose a communication made by his client to him"][10] is very clear and explicit. Disbarment or suspension from practice would be the penalty of such an act.'[11] Whether House believed that Patrick could waive the privilege is not clear. The better opinion is that Patrick could have waived it.[12]

Some editorial writers considered Jerome's tactics entirely unfair. 'The rule which forbids a prosecutor in any way to twit a defendant for not taking the stand in his own behalf,' the *Tribune* said, 'should likewise forbid the issuing of any "dares" to waive any other constitutional right.'[13]

Edgar Kohler, who had been assisting Olcott, although not taking part in the examination of the witnesses, wrote to Senator Hill in South Carolina to tell him about the proceedings thus far. 'The course pursued by Mr. Jerome and countenanced by the Recorder,' he wrote, 'of con-

stantly challenging Patrick to waive the privilege of confidential communications with Mr. House, his former attorney, seems to me grossly
improper and presents an additional problem for defendant's counsel,
the attempt to solve which is both perplexing and embarrassing.' Kohler
also told Hill what was apparent from the press report, that 'the Texan
affiants were certainly a rather disreputable lot and the case has, I fear,
lost in public sympathy, by reason of that fact.' 'Nevertheless,' he added,
'we hope that the medical side of the case, which will be taken up at
the adjourned hearing, commencing Tuesday, April 3rd, will score solidly
in our favor.' He warned Hill that 'indications of the Court being likely
to look with favor upon the granting of a new trial are, however, conspicuous by their absence.'[14]

Milliken also wrote to Hill:

Of course you have heard all about the witnesses that Railley took to New York;
no doubt they were a bad lot, and Railley ought to have had better sense than to
impose such men as they upon us, but I think there is no doubt that they talked
with Jones and that what they testified to was the truth, but their characters were
so bad that they did not do Patrick any good.

Milliken returned to Texas for further evidence and wrote Hill more
optimistically: 'I have some good witnesses that I will bring to New
York ... who will contradict Mayor Rice when he swears that he did
not know Jones.' Moreover, other reputable witnesses, he said, such as
the ex-chief of police of Houston would come to New York to testify
that Jones had admitted that Patrick was innocent.

Another important potential witness, Milliken wrote, was J.B. Brockman:

The best evidence that I have so far discovered is that of J.B. Brockman, the
leading criminal lawyer of Texas, who resides at Houston. Jones' brother who
swore he sent the chloroform to him in New York went to Brockman after he returned from New York and asked Brockman if he could be prosecuted in Texas
for perjury that he committed in New York; Brockman asked him what he had
been committing perjury in New York about and he then told him that he did
not buy any chloroform in Texas or anywhere else and ship to the valet at any
place, in fact he admitted that he committed perjury. This confession was not
made to Brockman while Brockman was occupying the position of counsel; he
received no fee or retainer of any character, just happened to know this fellow

whom he met on the streets, and is bound by no privilege whatever not to reveal what was said to him. Brockman is willing to make an affidavit and go to New York and testify about this matter. He is also inclined to believe that he can induce this fellow Jones to make an affidavit to that effect.

The press were, of course, continually speculating about the whereabouts of Charlie Jones and whether he would appear. The *Times* reported rumors that he was in Louisiana, where he was said to have interests (along with a plantation in Cuba), and would appear to testify when needed. Many news reports mentioned sudden wealth. Hearst's *Evening Journal* at one point reported that he was on his way to New York, and Pulitzer's *World*, not to be outdone, said that a 'high official' in the DA's office confirmed that Jones was already in New York. Other newspaper reports had Jones in such places as Russia, Mexico, Panama, and closer to home in the Humble Oil fields. Other reports claimed Jones had been murdered by the 'irate father and brother of a girl he wronged.'

The *World* sent a reporter to Texas to track him down, without success. Witnesses told the reporter that 'Jones claimed to us that Jerome, whom he described as a terrible man, had got him into his clutches, and that the only way to escape was to confess to a crime he had never committed ... Jones said he would be willing to do two or three years in the penitentiary to save Patrick, but that if he went back on his evidence in court, Jerome would surely give him the limit of the law for perjury and might even try to put him on trial for murder.' Many persons thought that Jones was 'hiding in the wilds of the Cedar Bayou country ... with its lagoons and marshes, bordered by thick patches of timber and heavy underbrush, that is almost impenetrable.' Jones' father would not help the reporter: 'We owe nothing to Patrick and he will have to look out for himself and fight his own battle.'[15]

# 83. Still More Evidence

Neither Jones, Brockman, nor House was in court when the hearing recommenced on 1 April. Jones was nowhere to be found; Brockman said he was unable to come to New York; and Patrick would not give House permission to testify.

The district attorney requested a further adjournment of two weeks to test the medical evidence. Olcott did not object, provided that some of the further Texas witnesses could first be heard.

Corporal Alex B. Stanbery, Rice's former valet, whose affidavit had been procured by Milliken in San Francisco, was called. The army had arranged to send him back from the Philippines for the hearing. For two days, Jerome challenged his credibility. On the first day, wearing his khaki uniform, he was questioned about a series of letters he had written to a friend and had asked to be burned, showing that he was trying to extract money in connection with the earlier will litigation. On the second day, having switched to his blue garrison uniform – no detail was too minor for the press – he was asked by Jerome about his previous criminal record:

'I object,' he began and then asked Goff: 'Do I have to answer all questions?'
'Unless they tend to incriminate or degrade you, yes,' explained the Recorder.
'Then I object on that ground. This one tends to disgrace me.'[1]

Several other witnesses with apparently good reputations also claimed that Jones denied that Rice had been murdered. One of these, a physician, Dr Solomon Williams, now a postmaster, who knew Jones well, said that Jones admitted to him that Rice died a natural death.

Goff granted Olcott permission to present several new affidavits, but warned him: 'This is positively the limit, Mr. Olcott. No more affidavits will be admitted.' Jerome had been objecting to the introduction of further evidence, stating: 'Where, when and how will this end if they are permitted to get new witnesses whenever others are torn to shreds and some of them are put in jail? The State of Texas is large and they can get new witnesses as long as Milliken's bank roll lasts.'[2]

Two of the new affidavits were designed to show that Mayor Rice in fact knew Jones. One of the witnesses, John Giesberg, was a marble cutter from Houston who claimed he saw Mayor Rice and Jones on a streetcar and distinctly heard Rice ask Jones if he needed any more money. The other witness was Anna Wright, the mother of the eighteen-year-old whom Jones was alleged to have made pregnant. She claimed that she saw Mayor Rice and Jones talking at Morgan's Point in the summer of 1904. She also testified that Jones said to her that he did not commit a crime. Jerome, of course, brought out that it was natural for Jones to deny he was a murderer when speaking to his girlfriend's mother and that Mrs Wright was now just trying to get even with Jones for the way he had treated her daughter. Finally, Robert Adams, a deputy sheriff of Galveston County, testified that he had gone to see Lafayette Jones after J.B. Brockman declined to go to New York and Lafayette said to him: 'No, I did not send the chloroform but I will not make any statement about it nor talk about it further.'[3]

The hearing to consider the medical evidence was to recommence on Monday, 23 April, but was adjourned until Wednesday because of the funeral of Judge McMahon, the judge that the defense had wanted to hear the new trial motion.

Kohler, it will be recalled, had written to Senator Hill: 'we hope that the medical side of the case ... will score solidly in our favor.'[4] He proved to be correct. The evidence tended to back up the Medico-Legal Society's report released at the beginning of the hearing, which had stated: 'It is simply impossible now, with the light thrown on the case by the investigation before the Select Committee of the Medico-Legal Society, for any fair, unprejudiced mind to regard Patrick guilty of the death of Rice.'[5]

Dr Albert T. Weston was the key witness for Patrick. A coroner's physician in Manhattan since 1889, the 1882 graduate of New York University Medical College claimed to have examined upwards of twenty thousand dead bodies and performed perhaps twenty-five hundred autopsies.

At the request of the defendant, he had performed twenty-one experiments on cadavers for the purpose of ascertaining the course which embalming fluid would follow through the body when injected into the right brachial artery. He swore that embalming fluid 'can and does reach the lungs when such fluid is injected into the right brachial artery in the same manner described by the embalmer.' His experiments with the Falcon embalming fluid and other fluids 'produced in the lungs a condition of congestion and oedema not distinguishable upon examination from the condition of congestion and oedema described' by the witnesses at the trial. He 'absolutely disagreed' with Dr Loomis' evidence at the trial that embalming fluid could 'never' reach the lungs.[6]

For three days, Jerome cross-examined Weston, attacking his integrity. Twelve of the experiments, he brought out, were done for a fee while Weston was supposed to be performing his official duty as coroners' physician on 'coroners' cases.' In six of these cases he had injected the embalming fluid before opening the lungs:

'How do you square your duty as a Coroner's physician with the injection of a fluid that would destroy the evidence of the cause of death?' asked Jerome.

'I have no explanation,' said Weston.

'If a crime had been committed in any one of these cases, your experiment would have made it impossible to determine that fact?'
'It would have made it difficult to tell.'[7]

Jerome announced that he would take action against Dr Weston and would ask for his removal from office.

Another witness, Dr George D. Stewart, a professor of anatomy and clinical surgery at New York University Medical College, agreed with Dr Weston. He had conducted seven experiments, and said that Dr Loomis' statement 'is so absurd that I believe that Dr. Loomis inadvertently made it.'

The president of the American Medical Association, Dr John A. Wyeth,[8] the author of a textbook on surgery and the senior professor of surgery at the New York Polyclinic Medical School and Hospital, gave similar evidence and added that in his experience chloroform never produced a noticeable congestion of the lungs.

Several embalmers supported Dr Weston. Dr Carl Barnes, the head of the Barnes School of Anatomy, Sanitary Science, and Embalming in Chicago, said that he had performed over two hundred autopsies and had embalmed over a thousand bodies. Five hundred of the embalmings had used the process involving the right brachial artery. Dr Howard Eckels, the embalmer from Philadelphia who had been a member of the Medico-Legal committee, naturally agreed with the new medical evidence.

An anaesthetist at New York Hospital and Mount Sinai Hospital, Thomas L. Bennett, who had administered anaesthetics in over twenty thousand cases, testified that a cone of chloroform placed on a person's face as Jones had said 'would invariably cause excessive choking.' It was 'absolutely impossible' to be done as Jones described. Moreover, when a room is lit by gas – and there was further evidence that Rice's apartment was so lit – the gas is 'exceedingly pungent, irritating and persistent' and so would easily have been detected by Dr Curry.

Finally, a new and important feature was introduced. Rice's embalmer, John Potter, swore that when he picked up Rice's body 'rigor mortis had set in completely': 'the body was rigid and stiff from head to foot to such a degree as not to bend in lifting it and carrying it from the couch to the table on which I placed it.' Dr Weston explained the nature of rigor mortis and concluded that 'such a condition of absolute rigidity could not have occurred unless life had departed for at least four hours before the time Potter made observation of the body of William Marsh Rice.' Thus, if the facts were as Jones said, Rice was already dead. Jerome put to Weston some medical texts indicating that rigor mortis might in exceptional cases set in earlier.

Only two medical witnesses were called by Jerome. Dr Hamilton Williams, a coroner's physician from 1888 to 1902, now retired, who had given important evidence for the prosecution at the trial, had recently conducted eight experiments upon dead bodies. 'In the result,' he swore, 'I am convinced that through no process of embalming in which "Falcon" fluid is used ... as in the case of the body of William Marsh Rice can congestion of the entire lung be produced or simulated.' A similar conclusion was reached in an affidavit filed by Dr Robert Kemp, a professor of gastrointestinal diseases at the New York School of Clinical Medicine, who had assisted Williams with the experiments. And Dr Otto H. Schultze, who had graduated from the New York College of Physicians and Surgeons and was now a coroner's physician in Manhattan, testified that he had conducted two thousand autopsies, many after the deceased had been embalmed through the brachial artery, and 'in no case was any effect shown in the right side of the heart,' which would have been the case if the fluid had passed through the lungs.

The evidence was now all in. Olcott asked the recorder for the appointment of some eminent physician to conduct experiments to determine whose medical evidence was correct. Could embalming fluid enter the lungs? Jerome objected: 'Unless a stop be put to such tactics as these, Patrick will die of old age at Sing Sing before this issue before your Honor is decided.'[9]

Goff agreed with Jerome and rejected the request. Jerome ended the proceedings with a motion of his own:

During the four years Patrick has sat in the shadow of death while every procedure known to the law has been employed by his counsel to stop the progress of justice, the lips of the defendant in this case have been sealed.

There has been all that time in this city a man who, if his lips were not sealed, would tell the whole miserable story of how Rice came to his death, as he heard that story from Valet Jones in the presence of Patrick in the Tombs. I refer to Lawyer Frederick House, who was counsel for Patrick and Jones. I ask at this time if the defense will unseal his lips by waiving the professional privilege and allow him to come here and tell his story.

'I object to this miserable grand-stand play of the District Attorney's!' shouted Mr. Olcott, interrupting Jerome's speech.

'Now, your Honor,' said Jerome, 'am I to be addressed that way in court?'

'Oh, you know, Mr. Olcott,' said the Recorder, 'that there is no jury present and that this court is not susceptible to be influenced by remarks made by either side when they are not backed by evidence. I think so far justice has been done to every one concerned during the long time this matter has been before the court.'[10]

The recorder asked both sides to present briefs and the hearing ended.

Governor Higgins, at the request of all counsel, reluctantly granted another extension until 18 June 1906. 'The delay in this matter has been exceedingly unsatisfactory to me,' he wrote counsel and the judge, 'as I had no reason to expect such an extraordinary procrastination of the matter.' He was, he warned, 'not disposed to grant any additional reprieve.'[11]

# 84. Goff's Ruling

Olcott did not hold out any hope that Goff's ruling would be favorable. 'I am just finishing before Goff,' he wrote to Senator Hill, 'and there is no chance of his granting the motion.'[1]

The law did not permit an appeal from a denial of a motion for a new trial. (Today, however, the Criminal Procedure Law of New York specifically permits an appeal to the Court of Appeals from a denial of such a motion in a capital case – even though capital punishment has been abolished in the state.)[2] In anticipation of a denial, Olcott, with the help of Louis Marshall, had prepared a legislative bill allowing an appeal in such a case. The bill, introduced by Assemblyman Wade and known as the Wade Bill, was passed by the New York Legislative Assembly and a similar bill was passed by the Senate.[3]

Would Governor Higgins sign the bill? Olcott, accompanied by his law partner, ex-governor Black, went to Albany to try to convince Higgins that he should sign it. Hill was asked to speak to Higgins' legal counsel.

Higgins, however, vetoed the bill and the similar Senate bill at the end of May, stating: 'I disapprove them for the reason that they introduce a new procedure to our criminal law and tend to defer indefinitely the termination of a capital case ... Rice, of whose murder Patrick is accused, died on September 23, 1900, nearly six years ago. The law's delays in this case seem to me little less than scandalous.'[4]

'The law's delays' was then a current topic of discussion in legal circles and in the public press.[5] Comparisons were made by many with the administration of justice in England, which in 1906 did not provide for an appeal from a conviction or a motion for a new trial. Many, including a US Supreme Court judge,[6] had been urging that the United States adopt the English system. Others, referring to the alleged miscarriages of justice in England in the Adolph Beck and Florence Maybrick cases, thought that the American system was preferable. 'A murder trial is, after all, just like fox chasing,' said an unnamed prominent criminal lawyer about the Patrick case, 'only in America we catch the quarry, let it get loose for another short dash, and then perhaps it slips away altogether from the hounds in the long run. In England, when the game is run to cover, there is either a quick "kill" or equally quick mercy.'[7] 'If our procedure allows too many trials,' the New York *Times* editorialized, 'theirs allows too few.'[8] In 1907, England changed its practice and introduced regular appeals from convictions in criminal cases.[9]

On Sunday, 10 June 1906, Hill met with Senator Lindsay and Milliken in Albany to plan the next step after Goff's expected ruling. Olcott had a prior engagement and could not be there, although he met with Lindsay in New York City earlier in the day. Because of Milliken's dislike of Kohler, he was not invited, but Hill had met with him privately the previous day. The Sunday meeting concluded that a writ of error to the United States Supreme Court should be taken. As previously mentioned, Olcott's strategy had been to use the new trial motion to 'lay the foundation' for an appeal to the Supreme Court of the United States. Lindsay expressed the view that there was 'one chance out of three that the Supreme Court will hold that Patrick has not been tried by due process of law.'[10] Milliken wanted Hill, who was now feeling somewhat better, to be associated with Lindsay on the appeal, but for health reasons Hill said he could not do it.

Goff gave his judgment Monday morning, dismissing the motion for a new trial:

It is now over four years since judgment was pronounced upon the defendant, and during that period he has, through the most skilful and resourceful efforts of successive counsel, eminent in their profession, suspended its execution, and now, for the second time since that judgment, he seeks a retrial and re-examination of all the issues that were disposed of by the verdict of the jury.[11]

The question to be answered, Goff said, is whether 'there arises a reasonable presumption that on a new trial the verdict of the jury would be different.' He held that it would not. The evidence of Jones' admissions was, in his view, not believable:

It would be taxing human credulity to a point beyond forbearance to even ask twelve men in a jury box to give credence to the witnesses who have testified to the alleged admissions of Jones.

Apart from the inherent improbabilities of their stories, the trail of a common design and purpose was unmistakable. From the first witness, who confessedly perjured himself, to the last, there was little difference in either degree or kind. With some few exceptions, they were shown to be persons of bad repute and unworthy of belief.

Patrick's medical evidence was also dismissed as unsatisfactory:

All of these experiments were made in a desultory and fugitive manner in the City Morgue upon the unknown dead with a singular disregard of those precautions for accuracy of tests, observations and noting results ...

It would seem that where a new trial is sought on the ground of newly discovered evidence obtained by experiments, that the method of investigation, the tests applied and therewith the character and sufficiency of the results arrived at, should be scientifically flawless and so invariable and inevitable as to demonstrate a law rather than furnish occasion for speculation.

He concluded his judgment by stating: 'On no one of the grounds urged in the motion is there sufficient cause to grant a new trial, and, therefore, it is denied.'

Warden Johnson of Sing Sing immediately started making plans to test the equipment and send out notices for the execution that was to take place the following Monday. Patrick told the warden that it was a waste of effort, but the warden said he was obligated to proceed unless there was an order of the court. 'Well, of course, you can do that,' the press reported Patrick as stating, 'but I merely wanted to give you my legal view of the case and perhaps save you some trouble.'[12]

# 85. Writ of Error

Just after Judge Goff's decision was announced, Senator Lindsay and Archibald Shenstone boarded the early evening train from New York for Canton, Ohio, to seek a writ of error from Supreme Court Justice William Rufus Day. Lindsay had sent him a telegram saying they were coming. It was reported that no Supreme Court judge was resident in Washington at the time. Justice Rufus Peckham probably had been the judge assigned to hear such applications during that period, but he was not well and had gone to Rhode Island. He later wrote to Justice Day thanking him for taking on Patrick's application.[1]

Justice Day, who had been appointed to the Supreme Court by President Theodore Roosevelt in 1903, had practiced law, specializing in criminal law, in Canton for over twenty-five years and as a judge continued to spend summers with his family there. The son of a chief justice of Ohio, he had been a member of the Sixth Circuit Bench for four years before his appointment to the Supreme Court.[2] The Sixth Circuit included Senator Lindsay's state of Kentucky.

It is not clear why Justice Day was selected. It could have been a question of availability, but it is more likely that he was seen as a strong judge – the right judge for the application. The taciturn, self-effacing Justice Day had written a judgment in a state tax sale case two years earlier giving a liberal view of the Fourteenth Amendment due-process clause.[3] Moreover, Senator Lindsay probably knew Justice Day. For several years in the late 1890s, while Lindsay was a senator in Washington, Day was an assistant secretary and then the secretary of state in the McKinley administration.

The two lawyers had several meetings with Justice Day. They no doubt stressed the many federal 'due process' points that had been developed by Olcott and Kohler on the recent unsuccessful motion for a new trial. These included the allegations that there was not a 'fair and impartial trial,' as required in some of the earlier US Supreme Court cases;[4] that counsel at trial had been refused permission to inspect the grand jury minutes, a point brought to Lindsay's attention by Patrick's trial lawyer, Robert Moore; that some of the evidence violated Patrick's attorney-client privilege and his protection against self-incrimination; that at the new trial hearings he was not present to confront the witnesses against him; that the trial violated his right to a speedy trial; and, finally, that granting Jones complete immunity was a denial of the due-process and 'equal protection of the laws' provisions of the Fourteenth Amendment.

The following afternoon, Justice Day announced, without reasons, that he was granting the writ. The writ operated as an automatic stay on Patrick's execution. At Day's insistence, the writ of error was directed to the trial judge, rather than to the Court of Appeals, as Lindsay and Hill had planned.[5] The writ was then served on the warden of Sing Sing, which brought his plans for an execution to a temporary halt. The appeal would be placed on the list of cases for the October 1906 term of the Supreme Court. Justice Peckham remarked in his letter to Justice Day, 'we will listen to the words of wisdom which will fall from the lips of counsel in his behalf this coming fall,' and then added that Patrick has put up 'a good fight, at any rate.'[6]

Several weeks later, another inmate of Sing Sing, John Johnson, would also be saved from the electric chair by a writ of error, but in his case it would be dramatically delivered to the penitentiary at 5:30 in the morning – thirty minutes before the execution was to take place. Patrick had a particular interest in Johnson because six months earlier he had acted as Johnson's counsel in drafting documents for an appeal from his murder conviction. The formal documents had been signed, 'Albert T. Patrick, attorney and counsellor-at-law, now residing in the State Prison, in Sing Sing, N.Y.'[7] Another inmate, Michael Bruesh, had received similar legal advice from Patrick, dictated through the bars of their cells, which resulted in a new trial and life imprisonment. Bruesh left the death house, telling the press: 'It's like being born all over again to get out of that death house at Sing Sing. If it hadn't been for Albert T. Patrick, I would have gone to the electric chair long ago.'[8] As it turned out, Johnson was not as lucky. His eventual appeal to the United States Supreme Court would be dismissed the following year and he would be executed.[9]

Patrick had his own idea on what the next step should be: as we know, he wanted a writ of habeas corpus in addition to the writ of error. He wrote to Senator Hill: 'I am preparing a petition for a writ of habeas corpus to the U.S. Circuit Court upon the ground that the court of conviction was without jurisdiction to convict.'[10] He asked Hill not to obstruct his proposed action: 'I do not ask my counsel to approve of, or take any part in, my habeas corpus proceedings. I do ask, and I have a right to ask, that they do not obstruct or discountenance me in any way in such proceeding.'

# 86. More Experiments and Petitions

A meeting of embalmers was held in New York City for four days in the second week of August 1906 attended by over one hundred embalmers from New York and surrounding states. The purpose of the meeting, which was organized by Clark Bell, the president of the Medico-Legal Society, was to demonstrate the fact that embalming fluid when introduced through the right brachial artery will enter the lungs. Not only was such a demonstration designed to help clear Patrick, but it was also designed to put pressure on the New York State Legislature to pass a law banning the use of poisonous substances such as arsenic and mercury, then commonly used in embalming solutions, by embalmers and thus covering up possible criminal poisonings. New Jersey and several other states had already passed such a law and New York did so shortly afterwards. The embalmers were interested in upgrading the status of their profession. A start had been made in 1905 when a law was passed requiring embalmers not already practicing to obtain a state license.[1]

The demonstration took place before a large crowd of embalmers at Frank E. Campbell's funeral parlor on 23rd Street. (Today situated in upper Madison Avenue, Campbell's is considered by many to be the most prestigious funeral establishment in New York.) Frank Campbell described in a letter to Clark Bell what had taken place at the demonstration:

I witnessed an operation of embalming on August 9th in my establishment with many other undertakers whom we invited there for the purpose of discussing scientific problems in embalming, these operations having been performed by Prof. H.S. Eckels, of Philadelphia, and Prof. Chas. A. Genung, Waterloo, N.Y. The body that was demonstrated upon was of about the same size and general condition as was the body of William M. Rice, according to the description given by the witnesses who have testified in this case. With this subject, the fluid was injected into the right brachial artery, the lungs and heart were exposed to view, and I carefully observed the filling of the blood vessels as the injection continued. I also saw that the tissues of the lungs became expanded by the further injection of the fluid and made close observation upon the appearance of the lungs after the injection of a half a gallon of fluid into the brachial artery and found that a congestion of blood in the lungs had been produced and that upon a close examination the odor of embalming fluid was readily perceptible therein. This operation was before a large audience of practical embalmers. It was a complete demonstration of an actual fact, that the fluid did enter and permeate the lungs and was not a matter of opinion, or that permitted an expression of opinion. It was a demonstration.[2]

Clark Bell wrote a strong editorial in the *Medico-Legal Journal* stating that what was shown 'is an indisputable fact within the personal knowledge of every experienced embalmer.' The demonstration 'makes it positive and certain that the medical evidence of Drs. Loomis, Williams and others, in which their opinion was allowed to be stated to the jury, that the embalming fluid did not and could not in such a case enter the lungs, was valueless.'[3] Bell and the Medico-Legal committee felt that a free pardon was close at hand.

The medical profession also supported Patrick's position. Over the summer, a petition had been circulated to all the doctors in New York State asking for an independent commission of inquiry into the medical aspects of the case. Nearly thirty-five hundred physicians signed it. Samuel B. Thomas claimed that only four had returned it, refusing to sign. The *Times* editorialized: 'it will be difficult for the Governor or the general public to dismiss as unimportant the fact that 3,500 doctors, representing 550 cities and towns in the State, have united in declaring that the "expert testimony" upon which the conviction of ALBERT T. PATRICK was so largely based does not seem to them good evidence or in accord with their knowledge and experience.'[4] Four of the signatures were from Governor Higgins' hometown of Olean.

The carefully drafted petition stated:

We, the undersigned physicians of New York State, have read the medical testimony presented on a motion for a new trial to Recorder Goff in the case of Albert T. Patrick, charged with the murder of William Marsh Rice.

The conclusions of the experts who testified on the motion are quite at variance, and the questions are novel as well as grave and important to the members of society, and especially to the defendant, and therefore should be justly solved. To this end, we petition your Excellency to appoint a commission, composed of disinterested experts selected from the medical profession, to examine impartially into the questions at issue and report their findings at as early a date as possible, and thus avoid the possibility of mistake in the case of Patrick, as well as to get a final and just solution of the question.[5]

Hill had prepared an eight-page memorandum showing that many previous governors, including on a number of occasions Hill himself, had appointed such a fact-finding commission. 'There can be no doubt whatever,' Hill argued, 'of the lawful authority of the Governor in cases of applications for clemency' to appoint such a commission.[6] The appointment, Hill wrote, could be 'under an implied or inherent power vested in the Executive to do whatever was desirable, appropriate or necessary to enable him the better to discharge the delicate and important power of pardon solely vested in him by the Constitution.' Or, Hill argued, it could be under an 1887 statute which permits the 'subpoenaing of witnesses and the production of books and papers in any matter arising before the Governor upon an application for Executive clemency.'[7]

The petition was presented personally to the governor by Samuel B. Thomas and Frank G. Logan, a wealthy retired broker and patron of the arts from Chicago,[8] who was a business associate of Milliken's.

The problem, Governor Higgins told the press after Logan and Thomas had gone, is that 'I know of no authority vested in me by which I could appoint the commission for which they asked, nor of any jurisdiction on my part over the case in the absence of a definite application for a pardon as executive clemency.'[9] He claimed he did not have such an application from Patrick.

The Medico-Legal Society immediately started another petition for a pardon for Patrick. We can, Bell wrote to the governor, 'lay before you ten thousand names in ten days for his full pardon.' Bell said that they would delay the petition if the governor wanted to wait until the federal courts had disposed of the issue. E.W. Huffcut, counsel for the governor, replied to Bell:

Dear Sir: Referring to yours of October 19th, addressed to Governor Higgins, I am instructed to say that it is not the intention of the Governor to take any action in the Patrick case pending the hearing upon it in the Supreme Court of the United States.

> Very truly yours
> E.W. Huffcut
> Counsel for the Governor

The Medico-Legal Society therefore suspended its action on the application for a pardon.

It was now up to Patrick and his advisers to decide what to do. Should they apply for a pardon and, if so, to whom?

# 87. The New Governor

Patrick did not think it was wise to apply to Governor Higgins for a pardon. Higgins, he said, seemed to have been hostile to him at all stages, including vetoing the bill that would have allowed an appeal from Goff's latest ruling, rejecting the recent massive petition by the medical profession for an independent inquiry into the medical aspects of the case, and several weeks earlier turning down Patrick's petition to have Jerome removed from the case because of personal bias. 'Friends of mine who are near to the Governor,' Patrick wrote Milliken, 'advise me to make no applications to him [Governor Higgins]. I fear that he is "weak" and is under the influence of my adversaries, that he hasn't the nerve to resist their power and influence.' The federal courts would, he believed, see that justice was done: 'I suggest that I be permitted to, or that my counsel make a statement to the public that I and my counsel have every confidence that the Federal Courts will liberate me and that I am unwilling to seek a pardon from Governor Higgins.'[1]

Moreover, he went on in his letter to Milliken, there is an election soon in New York and therefore 'in a month we will know who is to be the next Governor. Let us wait a month anyhow and then decide.'

Governor Frank Wayland Higgins had decided not to seek reelection as governor. The fifty-year-old wealthy businessman from Olean, New York, where he was always known according to the *Times* obituary as 'plain Frank Higgins,' was not physically well when he became governor two years earlier and this condition had continued throughout his mediocre administration. He would in fact die of heart failure the month after his successor's inauguration.[2]

The key question for Patrick and his advisers was: who would be elected his successor? Higgins did not attend the Republican convention at Saratoga. The *Times* reported that there 'appears to be a very widespread demand for the nomination of ex-Governor Frank S. Black. In fact, the talk throughout the crowds tonight is that Black will be the nominee.'[3] Of course, no one would have been better for Patrick's cause.

In the end, however, Charles Evans Hughes, with the strong backing of President Theodore Roosevelt, was the Republican nominee. Hughes, who eventually became the chief justice of the United States, was an excellent, tough-minded lawyer. He had been the gold-medalist from Columbia Law School in 1884, and for several years had been a professor of law at Cornell Law School. One perhaps fatal drawback from Patrick's perspective, however, was that he had been a junior partner for several years in the famous Carter firm, in which William Hornblower and James Byrne had been partners. Patrick knew Hughes because he had attended Hughes' Bible class in the 1890s at the Fifth Avenue Baptist Church.[4]

One of the possible Democratic candidates for governor was District Attorney William Travers Jerome. If elected, he said, he would be 'anti-bossism,' referring to Hill and others, and would ensure that the Democratic Party of New York was 'held together by principles, not by peanut patronage and petty dole.' Tammany Hall, he said, was a 'quasi-criminal conspiracy.'[5]

The Buffalo convention, however, with the support of Tammany Hall, chose the newspaper baron William Randolph Hearst. Jerome publicly described Hearst as a 'person intellectually sterile, socially vulgar, and morally obtuse.'[6] The Buffalo convention, Jerome said, was a 'fake' and he would work to secure the election of Hughes.[7] A Hearst victory would be very favorable to Patrick's interests. As the *Fort Worth Record* stated: 'Mr. Hearst is known to oppose capital punishment; he is known to have been very, very slow to urge the execution of individuals, either personally or in his newspapers ... Many there are who think that in the event of the election of Mr. Hearst as governor there will be little doubt about his granting Patrick a new trial ...'[8]

The strategy was therefore to wait until the new governor was elected. 'If Hughes is elected,' Milliken wrote to Hill on 1 November, 'I see but one thing to do, and that is, go to Higgins as quickly as possible. If Hearst is elected, then I am willing to let the case go to the Supreme Court, and take chances upon getting some favors from Mr. Hearst, should we have to go to him.'[9]

A week later, Hughes won the election. He defeated Hearst for governor by a plurality of nearly sixty thousand votes, while every other state official elected was a Democrat.

# 88. Application for a Pardon?

'Patrick's fight for life,' the *World* wrote, 'is the most remarkable of its kind ever made in this country.'[1]

On Tuesday, 8 November 1906, the day after Hughes' electoral victory, Patrick's sisters May Milliken and Emma Patrick (now married to Robert Jamison, a North Dakota banker) went to see their brother, Albert, to try to convince him to allow a petition for clemency to be sent to Governor Higgins on his behalf.

Hill's approach, 'carefully drawn' to overcome what he referred to as 'the obstinacy of Mr. Patrick,' was to have the family present a petition – signed by Patrick's mother, wife, and four sisters, in that order – and to have Patrick ratify the petition, while still protesting his innocence.[2]

Patrick, however, was opposed to the making of a family application as 'it gives to the matter an air of despair and pleading for mercy which is unwarranted.' His sisters pleaded with him, however, and he finally agreed to draft an application for a pardon in his own name and to consent to the withdrawal of the writ of error. The case, number 336 on the Supreme Court's calendar, would probably not be reached before the next October term of the court. The withdrawal of the writ was not a major concession because Patrick had always felt that the proper legal approach was to file a writ of habeas corpus, which, he wrote Hill, he still intended to do. Milliken wanted to stay out of the question of the withdrawal of the writ because, as he wrote to Hill, 'Higgins might give no relief, and if matters came to the worst, the balance of the family would for ever blame me for having the writ of error withdrawn.'

The two sisters brought back with them a petition signed by Patrick that asked for a pardon, but had included the crucial words 'and not otherwise.' The petition read as follows:[3]

The Governor of the State of New York,
                    Albany, N.Y.
Sir: –

While solemnly protesting my innocence and having confidence that the Federal Courts would eventually declare my trial unfair and conviction unjust and illegal and that upon a new trial my innocence would be conclusively established; yet in view of the enormous expense and unending delay of legal proceedings, and at the earnest entreaties of my faithful wife, my bereft little children, my aged mother, my anguished sisters and other dear relatives and faithful friends, whose wishes and interests under the circumstances I cannot disregard, I yield

with reluctance my own judgment and inclinations in the matter and hereby
apply to you for a free pardon and not otherwise, upon the ground that the
newly discovered medical and other evidence proves that there was a fundamen-
tal mistake of fact and a miscarriage of justice in and by my conviction, sufficient
to restore my presumptive innocence and to warrant a pardon.

Respectfully,<br>
Albert T. Patrick.

Sing Sing Prison
  Ossining, N.Y.,
    November 8, 1906.

Hill knew that the governor and his legal counsel, Huffcut, would
not accept that wording as it limited the governor to granting a free
pardon, and Emma Jamison returned to Sing Sing and persuaded her
brother to delete the words 'and not otherwise.' A new petition dated
15 November was signed by Patrick. He left it up to Hill's discretion
to decide whether to present the petition, stating: 'You are on the ground
and will have the opportunity of determining the lay of the land and
the chances of a *pardon*. My own opinion is that if you urge that and
that alone, without suggestion of compromise you will get it ... Somebody must decide it, and I have chosen you to make the decision
– whether you will apply or not.'[4]

Whatever Hill decided to do, Patrick wanted it clearly understood
by Hill that 'no one has any authority from me to seek or accept anything
less than a full pardon.' If a commutation came rather than a pardon,
he wanted to bring further legal proceedings. It would not be 'such a
serious injury to me if done over my protest,' he wrote Hill, 'but if
upon my application it would be irreparable.' 'I am either innocent or
guilty,' the *Evening Journal* quoted him as saying under his byline: 'If
guilty let the law take its course. If innocent, as I know I am, I must
be set free.'[5]

Kohler and Olcott felt it was not wise to abandon the writ of error.
Kohler wrote to Hill: 'I am not the only lawyer familiar with the Patrick
case, who believes that the appeal to the U.S. Supreme Court has merit,
and, if properly conducted, affords at least a fair prospect of success ... Since when is it the law that an appeal from a judgment of death
must be abandoned before the Governor has jurisdiction to exercise executive clemency?'[6]

The arrangement for the withdrawal of the writ of error may have
been suggested by one of Milliken's emissaries, H.H. Kohlsaat. He was

an influential wealthy publisher from Chicago – he once tried to buy
the New York *Times* and the New York *Tribune* – and was probably
a business associate of Milliken's. He seemed to know a great number
of influential people; one of his books is entitled *From McKinley to Harding*,
and when he died in 1924 Herbert Hoover said, 'Mr.
Kohlsaat has been a valued friend of every President since McKinley.'[7] It is known
that Kohlsaat saw Jerome and discussed the requirement that the writ
of error be withdrawn. He also seems to have silenced Jerome's public
comments on the case. Moreover, he kept in contact with Higgins' counsel,
E.W. Huffcut, wiring Milliken a week before the election of Hughes
that he was going to see Huffcut in Ithaca: 'I want Huffcut to be primed
before he goes to Albany, which he will probably do immediately after
election.'[8]

The press wrote that rumors were circulating in Albany and New
York City that Governor Higgins was about to commute Patrick's sentence.
The *World* had a headline stating: 'Lawyer Patrick Wins His Great
Fight for Life.' The *Times* more cautiously reported that 'from a reliable
source it was learned that Gov. Higgins gave a definite promise to commute
the sentence of Patrick two weeks ago.'[9] (On the same page of
that issue of the *Times* containing a two-column story on Patrick – it
is worth noting as an aside – is a very obscure item stating that the
prosecution hoped to complete its evidence that day in Herkimer, New
York, in the Chester Gillette murder case. Twenty years later, the Gillette
case would achieve a fame far greater than Patrick's when Theodore
Dreiser wrote *An American Tragedy* based on it.)

Governor Higgins said from his hometown of Olean that there was
'no authority for the statement. I cannot now say whether I will take
action in Mr. Patrick's case or not.'[10] His office in Albany put out a
release stating that the report was 'absolutely and unqualifiably false.'[11]

Patrick himself did not know what was going on. He wrote to Hill
on 30 November: 'I am so in the dark that I do not know what if anything
I should do.'[12] He had just completed his fifth Thanksgiving in solitary
confinement.

# 89. Governor Higgins

Governor Higgins and his wife came to New York in early December
for Christmas shopping. He was besieged by reporters at the Waldorf-Astoria,
asking whether he had reached a conclusion on the Patrick case.
'All reports that I have decided to pardon Mr. Patrick, or have denied

the application for a pardon, are erroneous,' he said: 'I have reached no conclusion and must decline to say anything more about the case.'[1] The governor and his advisers were not willing to deal with the issue until the Supreme Court case was withdrawn.

On 13 December 1906 the Supreme Court of the United States, on a motion by Senator Lindsay, dismissed Patrick's writ of error. That evening, Governor Higgins, who was back at the Waldorf-Astoria, told the press: 'I have seen no one in connection with the Patrick case since the action of the Supreme Court in Washington, and no application of any sort has been made to me.'[2]

Kohler expressed his concern that the writ of error and stay had now been withdrawn and 'executive clemency is by no means yet assured.' Kohler suggested to Hill that he could get letters to the governor from such leaders of the bar as Joseph H. Choate, Paul Cravath, 'and possibly – as act of conscience – William B. Hornblower.'[3]

Behind the scenes, the governor's legal adviser, Ernest W. Huffcut, was playing a major role. Huffcut was then the dean of the Cornell Law School. A graduate of Cornell's first law class in 1888, he took Charles Evans Hughes' position at Cornell in 1893 and became dean in 1903. The author of five books on commercial law subjects, the forty-six-year-old Huffcut was understandably known in Albany as 'the Dean.'[4]

It was perhaps Huffcut more than Higgins who had to be convinced. Milliken arranged for Dr James Ewing to send a letter to Huffcut. Ewing, it will be recalled, was a distinguished professor of pathology at Cornell and one of the founders of the Memorial Sloan-Kettering Hospital and the American Cancer Society, and had given evidence for Patrick at the trial. 'I concluded,' Milliken wrote Hill, 'that I could not get anything more convincing to Huffcut's mind, than a declaration from one of the Professors of his own University.'

Ewing's letter was a persuasive one, arguing that Rice had died a natural death: 'I had several quiet conversations with Dr. Curry about the case, and became convinced that the Doctor was honest, and had reached a correct conclusion, regarding the conditions before death.'[5] He reviewed the medical evidence and concluded: 'I am quite familiar with all the medical evidence in the case, and have considered, and reconsidered it many times in the past four years. I have concluded that this medical evidence clearly demonstrates the existence of a critical moribund condition resulting from natural causes, and strongly favors the diagnosis of death, from natural causes.'

Finally, he criticized the practice of calling medical evidence – a practice still, of course, in existence today:

The medical history of the Patrick case demonstrates what every thinking person has long known, that the present practice of calling expert medical testimony in homicide cases is a disgrace to our civilization. The bearded ignoramus, the busy practitioner, the half trained pathologist are called at random, and the testimony of each is given equal weight by the lay Judge and jury, or is estimated by law standards. I would urge upon you, as a jurist, that of all branches of medicine, experimental pathology is the most highly technical, expert and difficult, requiring rare natural gifts, and long and critical training. Only one man in America has even the title, that in our own University.

Olcott, who, it will be recalled, had once been the district attorney of New York City, directed his own letter to Huffcut, after first clearing it with Hill, stating that his 'professional connection with the Patrick case has practically ceased' and so he feels more free to offer his 'personal opinions and belief':

I believe that Patrick is as guiltless of the alleged murder of Rice as you or I. I believe he was falsely convicted by perjured testimony as to facts, and mistaken opinions as to theories. I think the story of Jones, and the corroborative testimony of the prosecution's experts, alike impossible. The attitude and the statements of the prisoner to me have all been persuasive to my mind of his complete innocence.[6]

Most importantly, Olcott dealt with what lawyer House had been told, an issue that had been repeatedly stressed by Osborne and Jerome. Olcott wrote:

The so-called House episode, with which you have been made familiar, is hard to fathom and difficult to analyze; but Mr. House (not-withstanding his insistent reticence as to the much-talked-of professional communication with his then clients, Patrick and Jones) has solemnly assured me of his belief that Rice was not murdered and that Patrick is not guilty of any degree of homicide.

Patrick sent Huffcut House's opening address at the trial and a later affidavit, both of which appear inconsistent with a belief by House that Patrick confessed to him.

In a letter to Hill dated 24 November 1906, Patrick emphatically stated that he was innocent and had never confessed to House, but he admitted that Jones had done so, stating: 'I make no question that Jones, while under the influence of Baker and Osborne ... did tell me and House on October 31 that he used chloroform.'[7] He went on to state that although he had 'absolutely nothing to conceal' he would 'not consent to permit House to testify for reasons which are satisfactory to me.' But, he wrote, he asked his wife 'to obtain from House a statement ... that I never confessed any crime to him in any way.'

Several days later, Patrick wrote to Hill that Olcott advised Mrs Patrick not to see House or to ask him to make a statement. House, he wrote, was a 'nervous wreck,' and reporters were watching him and Mrs Patrick. He explained to Hill why he was worried about House and had brought in Moore as the senior counsel at trial: 'One of my reasons for dispensing with Mr. House's services was that I was informed very credibly that he was a morphine fiend and was unreliable in his statements ... A few months after my arrest I read in the newspapers that Mr. House was found speechless and mindless wandering about the streets.'[8] Moreover, Patrick believed that House was 'in league with my adversaries.' While House was his and Jones' counsel, House was 'in consultation' with the district attorney in a case in which he, House, and another lawyer had been retained by the DA 'for Miller of the Franklin syndicate.' Patrick went on: 'At the time House was said to have taken $17,000 of the funds as a fee. Armour [the cocounsel] was indicted and convicted for receiving stolen goods; House was not!'

In an earlier long letter to Governor Higgins, which was published in the *Albany Argus*, where Hill obviously had influence, Milliken wrote that before he agreed to support Patrick he had gone to see House with a waiver from Patrick. House, he said, confirmed Patrick's version that he, Patrick, never confessed and that when Jones told about the chloroform, Patrick had said: 'Mr. House, this is the first time that I have heard of this.'[9]

Milliken visited Huffcut at Ithaca to go over Patrick's case. At one point, according to Milliken, Huffcut turned to him and said: 'Mr. Milliken, I am very frank to tell you that Governor Higgins believes Patrick made a confession to his attorney, Fred House.' Milliken had with him a letter from House to Patrick, given shortly after the trial, in which House had stated: 'There is no doubt in my mind as to the final outcome of your matter. Now, just keep up your courage, and don't worry. You surely are bound to win in the end.' According to Milliken, Huffcut studied the letter for five minutes and stated: 'Mr. Milliken, I do not believe any reputable lawyer would write such a letter as this to a man that he knew was a self-confessed murderer.'[10]

Governor Higgins' papers have not survived in the archives in Albany and his personal papers at Syracuse University do not refer to the Patrick case, so it is not known what other letters and documents were sent. A few months earlier, it will be recalled, thirty-five hundred New York doctors had signed a petition on Patrick's behalf, and at the beginning of the year Dr Allan McLane Hamilton had sent a petition containing the signatures of many leaders of the legal and medical community as well as public figures such as ex-president Cleveland and Mark Twain. It is also likely that the Houston criminal lawyer J.B. Brockman sent a letter to the governor saying that Jones' brother told him that he lied when he testified that he sent chloroform from Texas to his brother Charlie in New York.

There is also a long twenty-five-page handwritten letter in the Hill papers from Patrick to the governor, which Patrick had asked Hill to send on to the governor with his application for a pardon. The letter ends as follows:

A bamboozled jury has found against me, a partisan judge has thrice pronounced judgment upon me, an unscrupulous prosecutor has continually denounced me in the newspapers, four judges of the Court of Appeals have given equivocal and colorable reasons for finding my guilt proved and trial fair, and yet such is the power of truth, that faith in my innocence grows stronger each day ... Strike loose my chains and unlock my prison door and the world will acclaim my innocence.[11]

The fact that a signed copy of the letter is in the Hill file probably means that Hill never sent it to the governor. Another document in Hill's files is the first twelve pages of a historical narrative of Patrick's early life, which he never completed.[12]

Hill himself had prepared a lengthy personal letter to the governor while he was recuperating in the South. He started the letter by stating: 'This is a most extraordinary case. Probably no criminal case in the country has attracted more widespread interest on the part of the legal profession, the medical profession, distinguished citizens, and the people generally ... The criminal annals of the country do not disclose any analogous case.'[13] His forty-two-page handwritten draft – and the fact that there is only a draft in the file is some indication that the letter was sent – ends with what Hill describes as 'a word personal to myself':

This is the first time since my retirement from the Governorship that I have made, endorsed, or advocated an application for Executive Clemency. From an experience of seven years in the Executive Chair I keenly realize the difficulties and responsibilities incident to the proper exercise of the pardoning power. I have no regrets to express over the cases in which I took the merciful side, and my only regret is that in some instances I was not more liberal.

Governor Higgins, he urged, has a duty to exercise 'such clemency as to him may seem appropriate ... I am sure that he will never regret such action.'

On Monday, 17 December 1906, Patrick's petition for a pardon was given to the governor. The next day, the governor and Dean Huffcut were invited to an embalming demonstration at the 19 December meeting of the Medico-Legal Society. 'The Society has its December dinner tomorrow evening,' the New York *Mail* reported, 'but the invitation does not specify whether the embalming and autopsy will take place before or after the dinner.'[14] Neither Higgins nor Huffcut attended.

On Thursday morning, 20 December, Patrick wrote to Hill that he was very worried about a commutation to life imprisonment, rather than a pardon: 'I am not and have not been alarmed at anything except the possibility of commutation. That I fear and dread ... I realize that if he commutes I cannot prevent it, but for moral effect, even if it be legally futile, I shall make a formal protest.'[15] Mrs Patrick expressed optimism to a reporter for the New York *American*: 'Far from asking for a commutation of sentence for Mr. Patrick, let me tell you I have much more encouraging hopes than that. I am expecting my innocent husband's freedom.'[16]

At noon on the 20th, Governor Higgins announced from Albany that he was commuting Patrick's sentence to life imprisonment and issued the following memorandum:

Albert T. Patrick has been convicted of the murder of William M. Rice, and the judgment of conviction has been affirmed by a divided court. It is not claimed that Patrick committed the murder in person, but that he procured the act to be done. He has been convicted principally upon the testimony of Charles F. Jones, who confessed that he murdered his master while he lay asleep, instigated thereto by Patrick, and Jones by this testimony has purchased his own immunity from trial or punishment. Neither this fact alone, nor the review of any of the facts already passed upon by the courts at some stage of these proceedings, would seem to me to warrant interfering with the judgment of death pronounced against the defendant, but three of the seven Judges of the Court of Appeals were so strongly of the opinion that errors were committed at the trial which were substantially prejudicial to the rights of Patrick that I feel that the death penalty ought not, under all the circumstances, to be inflicted.

In view of these facts and the grave doubts expressed by these Judges, I am satisfied that I ought to relieve the defendant from the extreme penalty of the law and commute his sentence to imprisonment for life.[17]

The New York *Times* reported that this was 'probably the most remarkable legal fight to save a man's life ever entered into in the criminal history of this State, if not in the United States.'[18]

# PART SEVEN
# Conclusion

Sing Sing Penitentiary at about the turn-of-the-century.

New York District Attorney Charles
Whitman, about 1910.

Houston criminal lawyer J.B.
Brockman, about 1910: *Houston Daily
Post*, 27 October 1910.

Governor John A. Dix (at wheel) and Mrs Dix about 1912, along with
'Cigarette,' the French poodle, and 'Bud,' the bulldog, in their Lozier car: New
York State Library, Albany.

Mrs Albert T. Patrick: New York *Times*, 28 November 1912.

Entrance to Rice University, Houston, today.

Statue of William Marsh Rice as a young man at Rice University.

# 90. Reactions

Immediately after receiving word of the commutation, Mrs Patrick left for Sing Sing on the 2:06 p.m. train from Grand Central Station. She drove up from the station in one of the horse-drawn station hacks and was taken immediately to her husband, who apparently had not yet been informed of the news. Whatever their private one-hour conversation may have been, Patrick's public response was one of great disappointment. A letter to his wife was immediately released to the press: 'It is needless to say that I am bitterly disappointed at the miscarriage of my hope for freedom, but I am not discouraged. I shall formally protest for its moral, even though it may have no legal effect ... I shall forthwith petition the incoming Governor to right this wrong.'[1] When Governor Higgins heard that Patrick was protesting the commutation, he remarked to the press: 'Patrick will have to be careful or he will find himself at Matteawan [the institution for the criminally insane]. He has apparently lost his head.'[2] The warden of Sing Sing, however, assured the press that Patrick showed no signs of insanity.

Patrick was, in fact, disappointed in not receiving a full pardon. He wrote to Senator Hill: 'This is a bitter disappointment to me ... I tried to force Gov. Higgins to pardon me but I failed.'[3]

Milliken immediately wired Patrick, after receiving the news of the commutation: 'Don't write or say anything, before getting letter from me; the fight will still go on.' In his letter to Patrick, Milliken wrote:

I know that you will be very much disappointed, because you did not get a pardon; I hoped that you would, but I did not expect it ... To grasp the true situation that your case presents, requires a careful study of the record, which you could not expect a Governor to make, especially Gov. Higgins whose health is not very good.

May and I feel very grateful to Gov. Higgins for what he has done, and I trust that you will not be ungrateful enough to condemn him for not pardoning you. You cannot possibly gain anything by such conduct, and you might prejudice Gov.-elect- Hughes against you. I know that you have suffered a long time, but bear it a little while longer, for in the end you must be vindicated.

Rest assured that this fight will go on. Now that your sentence has been commuted to life imprisonment, Jones will begin to demand from Baker, and his pals, the part of the Rice estate that was promised him, as the price of his perfidy and perjury, and the old adage of 'when thieves fall out, honest men get their just dues' will again be demonstrated.

In a letter thanking Governor Higgins for the commutation, Milliken wrote: 'Patrick is the victim of as foul a conspiracy as ever was concocted to deprive a man of his life and liberty.' 'James A. Baker of Houston, Texas is the main man who has been instrumental in prosecuting Patrick ... I am satisfied that this man is at the bottom of Patrick's woes and I am determined to expose him, if I live long enough. I am satisfied that he corrupted Jones.'

Milliken also wrote to Jerome, thanking him for not opposing the commutation and again expressing his belief in Patrick's innocence: 'As I told you, I believe him innocent, and I propose to continue fighting on that line, until I either prove it, or die.'

Milliken brought up the question of House's failure to testify and told Jerome that it was he, Milliken, who would not permit House to take the stand: 'Patrick was willing to waive House's privilege, and let him take the stand, but I forbid it, because I had information in my possession, that I have never made public, and which even Patrick does not know. I have a score to settle with House, before the Bar Association of your City, before I am done with the Patrick case.' Milliken never stated what his complaint was and never proceeded before the Bar Association. Within a month, House was appointed a city magistrate and six months later he was elected president of the Board of Magistrates.

Finally, Milliken wrote to Dean Huffcut, thanking him for his role in the commutation and stating: 'We can never tell in this life, where our paths may lead; most often they go in an unexpected direction and it may be that sometime, I may be able to do you a good turn. I trust, however, that you may never have the same kind of trouble that I have had ...' As it turned out, less than five months later, Huffcut committed suicide. Governor Hughes, for whom he had continued as counsel, thought that Huffcut's suicide by a handgun was the result of overwork. His suicide note to his sister – he was not married – showed, however, that he had been contemplating suicide for some time: 'Good bye. I don't want you or any of the others to be troubled about this. I've really postponed it often on account of others, but this time I am doing it. After all, in the end one must have his own way of escape.'[4]

The press gave extensive coverage to the commutation. Many newspaper editorials seized on the financial resources that had been available to Patrick. 'Is the chance equal,' the *Evening Sun* asked, 'as between those who have the money to pay for eminent legal services and for those who have not?' The *Fort Worth Record* put it more starkly, stating, 'It is impossible to hang a rich man.' Nobody expected that this was the last that would be heard from Patrick. 'It is to be feared,' the *Tribune* stated, 'that before very long we shall begin to hear appeals for his release.' And the New York *Times*, which approved the commutation, said:

Patrick was indicted for murder, and he is either innocent or guilty. In other words, he should have been put to death or set at liberty. Life imprisonment is wholly illogical under any even moderately strict interpretation of the law, and we are fairly well convinced that the present determination is only a step toward the release which should be his if he did not procure the killing of the old Texan, Rice.[5]

The *American Lawyer* agreed that a compromise was not just: 'There is no middle course. There is no such thing as splitting the difference and calling it a life imprisonment case.'[6]

Patrick was officially informed of the commutation by Warden Johnson the following afternoon, Thursday, 21 December 1906. The warden told the press that Patrick had spent the morning in his cell working on a writ of habeas corpus to the federal courts and a letter of protest which he handed to the warden at the time of his removal from the death house. The letter read:

Please take notice that I reject the warrant of the Governor of the State of New York now in your hands, commuting my death sentence to imprisonment for life, and that I refuse to accept or take any benefit under the same, and that I protest against the execution thereof, upon the ground that said warrant of the Governor, as well as the judgment of conviction upon which it is founded, is contrary to law and void.[7]

Patrick said good-bye to the nine other occupants of the death house and was taken to the main prison – the prison often referred to as 'the Big House.'

Sing Sing housed nearly fourteen hundred prisoners in its twelve hundred cells. As noted earlier, it was built in the 1820s and was strongly condemned by a series of commentators, studies, and reports in that very year, 1906. The New York *Times* summed up the prevailing view in an editorial the week of Patrick's transfer, stating that Sing Sing was 'disgraceful to our civilization in construction and sanitary arrangements.'[8] And Mrs Florence Maybrick, who had recently been pardoned in England for the murder of her husband and had subsequently visited twenty-four prisons in the United States, stated in a speech on the very day of his transfer that at Sing Sing 'strong men are shut up in cells, six feet by three, without ventilation, sanitary provisions, or water for thirteen hours a day' and that 'at high tide one could write one's name on the wall in the moisture.'[9]

The State Prison Improvement Commission appointed by Governor Higgins had reported the previous January that Sing Sing was entirely inadequate and should be replaced by a new building on a new site. It noted the peculiar odor of foulness in the cells and their confined dimensions: 'The dimensions of the cells at Sing Sing are: depth, 7 feet; width, 3 feet and 3 inches; height, 6 feet and 7 inches, giving for each cell a cubic space of 168.67 feet, much too small to house an adult person during the fourteen hours which each prisoner is usually required to remain in his cell daily and on Sundays and holidays additional hours.'[10] As a result, an Act was passed and a five-hundred-acre site was selected on the West Bank of the Hudson River, opposite Sing Sing. Over the next few years, the project became controversial: architects were unhappy with the method of selecting an architect, bringing a court action; and there was concern that the site was marshy, with a 'swamp river' running through it. In 1911, Governor Dix abandoned the project and took steps to improve Sing Sing and rebuild a new prison for those awaiting death.[11] As previously mentioned, Sing Sing is still in active use today.

The barber, following the prison regulations, shaved off Patrick's mustache and cropped his hair. His height was recorded as 5 feet 6 1/2 inches and his weight 171 pounds, four pounds heavier than when he first arrived. He was given the standard gray uniform with white metal buttons and a matching cap, the stripes being reserved for repeat offenders. Most of the inmates in Sing Sing were first offenders; second offenders were sent to Auburn.[12] The many New York lawyers convicted of crime – and this now included Abraham Hummel of Howe and Hummel fame – were therefore congregated in Sing Sing, as the press liked to point out.[13] Four small red shapes were sewn on the left sleeve of Patrick's uniform to indicate the number of years he had been in Sing Sing. In April, he would receive a star marking five years' imprisonment.

He was shown through the door and sash factory where he would be working. Under New York's 'State use' law, prison labor could only be used for government purposes and could not compete in the commercial world.[14] The *Times* reported: 'On arriving at the workshop Patrick at once became an object of intense interest to the convicts at work in the place. The men are not supposed to raise their eyes or look around them while at work, but none of them could resist the temptation to steal a glance at the noted prisoner, and the Warden overlooked this infraction of the rules for once.'[15] When the men had finished their work, they, along with Patrick, marched back to their cells. In 1900, a simple march had replaced the famous lock-step shuffle.[16] On the way back to their cells they received a chunk of ginger bread and some tea to take into their cells for supper. Life would be different from what it had been in the death cell. He would not have a large cell or good food; his 150-volume library would be taken away; and visits from his wife and others would be strictly limited.

Patrick was placed in cell no. 1074 in gallery 22.[17] At 6:30 the next morning, he marched silently – the silent system was then still in effect[18] – with his other cell-mates for breakfast, consisting of coffee and bread. He would begin the first full day of his life term by carrying lumber in the door and sash factory.

# 91. Hughes' Tenure Begins

Although Patrick had said that he would 'forthwith petition the incoming Governor to right this wrong,'[1] it was not until June 1907 that he applied to Governor Hughes for a full pardon.[2]

Hughes had, however, received a great number of letters from others seeking a pardon for Patrick. The Medico-Legal Society continued its agitation to free him. Clark Bell, its president, issued a statement that Patrick's innocence was 'a matter of absolute scientific demonstration.' 'The time has now come,' he wrote, 'when the Medico-Legal Society has asked me to call upon all men and women who believe and desire that the Governor should promptly pardon this man, who is guiltless of the death of Rice and who is now serving a life sentence in prison for a crime that he has never committed.'[3] The *Medico-Legal Journal* urged its medical members to secure signatures: 'it is your duty now in securing the names of medical men ... to the petition this Society will lay before the Governor for the full pardon of Patrick.'[4]

And the Medico-Legal Society also urged the embalmers in the United States to obtain signatures: 'The prominent part taken by your profession in demonstrating the innocence of Albert T. Patrick ... makes it a public duty for embalmers to sign the appeal for the pardon of Mr. Patrick, and to induce their patrons to do so.'[5]

The monthly journal, the *Sunnyside*, which claimed on its masthead to be 'the Oldest and Leading Embalmers' Journal in the World,' took up the cause. In an editorial in its February 1907 issue, it stated: 'there is not a scintilla of evidence that murder was committed.' A new expert, Dr William Smith of Kirksville, Missouri, appeared. Dr Smith happened to be in New York around the time of the commutation and read of the embalming issue. He contacted Olcott, Patrick's lawyer, and told him that in 1898 he had published an article in the *American X-ray Journal*[6] showing precisely what Patrick was claiming. He had injected a special solution into a dead body through the right brachial artery and then, using the newly discovered X-ray technique, obtained pictures of the circulation of the solution in the body. 'Simple embalming fluid,' he told the *Sunnyside*, 'will enter the lungs ... in every case, and I speak as one knowing.' He concluded by stating: 'I leave the pictures to speak for themselves; they tell more than I can. These pictures are the only ones of the kind in the world ... and it is strange, indeed, that what I did eight years ago, with no thought of its ever being used on such an occasion, by the merest chance came to my remembrance last week.'[7]

Dr Smith was a medical graduate of the Royal College of Physicians and Surgeons of Edinburgh, where he studied and worked with Sir Joseph Bell, the original of Sherlock Holmes.[8] For six years he was a demonstrator of anatomy in the American School of Osteopathy in Kirksville, Missouri, where he had dissected over a thousand bodies. 'Had a student in his second term,' he said, 'stated to me that "under no circumstances or in any way could embalming fluid reach the lungs," he would at once have been put back in his studies for six months.'

Dr Smith must have sent a copy of the article to Dr Bell at Edinburgh University, requesting his intervention in the case. Bell, in turn, asked some of his colleagues for their opinions. The May issue of the *Sunnyside* contains photographic excerpts from letters from Dr Bell and others, stating that Dr Smith was indeed correct in expressing the opinion that embalming fluid enters the lungs.[9]

One of the letters reproduced was signed by Sir Arthur Conan Doyle. 'I am much interested in your letter,' Conan Doyle had written to Dr Smith, 'and from the circumstances as stated there certainly seems to have been a gross miscarriage of justice.' This letter, apparently unknown to present-day Sherlock Holmes scholars, is not mentioned in the biography of Dr Joseph Bell,[10] or in a recent book on true crimes in which Conan Doyle became involved.[11] Indeed, the Patrick case may possibly have been the only American case in which Conan Doyle became directly involved. Embalming, however, does not play a part in any Sherlock

Holmes story, although the use of 'a chloroformed sponge' is briefly mentioned in a story published after 1907.[12]

New scientific techniques played a role in another way. Patrick's contention that the 1900 will was genuine was given a boost by the emerging science of fingerprinting which had just recently been introduced into police forces – Scotland Yard had not employed fingerprinting until 1901 and it was not until 1908 that the technique helped solve a murder case in New York City.[13]

Albert H. Hamilton, a forty-five-year-old pharmacist, who owned a drugstore in Auburn, New York, had started to become involved as a forensic expert in analytical chemistry and microscopy. He later sold the drugstore and devoted himself entirely to his new profession. In his obituary in the *Times* in 1938, he was noted as 'one of the recognized authorities in handwriting, bullet and gun identification,' having appeared as an expert witness in nearly three hundred homicide cases.[14]

Hamilton had written to Patrick in Sing Sing in 1904 saying that the case against him 'hinges upon the presumption by the Courts that a man in the ordinary writing of his signature upon the same or subsequent days does not and cannot write his name two or more times exactly alike.' 'What I wish to call to your attention,' Hamilton wrote, 'is that this assumption is not correct.'[15] Hamilton had made a study of the subject in another murder case and wrote to Senator Hill:

I am just completing a systematic record of the study of over 20,000 check signatures written by various businessmen, and find the following facts – that the ability to write two to four and even six check signatures so near alike upon the same day that they will superimpose to an extent of 80 to 90% is common to many businessmen. I have records of all these occurrences and it is a complete exposure of the fallacy and absurdity of statements claimed by experts in the Rice case and accepted by courts as facts.

The appearance that the signatures superimposed was, he said without explanation, 'due to an optical illusion practiced through the art of the photographer.' On his own initiative, Hamilton examined the expert testimony and signature exhibits in the Rice case in the Court of Appeals office and told Hill that he 'was much surprised to find the disputed signatures do not superimpose ... as closely as some of the standards.' Although Patrick wanted to involve Hamilton in the case, Hill did not choose to do so, preferring instead to concentrate on the medical evidence.[16]

But it was Hamilton's accidental discovery two years later of what he alleged was Rice's fingerprint in ink above his signature in the 1900 will which brought him into the case. Hamilton wrote to the *World*, stating that this was 'conclusive evidence ... that this signature is genuine.'[17] He claimed that Rice had the habit of blotting the ink in his signature and in other places with his forefinger, and this could be seen in his final signature on the 1900 will and also on an admittedly genuine document signed on the same date, 30 June 1900. 'The same finger of the same person,' he stated, 'made both prints.'[18] Hamilton told the *World* that he had sent this new information to Judge Goff, but his letter was not even acknowledged. 'I am in no way connected with either side of the Rice case,' he told the *World*. Samuel Bell Thomas, acting for Patrick, immediately established contact with Hamilton.

Meanwhile, Milliken was attempting to get evidence in Texas concerning Jones. 'I think that in a short time,' he wrote Hill on 6 March 1907, 'I will be able to land Jones alright.' Milliken, however, may have had more than Patrick's welfare at heart. He had taken an assignment of Patrick's interest in the Rice estate and wrote to Hill: 'I have been told that if Patrick should gain his freedom ... suit could be brought to set aside the probate of the will of W.M. Rice. I wish you would let me know if such a suit as this could be maintained under the laws of the State of New York.'[19] 'There is no use of wasting your money in schemes which have no substantial foundation,' was Hill's reply.[20]

Relations between Senator Hill and Milliken cooled the following month, however, when Hill sent a bill for $7,500 for his services after the appeal. Milliken replied that he was 'somewhat astonished at the bill that you have rendered me.' Hill answered: 'there can be no doubt of your legal liability therefore and I must insist upon receiving such compensation.' Many months later, Hill's account still had not been paid. Over the summer, the reduction plant for Milliken's Golden Cycle Mine in Cripple Creek burned down without adequate insurance and Milliken wanted time to negotiate a settlement with Hill. This souring of relations meant that Hill was no longer a central figure in the case, and so the rich information on the case preserved in his files subsequently becomes relatively sparse.

The Rice Institute in Houston had now settled the major litigation with Rice's relatives over his estate, had chosen a new site for the campus instead of the confined six acres that Rice had provided, and was taking steps to appoint a president. Later in 1907, Professor Edgar Odel Lovett, the head of the Department of Astronomy at Princeton, was chosen as president – he remained in the position until 1946 – and in 1908 the present three-hundred-acre site then outside the city limits was selected.[21]

The newspapers in Texas were enthusiastic. 'All obstacles have been overcome and ... during 1907 one of the greatest schools in the United States will be born in Houston,' said the *Galveston News*: 'The endowment makes possible the founding of a school greater than any in the South and equal to any in the United States with the single exception of Leland Stanford University in California.'[22] The *Houston Chronicle* was even more eloquent: 'It would be the greatest institute of learning in this entire country, and could be made far ahead of either Princeton or Yale.'[23] The *Houston Post* noted that the institute would be 'absolutely free to white boys and girls of Houston, first, and then free to white boys and girls of Texas.'[24]

The Rice trustees were obviously concerned about Patrick's commutation and the renewed agitation for a pardon. A series of articles emanating from New York, published in the *Houston Post*,[25] were particularly disturbing. Samuel Bell Thomas was quoted as the source of the stories which stressed that the new fingerprint evidence proved that the Patrick will was genuine. One article alleged that because the Patrick will had 'deprived interested parties in Texas of a vast fortune he had to be put to death to enable them to acquire possession of it.' 'It is asserted,' the *Post* went on, 'that the fees paid to the lawyers in New York representing the estate are the largest fees ever paid attorneys in connection with any criminal case in the history of the world.' Thomas told the *Post* that proceedings might be brought in Texas with respect to the will; the normal statute of limitations in Texas, he said, would not apply to someone in Patrick's position.

Baker spoke to Colonel R.M. Johnston, the editor-in-chief of the *Houston Post*, about one such article and later wrote to him when another appeared:

In view of the fact that the so-called Patrick will was pronounced a forgery by all of the courts of New York through which it passed, and that Patrick is now serving a life term in the penitentiary for the murder of Mr. Rice, it seems to me that communications such as the one enclosed ought to be suppressed. They do no good and are calculated to keep alive issues that have been settled in our courts.[26]

The district attorney's office in New York also took steps to control the damage. Arthur Train, an assistant district attorney in New York with a journalistic flair, published an article in the May issue of the monthly *American*[27] in which he argued that Patrick's guilt was clear. The title of his article shows its flavor: 'The Patrick Case Complete: In Which an Ingenious Conspiracy Crumbled, and a Famous Murder Was Exposed.' Mrs Patrick sent a long letter to the press in which she stated:

I warn the public that the article besmirching my husband, which has been inspired by the chief bloodhound of the law and put into libellous and odious print by one of his underlings, has for its aim and object the further poisoning of the public mind with a view to influencing another jury in the dastardly work already mapped out for it. The judicial crime committed against Albert T. Patrick is to be followed, if possible, by another similar crime against two of the witnesses who dared to tell the truth in his behalf and who swerved not a hair's breadth, in spite of threats, persecution, arrest and third degrees like those under which Jones, the secretary of William M. Rice, broke down and perjured his cowardly soul four or more times in succession.[28]

The *Evening Journal*, suspecting that this was Patrick talking, commented that her language is 'very like that used by her husband.'[29]

The 'chief bloodhound,' Jerome, took steps to try to ensure that Jones' evidence would be available on any new trial. Jerome went to Albany to ask for passage of an amendment to the Code of Criminal Procedure to provide that if a court stenographer should die, any person who was able to read the shorthand notes would be competent to do so at a subsequent trial.[30]

On 21 July 1907, a *World* reporter interviewed Patrick in Sing Sing. Patrick was still in the door and sash department, but he was no longer hauling lumber; not surprisingly, he was now handling the books of the department. Patrick outlined to the reporter his views on penology and corrections: how there should be greater use of parole (it did not apply to lifers) and more indeterminate sentences – ideas that were then current among criminologists.

He told the reporter that he was hoping for the pardon he had applied for the previous month:

'How do you hope that can be accomplished?' asked the *World* reporter.

'Governor Hughes can do all that. He is a first-class lawyer, and besides, an honest and upright man. All I want the Governor to do is to look into my case, read the papers on file in the office, and I have no fear as to the final outcome.'[31]

Patrick also outlined his planned application to the courts:

I hold that I am confined in State prison in an illegal way, because the Governor granted me something for which no application had been made. Under the Constitution of the United States no man can be confined in an illegal way in any penal or other institution. Therefore I will apply for a writ of habeas corpus in a United States court, and I believe I will be discharged.

# 92. Court Proceedings

It was not until the following spring of 1908 that Patrick applied to the Federal Circuit Court for the Southern District of New York for a writ of habeas corpus. He was assisted by his friend, William L. McDonald, a New York lawyer who had been in his law class at the University of Texas.[1]

The motion came before Circuit Judge E. Henry Lacombe, who had been appointed to the circuit court in 1887 after being the corporation counsel for the City of New York. (On the creation of the Circuit Court of Appeals in 1891 he was appointed to that bench, remaining until he retired in 1916.)[2]

Patrick alleged in his petition[3] that there was a conspiracy against him involving James A. Baker, Jr, Judge Goff, District Attorneys Jerome, Osborne, and Garvan, and the members of the Court of Appeals who had held against him. These persons, Patrick alleged, 'knowingly, wilfully and corruptly conspired, confederated and acted together,' *inter alia*, for the purpose of depriving him 'of his life and liberty without due process of law,' contrary to the US Constitution. Their main motive, he said, was to prevent him from properly litigating and enforcing his claim to the Rice estate. Because of the conspiracy, he went on, 'it is wholly impracticable for your complainant to obtain any redress, hearing or just conclusion of law or fact from the State officers or tribunals, and an emergency exists which makes relief by this Court imperative.' Patrick was obviously trying to fit his case into the very narrow confines of the existing habeas corpus jurisprudence.[4]

Patrick also claimed that life imprisonment could not be imposed on him because 'life imprisonment, as administered and applied in the prisons of the State of New York, is a greater, not a less, punishment than the death penalty.'

On 15 June 1908, Judge Lacombe, sitting in the since-destroyed five-story federal Post-Office Building[5] at the lower end of City Hall Park, without bringing Patrick from Sing Sing or giving notice to the district attorney and without reasons, dismissed the petition.[6]

An appeal was brought by Patrick and McDonald to the Supreme Court of the United States. 'Well, here I am again, Mr. McKenny,' Patrick wrote to the clerk of the Supreme Court; 'this time I believe right and to stay to the end.'[7] Patrick added a further original motion of habeas corpus and asked for an expedited hearing. He also added an allegation against the administration of Sing Sing, stating that it

is managed and conducted by the prison authorities with the intent and effect of injuring the convicts there confined, mentally, morally and physically, generally to their utter ruin, under color of arbitrary and unworkable rules, enforced at discretion; whereby the prison authorities hold an arbitrary and irresponsible control over the prisoners, exercised with arrogance, contempt and malignity.[8]

The hearing was scheduled to take place in November 1908. Edgar Kohler and Olcott tried to talk Patrick out of proceeding with the Supreme Court appeal, and Kohler remarked in a letter to Hill that 'Patrick has been his own lawyer in this matter ... with a proverbial result.'[9] Patrick's appeal, Kohler said, was based on an inadequate record and made allegations 'so sweeping and in a manner so bold as to divest the case of the slightest chance of obtaining a patient consideration from any court.' This would be unfortunate, he said, because the case raised 'several grave federal questions.' The present appeal, he said, 'will lead to the almost inevitable dismissal of his case by the Supreme Court.'

The New York district attorney's office had a technical objection to the proceedings, bringing an application to dismiss Patrick's appeal on the basis of a recently enacted federal statute that stated that appeals to the Supreme Court in criminal cases were to be accompanied by a certificate from the lower federal court or a justice of the Supreme Court to the effect that 'there exists probable cause for an appeal.'[10] When McDonald commenced his argument on 9 November for an early hearing of the case before the full Court, he was summarily stopped by Chief Justice Fuller, who turned to Assistant District Attorney Robert C. Taylor to first argue his application to quash the proceedings.[11]

The seventy-six-year-old Melville W. Fuller had been chief justice of the United States since 1888 and ran the court with a strong and efficient hand.[12] He and his brethren were obviously unsympathetic to Patrick for the reasons Kohler had given, but they were also opposed to widening challenges to state criminal proceedings in the federal courts.

This was an age of crime control, not one of due process.[13] The very day that Patrick's appeal was argued, the Supreme Court released their decision in *Twining* v. *New Jersey*,[14] in which they gave a very narrow interpretation to the words 'due process of law' in the Fourteenth Amendment, holding in that case that the right against compulsory self-incrimination in the Fifth Amendment did not apply to the states. (It was not until *Mapp* v. *Ohio*[15] in 1961 that there was a wholesale incorporation into the Fourteenth Amendment of the earlier provisions of the Bill of Rights.) On 16 November 1908, the Supreme Court, without reasons, unanimously dismissed Patrick's appeal for 'want of jurisdiction' and denied his application for a writ of habeas corpus.[16]

Patrick wrote to the clerk of the Supreme Court saying that he would start again in either the circuit court or the state court and added a light-hearted postscript: 'Please keep your eye on Congress and don't let them furtively pass any more laws to obstruct my getting a day in court.'[17]

A new application for a writ of habeas corpus was filed by McDonald on Patrick's behalf in early 1909 in the state court before Justice William Gaynor[18] of the Second Department of the Appellate Division of the New York Supreme Court, sitting in Brooklyn. Patrick's argument – described editorially by the *Times* as having 'a characteristic audacity and ingenuity'[19] – centred on the fact that Governor Higgins had no right to commute the sentence because life imprisonment is worse than death. The *Times* conceded that for some persons 'many weary years of [imprisonment] might be acutely painful enough to make such leniency as Patrick received mean an intolerable increase of suffering.'

Gaynor, later that year elected mayor of New York City, had apparently previously discussed the issue with McDonald privately and thought the question a very important one which should come before the full appellate bench.[20] He therefore issued a writ of habeas corpus to have Patrick appear before the full bench of the Second Appellate Department.[21] One of Milliken's personal lawyers from St Louis, Tyson S. Dines,[22] met with McDonald and formed a poor impression of him as 'inexperienced, illogical and at times irrational.'[23] Dines, however, thought the argument a good one: if they could establish that the governor could not substitute life, they could then argue on double-jeopardy grounds that Patrick could not be executed after he had already served time under a life sentence. Milliken wrote to Senator Hill asking him if he would be willing to appear on the appeal. Milliken, however, had still not paid Hill's $7,500 bill for his activity in obtaining the commutation and Hill was obviously not willing to get involved in further proceedings.

The appeal was heard in the Brooklyn Borough Hall. Patrick was brought from Sing Sing – his third trip out of the prison since he was incarcerated. For over three hours, Patrick argued his appeal before a crowded courtroom. Assistant District Attorney Taylor pointed out the consequence of Patrick's argument: 'If the Governor's act was invalid the sentence remains. If he refuses the commutation – it is hard for me to say it, but I must do so – there remains the judgment of death. The courts can again fix a date for the execution of the sentence in this case.'[24] At this point, the press heard Patrick state in a low tone of voice, echoing Patrick Henry's famous remark: 'I want liberty or death.' 'Liberty or Death, Patrick's Demand' was the *Times* headline the next day.

The court asked for written briefs. Warden Frost of Sing Sing, in compliance with the court's direction, relieved Patrick from routine work so that he could devote himself to preparing the brief. On Friday, 4 June 1909, Justice Almet F. Jenks,[25] a former assistant district attorney and corporation counsel in Brooklyn, delivered the unanimous judgment of the court:

I have no doubt that the Governor had the power of commutation in this case. I find no force in the contention that there cannot be a commutation of the punishment of death to that of life imprisonment, because commutation implies a less punishment, but life imprisonment is a greater punishment than death. The degree of a punishment is not determined by the individual preference of a convict. It is the common judgment of man that to deprive the criminal of his life is the greatest punishment known to modern times.[26]

McDonald announced that they would seek leave to appeal to the New York Court of Appeals.

A further habeas corpus motion was later brought to the Appellate Division in Brooklyn to add an argument that was said to have been overlooked in the earlier appeal, that is, that Justice O'Brien of the Court of Appeals had no authority to grant a stay of execution in 1904. After a two-hour argument by Patrick – another trip from Sing Sing – and without calling on the district attorney, Justice Jenks dismissed the motion.[27]

Patrick returned to Sing Sing to face his eighth Christmas there. The institution was now severely overcrowded. There were 1,875 prisoners in 1909, 350 more than at the same time the previous year. Convicts were being housed in the auditorium – actually the Protestant chapel – and as a result the annual vaudeville show had to be canceled.[28]

# 93. Meyers and Short

On 1 January 1910, Charles Seymour Whitman took office as the district attorney of New York. Jerome had hoped to have a third term in office, but the reform groups which had backed him turned to Whitman, a Republican, who was nominated as their candidate. The unsuccessful Democratic candidate was George Gordon Battle, who had acted in 1900 as Jones' counsel.[1]

Whitman, a law graduate from New York University, who in 1915 would become governor of New York, had, like Jerome before him, been a crusading magistrate. He personally conducted raids against 'Tenderloin' saloons and established the first night court in New York. In 1907 he had been elevated by Governor Hughes to the Court of General Sessions.[2]

One of his first tasks as district attorney was to clean up the backlog of criminal cases in the courts. The indictment against Patrick, Meyers, and Short for forgery and against Meyers and Short for perjury had been held in abeyance for almost ten years. The forgery charge against Jones had been dropped in 1901. On 5 January, Whitman assigned Assistant District Attorney William A. De Ford to look into the question of whether proceedings should now be brought.

For the past three years the district attorney's office had said they were now ready to try these indictments, but proceedings were never in fact brought. When Patrick's sentence was commuted in December 1906, Jerome announced that the trials for forgery and perjury would shortly commence. Meyers, who was still practicing law in New York, wrote to Senator Hill asking if he would serve as senior counsel for Short and himself in the expected cases. The Kohler brothers had already been engaged to assist in the defense. The funds would come from Milliken. Milliken had earlier put up the $15,000 bail when they were arrested and had set aside $7,500 for their defense.[3]

Milliken apparently believed that they were innocent. Immediately after Patrick's commutation, he wrote to Jerome saying: 'there has always been one mysterious thing to me in the Patrick case, and that is the conduct of Meyers and Short.'

In my own honest opinion, Meyers and Short are absolutely innocent of any wrong-doing in this matter. I have put every pressure to bear on them that I can, to get at the truth. They have been imprisoned, and importuned, and persuaded by others, to make a confession if they had done wrong, but they have resisted every effort, that has been made to induce them to make a confession. There was no motive for those boys to either commit forgery, or perjury, and I do not believe they did.[4]

After Short was released from custody, he took a job working for one of Milliken's companies in Philadelphia. Milliken told Jerome: 'every transaction that we have had with him has been on the level and I believe him perfectly honest and upright.'

In early 1908, Jerome became serious about the cases, removing them into the Supreme Court for trial.[5] But because of the press of other cases they could not be tried before the summer recess. Assistant Attorney Garvan wrote to Byrne:

On account of the condition of the calendars at this time it has been impossible to try the Meyers and Short cases. However, they must be tried in the fall, probably in October. I regret this delay but, as heretofore, will expect that during the summer months you will preserve all the evidence to be needed by me intact and will give to this office the same earnest support and assistance which you have given in the past.[6]

Byrne then wrote to Baker: 'What action do you desire us to take?' The Rice trustees told Byrne: they would 'be glad to have you co-operate with Mr. Garvin in the prosecution of Meyers and Short,' but 'would like to know what charge you will make for your professional services.' 'We should judge that our fee would be somewhere from $10,000 to $15,000,' Byrne replied, and if there was a later dispute they would allow Mr Lovett, Baker's former partner, to arbitrate. Four months later, after much hesitation, the trustees authorized Byrne's terms, but wanted to make it clear that it was the DA's prosecution and not theirs: 'whether the prosecution shall be continued or discontinued,' Baker wrote, 'about which we have heard there has been some uncertainty in the minds of the New York authorities, is a question the Trustees think should be determined by those authorities, and no one else ... You should do nothing which might be construed as stirring up or urging on of the prosecution by the trustees.' In a separate letter to Byrne, Baker expressed his personal view that they 'should be prosecuted to the full extent of the law.'

Several months later, however, the district attorney's office informed Byrne that the exhibits in the Patrick case could not be found. The exhibits had been kept in the safe of the clerk of the court, but the particular employee who was in charge of the Patrick case was now dead. Nevertheless, Jerome informed Byrne that it was still his intention personally to proceed with the prosecution. But he did not do so, and the cases were therefore still pending when Whitman took office.

Assistant District Attorney De Ford reported to Whitman in March 1910 that proceedings should not be brought against Meyers, Short, or Patrick for these further charges. 'These cases,' he said, 'have been pending for trial for the period of about nine years. I can find no justification for their not having been moved for trial immediately after the affirmance of the judgment' in Patrick's murder case. He then analyzed the evidence. Even if Jones could be found, his 'evidence would be of little value' because 'he is a self-confessed murderer' whose 'testimony ... was paid for by immunity.' Besides, he has probably 'given to the friends of Patrick a written denial' of his testimony.[7]

Moreover, and most importantly, the exhibits, with the exception of the 1900 will, could still not be found. Garvan, now in private practice, wrote that the last person to have the exhibits was the clerk, 'a man of the highest integrity,' who was now dead. In the declining years of the clerk's life, Garvan speculated, 'he either took them to his house, working on the case on appeal, or has carefully placed them in some place where they cannot be found.'

In spite of these problems, De Ford wrote, 'a case could be made out against the defendants which would probably result in their conviction.' However, he went on to say, 'the preparation and the presentation of the proofs would require enormous labor and large expense.' Moreover, he concluded, 'I am not satisfied that it would be just to the defendants, or sound practice, to put them on trial upon these charges in consideration of the long lapse of time.' In any event, he said, Short 'has probably learned his lesson' and steps could be taken to have Meyers disbarred.

Whitman accepted his recommendation that bail be discharged and so recommended to the court. The loss of the exhibits was not disclosed to the court or the public – all that was stated was that Jones's evidence was of 'little value' and that 'other evidence in the case is not now available.' No disbarment proceedings were ever taken against Meyers.

After the bail had been discharged, Byrne wrote to Baker saying that the defendants would undoubtedly now move that the indictments be dismissed, particularly Meyers, who 'is practising law here and stands well with the judges of the City Court.' 'Is it your desire to oppose the dismissal?' Garvan asked. Baker replied: 'the Trustees are not disposed to interfere in any particular way in whatever action the District Attorney decides to take.'

On 16 May 1910, with the approval of the district attorney, the indictments against Meyers and Short were dismissed, and a month later the forgery charge against Patrick was similarly dismissed. They could now never again be charged with these specific offenses.

# 94. J.B. Brockman

The next step in Patrick's fight for a pardon was to try to get Charlie Jones or his brother to swear that they had lied at Patrick's trial. In September 1910, Mrs Patrick went to Houston to work with the leading criminal lawyer in Southern Texas, J.B. Brockman, to secure affidavits from the Joneses. Milliken had discussed the financial terms for Brockman's assistance when he had met him in Dallas several months earlier.[1] The precise terms of the arrangement are not known, but it is known that Brockman charged very high fees – in one criminal case receiving over $30,000.

Milliken wanted affidavits from the Joneses, not from persons to whom they had allegedly spoken. The disastrous experience with Joe Jordan and the other Texans at the motion for a new trial in 1906 was still fresh in everyone's memory.

Several years earlier, Jones' brother-in-law, West, had visited Milliken in St Louis to sound out the possibility of a retraction from Jones. Milliken was in Colorado at the time and Charles Tinsley, who had helped get the witnesses from Texas for the new trial motion, saw West. Tinsley later told Milliken that Jones claimed that the conviction was 'a job put up by Baker and Osborne.'[2] Jones' father was told, according to West, that if his son 'did not implicate Patrick for the death of old man Rice they would send Jones to the electric chair.' The information was sent by Milliken to Judge Lewis Fisher of the 17th Judicial District of Texas, a friend of Patrick's, to try to get affidavits, but nothing seems to have come of this.

And in late 1909 another attempt was made by some unidentified Texans to procure affidavits. In a letter to Senator Hill – his final letter in the Hill papers – Milliken states: 'I have had a number of overtures made to me by people from Texas to procure an affidavit from Chas. F. Jones exonerating Patrick; two men were here yesterday, one of whom was here last month. They claim that for a consideration they could deliver Jones' affidavit completely exonerating Patrick, but they want an exorbitant price for their services.'[3] He told Hill that he was trying to obtain affidavits from 'a reliable source.'

That reliable source was probably J.B. Brockman. It is not possible to be definite about this next stage because the main source of information is a memorandum to file prepared by Captain Baker, who was careful to leave blanks instead of names for most of the characters. Milliken had arranged for one of his Colorado Springs lawyers to see a 'Colonel,' probably Colonel Holt, and another person, probably J.B. Brockman, to induce them to try to find Jones. In a letter to the Colorado Springs lawyer, Milliken wrote:

If you succeed in finding Jones and induce him to make an affidavit I want you to impress upon his mind the fact that I will protect him and do my best to aid him in removing the disgrace that must ever be uppermost in his mind. You may say to him that I had a conversation with Mr. Jerome last January in the presence of Saml. Bell Thomas of New York City. In that conversation I asked him if he would prosecute Jones if he would come out and say that the statement of his alleged killing of Rice was false and Jerome promised me in Thomas' presence that he would not prosecute Jones and that if there was a conspiracy for Jones to perjure himself that he would let Jones go free and prosecute the men higher up. I think that it would be best for you to have Jones come to St. Louis where his affidavit can be drawn and from which place he can more easily reach Colorado where I can find employment for him.[4]

Colonel Holt, it seems, made a copy of this letter and showed it to Baker, one of the 'men higher up.' He did so, Baker noted in his memorandum, 'because of his personal regard for me and the Institution of which I was a trustee.' Baker recorded that Jones would be offered $25,000 to make the affidavit and that Jones had been located by the Patrick interests in Texas, living under the name Lashwell. The colonel promised to keep Baker 'posted from time to time about what was going on.'

Brockman had apparently procured an affidavit from Fayette Jones to the effect that he had never sent chloroform to his brother. The affidavit had been mailed to Milliken in St Louis, but it had never arrived there. As a result, Mrs Patrick was sent to Houston to work with Brockman to obtain and bring back the crucial affidavits. Milliken, of course, suspected that Baker and his group had intercepted the earlier communication.[5]

James B. Brockman was an exceptionally busy and successful lawyer. He had pending at the time eighteen capital cases and as many as two hundred and fifty civil cases. The *Houston Post* said that in the past four years he was reported to have lost only one criminal case, and in that case his client was eventually pardoned. Born in Georgia, the forty-eight-year-old Brockman had traveled with his blind mother to New York State after the Civil War and eventually became a lawyer in Elmira, New York. He had come to Houston in 1895. One of his major pending cases involved the defense of Earl McFarlane, who was accused of murdering the night chief of the Houston Police Force the previous spring. There was so much gunplay in Houston at the time that Mayor H.B. Rice later that month had personally brought to Houston two crack-shot former Texas Rangers, Henry L. Ransom and Jules J. Baker, to help restore order. They were to perform whatever duties were assigned to them by the mayor.[6]

On Sunday, 23 October 1910, Brockman went to Galveston. Mrs Patrick wired Milliken that Brockman had finally gone to obtain the affidavits. He stayed in Galveston three days, returning to Houston late Tuesday.

Brockman spent that evening in his law office and then had a drink in a nearby saloon. At 11:40 p.m., while crossing the road at the corner of Franklin Avenue and San Jacinto Street to get a tram to his house, he was shot with a .45 by Special Officer Henry Ransom, who was accompanied by Jules Baker.[7]

The wounded lawyer was taken to the hospital. Justice McDonald was immediately called and Brockman gave a dying statement: 'I have been in Galveston ... and had gone to my office ... I walked across the street to the corner where I was to get the car. I saw Ransom and a man whom I have often seen with him. I said "Good evening, gentlemen," and Ransom pulled his gun and began shooting ... I have never spoken a half-dozen words to him in my life. I scarcely knew him.'[8] Four bullets entered Brockman's body, two from the back. Brockman had a gun on him, but claimed he had not drawn it.

The surgeons held out no hope and twelve hours later, in the presence of his wife and young daughter, he died. Ransom and Baker were charged with murder. The grand jury released Baker, but found a true bill against Ransom. Ransom made a brief statement for the press, claiming self-defense: 'All I care to say at this time is that I regret the circumstances which forced me to shoot Attorney Brockman. I had to kill him or be killed by him.'[9]

Mrs Patrick returned to New York without the affidavits. In a three-part series of articles in the New York *Times* in December 1910, obviously engineered by Milliken, the allegation was directly made that Brockman was murdered by the Rice interests in Texas. Mrs Patrick prepared an affidavit, reproduced in the *Times*, in which she said that Brockman had told her that 'neither his life nor mine would be safe if it were known that I was there and he was aiding me.'[10]

Patrick gave a lengthy interview to the *Times* in the warden's office at Sing Sing: 'a remarkable story ... told by a remarkable man,' said the *Times*. He claimed that the Rice interests had no doubt intercepted his wife's telegram to Milliken and the letter she sent to him which he never received. The Rice interests therefore knew that Brockman was getting the affidavits, 'affidavits which would prove that Fayette Jones never sent those two bottles of chloroform to his brother.' Brockman, Patrick said, was murdered. The lawyer 'had already incurred the animosity of Captain Baker and the other Rice Institute Trustees by threatening a suit for an accounting of the $3,500,000 spent by Baker in the last eight years out of the Rice estate.' If he were pardoned, Patrick told the *Times*, he would bring a civil suit. 'Naturally, I would push it to the end,' he added.

Captain Baker in Texas claimed that he had not known until after Brockman died that he was getting affidavits on Patrick's behalf. And Mayor Rice told the *Times*: 'The idea that Brockman should have been killed because of any connection he might have had with the Patrick case is too absurd to be considered.'

Several months later, the thirty-eight-year-old Ransom was tried for murder. Approximately three hundred jurymen were questioned before a jury of twelve was chosen. The prosecution, in an amazing concession, agreed that Ransom's character was good and that Brockman was a man of violent and dangerous character who habitually carried a pistol and frequently engaged in altercations upon slight provocation and sometimes even without provocation. Jules Baker and Henry Ransom entered the witness box, both claiming that Brockman had reached for his gun and that Ransom shot in self-defense. After deliberating for twenty-three hours, the jury brought in a verdict of not guilty.[11]

The following year, Mayor Rice appointed Ransom as the chief of police of Houston, but he was later removed from the position. In 1918,

Captain Ransom, once again a Texas Ranger, was shot and killed in Sweetwater, Texas, possibly accidentally. 'The gun fighters all go the same route, sooner or later,' the *Houston Chronicle* reported as the general opinion on Main Street.[12]

# 95. Governor Dix

The series of articles in the *Times* in December 1910 confirmed the concerns of Baker and the other trustees of the Rice Institute that they were in for trouble. Baker wrote to Byrne and Lovett, Baker's former partner: 'the trustees have every reason to believe that Patrick's friends are working in season and out of season for his pardon and that he will probably be pardoned unless some effort is made by someone to lay before the Governor those facts and circumstances going to show conclusively his guilt.' 'Knowing Patrick as they do,' Baker wrote, 'the Trustees feel that if he is ever pardoned he will commence some character of litigation – exactly what they do not know.'[1] Their suspicion of further action was again confirmed by news from Byrne that Milliken had recently been in the surrogate office in New York City getting copies of the relevant papers.

Byrne and Lovett wired Baker in cipher, saying that he should arrange for an interview to be published in the *Times* to counteract the recent articles. Baker, they said, should come to New York as soon as possible and have the interview there. They could then also discuss other steps that might be taken. Jerome and Garvan were leaving the district attorney's office at the end of the month; Osborne had left several years earlier. The DA's office, therefore, no longer had a good grasp of the case. Baker said that he would try to come.

A new governor, John A. Dix, had been elected to take office on 1 January 1911. Baker was particularly worried about what he might do.

Governor Hughes had resigned as governor of New York to take Justice Brewer's position on the US Supreme Court. He would apparently have had no difficulty in being elected to a third term as governor, but he was tired of politics and President Taft dangled the prospect of Hughes later becoming the chief justice when Chief Justice Fuller left the Court.[2] As it turned out, Edward D. White of Louisiana (who had been on the court since 1894) was made chief justice in 1910 and Hughes left the bench in 1916 to run unsuccessfully against Woodrow Wilson for president. He would, however, later return to the Court as chief justice in 1930. From Hughes' resignation in October 1910 until Dix took office, the lieutenant governor and former state senator Horace White was acting governor. Although the petition to White for a pardon was prepared by the Medico-Legal Society, with a supporting affidavit by Patrick, it seems that it was submitted too late for Governor White to deal with it. White turned the matter over to Dix, stating that he had 'serious doubts as to the justice of the conviction.'[3]

Dix was the first Democratic governor of New York in fifteen years.[4] An industrialist from Albany, who owned one of the largest wallpaper manufacturing concerns in the United States, Dix had not entered politics until he was elected as a delegate to the Democratic National Convention in 1904. The *Times* strongly supported his candidacy, stating, 'Mr. John A. Dix seems to be a man of just the sort now needed at the head of the affairs of the State.'[5] The voters agreed and Dix defeated the Republican candidate, Henry L. Stimson, who went on to hold many important cabinet posts in Washington, including secretary of war during the Second World War. The *Times* had said that the election was an even-money bet, although it pointed out that it was hard to place such a bet because of Hughes' antigambling laws. Former governor Hill died several weeks before Dix was elected and so never experienced the triumph of the return of a Democrat to the governorship.

Another person who actively supported Dix was Charles F. Murphy, better known as Boss Murphy of Tammany Hall.[6] Captain Baker in Texas wrote to Byrne about a troubling 'report emanating from New York, and from one said to be a kinsman and close friend of Charles Murphy, that Patrick will be pardoned by the incoming Governor, not later than the first of March.'[7]

Baker wanted to know what Byrne would charge for an opinion on whether Patrick, if pardoned, could upset the 1896 will and whether Byrne thought that the trustees 'ought now to employ someone in New York whose relationship to the incoming Governor is such that he could go and talk to him about this rumor and secure a promise from the Governor ... that he would be notified of any application for a pardon, and that he would be given full opportunity to offer any evidence or reasons to show why a pardon should not be granted.' Baker suggested that 'instead of giving some person a continuous employment to look after this matter, it might be better for the Trustees to make such employment with the beginning of each incoming administration, so as always to have a man who is in touch with the particular administration in power at the time he is called upon to act.'

Byrne replied that all that need be done was to tell the governor's counsel that the district attorney's office should, as was the normal practice, be notified before any step to pardon Patrick was taken. Baker was satisfied with the response, stating:

I did not understand that all applications to the Governor for pardons are generally referred to the District Attorney, or that it is usual for the Governor to consult him before finally acting on such applications. If this is true, I think it would be wise for the Trustees to leave to the District Attorney's office the matter of resisting any application for a pardon that may be made on behalf of Patrick and permit him to resist it at his own time and in his own way.[8]

The fee for an opinion on whether Patrick could attack the will would, Byrne wrote, be $2,500. It was some time, however, before the trustees authorized the expenditure. Byrne's thirteen-page opinion stated that Patrick was not bound by the two-year statute of limitation, but he would be blocked by the language of the section that said that the challenge to a will could only be made by 'any person interested as devisee, legatee or otherwise.'[9] In a rather technical and not very convincing opinion, Byrne argued that Patrick was interested in the 1900 will, not the 1896 will, and so could not challenge the probate of the latter. In any event, Byrne concluded: 'If it should ever be held at any time in any proceeding that Patrick might again try the validity of the alleged will of 1900, we should suppose that in view of the language of the Appellate Division, any jury would find against Patrick, and if it did not, any trial court would set aside a verdict in his favor.' Finally, on a practical level, Byrne stated that he could not 'conceive any of these people in whose favor the Statute of Limitations has run [on the criminal charges] exposing themselves to prosecution for the fresh crimes of conspiracy and perjury that they would have to commit to make out even a prima facie case.'[10]

Baker heard a further rumor in Texas that a full pardon would be granted by Dix on 22 February 1911. 'I hope you will keep in touch with everything pertaining to the effort of Patrick to secure a pardon,' he wrote to Byrne, 'so that at the proper time and in the proper way, proper steps may be taken to thwart it.' Byrne replied that the district attorney's office had not heard of an application, and the governor's legal adviser told Byrne that 'any such application would be referred to him [the adviser] and that in regular course it would be referred to the District Attorney and he knew no reason why regular course should not be followed.'

The 22nd of February 1911, the date of the possible pardon, was a particularly important date for the Rice Institute because that very day had been selected for the laying of the cornerstone for the first major building on the new three-hundred-acre site. The architect, Ralph Adams Cram,[11] a Bostonian with a Princeton connection, had designed the intricate and distinctive buildings on the Rice campus. He had recently completed St Thomas Church on 5th Avenue at 53rd Street in New York City – the most important Gothic design in New York since St Patrick's Cathedral – and was then working on the completion of the Cathedral of St John the Divine at 112th Street and Amsterdam Avenue.[12] Cram, without ever actually visiting Houston, rejected the Northern Gothic and, in the words of President Lovett, chose features 'based on the Southern development during the 11th and 12th centuries of the architecture of the Byzantine and Carolingian epochs.'[13]

Baker and the trustees could not risk a public ceremony on the very day of a possible pardon and put it off. No pardon, however, was granted on 22 February. The trustees decided on 23 February to reschedule the event to 2 March, the anniversary of Texan independence. President Lovett wrote the trustees that it would be 'a quiet, informal one. There will be no invited guests, not even representatives of the press.'[14] The cornerstone contains a history of the institute, written by Baker, which briefly recounts the events in the murder case: 'Jones afterwards confessed, and Patrick was tried and was convicted and sentenced to be electrocuted. Afterwards, his punishment was commuted to imprisonment for life.'[15] No doubt, the trustees wondered whether there would be more to be added to the story.

Patrick's supporters were organizing their forces for an application to Governor Dix for a full pardon. The Medico-Legal Society sent out fourteen thousand postcards to physicians asking for their support, and the embalmers associations were continuing their demonstrations that embalming fluid in fact reached the lungs.[16] Another demonstration on a fresh cadaver was held in Albany on 19 April 1911, to which Governor Dix had been invited. The embalmers again passed a motion for an 'unconditional pardon': 'We, the New York State Embalmers' Association, as practical embalmers, know that embalming fluid circulates in and suffuses the lungs of such body as freely as the blood does during life.'[17] Moreover, Dr Hamilton Williams, the former coroner's physician, who had given important evidence at the trial and on the motion for a new trial, told the district attorney's office that they could no longer count on his support. Milliken had obviously got to Williams, Byrne wrote

Baker. Byrne also wrote that he had heard that Jones wanted $60,000 for a recantation, but that Milliken considered the figure too high.[18]

Much of the new activity was being organized by a New York lawyer, George Francis O'Neill – described by the *American* as 'a brilliant young New York attorney'[19] – who had become involved in the case as a medicolegal expert. And Robert Moore, who had been Patrick's counsel at the original trial, again got back into the case. He obtained and sent to Governor Dix a statement from five of the jurors at the trial – another five were now dead – declaring that they would have returned a different verdict if they had been acquainted with the action of the embalming fluid.[20] Moreover, the foreman of the grand jury that had indicted Patrick swore an affidavit that he believed that Patrick's conviction was 'a gross miscarriage of justice.' 'I can say with the most positive assurance,' stated Colonel William C. Church, the editor of the *Army and Navy Journal* and a founder of the National Rifle Association, 'not only that Patrick was not guilty of the murder of William Marsh Rice, but that there was no murder in the case.'[21]

Patrick's appeal to the New York Court of Appeals from the dismissal of his habeas corpus motion by the Second Department of the Appellate Division was to be heard in the spring of 1911. Coupled with this was a further appeal to the Court of Appeals from disbarment proceedings that had been taken against Patrick in 1910 in the First Appellate Department in Manhattan. That court, the same one that had upheld the 1896 will, had agreed with counsel for the New York Bar Association that the New York statute stating that an attorney convicted of a felony should be disbarred was mandatory. There was no discretion, the court held.[22] Why the Bar Association waited until 1910 to bring disbarment proceedings is not clear.

Unlike in Patrick's earlier appeal to the Court of Appeals, this time Chief Judge Cullen did not grant Patrick permission to be present.[23] As it turned out, the appeal did not proceed as planned, but was adjourned from time to time until the fall. Attention had shifted to Governor Dix.

Just prior to the scheduled court hearing, Patrick's new counsel, George Francis O'Neill, had met with Governor Dix to try to fix a date when Patrick could appear personally before the governor in Albany to argue that an unconditional pardon should be granted. He also presented the governor with further evidence, including handwriting expert Albert H. Hamilton's opinion that the 1900 will was not a forgery. O'Neill returned to New York and told the press that unfortunately the governor was so busy with legislative matters that no fixed date could be set, but he hoped the governor would give Patrick a hearing in the near future.[24]

During the summer of 1912, Milliken met with Governor Dix at the governor's summer home on a high plateau overlooking the Hudson River. The only record of that meeting is Milliken's later statement to the press that he met the governor 'with some mutual friends': 'I had a brief interview with him about the injustice that had been done to Mr. Patrick, and he assured me he would take up the matter and give it his closest attention, and that I could depend upon him doing what he thought was right and proper.'[25]

Although Governor Dix sought the Democratic renomination for governor that fall, the convention chose William Sulzer. Many of the delegates felt that Dix was too much in Boss Murphy's pocket. Sulzer won the election over the Republican candidate, Oscar S. Straus, the former ambassador to Turkey – the Democratic candidate for president, Woodrow Wilson, also won over Taft and Teddy Roosevelt – and would take office on 1 January 1913.[26]

In the second week of October 1912, the Rice Institute had its formal opening. Seventy-seven students had started classes the month before.[27] Distinguished guests from around the world attended – 'an array of learning such as has seldom been assembled in the United States,' said the *Times*.[28] The first day of the four-day celebration included a speech by Mayor Rice and an evening reception at the home of Captain Baker. There was an obvious feeling of pride in the establishment of the institute and optimism for its future.

At six o'clock Wednesday afternoon, 27 November, as he was leaving the Capitol in Albany, Governor Dix announced that he was granting Patrick a full pardon. 'There has always been an air of mystery in this important case,' Dix said, and quoting the minority opinion in the Court of Appeals, he went on to say that 'the atmosphere that surrounded the defendant showed that a fair and impartial trial was scarcely possible': 'During this past year I have given much consideration to this case, and am convinced the defendant is entitled to have a full pardon ... I trust that Mr. Patrick will devote his energies to a complete vindication of his declared innocence.'[29]

# 96. Leaving

Patrick's formal pardon was mistakenly placed in the ordinary mail later that same day, rather than, as usual, carried by a special messenger to Sing Sing. The next day was Thanksgiving, however, and mail would not be delivered on the holiday. All Wednesday evening, officials in the governor's office tried to contact the warden, but the person who answered the phone in Sing Sing would not rouse him, claiming that anyone could call claiming to be the governor. Finally, at 1:30 in the morning, the Ossining police got through to the warden, who made special arrangements the next morning to retrieve the pardon from the closed post office.[1]

Mrs Patrick had been visiting her husband on the day of the pardon on one of her permitted monthly visits. She had returned to New York on the 4:09 from Ossining. At 8:30 that evening she received word from George Francis O'Neill that her husband had been pardoned.

Patrick received official word of the pardon the next day, shortly after three in the afternoon. He had eaten the Thanksgiving meal of chicken fricassee with his fellow inmates. The former inmate 53448 quickly changed from his prison garb into the black suit supplied by the state. He was now fifteen pounds heavier than when he arrived there and had acquired steel-rimmed glasses. For the past two years he had worked in the prison hospital, helping the eye specialist with the instruments and the clinical records, and was given the special privilege of sleeping in the dormitory of the hospital. Like all inmates, he was given $10 in cash, 67 cents for train fare to New York City, and 1½ cents for each day worked, making a total of about $50. 'No man ever left Sing Sing with a better prison record,' said the warden: 'In all the years he has been here he has not had one demerit against him.' Patrick took with him a small paper box a foot square containing his papers.[2]

The press, with a battery of photographers, were waiting for him at the front entrance to Sing Sing. The *World* described Patrick's slight hesitation as he left the penitentiary: 'He stopped at the top of the stairway and just looked.'[3] Patrick shook hands with the reporters, but refused to answer their questions. He needed time, he said, to gain a proper perspective: 'I don't think I care to make a statement ... I expect always to continue to fight for my vindication, and to fight to clear my name of the unjust stigma which has rested upon it ... All I can say now is that I am going back to my wife, who is ill.' At 4:35 in the afternoon, he entered an automobile – driven by a former cell-mate of his who was now working for Milliken – that had been waiting for him since early in the morning for the forty-mile trip back to New York City. His black-gowned, heavily veiled, ailing wife was waiting for him at her ground-floor rear apartment at 180 Claremont Avenue at 125th Street in Harlem. He had a second Thanksgiving dinner with her and his elder daughter, Lucille. His mother and his younger daughter, Lillian, were living in Denver with one of Patrick's sisters.

As in Sing Sing, he was awake at 6:30 the next morning; later that morning he went to Olcott's office on Broadway to meet the press. 'I am convinced that he is an innocent man,' Olcott told the press, 'and that his conviction was a miscarriage of justice.'[4]

'Have you been railroaded to a conviction?' Patrick was asked.

'I have made that charge in court,' Patrick replied: 'By a conspiracy between the trial judge and ...'

'I wouldn't say just that,' interjected Olcott, 'say instead that there was a conspiracy among the trustees of the Rice will.'[5]

Patrick was, of course, asked about further proceedings:

'Will you make a fight for the Rice millions under the will?'

'I have never made any claim to the Rice millions. I was merely the executor of a trust ... a trust that was to resemble the Sage Foundation.'

Olcott was asked if he would move to have the 1900 will probated.

'That is a mighty good guess,' he responded.

'Wouldn't a suit be barred by time?'

'The Statute of Limitations does not, I believe, run against a man in the death house at Sing Sing,' Olcott correctly observed.[6]

Olcott was asked his opinion about when proceedings would be started. 'I believe Patrick when he says the will was not forged, but I have not had time enough to consider a line of procedure,' Olcott replied. 'If Patrick could wait 12 years to get out of Sing Sing he certainly can wait more than 12 hours to arrive at a decision on future action.'[7] One danger, Olcott said, was that there could be new charges of uttering a forged document and perjury. 'There isn't any danger. I am not afraid,' Patrick stated.

Patrick's seventy-seven-year-old mother was interviewed in Denver. Her son, she said, 'has a mission of some kind – a trust to fulfill, he calls it, something old man Rice entrusted to him to do.' Her son, she said, was innocent: 'It was that man Baker who was at the bottom of it – he caused all my son's trouble. He wanted to get him out of the way ... I knew when he denied having poisoned Mr. Rice that he told the truth. We mothers know.'[8]

Robert Moore also expressed his personal belief in Patrick's innocence, stating: 'It was an unjust conviction. I feel that a twelve-year wrong has been righted. Patrick is innocent. Of that I am certain.'[9] Milliken was so sure of Patrick's innocence, he told the press, that he would 'turn over $100,000 to any good charity if Patrick doesn't prove his guilt-lessness absolutely in one year of his release.'[10] And David Short, now a successful businessman in Philadelphia, told the press that he was prepared to swear again that he witnessed Rice signing the 1900 will.

Several days later, the press reported that Milliken had sent a telegram to Patrick disapproving his plan to contest the will: 'The newspapers here report that you have retained William M.K. Olcott to start litigation against the trustees of the Rice estate. Such action is suicidal. I shall not aid you in it or give it countenance in any manner. I advise you to stop talking to the newspapers. Go hide yourself.'[11] Mrs Patrick, who because of her illness had refused to talk to the press, said that Patrick had never received such a telegram and that she had a telegram from Milliken saying he had never sent it. 'Mr. Patrick,' she said, 'is a man to command and not to be commanded.'[12] And the day after the supposed telegram, Milliken told the *Times* that he was 'not going to attempt to prevent Patrick from seeking to establish his claim to the Rice estate at some future date, but would do all in his power to prevent his taking any action at this time.'

Neither District Attorney Whitman nor any of the former prosecutors had been notified that a pardon was about to be granted. Jerome told the press that he had in fact been in Albany and seen the governor the very day that the pardon was granted and 'knew nothing about it until I got back here tonight.'[13] All he would say was that he was 'amazed' and wanted the pardoning powers taken out of the governor's hands and given to a pardoning board.[14] Arthur Train also expressed amazement: 'It seems amazing to me that Patrick should get off after serving only seven or eight years in prison, when for the forgeries that he committed he could have been sent to jail for life.'[15] Francis Garvan said

that the pardon was 'an insult to Judge Goff, who tried him, an affront
to the District Attorney and an outrage against the people of New York.'
If the governor had desired to know the truth, Garvan stated, 'he could
have called Patrick before him for examination by his own counsel and
then for cross-examination by representatives of the people.'[16] He noted
that Chief Judge Cullen and Judge O'Brien, who had dissented on the
criminal appeal, had joined with the court in declaring the Patrick will
a forgery. 'I should like to know,' Garvan went on to say, 'what influences, other than the "informed conversation" with Mr. Milliken, Patrick's millionaire brother-in-law, led Governor Dix to make up his mind
for a pardon.'

Judges Goff and House were asked for their reactions, but declined
to comment. House said that 'he had never been released by Patrick
from his obligation to keep silent on the subject.'[17]

No paper was able to locate Charlie Jones for his comment. 'What
became of Jones, the valet, is not known,' said the *Times*. But the next
day the paper carried a special report from Houston stating that 'after
making the confession which obtained his release, Jones came to
Chambers County, Texas, and became the teacher of a Sunday school.
He died a few years later.'[18]

Baker refused to comment publicly.[19] 'I have nothing to say,' he told
the representative of the New York *Times*. But William Hornblower,
who had argued the invalidity of the 1900 will, released a statement
to the press, agreeing with Milliken's supposed telegram that it would
be 'suicidal' for Patrick to attack the 1896 will. 'In all my professional
experience,' said Hornblower, 'I have never known a case more conclusively proved than the case against Patrick as to the will of 1900.'[20]
James Byrne did not make a public statement but wrote to Baker that
he thought a suit by Patrick was unlikely: 'I should think it very unlikely
that Patrick, after his years in Sing Sing, would now seek to regain his
place there by committing perjury in an effort to carry out his original
plans to get possession of Mr. Rice's money.'[21]

Baker, always a pessimist, thought that it was likely that Patrick would
sue. He wrote Maurice Lombardi, one of the Rice Institute trustees: 'That
Patrick will attempt to re-open the proceedings in New York which resulted in the finding that the so-called Patrick will was a forgery, and
the 1896 will was the genuine will of Mr. Rice, I have no doubt. There
is nothing for the Trustees to do but to sit steadily in the boat and await
developments.' Lombardi, a principal in the *Dallas News*, had expressed
the views of other trustees in saying that 'there is no telling what a fool

Court might do if the case ever gets there.' Other persons who had dealings with the institute were worried: 'We cannot buy into a lawsuit,' said one person, who stated that 'the general opinion in Houston is that Patrick will recover all that land.'[22]

Baker wrote to Byrne, asking for his help: 'I hope you will ... be prepared to cooperate with us in any litigation that may follow Patrick's release. That he will institute litigation of some kind, I have no doubt.'[23] As to Milliken's telegram to Patrick that it would be 'suicidal' to sue, Baker stated that he doubted Milliken's sincerity and that 'even if he has given such advice, I am quite sure Patrick would not follow it in any event.' Baker's former partner, R.S. Lovett, the chairman of Southern Pacific, wrote Baker that Patrick was 'such a reckless rascal that he is liable to attempt anything.' His release now, Lovett thought, was, in fact fortunate, because witnesses were still alive who would successfully resist a lawsuit by Patrick.

Editorial comment in what the *Denver Post* described as 'America's most remarkable murder case'[24] was somewhat mixed, although as one journal stated, 'on the whole, the weight of journalistic opinion is adversely critical.'[25] Some, such as the New York *World*, expressed the view that 'it is difficult to find fault with the Governor's action,' but most agreed with the *New York Press* that this was 'a grievous abuse of the pardoning power.' A writer in the *Journal of Criminal Law* described it as 'one of the most striking abuses of executive clemency in recent times.'[26] Many papers agreed with Jerome that what New York needed was a pardoning board, which then existed in several other states. 'The need of a rightly constituted Board of Pardons in this State was never more clearly shown,' said the *Times*. The paper was critical of Dix's action because Dix 'cast doubt upon the proceedings of the trial court' and yet withheld from the public 'the facts on which he bases his conclusions.' 'The editorial from the New York *Times*,' Baker wrote to Byrne, 'I believe reflects the sentiment of the best people everywhere.'

The press questioned Governor Dix at the Waldorf on the weekend on his way back to Albany from the Army-Navy football game in Philadelphia. He agreed with the press that a pardoning board would be desirable, stating that 'the Governor should not be compelled, as he is, to bear the full pardoning responsibility.'[27] (A pardoning board has, in fact, never been set up in New York.)[28] Dix did not go into the factors which had influenced him. Several days earlier, though, he mentioned that he became familiar with the case even before he became governor through Dean Ernest Huffcut, who was a college friend of his from Cornell:

Dean Huffcut visited my house frequently while Governor Higgins was considering the case. Dean Huffcut told me that Governor Higgins believed Patrick innocent of murder, but thought he ought not to have a pardon at once ... He further told me after Governor Hughes came into office that he was going to press for a full pardon for Patrick, but just as he was about to do this his life ended in the tragedy of which every one knows.[29]

On Friday, 6 December 1912, Patrick left New York by train for the Millikens in St Louis. He sent a letter to his counsel, Olcott, which was then released by Olcott to the press:

Since my release from prison I have been devoting myself entirely to my wife, whom I found in a very weakened and nervous condition – so much so that it has been impossible for me to attend to any other business. It is her desire to go West to her son, who is married, and her grandchild, whom she has never seen, in an effort to recuperate her health; and I leave tomorrow to make suitable arrangements for her to follow me, leaving her, meanwhile in the care of my daughter ...

I hope soon, but after full conference with you and those representing interests allied to myself, to commence legal proceedings to vindicate myself as to all of my relations with William Marsh Rice.[30]

'Another chapter added to one of the most remarkable trials in all history,' said the *Houston Chronicle*.[31]

# 97. Tulsa, Oklahoma

After spending the night at Milliken's mansion at 1150 Belt Avenue (today, an empty lot), Patrick, accompanied by his sister May, went to the Millikens' country home at Crescent, Missouri, to gather his strength. Mrs Patrick joined him there. They did not go farther west to Denver, as planned. Mrs Patrick's condition was deteriorating and so Patrick's mother and sixteen-year-old daughter, Lillian, joined them for Christmas in St Louis. The press described Patrick's joyous Christmas with his family, but it was in fact not a happy event. Mrs Patrick was taken to the Deaconess Hospital in St Louis and was diagnosed as having inoperable abdominal cancer.

There was a rumor reported that Patrick would be taking a job in Milliken's firm at the St Louis Merchant's Exchange, but in early 1913 he went to Tulsa, Oklahoma, to look after Milliken's oil interests there.

On the advice of her doctors, Mrs Patrick spent much of the next year with her son and granddaughter in the State of Washington. In November 1913, her condition further deteriorated and Patrick brought her back to Tulsa to die. Patrick and his elder daughter, Lucille, who was seeking a divorce and was now living in Tulsa, and Mrs Patrick's son and daughter-in-law attended her constantly in the Tulsa Hospital. She died on Friday, 19 December, at the age of fifty-four. 'Her husband, the noted lawyer, was at her bedside when she passed away,' stated the *Tulsa Daily World* in its headline story that day.[1] She was buried at Oak Lawn Cemetery in Tulsa. Her tombstone reads:

ADDIE SHARPE PATRICK
January 15, 1859
December 13, 1913

About a year later, Patrick left Milliken's employment and went into the oil business on his own. The 1914 Tulsa City Directory shows him in the Bliss Building as president of the Patrick Oil Company and the Patrick Drilling Company. Why he no longer worked with Milliken is not known.

Milliken's oil holdings in Oklahoma were now very valuable. Indeed, they were sufficiently valuable that Milliken's brother-in-law in Denver, Leonidas Hill, demanded an accounting for the twenty thousand shares of Milliken Oil that he had given to Milliken in 1907 to help defray the cost of Patrick's defense. Hill had been the one to have first staked the claim many years earlier and had turned to Milliken for financial help. The dispute led to a lawsuit by Hill in the federal courts in Denver. Milliken claimed that 'Mr. Hill's contribution towards Mr. Patrick was a bunch of oil stock that was worthless at the time he contributed it.'[2] The Denver court agreed and dismissed the suit. The following year, Milliken sold his oil interests in Oklahoma to the new Sinclair Oil Company for $10 million.[3]

Ever since Patrick had been pardoned, there was speculation on Governor Dix's motive for doing so. The pressure for an explanation was such that Governor Sulzer, who later that year was impeached for corrupt practices and left office,[4] opened the Patrick pardon file to public scrutiny as soon as he took office. The box containing the petitions and correspondence, which no longer can be found in the archives in Albany, was said to be as big as a trunk.[5]

No evidence not already known was found in the material. There was, however, an emotional letter from Patrick to Colonel Joseph F. Scott, the state superintendent of prisons, who was said to have had considerable influence with Dix, in which Patrick sought release for the sake of his family: his wife's health, Patrick wrote, had 'been shattered by her sacrifices and the continued alternation of hope and despair'; his aged mother continually wrote to him expressing her hope that he would soon be free to comfort her in her declining years; and his elder daughter Lucille was getting a divorce and had 'become infatuated with another stripling.'[6] Patrick told Scott that what he wanted was an 'unconditional commutation,' which, unlike a pardon, would not imply an admission of guilt. There is some indication that Patrick was offered a pardon by Dix even earlier in Dix's tenure, but Patrick had refused it.[7] If so, perhaps his wife's condition caused him to change his mind.

Stories appeared in the press that Dix had pardoned Patrick because Milliken had promised to arrange support for Dix's nomination for vice-president of the United States at the Democratic convention in Baltimore in June 1912. 'I have read today's article,' Milliken told the press. 'It is all tommyrot from beginning to end.'[8]

A more serious allegation occurred in November 1914, when a mining promoter, George C. Goodrich, alleged in Hearst's New York *American*[9] that Dix had granted the pardon in exchange for an option to friends of Dix on Milliken's famous Golden Cycle Mine in Cripple Creek, Colorado. The mine, which Milliken had acquired in 1900, was described by the press as 'the greatest producer of gold in the Cripple Creek district,' which many thought was 'the richest gold mine camp in the world.'[10]

Over the years, many persons had attempted to consolidate the gold-mining interests in Cripple Creek so that tunneling could be properly coordinated and the rich deposits recovered.[11] Goodrich, on behalf of William Nelson Cromwell, of the law firm of Sullivan and Cromwell, had been trying unsuccessfully to acquire the Golden Cycle Mine from Milliken since 1907. Then, in early 1912, acting for Joseph Walker and Sons, said to be 'one of the oldest and most influential firms in the financial district of New York,'[12] he again tried to acquire the mine from Milliken. He induced Milliken to come to New York to discuss the matter with the Walker firm, but Milliken claimed he was not interested. The following conversation then took place between Goodrich and Joseph Walker, according to Goodrich's sworn affidavit, reproduced in the press:

Walker then said: 'Milliken is a brother-in-law of Patrick, isn't he?'

'Yes,' I answered.

'I understand he has been working to secure Patrick's release,' said Walker.

'Do you think Milliken would be grateful and feel obligated to the man who would procure Patrick's pardon?' asked Walker.

'In my opinion there is nothing in the world he would not do for that man,' I replied.

Walker leaned forward and said slowly and impressively: 'I can get my friend Governor Dix to pardon Patrick.'     ·

I was incredulous. I told Walker so.

Walker smiled.

'You don't understand our connections with Dix,' said Walker. 'You don't realize how closely allied Dix is with our firm. Dix's closest friends on earth are Horace G. Young of Albany and Mr. Young's father-in-law, Oscar L. Hasey, one of the wealthiest men in Albany. Mr. Young's son is Clarence H. Young, a member of our firm. These men are all associated with me in this proposed merger and most anxious to see it succeed, Governor Dix transacts business through my office. One of my partners recently did the governor a great favor.'[13]

Patrick was interviewed about this account in his office in the Hotel Tulsa, where he also had his residence. He had not made a statement to the press in almost two years. He did not know Goodrich, he said, adding that he had 'put out of his mind all thoughts of his past in order to avoid the sense of compelling obligation constantly impressed upon him by the fact of his unjust conviction and by failure to obtain a fair and honest administration of justice.'[14] Patrick thought that the animus behind the whole affair was William Randolph Hearst's enmity for Governor Dix.[15]

The Walker firm denied Goodrich's allegations, as did Dix and Milliken. 'This man Goodrich,' Milliken said, 'is simply sore at me because I would not give him an option for the purchase of the Golden Cycle gold mine for $6,000,000. I did, later, give the option to the New York firm, but that was a straight out business proposition, and the name of Patrick was never mentioned in connection with the deal, and so far as I know was never thought of.' It was Kohlsaat, he said, who suggested that he see the governor. Goodrich's story 'is made out of whole cloth.'[16]

Ex-governor Dix said that he did not know until much later that Milliken owned gold mines. He did not deny, however, that it was his best friend, Horace Young, the president of the Albany Trust Company, who had introduced him to Milliken and was with them when Milliken met Dix in the summer of 1912 at Dix's summer home.[17] There could have been truth in Goodrich's story of influence peddling, even if Dix did not know of it.

Governor-elect Whitman, who was still the district attorney, began an investigation and Assistant District Attorney Delehanty examined a number of witnesses. Nothing was brought to light, the DA said on 23 November, except coincidences and hearsay testimony, and nothing that was submitted showed that ex-governor Dix had any knowledge of a conspiracy to obtain the pardon of Patrick. The two-year statute of limitations – two years after the pardon was granted – operated at the end of that week to prevent a conspiracy charge.[18] No file now exists in the New York archives relating to this investigation.

# 98. Later Career

There are very few documents available relating to Patrick's later career, so that the following outline contains only those matters that happened to appear for the most part in newspapers and government files. The Rice archives do not contain any documents after 1915. Baker's last letter in the file, dated 26 January 1915, ends by stating: 'I have heard nothing very direct from Patrick for a long time. I am advised that he is in the oil business in Oklahoma ... I hope the Institute will not be troubled with him again.'[1]

Just before Christmas 1916, the fifty-year-old Patrick became engaged to twenty-six-year-old Verna Lucille West, the daughter of a Tulsa oil operator. They were married in June 1917.[2]

In the spring of 1917, Patrick applied for a commission as a major in the Quartermaster Department of the US Reserve. On 11 March, he wrote to the attorney general of the United States, Thomas W. Gregory, who had been a contemporary of his at the University of Texas Law School, accurately predicting that the United States would be at war with Germany in the 'next few weeks' (war was declared on 6 April). The nation, he said, must make 'preparations to resist invasion and local treachery.' 'I feel that my service to my country would be of value in such preparation,' he went on. The attorney general forwarded Patrick's letter to Newton D. Barker, the secretary of war, reminding him about Patrick's past trouble and concluding: 'I do not know whether he was guilty or not, and I really have no comments to make in regard to this letter except to say that Patrick has had the character of military experience stated by him, and that he was an extremely efficient captain of a company in my town for a long while, serving with considerable distinction with the militia of our state in various capacities.'[3] There is no indication that Patrick ever received a commission. It is known, however, that he organized an ambulance unit during the war.[4]

Mr and Mrs Patrick moved to Fort Worth, Texas, in 1919, where Patrick became general counsel to the Livingston Oil Company, moving back to the company's head office in Tulsa in 1921. A salesman from Detroit met Patrick in Tulsa in 1921 or 1922 and recorded his recollection as follows: 'Mr. Patrick intrigued me a great deal with his appearance, his bedroom slippers he wore in the office, and his general suspicious demeanor while talking to me.'[5]

At about that time, Patrick applied to be admitted to the Oklahoma Bar. He was refused admission by the Supreme Court of Oklahoma on the recommendation of the Oklahoma State Bar Commission on the ground that he had been disbarred in New York and first had to remove that obstacle.[6] The problem, Patrick argued, was that according to New York law he would have to return to New York for six months and undertake to remain there for the future before New York would consider reinstating him. His pardon, unlike a successful appeal, did not operate as an automatic reinstatement in New York.

He was admitted to the Federal Bar, however, and practiced in the Eastern and Northern District federal courts of Oklahoma and the fifth and eight circuit courts in Fort Worth and St Louis, respectively. He was also admitted to the Treasury Bar and the Supreme Court of the United States. His letterhead was careful to make it clear that he did not practice in the Oklahoma state courts.

In 1926, a reporter for the *Houston Press*[7] interviewed Patrick in his office on the sixth floor of the Mid-Continent Building in downtown Tulsa.[8] Apart from practicing law in the federal courts, he was involved in the oil business, was part-owner of an auto-supply company, and had three cars, including a 1917 Packard. The reporter described Patrick, now known by his associates as 'Judge Patrick,' as a 'stout, well-dressed, prosperous-looking business man.' He also reported Patrick's strong views about the judicial system. 'The trouble with our judicial system today,' Patrick is reported to have said, without specific reference to his own case, 'is that our courts are corrupt ... Our district attorneys, our big lawyers and the big moneyed interests are in league with each other.' He did not wish to talk about the case except to maintain that Rice's death was due to natural causes, adding: 'Jones could not have chloroformed Rice the way he described it on the witness stand. I know, because I have studied the medical reactions of chloroform. I have also studied handwriting and my contentions that I had not forged Rice's name are borne out by what I have found.' Patrick claimed to have 'evolved a new form of religion, a modernization of the application of the Holy Trinity.' 'I believe,' Patrick said, that 'the world is on the verge of a moral and religious upheaval.'

On 24 February 1930 – the very first day that Charles Evans Hughes sat as the chief justice of the Supreme Court – an order was made by the Supreme Court to suspend Patrick from practicing before that Court unless he could show 'good cause to the contrary.'[9] Patrick received the order on 27 February – he had no previous knowledge of the proceedings – and reacted angrily. He wrote the same day to the clerk of the Supreme Court asking him to send him 'at once a complete record of the suggestion or application on which said order was made, so that I may know the real nature of the accusation and the names of my accusers or instigators.'[10] The next day, he wrote to the solicitor general of the United States, Charles E. Hughes, Jr,[11] the son of the chief justice, asking him not to take part in the proceedings so that the chief justice would be able to preside over the hearing. His conviction, Patrick wrote, was 'pursuant to a general conspiracy to murder me under color of the law in order to defeat a will involving millions of dollars, nearly four millions of which was diverted and divided among the conspirators.' He did not claim, however, that it was the Texas interests that had brought these disbarment proceedings; rather, he wrote: 'I assume that these proceedings were instigated by Oklahoma influences which I have antagonized.' Hughes, Jr, replied that he had resigned as solicitor general and would therefore not be taking part in the proceedings.[12]

On the same day that he wrote to the solicitor general, Patrick wrote a stinging letter to the Supreme Court of Oklahoma, accusing the Board of Governors of the Oklahoma State Bar and the State Bar Commission of bias and asking for the disbarment of one of its members, Edgar de Meules,[13] and his senior law partner, George Ramsey,[14] a member of the bar's Legal Advisory Committee. That letter was sent on by the Oklahoma Supreme Court to the Board of Governors of the state bar, which demanded that Patrick appear before them to support his allegations.

De Meules had been the chairman of the Bar Commission since 1916 and it was he who had refused Patrick's application for admission in 1921 and subsequently. De Meules and Ramsey, Patrick alleged, had framed a regulation aimed at him personally that a disbarred lawyer first had to return to his home state and clear up the disbarment before he could be admitted in Oklahoma. Patrick alleged in his lengthy submission that de Meules had been fraudulently admitted to the Bar of the Indian Territory (which subsequently formed part of Oklahoma) in 1905 by failing to disclose that he had been convicted of embezzlement, a felony, in his home state of Iowa while a law student at the University of Michigan.[15] He was thus prevented from obtaining his Michigan degree and even though he was subsequently pardoned still had not been granted the degree. There were a number of other serious allegations of improper practice at the bar, including, for example, theft of exhibits. The document was mailed by Patrick to one thousand lawyers, judges, and prominent businessmen in Oklahoma, a tactic which had proved successful for Patrick in earlier years.

After an all-day hearing before the Board of Governors, it was clear to Patrick that the board had not vindictively sent his name to the US Supreme Court, but that it was done by the secretary of the board pursuant to a standing rule that all disbarments be sent to the Supreme Court. Under these circumstances, Patrick withdrew his allegation against the board and did not want to proceed against de Meules and Ramsey at this time 'for the simple reason,' Patrick said, 'that I would be undertaking something that would interfere with my own affairs,'[16] that is, the Supreme Court hearing.

The board concluded, however, that there should be a full hearing, whether Patrick wanted one then or not. De Meules and Ramsey requested that the hearing be a public one. Both the defendants were important members of the Oklahoma Bar. Ramsey had been the president of the Oklahoma State Bar Association and served briefly as a justice of the Oklahoma Supreme Court. A book entitled *Oklahoma Leaders*, published in 1928, stated: 'probably no man in Oklahoma has left a deeper impression upon the state than he, considering the important part he has played in establishing the law of oil and gas and Indian land titles.'[17] Ramsey's partner since 1914, de Meules, had been the president of the Oklahoma State Bar Association in 1927.

The hearing commenced on 27 June and went from ten in the morning until eleven at night. Further evidence was heard on 28 June and 5 July. The testimony of 112 witnesses was heard or read. On 26 July 1930, the board, in a lengthy judgment, unanimously dismissed the charges, concluding: 'We find from the evidence that all the charges against both respondents have in each and every particular been disproved beyond all reasonable doubt, and that the action of Patrick in making such charges was malicious and without probable cause to believe the truth thereof.'[18] As to whether de Meules had been properly admitted to the Oklahoma Bar, the board stated: 'We find from the evidence that the said Edgar A. de Meules was regularly and legally admitted to the practice of law in the United States Court for the Western District of the Indian Territory, and is now a member in good standing of the State Bar of Oklahoma.'

In the meantime, the Supreme Court of the United States referred the question of Patrick's disbarment to a special committee. On 22 April 1930, Chief Justice Hughes appointed three distinguished members of the New York Bar – Nathan L. Miller,[19] a former governor of New York; Charles C. Burlingham,[20] president of the Bar of the City of New York; and Henry W. Taft,[21] president of the New York County Lawyers Association, who had worked in the same firm with Hornblower and Byrne many years earlier – 'to make a report and recommendation' to the Supreme Court.[22] Patrick was reported in June as having spent several hours in Governor Franklin D. Roosevelt's office in Albany looking over records. Hearings were held by the committee in September 1930. Patrick appeared by counsel and in person and argued that the free pardon absolved him of the order of disbarment – a difficult argument, considering that the Supreme Court had previously held that a pardon does not blot out guilt[23] – and that, in any event, not being a resident of New York, he could not apply to the Appellate Division for reinstatement. Section 88 of the Judiciary Law of New York provided that: 'Upon a reversal of the conviction for felony of an attorney and counsellor-at-law, or pardon by the president of the United States or governor of this state, the appellate division shall have power to vacate or modify such order or debarment.'[24] The Special Committee held that Patrick did not have to be a resident to apply under section 88, and that because he had not done so he had 'failed to show good cause why he should not be disbarred as an attorney and counsellor-at-law.'[25] The committee's report was submitted to the Supreme Court, which, on 24 November 1930, without reasons, ordered 'that the said Albert T. Patrick be, and he is hereby, disbarred, and that his name be stricken from the roll of attorneys admitted to practice in this Court.'[26]

'And thus ended,' said Henry W. Taft in his memoirs, 'the last attempt of Patrick to reinstate himself as a lawyer in good standing and entitled to the rights and privileges of a member of the bar.'[27]

# 99. Final Exits

What finally happened to the many characters in this saga? In this section, I will give brief answers about some of the principal players.

First, the police. Captain George 'Chesty' McCluskey, otherwise known as 'Gentleman George,' who was in charge of the investigation in 1900, rose to be a police inspector and died at the age of fifty-one in December 1912, a few weeks after Patrick was released from Sing Sing. Although a police officer for his entire working life, he left an estate said to be valued at $1 million.[1] Detective Sergeant James Vallely, who worked on the case under McCluskey, became a captain, later retiring to Houston, where his son lived. He died there in 1937 at the age of eighty-three.[2] Whether he ever visited the Rice Institute is not known.

The key judges in the case continued in office until the age of retirement. Recorder Goff, who had conducted the trial, was elected a judge of the New York Supreme Court in 1906 and served in that capacity for thirteen years until he retired at age seventy.[3] He died in 1924 at the age of seventy-eight. Judge Denis O'Brien, who wrote the principal dissent in the Court of Appeals, retired from the court in 1907 and died two years later.[4] And John Gray, who wrote the majority judgment, died in 1915, the year after he retired.[5]

The principal district attorneys in the story, Jerome, Osborne, and Garvan, all went into private practice after they left the district attorney's office. William Travers Jerome left the office at the end of 1909, when Whitman became the district attorney. He joined several of his former assistants in practice and eventually made a considerable amount of money through his involvement in the movie Technicolor process. At the time of his death in 1934, at the age of seventy-five, he was the chairman of the board of Technicolor Inc. He died in New York at his home, a brownstone at 125 East 36th Street. The *Times* noted that his son and daughter-in-law were with him at the time, but that his widow was ill at their country home. What the *Times* did not know, or more likely did not wish to disclose, was that his home was one that he shared with his 'friend,' Mrs Ethel Stuart Elliot, who would undoubtedly also have been there at the time. Mrs Elliot, whom he had met while he was district attorney, was 'from then until his death,' according to his biographer, 'the most meaningful and comforting element in Jerome's life.'[6]

The prosecutor at the trial, James Osborne, left the district attorney's office in 1902 and entered private practice. He was given a number of special assignments by the state and federal authorities. In 1913, for example, he was appointed special attorney general to investigate the condition and the treatment of prisoners at Sing Sing. Patrick, of course, had left the previous year. Osborne, always a fierce competitor, took up tennis at the age of fifty-three and was scheduled to have a tennis lesson with the Forest Hills Club professional the day he died in 1919 at the age of sixty-one.[7]

Francis Garvan, who handled some of the later proceedings and was in charge of the Homicide Bureau, resigned with Jerome at the end of 1909 and later for a period of time practiced law with Osborne. During World War I, he became the custodian of alien property and after the war was an assistant attorney general of the United States in charge of the suppression of communism in America. From 1919 to 1923, apparently while holding these other offices, Garvan was the dean of the Fordham Law School. Because of his interest in German chemical patents, as the custodian of alien property, he became the president of the Chemical Foundation, designed to expand the scope and capacity of the chemical industries in the United States. Garvan's work in this field was sufficiently important that he was awarded the prestigious Priestley Medal by the American Chemical Society, the only layman up until then to have been so honored. He continued to be the president of the foundation until his death in 1937 at the age of sixty-two.[8]

The lawyer who first called in the police when Patrick attempted to have the checks cashed was James Gerard. He was elected a New York Supreme Court judge in 1908 at the age of thirty-nine, but resigned in 1913 to become the US Ambassador to Germany, leaving when diplomatic relations were broken off in 1917. Gerard became a national hero because he had stood up to the Kaiser, was frequently mentioned as a presidential candidate to succeed Woodrow Wilson, and was actually entered in one primary. His wife came from a very wealthy family, and he was heavily involved over the years in fund-raising for the Democratic party. In 1951, just before he died, he published a book, *My First Eighty-three Years in America*, in which he stated:

When I attended the Houston convention of the Democratic party in 1928, Captain James A. Baker, before his death perhaps the most distinguished lawyer in Texas, gave me a dinner and took me to see the beautiful buildings of the Rice Institute. It occupies more than three hundred acres in the city of Houston and has an endowment of more than $22,000,000 – a great tribute to the skill of

Captain Baker and his fellow trustees. The captain asked for my photograph to hang in the office of the Rice Institute. This, he said, was fitting, as the Institute might not have existed if I had not gone to see the district attorney in New York twenty-eight years before.[9]

The person in charge of the Rice litigation in New York, William Hornblower, continued to be one of the leaders of the New York Bar. It will be recalled that President Grover Cleveland had nominated him to be a justice of the US Supreme Court in 1893, but the Senate, led by Senator Hill, refused to confirm the appointment. In February 1914, although not well at the time, he was appointed by the governor of New York to be a judge of the New York Court of Appeals. He died after sitting as a judge for only one week.[10]

Hornblower's partner, James Byrne, continued to be one of New York City's most important corporate lawyers. He also took a particular interest in educational institutions and was on the Board of Governors of his alma mater, Harvard University, for a number of years – it will be recalled that he had established the Byrne Professorship of Administrative Law at Harvard Law School in 1917 – and was on the Board of Regents and eventually the chancellor of the University of the State of New York. He died in 1942 at the age of eighty-five.[11]

Turning to Patrick's lawyers, we have already seen that Frederick House was appointed a city magistrate in 1907. In 1917 he was reappointed for a further ten-year term and was assigned to the Traffic Court. He died in office in 1925 at the age of sixty-eight. During the almost twenty years he served as a magistrate, he was said to have handled over 350,000 cases. He left no descendants and as far as I have been able to discover no record of what Patrick had said to him in the Tombs.[12]

Robert Moore's reputation as a criminal lawyer continued to grow both in New York City and in Upper New York State. He was the counsel of choice for persons charged with crime from the Chinese community. Late Saturday evening on 26 November 1921, he had left his new home on Riverside Drive to purchase two quarts of ice cream for some guests he and his wife were entertaining. As he was crossing the road to the drugstore, he was hit by an automobile, suffering a compound fracture of the skull, and died several hours later at the age of fifty-five. The driver was arrested for homicide, but whether he was convicted is not known.[13]

Senator Hill, as we know, died in 1910, just prior to Governor Dix's electoral victory.[14] William Olcott, who handled the later motion for a new trial, continued to practice law and look after his large business interests until he died at age seventy in 1933.[15] Edgar Kohler became the assistant corporation counsel for New York City in 1918, remaining there until 1932. He then practiced law until he died in 1941. Like his brother, Max, he was heavily involved in Jewish affairs.[16]

Let us now examine the final days of those characters in the story who had a personal stake in the proceedings. Foremost among them, of course, is Albert T. Patrick.

Patrick, as previously mentioned, was no longer entitled to practice law. In the 1931 Tulsa City Directory he is still listed as a lawyer. The following year, however, the listing shows him working in 'sales and service' for the Oldsmobile Company of Tulsa. In 1934, the listing simply says 'oil,' and in 1936, 'mechanical engineer,' apparently selling air-conditioning units. His name is not in the 1939 directory.

In 1939, in semiretirement, the seventy-two-year-old Patrick and his wife moved to Wetumka, Oklahoma, a small community about eighty miles south of Tulsa. There, he hoped to apply his own theory of 'human progress' – basically, the Golden Rule – to show how to make the world a better place. In a speech to the Wetumka Chamber of Commerce on his so-called Human Progress League, he pointed out that 'our troubles are due first to the amazing fact that humanity has never made a logical definition and general rule of right and wrong.'[17] The *Wetumka Gazette* described this as a 'singular philosophy ... fringing on a theological plane.'[18] It was also connected with his desire to be vindicated in the eyes of the public for the events that had taken place many years earlier. He pleaded for a congressional investigation, he told the *Tulsa Daily World*, to reveal the 'corruption and grafting' which surrounded his trial and imprisonment. 'The force which was fed by the Rice millions is still a dominating power in American politics today,' he said: 'They name judges and they rule men.'[19] Patrick never pursued a claim against the Rice Institute.

A little over a year later, he entered a Tulsa hospital for a prostate operation and was recovering from it when he contracted bronchial pneumonia and died at the age of seventy-three. 'Famous Murder Case Principal Dies Here,' headlined the *Tulsa Daily World*.[20] His wife and his daughters, Lucille and Lillian, and a few others attended his funeral and he was buried beside his second wife, Addie Patrick, in the Woodlawn Cemetery in Tulsa. Below her name on the tombstone is carved:

## ALBERT T. PATRICK
February 26, 1866
February 11, 1940

His antagonist, James A. Baker, died the following year at the age of eighty-four.[21] His funeral procession was two miles long. He had continued as the chairman of the board of the Rice Institute until his death, participating in the graduation exercises the previous spring. As the head of Baker and Botts and the longest-serving active lawyer in Houston, he was considered the dean of the Houston Bar. 'Few men have had so much influence on Houston, its growth and development as had Captain Baker,' stated the *Houston Chronicle*.[22] 'There is no place of greater opportunity in the country,' he had told the press on his eightieth birthday.[23] Five children survived him, and he left an estate of over one and one-half million dollars. His eleven-year-old grandson, James A. Baker III, the former secretary of state (now in the Washington office of Baker and Botts), was left $10,000.[24] The most interesting case in his career, Captain Baker said shortly before he died, was the Rice-Patrick case.[25]

Patrick's favorite sister, May Milliken, died in 1942 at the age of seventy-two.[26] Her husband, John T., had died in 1919. The *St. Louis Globe-Democrat* had a two-inch headline, 'John T. Milliken is dead,' and the *St. Louis Republic* said that Milliken was 'recognized as the wealthiest man in St. Louis,' leaving an estate that the paper estimated as between twenty-five and thirty million dollars.[27] In fact, the estate, although in the multimillions, was worth far less than that. When his holdings were made public, the press noted with disdain that it contained no Liberty Bonds, even though he had said during the last bond campaign that 'Liberty Bonds were the finest investment on earth.'[28] His property was left to his wife and three children. Washington University had received a gift several years earlier of $166,000, and the department of internal medicine at the Medical School is officially named the John T. Milliken Department of Medicine.[29] His chemical plant was sold to the Abbott Laboratories in the 1920s. He and his wife built a magnificent twenty-two-room home at 35 Portland Place, with nine and one-half bathrooms, an elevator, and a ballroom. The ballroom is still used today by the present occupants for lavish entertainments.[30]

The New York *Times* did not note the connection of Morris Meyers to the Patrick case when it reported his death in 1956 at the age of seventy-eight. 'Morris Meyers, a lawyer specializing in real estate,' the obituary stated, 'died yesterday in a nursing home in Huntington, Long Island, after a long illness ... He is survived by his widow, Selma, and two sons.'[31] Nor had the *Philadelphia Inquirer* noted David Short's connection with the case when he died in 1928 at the age of fifty-eight. Indeed, it did not even mention that he had lived in New York, simply stating that he 'came to this city early in life.'[32] He had become a very successful businessman in Philadelphia, having been the founder and president of the West Electric Hair Curler Corporation for twenty-five years. He left a very considerable estate, which included a Lincoln limousine and a cabin cruiser, to his wife and two children.[33]

Charlie Jones continued to live in the Baytown area where he was born. Earlier reports of his death were mistaken. He never married and lived with his brother in his parents' home. After the Second World War, oil was discovered on his property and he owned six or seven producing wells. He was described as an 'unassuming, but shrewd and intelligent businessman.'[34]

On 16 November 1954, at the age of seventy-nine, he killed himself with his own .38 revolver. The *Baytown Sun* reported the next day: 'Baytown police said Jones apparently had held a mirror before his face while lying on his back in bed, put a pistol to his head and pulled the trigger. The bullet entered above his right ear and emerged above the left.' A coroner's inquest declared that it was suicide.[35] Jones had been ill for some time and had told his neighbors that he would make sure that he would never become dependent on others. The press gave extensive coverage to the story. The headline in the *Baytown Sun* read: 'Suicide Is Final Chapter in W.M. Rice Murder Case.' There was a private graveside service. His home and his property were left to his nephew, Robert Busch, who worked in a bank in Houston.[36] Busch was still alive at the age of eighty-eight several years ago, but did not wish to talk to me by telephone about his Uncle Charles.

Finally, we come to Patrick's family. After his death, his third wife, Verna Patrick, moved back to Tulsa and worked as the court clerk there for many years. Although Patrick had left a one-page simple will, prepared many years before he died, leaving everything to his wife, it was not probated until his late parents' farm in Texas was sold many years later. The fact that Patrick's will was not probated indicates that he probably had little wealth at the time of his death and therefore nobody had an interest in seeking probate. Mrs Patrick moved to Coffeyville, Kansas, in 1961 to live with her sister and died in 1965 at the age of seventy-five.[37]

Patrick's elder daughter, Lucille, married again, but apparently did not have any children. She was living in Louisiana when her father died. She did not survive into the 1970s.[38]

The younger daughter, Lillian, was adopted by Patrick's sister, Emma Jameson, and married a naval physicist, T.B. Hill, who rose to become a vice-admiral in the navy. In 1952 he was the chief of staff of the Pacific Fleet. He died in 1957 and is buried in Arlington Cemetery.[39] Lillian died in a retirement home near Orlando, Florida, in 1980. The obituary in the *Orlando Sentinel Star* did not refer to the Patrick case.[40] They had three children, a son and two daughters, one of whom is still alive, living in retirement on Vancouver Island. She told me that she never met her grandfather, Albert, or her Aunt Lucille, and did not know about the case until she was in her thirties.[41]

# 100. My Exit

Now, for my own exit from the case. The reader will no doubt wonder whether I believe that Patrick was guilty or innocent. When I started researching the case, I was certain that Patrick was guilty of murder. All the accounts of the case take that approach. But as I worked my way through the documents and the years, I became far less convinced. In the end, like Patrick's own lawyers, Moore, Hill, and Olcott, I believe he was probably not guilty of murder.

Since writing the above, I asked three medical experts to read the manuscript and comment on the medical aspects of the case. All three agreed with Patrick's experts. Dr Frederick Jaffe, the former chief pathologist at the Ontario Centre of Forensic Sciences in Toronto, found the prosecution's medical evidence 'appalling from a contemporary perspective.'[1] Not only does chloroform 'not produce recognizable changes in the lungs,' Dr Jaffe wrote, but death from placing a cone containing chloroform on the face of a sleeping individual and then leaving the room 'is a very unlikely mode of death.' 'I thus have grave doubts,' he concluded, 'that a homicide had, in fact, been committed.'

Dr Alan Van Poznak, a professor of anesthesiology and pharmacology at the New York Hospital–Cornell Medical Center, expressed similar doubts.[2] In a detailed letter to me he stated, in part:

First of all, chloroform is non-flammable, which casts doubt on Mr. Jones' story that the saturated cloth burst into flame in the range. In addition, it would have been almost impossible to place a high concentration of chloroform vapor on the face of a normally sleeping person without having some reaction of suffocation and attempt to remove or avoid the offending vapor ... When Mr. Jones returned after about forty minutes, he said he found Mr. Rice in an unchanged position. Was Mr. Rice dead of natural causes before Mr. Jones put the chloroform to his face? And was any chloroform ever used?

Chloroform, Dr Van Poznak went on to say, would not affect the lungs. 'The medical "experts" who testified to the pulmonary irritant effect of chloroform,' he states, 'were absolutely wrong.' Further, the so-called experts were 'completely wrong' in claiming that the embalming fluid would not reach the lungs.

Dr Charles S. Hirsch, the chief medical examiner of New York City and a professor of pathology at the New York Hospital–Cornell Medical Center, agreed with Dr Van Poznak that chloroform 'is neither flammable nor a pulmonary irritant' and that it is 'probably safe to conclude' that the embalming fluid would reach the lungs.[3] 'In conclusion,' he wrote, 'I share your doubt about Patrick's guilt ... but prefer to conclude with a Scotch Verdict that Patrick's guilt was not proven.'

I also sent the manuscript to a husband and wife team of embalmers in Chicago, Edward and Gail Johnson, who are acknowledged experts on the history of embalming. They had absolutely no doubt that Patrick was innocent of murder, referring to the 'overwhelming and irrefutable proof of innocence.'[4]

If it is true that Patrick was not guilty of murder, was he guilty of participating in the forgery of the 1900 will and other documents? The handwriting expert at the Ontario Centre of Forensic Sciences suggested that I contact Paul Osborn in New York and Janet Masson in Houston. Both, he said, have excellent reputations as document examiners. Paul Osborn is the grandson of the expert, Albert Osborn, who played a major role in the case. He was, perhaps understandably, not interested in participating in any exercise that might prove that his highly respected grandfather might have been wrong.

Janet Masson was, however, intrigued by the case, read the manuscript, and examined in detail the photographic copies of the exhibits and other handwriting evidence in the archives of Rice University. Her detailed persuasive report to me supports the prosecution's case that the key documents were forged.[5] She states:

I find strong evidence to support the conclusion reached by Albert S. Osborn, John Tyrell and others that the four signatures on the 1900 will [and other documents] were not written by Mr. Rice. Not only are these four signatures unnaturally similar to each other, but they contain significant differences from the genuine signature of Mr. Rice ... Probably the most significant evidence that these signatures are not genuine is the presence and location of shading in the ink line ... The signatures on documents produced by Mr. Patrick do not contain this shading pattern ... The evidence validating the conclusions reached by Osborn, Tyrell, and others is just as powerful and persuasive today as it was when presented at the beginning of the century.

Ms Masson prepared transparencies for me of Rice's 'signatures' to the 1900 will for the purpose of superimposing one on the other. It is difficult not to agree with her conclusion that 'the four signatures were traced using the same presumably genuine signature as a model.'

She also commented on Albert Hamilton's claim that the Patrick will was genuine because Rice was in the habit of blotting the ink in his signature with his forefinger and an inked fingerprint appears on Rice's signature on the will. 'It is not clear,' she writes, 'that the mark is actually an inked fingerprint'; it 'may be the edge of the imprint of a seal.' (The actual 1900 will is no longer available, having disappeared from the New York City archives.) Moreover, she goes on, 'after reviewing a multitude of photographs of genuine and questioned signatures, I find no evidence whatsoever to support Hamilton's contention that Rice had a habit of using his forefinger as a blotter.'

Further, she also concluded that there is 'very strong evidence' that the letter allegedly from Rice requesting cremation was also a forgery. 'I am especially perplexed by the forged letter requesting cremation,' she wrote, acknowledging that she may perhaps be treading outside her specific area of expertise: 'What would be the need of such a letter if the death was due to natural causes?'

I still believe that Patrick was probably not guilty of murder. Rice was either already dead when chloroform was administered or, more likely, no chloroform was ever administered. Patrick was, however, probably guilty of fraudulently forging the will or at least of having Rice sign a document that he did not realize was a will. Perhaps Patrick hoped to negotiate a handsome settlement from Baker and the Rice interests, not expecting that the police would be brought in. My guess is that Patrick told House in the Tombs that he had nothing to do with Rice's death, but admitted to acting fraudulently with respect to the will and the other documents. He did not want House to reveal the conversation because he would lose any claim to the Rice millions and, moreover, be convicted of forgery. For similar reasons he did not take the stand at his trial. But why the cremation letter? Assuming it was in fact forged, one possible explanation for its preparation is that Patrick and Jones were, as Jones said, administering mercury and other drugs to hasten Rice's death. Cremation would destroy evidence of this. If so, Patrick would be guilty of attempted murder, not murder.

The chloroform theory emerged only after Dr Witthaus concluded that there was not enough mercury administered to cause death. If Jones did not actually administer chloroform to Rice, where did the chloroform story come from? It seems more than likely that it was planted in Jones' mind by Captain Baker, eagerly taken up by Jones, and willingly supported by the prosecution's 'experts.' Baker, it will be recalled, had an earlier relationship with Jones, having had private correspondence with him in early 1900 about Rice's 1896 will.[6]

We will never know the true story. Nor will we know whether Governor Dix was bribed or whether lawyer Brockman was deliberately killed by those supporting the earlier will. It is unlikely that a cache of conclusive documents will emerge from somebody's attic – although one never gives up hope of such a discovery.

This case, like the earlier *Lipski*[7] and *Shortis*[8] cases that formed the subjects of my earlier books, shows the inherent frailty and fallibility of the criminal process and the constant specter of error. All three cases show the danger of shifting the balance too far in favor of the prosecution and strengthen the arguments against capital punishment. As I stated in the Lipski book:

A trial may in theory be an objective pursuit of truth, but in practice there are many subjective factors which influence the course of events. Justice may in theory be blind, but in practice she has altogether too human a perspective. The ... story is, no doubt, more dramatic, and the wealth of material richer, than in most cases; yet, by looking at this extreme example one can better understand some of the factors that may influence any criminal trial.[9]

In the Patrick case we see such factors playing a role in the outcome as overly aggressive prosecutors with political ambitions, the influence of the press in molding public and professional attitudes, and the ability of the participants, in turn, to manipulate the press. We also see the power of money – vast fortunes were available to each side – to bring about results. In the early stages the wealth of those favoring upholding the 1896 will played a role in helping bring about the conviction by offering enormous support to the prosecution. In the later stages, Milliken's wealth financed the various steps towards the pardon. The ability to take these steps and to mobilize various professional and other groups, then and now, often depends on the money available. Further, one cannot discount the importance of the relationships between the various judges and counsel involved in the case: for example, the son of Judge Gray, who wrote the majority judgment against Patrick in the Court of Appeals, had earlier worked on the case for the prosecution; and Judge O'Brien, whose strong dissent probably saved Patrick's life, was one of Hill's closest friends. These are, perhaps, inevitable problems with any system of justice that has a human perspective. Recognizing the inherent fallibility of the process, however, helps keep us on our guard against miscarriages of justice.

Two other specific matters of concern arising from the Patrick case will be touched on here. The case shows the great dangers inherent in the manner in which the legal system uses expert testimony. The practice at the turn-of-the-century is not significantly different from the practice today. Expert witnesses can be bought, cornered, neutralized, and manipulated. As one legal scholar noted in a recent hundred-page article: 'this system should be changed. We ought to be able to do better.'[10] A number of solutions are possible, including, of course, giving the judge a greater role in the selection of experts. Another major concern shown by the case is the great danger of relying on an accomplice's testimony.[11] An accomplice such as Jones obviously has much to gain by supporting the prosecution. In the end, we have in this case the spectacle of Jones confessing – probably falsely – to murder and yet not being prosecuted for any crime.

Meanwhile the Rice Institute – now, of course, named Rice University – is flourishing. There is a statue of William Marsh Rice in the center of the campus. Many years ago, Rice's cremated ashes were removed from New York and placed at its base. On my first visit to Rice University several years ago, I asked a student where the library was located. His answer: 'Turn left at Willy.'

# Notes

Unless otherwise noted, the transcript and appeal documents are at the Association of the Bar of the City of New York Library; the Rice Papers are at the Woodson Research Center at Rice University; the Hill Papers are at the New York State Library in Albany; and the district attorney's files are at the Municipal Archives of the City of New York.

## PREFACE

1 *Denver Post*, 28 November 1912.
2 *Houston Chronicle*, 28 November 1912.
3 See A. Train, 'The Patrick Case, Complete' (1907) 64 *American Magazine* 97, reproduced in A. Train, *From the District Attorney's Office* (New York: Scribner's 1939), pp. 278–96; E. Pearson, *Five Murders* (New York: Doubleday 1928); R.C. Raby, *Fifty Famous Trials* (Washington Law Book 1937); F.X. Busch, *They Escaped the Hangman* (Indianapolis: Bobbs-Merrill 1953); C. Wilson and P. Pitman, *Encyclopaedia of Murder* (London: Arthur Barker 1961); A.F. Muir, 'William Marsh Rice and His Institute' (1972) 58 *Rice University Studies* 84 (edited by S.S. Morris); J.H.H. Gaute and

R. Odell, *The Murderers' Who's Who* (Montreal: Optimum 1979); *Crimes of the 20th Century: A Chronology* (Lincolnwood, Ill.: Publications International 1991) at pp. 22–3; E.W. Knappman, ed., *Great American Trials* (Detroit: Visible Ink Press 1994) at pp. 228–30; and J.R. Nash, *Murder, America: Homicide in the United States from the Revolution to the Present* (New York: Simon and Schuster 1980). The case is also the subject of a play, *The Rice Murder*, by J.D. Killgore (Houston 1985) and a movie by Killgore, *The Trust*, which premiered at the Houston International Film Festival on 23 April 1993.
4 *The Trials of Israel Lipski: A True Story of a Victorian Murder in the*

*East End of London* (London: Macmillan 1984; New York: Beaufort Books 1985).

5 *The Case of Valentine Shortis: A True Story of Crime and Politics in*

*Canada* (University of Toronto Press 1986).

6 *Fort Worth Record*, 30 December 1906.


## PART ONE: ARREST

### Section 1: A Death on Madison Avenue

1 See generally R.A.M. Stern, G. Gilmartin, and J. Massengale, *New York 1900: Metropolitan Architecture and Urbanism 1890–1915* (New York: Rizzoli 1983). For a description of the Berkshire see p. 282; see also 'The Berkshire' (1883) 14 *American Architect and Building News* 53–4, plates.

2 See D.C. Hammack, *Power and Society: Greater New York at the Turn of the Century* (New York: Russell Sage Foundation 1982) at p. 46.

3 Court of Appeals documents, Trial Transcript, p. 4120, Defendant's Exhibit No. 31.

4 Trial Transcript, p. 221.

5 See R.W. Habenstein and W.M. Lamers, *The History of American Funeral Directing*, rev. ed.

(Milwaukee: Bulfin 1962).

6 Technically referred to as a 'cannula.' I am grateful to Edward and Gail Johnson of Chicago, both practicing embalmers and historians of the history of embalming, for their help. In a letter to the author they point out that the 'embalming procedures described in the text are rarely employed today, though at the time were common.' Today, most embalmers use the carotid artery near the neck. Paul Faris and his colleagues at Humber College in Toronto permitted me to attend two embalmings, in one of which, because of my interest in the procedure, they used the right brachial artery procedure.

### Section 2: Certifying Checks

1 See New York *Saturday Standard*, 18 January 1902; New York *Journal*, 16 December 1900.

2 Trial Transcript, p. 4047, People's Exhibit D.

3 Evidence of David Short, Rice Papers, 'Chronological View of

the Facts in Respect to the Murder of William M. Rice,' p. 173, a document prepared by the prosecution from the evidence given at the preliminary hearing, hereafter cited as 'Chronology.'

## Section 3: Houston, Texas

1 See generally M.M. Sibley, *The Port of Houston: A History* (Austin: University of Texas Press 1968); D.G. McComb, *Houston: A History* (Austin: University of Texas Press 1981); M. Johnston, *Houston, the Unknown City 1836–1946* (College Station: Texas A. and M. University Press 1991).

2 See A.F. Muir, 'William Marsh Rice and His Institute'; K.J. Lipartito and J.A. Pratt, *Baker and Botts in the Development of Modern Houston* (Austin: University of Texas Press 1991); 'William Marsh Rice' in *The Handbook of Texas* (Austin: Texas Historical Association 1952).

3 Letter to Mrs L.M. McCraven, Houston, Texas, 16 August 1900, Rice Papers, File 36.14.

4 See Lipartito and Pratt, *Baker and Botts*. See also J.H. Freeman, *The People of Baker and Botts* (privately published by Baker and Botts, Houston, 1992), containing pictures and human-interest aspects of the firm.

5 Resolution of the Houston Bar Association, 3 October 1941.

6 *Texas Bar Journal*, 1941, p. 789.

7 See B.A. Olson, 'The Houston Light Guards' (1985) 7 *The Houston Review* 111.

8 See H.W. Baade, 'Law in Texas: The Roberts-Gould Era (1883–1893)' (1982) 86 *Southwestern Historical Quarterly* 161.

9 See generally G. Martin, *Causes and Conflicts: The Centennial History of the Association of the Bar of the City of New York 1870–1970* (Boston: Houghton Mifflin 1970); J.S. Auerbach, *Unequal Justice: Lawyers and Social Change in Modern America* (New York: Oxford 1976); G.W. Gawalt (ed.), *The New High Priests: Lawyers in Post-Civil War America* (Westport, Conn.: Greenwood 1984); R.L. Abel, *American Lawyers* (New York: Oxford 1989) at pp. 182 *et seq.*; C. Wilton, *Beyond the Law: Lawyers and Business in Canada 1830 to 1930* (Toronto: Osgoode Society 1990); M. Galanter and T. Palay, *Tournament of Lawyers: The Transformation of the Big Law Firms* (University of Chicago Press 1991).

10 Lipartito and Pratt, *Baker and Botts*, p. 22. See also S. Haber, *The Quest for Authority and Honor in the American Professions, 1750–1900* (University of Chicago Press 1991), pp. 206–39.

11 Lipartito and Pratt, at p. 6.

12 Rice Papers, File 63.1.

13 T. Petzinger, *Oil and Honor: The Texaco-Pennzoil Wars* (New York: Putman's 1987).

## Section 4: Telegrams

1 Trial Transcript, p. 3983.
2 Rice Papers, File 47.
3 See F. Meiners, *A History of Rice University: The Institute Years, 1907-1963* (Rice University Studies 1982), pp. 196 *et seq.*
4 *Times*, 11 July 1990.
5 Rice Papers, File 47.
6 *Ibid.*
7 See *Times*, 20 June 1932; *The Handbook of Texas*; D.L. Hofsommer, *The Southern Pacific, 1901-1985* (College Station: Texas A. and M. University Press 1986).
8 See *The Alcalde*, 30 October 1929.
9 Rice Papers, File 40.1.
10 Rice Papers, File 62.1.
11 Chronology, p. 230.
12 Rice Papers, File 62.1.

## Section 5: The Authorities

1 See J.W. Gerard, *My First Eighty-three Years in America* (Garden City, NY: Doubleday 1951), pp. 77-82.
2 *Times*, 7 September 1951; *National Cyclopaedia of American Biography*, vol. 49, p. 124.
3 *Times*, 29 May 1919.
4 See J.F. Richardson, *The New York Police: Colonial Times to 1901* (New York: Oxford 1970) at p. 276.
5 *Times*, 20 November 1937.
6 New York *American*, 18 December 1912.
7 *King's Handbook of New York City 1893* (reissued New York: Benjamin Blom 1972) at p. 525.
8 *Ibid.* at p. 527.
9 See A.A. Carey, *Memoirs of a Murder Man* (Garden City, NY: Doubleday 1930) at pp. 30-1.
10 *National Cyclopaedia of American Biography*, vol. 2, p. 217.
11 Habenstein and Lamers, *The History of American Funeral Directing*, pp. 453-4.
12 Trial Transcript, p. 4043.

## Section 6: Monday Evening

1 See Trial Transcript, testimony of Gerard at pp. 195-7, testimony of Vallely, pp. 208-9; Gerard, *My First Eighty-three Years in America*, p. 79; Chronology, pp. 236-52.
2 Chronology, Harold Stuart Acheson, p. 252.
3 Rice Papers, File 62.1.

## Section 7: The Funeral

1 New York *Herald*, 25 September 1900.
2 Stern, Gilmartin, and Massengale, *New York 1900: Metropolitan Ar-*

*chitecture and Urbanism 1980–1915*, pp. 156–7; (1900) 67 *American Architect and Building News* 63 (plate); (1901) 72 *American Architect and Building News* (plates). The architect was Cass Gilbert, who later designed the Woolworth Building, completed in 1913.

3 Chronology, p. 266.
4 *King's Handbook of New York City 1893*, p. 352.
5 *Herald*, 26 September 1900.
6 26 September 1900.

## Section 8: En Route

1 Rice Papers, File 62.1.
2 *Ibid.*
3 See W.Q. De Funiak and M.J. Vaughn, *Principles of Community Property*, 2nd ed. (Tucson: University of Arizona Press 1971) at pp. 72–3; H. Marsh, *Marital Property in Conflict of Laws* (Seattle: University of Washington Press 1952).
4 *Who Was Who*, vol. 4, p. 457.
5 See *The Campaigns of Walker's Texas Division by a Private Soldier* (New York: Lange, Little 1875). p. 54.
6 Hill Papers, George Arents Research Library, Syracuse University.
7 *Catalogue of the University of Texas for 1886–7* (Austin 1887), p. 86.
8 See S.O. Young, *A Thumb-nail History of Houston, Texas* (Houston: Rein and Sons 1912) at pp. 120 *et seq.* There was a competition in Houston in 1884 and one in Austin in 1888.
9 *Biographical Directory of American Congress 1774–1949* (US Government Printing Office 1950).
10 See *Galveston News*, 5 November 1893.
11 Rice Papers, File 62.2.
12 *Ibid.*
13 Chapter 360 of Laws of 1860.
14 Rice Papers, File 62.2.
15 *Ibid.*
16 *Ibid.*
17 Rice Papers, File 62.1.

## Section 9: Probings

1 *Times*, 8 September 1919; *Reports of the New York City Bar Association*, 1920, vol. 23, pp. 188 *et seq.*
2 See *People* v. *Molineux* (1901) 61 N.E. 286 (NYCA). See also L.P. Stryker, *The Art of Advocacy* (New York: Simon and Schuster 1954) at p. 40, referring to Osborne as a 'great advocate.'
3 *King's Handbook of New York*, p. 461.
4 *Times*, 24 September 1933.
5 Office of Chief Medical Examiner, 'General Information' pamphlet: established pursuant to the New York Laws of 1915. Autop-

sies are now performed in the
eight-story Chief Medical Examiner's building at 30th Street and
1st Avenue. For an excellent historical account of the medical examiner's office in the United
States, see the 1992 University of
Pennsylvania PhD thesis by Julie
Ann Johnson, 'Speaking for the
Dead: Forensic Scientists and

American Justice in the Twentieth
Century.'
6 *People* v. *Molineux* (1901) 61 N.E.
286 (NYCA).
7 Trial Transcript, pp. 239–40.
8 *Times*, 21 December 1915.
9 See G. LeBrun, *It's Time to Tell*
(New York: William Morrow
1962) at pp. 37 *et seq.*

## Section 10: The Press

1 Rice Papers, File 62.1. See generally C.E. Grinnell, 'Modern
Murder Trials and Newspapers'
(1901) 88 *Atlantic Monthly* 662.
2 See generally R. Ericson, P. Ba-
ranak, and J. Chan, *Visualizing
Deviance: A Study of News Organi-
zation* (University of Toronto
Press 1987); *Negotiating Control:
A Study of News Sources* (University of Toronto Press 1989);

*Representing Order: Crime, Law
and Justice in the News Media* (University of Toronto Press 1991),
particularly chapter 8.
3 *Times*, 25 September 1943.
4 See G. Borrie and N. Lowe, *The
Law of Contempt* (London: Butter-
worths 1973) at pp. 46 *et seq.*
5 *World*, 26 September 1900.
6 *Ibid.*

## Section 11: Explanations

1 26 and 27 September 1900.
2 *Ibid.*
3 The *World* reported, 29 September 1900, that 'there has never
been any express adjudication in a
case where a check has been presented after the drawer of a check

has died, but the best text writers
hold that the death of the drawer
revokes the authority of the
drawee to pay the check unless it
has been certified.'
4 *World*, 27 September 1900.

## Section 12: Baker Arrives

1 See Chronology, pp. 352 *et seq.*,
Trial Transcript, pp. 332 *et seq.*,
and Rice Papers, File 62.2 for
conversation between Baker,

Jones, and Patrick.
2 Rice Papers, File 62.2.
3 *King's Handbook of New York*, p.
522.

## Section 13: Gathering Documents

1 Rice Papers, File 62.2.
2 Trial Transcript, pp. 340 *et seq.*
3 Rice Papers, File 62.1
4 See Carey, *Memoirs of a Murder Man.*

5 Rice Papers, File 61.2.
6 *Times*, 28 September 1900.
7 Chronology, p. 366.
8 Chronology, p. 358.

## Section 14: Orren T. Holt

1 See *Houston Post*, 7 February 1992: the hotel was reconstructed in 1913; the present German owners are reported to have reduced the asking price from fifteen to four million dollars for the seventeen-story structure.
2 *Who Was Who*, vol. 4, p. 457.
3 Trial Transcript, p. 1373.
4 Trial Transcript, p. 3995.
5 Rice Papers, File 47.

6 *Ibid.*
7 Trial Transcript, p. 3967.
8 Rice Papers, File 47.
9 Trial Transcript, pp. 1347 *et seq.*
10 Trial Transcript, pp. 3116 *et seq.*; Rice Papers, File 9.6.
11 Material on her death was obtained from the Assumption Parish Library, Napoleonville, La.
12 Rice Papers, File 47.

## Section 15: Hornblower, Byrne

1 Trial Transcript, p. 3901.
2 *Times*, 29 September 1900.
3 *Times*, 17 June 1914; *Reports of the City of New York Bar Association*, 1915, pp. 186 *et seq.*; *National Cyclopaedia*, vol. 3, p. 466; O'Brien, 'The Nine Rejected Men' (1967) 19 *Baylor L. Rev.* 1 at pp. 14–16.
4 *Times*, 5 November 1942; *National Cyclopaedia*, vol. 3, pp. 467–8.
5 The first incumbent of the chair was Felix Frankfurter, who, coincidentally, had worked briefly for the Hornblower, Byrne firm after graduating from Harvard Law School fifteen years earlier. The unnamed partner who hired him had suggested that he change his name: see H.B. Phillips (ed.), *Felix Frankfurter Reminisces* (New York: Reynal 1960), pp. 37–8.
6 Rice Papers, File 62.2
7 *Ibid.*

### Section 16: McCluskey

1 *King's Handbook of New York*, p. 226.
2 New York *American*, 18 December 1912; Carey, *Memoirs of a*

*Murder Man*, pp. 45–6.
3 Rice Papers, File 62.5.
4 *Times*, 29 September 1900.

### Section 17: More at the Normandie

1 Memorandum by F.A. Rice, Rice Papers, File 9.6.

2 *Times*, 30 September 1900.

### Section 18: Handwriting Experts

1 Rice Papers, File 62.2.
2 *Times*, 6 October 1900.
3 Trial Transcript, pp. 1508–9.
4 *Times*, 30 June 1925.
5 'Biography of a Forged Will,' p. 12, prepared by the American Society of Questioned Document Examiners, 1951, in the Rice Papers.

6 See C. Carvalho and B. Sparkes, *Crime in Ink* (New York: Scribner's 1929) at pp. 49 *et seq.*
7 New York: Franklin 1971; first published by the Banks Law Publishing Co., New York, 1904.
8 *Times*, 6 October 1900.
9 Rice Papers, File 11.1.
10 *Times*, 6 October 1900.

### Section 19: Arrests

1 *World*, 5 October 1900.
2 Carey, *Memoirs of a Murder Man*.
3 Rice Papers, File 62.2.
4 Carey, *Memoirs of a Murder Man*, at p. 100.

5 *Miranda* v. *Arizona* 384 U.S. 436 (1966).
6 Rice Papers, File 14.1.
7 *World*, 5 October 1900.

## PART TWO: THE TOMBS

### Section 20: Arraignment

1 William McAdoo, *Guarding a Great City* (New York: Harper 1906) p. 135.

2 *Times*, 24 November 1925; *Tammany Times*, 27 July 1907.
3 Chronology, p. 420.

4  See C.H. Whitebread and C. Slo-
   bogin, *Criminal Procedure*, 3rd ed.
   (Westbury, NY: Foundation Press
   1993) at pp. 82 *et seq.*; *Strickland
   v. Washington* 104 Sup. Ct. 2052

(1984); *Regina* v. *Silvini* (1991) 68
C.C.C. (3d) 251 (Ont. CA).
5  *World*, 6 October 1900.
6  *Times*, 6 October 1900.
7  *Times*, 7 October 1900.

## Section 21: The Tombs

1  (London: Macmillan 1893), p. 71.
2  *King's Handbook of New York*, pp.
   493-4; *Times*, 7 and 29 September 1900 and 29 September
   1902; 'The New Tombs Prison,'
   *Charities*, 6 December 1902, pp.
   549-50; J.J. Munro, *The New
   York Tombs Inside and Out!*
   (Brooklyn: privately printed
   1909); C. Sifakis, *Encyclopaedia of
   American Crime* (New York: Facts
   on File 1982), p. 714; N. Silver,
   *Lost New York* (New York:
   Houghton, Mifflin 1967), p.
   105; 'City Prison, New York,'

*American Architect and Building
News*, vol. 56, 3 April 1897, p. 56
(plates).
3  *Herald*, 13 October 1900.
4  *Times*, 8 October 1900.
5  *World*, 8 October 1900.
6  *World*, 10 October 1900.
7  *Times*, 9 October 1900.
8  *World*, 9 October 1900.
9  *Herald*, 15 October 1900.
10  *Times*, 8 October 1900.
11  Rice Papers, File 62.3.
12  Rice Papers, File 62.4.
13  Rice Papers, File 63.1.

## Section 22: Short's Story

1  Rice Papers, File 10.9, for this and
   following quotes.

2  *Times*, 8 October 1900.

## Section 23: Jones' Story

1  15 October 1900.
2  Rice Papers, File 62.2.

3  *Herald*, 15 October 1900.
4  Rice Papers, Additional Papers.

## Section 24: Rice's Last Days: According to Jones

1  Rice Papers, Additional Papers.

## Section 25: Baker Settles In

1  Rice Papers, File 62.5.
2  Rice Papers, File 62.7.
3  Rice Papers, File 62.5.
4  Rice Papers, File 62.2.
5  *Ibid.*
6  Rice Papers, File 62.3.
7  Rice Papers, File 62.2.
8  Rice Papers, File 40.1.
9  Rice Papers, File 62.4.
10 See Lipartito and Pratt, *Baker and Botts in the Development of Modern Houston* at pp. 41-2.
11 *King's Handbook of New York*, p. 236.
12 Rice Papers, File 62.4.
13 Rice Papers, File 62.5.
14 Rice Papers, File 62.3.
15 Rice Papers, File 62.2.
16 Rice Papers, File 40.1.

## Section 26: Magistrate Brann

1  *People v. Molineux* 168 N.Y. 264 (NYCA 1901).
2  *Times*, 17 October 1900.
3  See generally S.R. Gross, 'Expert Evidence' [1991] *Wisconsin L. Rev.* 1113 at pp. 1130-1.
4  *Times*, 19 October 1900.
5  *Encyclopaedia of American Crime* at pp. 729-30.
6  See the *Times*, 16 December 1946; Clark Sellers, 'Albert Sherman Osborn: Questioned Document Pioneer,' *American Bar Association Journal*, December 1959.
7  Second edition (London: Sweet and Maxwell 1929). For a skeptical approach to expert evidence and, in particular, handwriting identification and the role of Osborn and Wigmore, see Risinger, Denbeaux, and Saks, 'Exorcism of Ignorance as Proxy for Rational Knowledge: The Lessons of Handwriting Identification "Expertise"' (1989) 137 *U. Pennsylvania L. Rev.* 731.
8  Rice Papers, File 11.1.
9  Rice Papers, File 13.
10 Rice Papers, File 62.4.

## Section 27: Committals

1  S. 208 of the New York Code of Criminal Procedure, 1881. An attempt was made to revise this code, David Dudley Field's Code, in 1900, but without success; see the *Annual Report of the Commissioners of Statutory Revision of the State of New York*, vol. 3 (Albany 1900); A. Chester, *Legal and Judicial History of New York* (reprinted, Buffalo: William S. Hein 1983), pp. 441-3. At the time, the accused could make a statement at the preliminary hearing, but not

under oath: ss. 203 *et seq*. See generally, re preliminary hearings, L.B. Orfield, *Criminal Procedure from Arrest to Appeal* (NYU Press 1947) at pp. 49 *et seq*. The present practice can be found in New York's Criminal Procedure Law, s. 180.60: see R.W. Vinal, *New York Criminal Practice Handbook* (Albany: New York State Bar Association 1991) at pp. 79 *et seq*.

2 *Times*, 25 October 1900.

3 Rice Papers, File 62.5.

4 *People* v. *McClafferty* 342 N.Y. 2d 208 (Crim. Ct., Queen's County, 1973): see Vinal, *New York Criminal Practice Handbook* at pp. 91–2.

5 Rice Papers, File 9.11.

6 Rice Papers, File 63.1.

7 Rice Papers, 9.9.

8 Rice Papers, File 9.11.

9 Rice Papers, File 62.5.

10 *Times*, 28 October 1900.

11 *Ibid*.

12 Rice Papers, File 9.11.

## Section 28: Confession

1 Trial Transcript, p. 597.

2 *Herald*, 29 October 1900.

3 Rice Papers, File 9.11.

4 Rice Papers, File 63.1.

5 Trial Transcript, People's Exhibit, p. 4090.

6 Rice Papers, File 14.1.

7 *Ibid*.

8 Trial Transcript, pp. 4095–6.

9 Rice Papers, File 9.11.

10 Rice Papers, File 63.1.

## Section 29: Bellevue Hospital

1 *Times*, 2 November 1900.

2 *King's Handbook of New York*, pp. 459–60.

3 See *American Bar Association Standards for Criminal Justice* (3rd ed., 1991), Standard 4-1.4, 'Public statements.'

4 *Times*, 2 November 1900.

5 *Times*, 3 November 1900.

6 *Ibid*.

7 See *People* v. *Rogers* 397 N.E. 2d 709 (NYCA).

8 Rice Papers, File 63.1.

9 Rice Papers, File 9.11.

## Section 30: George Gordon Battle

1 *Times*, 30 April 1949; *National Cyclopaedia of American Biography*, pp. 97–8; *City of New York Bar Association Reports*, vol. 102, 1949, at pp. 9 *et seq*. See also George

Battle, 'Three Notable Cases' in *Proceedings of the Virginia State Bar Association*, 1932, at pp. 254 *et seq*.

2 Rice Papers, File 63.1.

3 *Ibid*.

4 *Times*, 2 November 1900.
5 Rice Papers, File 63.1.
6 *Times*, 3 November 1900.
7 *Times*, 2 November 1900.

8 Trial Transcript, People's Exhibits, p. 3979.
9 Rice Papers, File 14.1.

## Section 31: Private Detectives

1 Rice Papers, File 53, for this and following quotes.

2 Rice Papers, File 32.2.

## Section 32: The Wills

1 *Herald*, 13 October 1900.
2 *Herald*, 11 October 1900.
3 Rice Papers, File 63.1.
4 Rice Papers, File 62.5.
5 Rice Papers, File 63.3.
6 Rice Papers, File 63.1.
7 See J.S. Auerbach, *Rabbis and Lawyers* (Bloomington: Indiana

University Press 1990) at p. 95: 'the foremost (and virtually the first) Jewish law firm.' See also L.S. Levy, *Yesterdays* (New York: Library Publishers 1954), pp. 32–43.
8 Rice Papers, File 63.2.

## Section 33: December 1900

1 Rice Papers, File 63.5.
2 Rice Papers, File 63.3.
3 Rice Papers, File 11.1.
4 Rice Papers, File 13.
5 Rice Papers, File 11.1.
6 *Ibid*.
7 Rice Papers, File 13.
8 *Globe and Mail*, 19 February 1944; H.J. Morgan, *Canadian Men and*

*Women of the Time* (Toronto 1912), pp. 520–1.
9 Rice Papers, File 32.2.
10 Rice Papers, File 11.1.
11 Rice Papers, File 63.2.
12 Rice Papers, File 53.
13 *Times*, 15 March 1920.
14 Rice Papers, File 32.2, for this and following quotes.

## Section 34: William Bacon

1 Rice Papers, Additional Papers.

2 Rice Papers, File 10.9.

## Section 35: Morris Meyers

1 28 September 1900.
2 6 October 1900.

3 Rice Papers, File 18, for the remainder of the section.

## Section 36: Jones: More Statements

1 Rice Papers, File 63.2.
2 Rice Papers, File 63.3.

3 *Houston Post*, 8 January 1901.
4 Rice Papers, File 14.1.

## Section 37: A New Charge

1 *Times*, 1 February 1919; see also *St. Louis Republic*, 1 February 1919.
2 Rice Papers, File 53.
3 Rice Papers, File 63.4.
4 *Herald*, 28 February 1901.

5 *Times*, 28 February 1901.
6 *New York Press*, 23 February 1902; *Times*, 27 November 1921.
7 *People* v. *Kennedy* 58 N.E. 652 (NYCA 1900).

## Section 38: The Preliminary Starts

1 *Times*, 7 April 1901.
2 *Times*, 19 January 1903.
3 *Times*, 19 and 20 February 1901.
4 *Times*, 14 February 1934.
5 R. O'Connor, *Courtroom Warrior: The Combative Career of William Travers Jerome* (Boston: Little, Brown 1963) at pp. 112–13. See also *National Cyclopaedia of Ameri-*

*can Biography*, pp. 149–50; New York City Bar Association, vol. 55, 1934, pp. 333–40.
6 Rice Papers, File 15.1.
7 *Times*, 27 March 1901.
8 Rice Papers, File 31.1.
9 *Times*, 30 March 1901.
10 *Times*, 31 March 1901.

## Section 39: Mrs Francis

1 *Times*, 2 April 1901.
2 Rice Papers, File 9.6.

3 *Ibid.*
4 Rice Papers, File 53.

## Section 40: Jones' Testimony

1 *Times*, 3 April 1901.
2 *Evening Telegram*, 3 April 1901.
3 S. 399 of the 1881 Code, as amended by chapter 360 of the Laws of 1882.
4 Criminal Procedure Law, s. 60.22. *Cf. Vetrovec* v. *The Queen* (1982)

67 C.C.C. (2d) 1, where the Supreme Court of Canada eliminated the judicially created corroboration rule, but partially brought it back in *Bevan and Griffith* v. *The Queen* (1993) 82 C.C.C. (3d) 310 (SCC). English

courts still apply the corroboration rule to accomplices: see *R.* v.
*Fallon* [1993] *Crim. L. Rev.* 591.

5 See T.J. Gilfoyle, *City of Eros:
New York City, Prostitution and the
Commercialization of Sex 1790–
1920* (New York: Norton 1992)
at pp. 203 *et seq.*

6 Detention of a witness was provided for in ss. 215 and 216 of
the 1881 Code. See now ss. 620

*et seq.* of the Criminal Procedure
Law. In fact the charge of forgery
against Jones had not been
dropped.

7 *Times*, 8 April 1901.
8 *Times*, 10 April 1901.
9 Rice Papers, File 11.
10 Rice Papers, Additional Papers.
11 Rice Papers, File 11.
12 Rice Papers, File 53.

## Section 41: Committal for Trial

1 *Times*, 10 April 1901.
2 Rice Papers, File 31.1.
3 *Times*, 11 April 1901.
4 *Sun*, 11 April 1901.

5 See chapter 36 of the 1880 Laws
of New York.
6 *Times*, 14 April 1901.
7 *Times*, 17 April 1901.

## Section 42: The Grand Jury

1 S. 258 of the 1881 Code: 'The
grand jury ought to find an indictment, when all the evidence
before them, taken together, is
such as in their judgment would, if
unexplained or uncontradicted,
warrant a conviction by the trial
jury.' See now s. 190.65 of the
Criminal Procedure Law. See
generally L.B. Orfield, *Criminal
Procedure from Arrest to Appeal*
(NYU Press 1947) at pp. 135 *et
seq.*; B.J. Shapiro, *'Beyond Reasonable Doubt and Probable Cause'*
(Berkeley: University of California Press 1991) at pp. 96–7. The
abolition of the grand jury was a
topic of discussion at the time in
the legal journals: see, for exam-

ple, F.A. Bregy, 'Should the
Grand Jury Be Abolished?'
(1901) 40 *American Law Register*
191; G. Lawyer, 'Should the
Grand Jury System Be Abolished?' (1905) 15 *Yale L.J.* 178.

2 Ss. 223 *et seq.* of 1881 Code: between sixteen and twenty-three
jurors are chosen by lot; now s.
190.05.

3 *Times*, 9 April 1901.

4 S. 244 of 1881 Code; now s.
190.20 of the Criminal Procedure
Law.

5 *Times*, 24 May 1917; *Who Was
Who.*

6 New York City Archives, District
Attorneys' Files.

7 S. 279 of 1881 Code.

8 S. 293 of 1881 Code; now s. 200.70 of Criminal Procedure Law.

9 *Evening Telegram*, 22 April 1901.

10 Unless he had given a written waiver: ss. 50.10(1) and 190.40(2) of the Criminal Procedure Law; see Vinal, *New York Criminal Practice Handbook* at pp. 119 *et seq.*

11 District Attorneys' Files.

12 See *People* v. *Rutherford* 62 N.Y. Supp. 224 (S. Ct. App. Div., 3d Dep., 1899); *People* v. *Steinhardt* 93 N.Y. Supp. 1026 (Sup. Ct., 1905). It is still relatively difficult for a defendant to inspect grand jury minutes: see Vinal, *New York Criminal Practice Handbook* at pp. 103–4 and 185. The so-called *Rosario* rule, however, requires disclosure of the pretrial testimony, including grand jury testimony, of any witness called at trial: see *People* v. *Rosario* 213 N.Y.S. 2d 448 (CA 1961).

13 Ss. 322 *et seq.* of 1881 Code.

## Section 43: Approaching the Trial

1 *Times*, 7 May 1901.

2 *Times*, 8 June 1901.

3 *Evening Journal*, 11 June 1901.

4 *Mail and Express*, 19 June 1901.

5 *Times*, 18 June 1901.

6 See the American Bar Association Project on Standards for Criminal Justice, *The Prosecution Function and the Defense Function* (Tentative Draft) (New York: ABA 1970), s. 5.10: 'The prosecution should not make public comments critical of a verdict, whether rendered by judge or jury.'

7 *People* v. *Molineux* 61 N.E. 286 (NYCA 1901).

8 *Sun*, 17 October 1901.

9 Rice Papers, File 64.5.

10 *Times*, 9 October 1901.

11 *Times*, 11 October 1901.

12 R.S. Skolnick, 'The Crystallization of Reform in New York City, 1890–1917' (PhD dissertation, Yale University, 1964) at pp. 260–1.

13 District Attorneys' Files.

14 S. 8 of 1881 Code: 'the defendant is entitled ... to a speedy and public trial.' See now s. 30.20 of Criminal Procedure Law; P.J. Galie, *The New York State Constitution: A Reference Guide* (New York: Greenwood Press 1991), pp. 31 and 48.

15 *Times*, 13 December 1901.

16 *Sun*, 3 January 1902.

## PART THREE: THE PROSECUTION

### Section 44: The Trial Starts

1 *Herald*, 25 December 1904.
2 *Times*, 10 November 1924; *National Cyclopaedia*, vol. 15, p. 254; *City of New York Bar Association Reports*, vol. 31, 1925.
3 L.P. Stryker, *The Art of Advocay* (New York: Simon and Schuster 1954) at p. 73.
4 *Evening Journal*, 25 January 1902; *Herald*, 21 January 1902.
5 *Evening Journal*, 21 January 1902.
6 See generally *Herald*, 25 December 1904.
7 *Times*, 21 February 1901.
8 The practice withstood a constitutional challenge in *People* v. *Conklin* 67 N.E. 624 (NYCA 1903) and much later by the US Supreme Court in *Fay* v. *New York*

332 U.S. 261 (1947). The abolition of special juries was recommended in the *Third Report of the New York Judicial Council* (1937) at pp. 121-8 and they were eventually eliminated in 1965 by the Judiciary Law of 1965. See generally L. Fleischer, 'Thomas E. Dewey and Earl Warren: The Rise of the Twentieth Century Urban Prosecutor' (1991-2) 28 *Calif. Western L. Rev.* 1 at pp. 23-6. A juror, however, could – and still can – be challenged because he or she did not believe in capital punishment: see s. 377 of 1881 Code and s. 270.20 of the present Criminal Procedure Law.
9 District Attorneys' Files.

### Section 45: Selecting the Jury

1 *Journal*, 21 January 1902, and *Times*, 22 January 1902.
2 Ss. 372 *et seq.* of 1881 Code; see now s. 270.25, allowing twenty peremptory challenges for a Class A felony.
3 Ss. 376 *et seq.* of 1881 Code; see now s. 270.20.

4 Rice Papers, jury selection transcript, for this and the following material.
5 *World*, and *Evening Journal*, 21 January 1902.
6 S. 414 of 1881 Code; see now s. 270.45.
7 *Mail and Express*, 25 January 1902.

### Section 46: Osborne's Opening Address

1 Trial Transcript, pp. 26-7.
2 See Trial Transcript, pp. 27-121, for Osborne's opening address.

3 *Times*, 24 January 1902.
4 *Evening Journal*, 23 January 1902.

## Section 47: Prosecution Witnesses

1 *Sun*, 26 January 1902.
2 Trial Transcript, pp. 122 *et seq.*, for this and other testimony.
3 *People* v. *Molineux* 168 N.Y. 264 (CA 1901). See Vinal, *New York Criminal Practice Handbook* at pp. 505 *et seq.*
4 *Evening Journal*, 27 January 1902.

## Section 48: The Second Week

1 Trial Transcript, pp. 219 *et seq.*, for the entire section.

## Section 49: Baker et al.

1 *Times*, 29 January 1902.
2 Trial Transcript, pp. 324 *et seq.*
3 *Evening Journal*, 29 January 1902.
4 *Herald*, 29 January 1902.
5 Woodson Research Center, Rice University, Emmanuel Raphael file. Raphael deserves more than the one sentence he receives in R. Winegarten and C. Schechter, *Deep in the Heart: The Lives and Legends of Texas Jews; a Photographic History* (Austin: Eakin Press 1990).
6 See F. Meiners, *A History of Rice University: The Institute Years, 1907–1963* (Rice University Studies 1982), p. 14.

## Section 50: The Third Week: Medical Evidence

1 Trial Transcript, pp. 574 *et seq.*
2 *Evening Journal*, 4 February 1902.
3 S. 416 of 1881 Code.
4 See New York Criminal Procedure Law, 1970, c. 996, ss. 270.30 and 270.35.

## Section 51: The Fourth Week

1 *World*, 11 February 1902.
2 Trial Transcript, pp. 659 *et seq.*
3 Rice Papers, File 32.6.
4 *Times*, 15 March 1921.
5 *Times*, 4 February 1902.
6 New York Laws of 1880, chapter 36, as amended by chapter 555 of the Laws of 1888. See *People* v. *Molineux* 168 N.Y. 264 (CA 1901); E.L. Fisch, *New York Evidence* (Pamona, NY: Lond Publications 1977) at p. 276.
7 Trial Transcript, pp. 787 *et seq.*
8 Rice Papers, File 32.6.
9 Rice Papers, File 64.8.

### Section 52: Jones Takes the Stand

1 *Evening Journal*, 18 February 1902.
2 *Evening Journal*, 27 February 1902.
3 Rice Papers, File 32.6.
4 *Times*, 20 February 1902.
5 *Times*, 21 February 1902.
6 Trial Transcript, pp. 1145 *et seq.*
7 *World*, 21 February 1902.

### Section 53: Cross-examination

1 Rice Papers, File 32.6.
2 *Times*, 26 February 1902.
3 Trial Transcript, pp. 1241 *et seq.*
4 *Times*, 27 February 1902.
5 Trial Transcript, pp. 1334 *et seq.*

### Section 54: More Evidence for the Prosecution

1 Trial Transcript, pp. 1516 *et seq.*
2 Rice Papers, File 64.6.
3 Rice Papers, File 31.1.
4 Rice Papers, File 32.6.
5 Rice Papers, Additional Papers.
6 Trial Transcript, pp. 1352 *et seq.*
7 *World*, 1 March 1902.

### Section 55: The People's Case Is Closed

1 Rice Papers, Files 32.6 and 64.2.
2 Rice Papers, File 31.2.
3 *Times*, 14 November 1901.
4 *Times*, 4 March 1902.
5 Trial Transcript, pp. 1425 *et seq.*
6 *Times*, 4 March 1902.
7 Trial Transcript, p. 1526.
8 Trial Transcript, p. 1553.

## PART FOUR: THE DEFENSE

### Section 56: The Defense Opens

1 Trial Transcript, pp. 1575–1633, for the entire section.
2 S. 399 of 1881 Code.
3 Vinal, *New York Criminal Practice* *Handbook* at pp. 512 *et seq.* See s. 60.22 of the Criminal Procedure Law.

## Section 57: Doctor Curry

1 Trial Transcript, pp. 1638 *et seq.*
2 Trial Transcript, pp. 1642–3; and

*Sun*, 7 March 1902.

## Section 58: Expert Medical Evidence

1 *Evening Journal*, 5 March 1902.
For contemporary discussions of
expert evidence, see Pritchard,
'Medical Evidence' (1900) 8
*American Lawyer* 556; Learned
Hand, 'Historical and Practical
Considerations Regarding Expert
Testimony' (1901) 15 *Harv. L.
Rev.* 40; note 'The Medico-Legal
Expert's Place' (1902) 54
*Independent* 1005; Frazer, 'Expert

Testimony: Its Abuses and Uses'
(1902) 50 *American Law Register*
87.
2 Trial Transcript, pp. 1733 *et seq.*
3 See Vinal, *New York Criminal
Practice Handbook* at pp. 377–8.
4 *Times*, 17 May 1943.
5 *Times*, 23 September 1915.
6 *Evening Journal*, 10 March 1902.
7 Hill Papers, Box 14, File 5.

## Section 59: More Defense Witnesses

1 Trial Transcript, pp. 1988 *et seq.*
2 *Times*, 15 March 1902.
3 Trial Transcript, pp. 2008 *et seq.*
4 *Times*, 15 March 1902.

5 *Sun*, 15 March 1902.
6 *Evening Journal*, 14 March 1902.
7 Trial Transcript, pp. 2029 *et seq.*

## Section 60: The Defense Closes Its Case

1 *Sun*, 18 March 1902.
2 Trial Transcript, pp. 2079 *et seq.*
3 *Saturday Standard*, 18 January
1902.
4 *Daily News*, 18 March 1902.
5 It would be the basis for a reversal
by the Court of Appeals if it was
stated in court: see Vinal, *New
York Criminal Practice Handbook* at
pp. 636–7.
6 See the American Bar Association
Project on Standards for Criminal

Justice, *The Prosecution Function
and the Defense Function* (tentative
draft) (New York: ABA 1970), s.
5.8: 'It is unprofessional conduct
for the prosecutor to express his
personal belief or opinion as to the
truth or falsity of any testimony
or the guilt of the defendant.' See
also standards 1.1 and 1.3 and
ABA Standards, *Fair Trial and
Free Press* (Approved Draft) (New
York: ABA 1968), and standards

8-1.1 and 8-1.3 of the ABA, *Right of Fair Trial and Free Press* (New York: ABA 1981).

7 Trial Transcript, pp. 2206 *et seq.*

8 *World*, 20 March 1902; *Sun*, 20 March 1902.

9 *Times*, 20 March 1902.

10 *Ibid.*

11 S. 393 of 1881 Code; see now s. 300.10.

12 See generally Vinal, *New York Criminal Practice Handbook* at pp. 315 *et seq.*

13 The accused was first permitted to testify in New York in 1869; Laws of New York of 1869, c. 678.

## Section 61: Rebuttal Evidence

1 Trial Transcript, pp. 2244 *et seq.*

## Section 62: Moore's Jury Address

1 Trial Transcript, pp. 2354 *et seq.*

2 S. 388 of the 1881 Code; see now s. 260.30 of the Criminal Proce-dure Law.

3 *Evening Sun*, 24 March 1902.

## Section 63: Osborne's Address

1 Trial Transcript, pp. 2294 *et seq.*

2 S. 393 of 1881 Code.

## Section 64: Goff's Charge

1 Trial Transcript, pp. 2652 *et seq.* The last sentence was perhaps un-duly more favorable to Patrick be-cause each question in the case – for example, the forgery of the will – does not have to be proven beyond a reasonable doubt: see *Morin* v. *The Queen* (1988) 44 C.C.C. (3d) 193 (SCC).

2 S. 393 of the 1881 Code; today, s. 300.10 of the Criminal Procedure Law provides that such an instruc-tion would be made by the judge only at the defendant's request.

3 Ss. 183 and 184 of the 1881 Penal Code; see now ss. 125.25 and 125.27 of the Penal Law.

4 S. 29 of the 1881 Penal Code; see now s. 20.00 of the Penal Law.

5 *People* v. *Ogle* 11 N.E. 53 (NYCA 1887); *People* v. *Eberhardt* 11 N.E. 62 (NYCA 1887); *People* v. *Elliott* 12 N.E. 602 (NYCA 1887).

6 Trial Transcript, pp. 2693 *et seq.*, citing *People* v. *Smith* 56 N.E. 1001 (NYCA 1900).

### Section 65: The Verdict

1 *Times*, 27 March 1902.
2 S. 450 of 1881 Code; now s. 310.80 of the Criminal Procedure Law.
3 *World*, 27 March 1902.
4 *Times*, 27 March 1902.
5 *Evening Journal*, 27 March 1902.
6 *World*, 27 March 1902.
7 New York *Commercial Advertiser*, 27 March 1902.
8 A declaration by a person since deceased to prove conduct was admitted by the US Supreme Court in the well-known case of *Mutual Life Insurance Co.* v. *Hillmon* 145 U.S. 285 (1892) and subsequently by the New York Court of Appeals in *People* v. *Conklin* 67 N.E. 624 (1903). See generally *McCormick on Evidence*, 3rd ed. (St Paul, Minn.: West 1984) at pp. 846 *et seq.* McCormick states at p.

847: 'it is now clear that out-of-court statements which tend to prove a plan, design, or intention of the declarant are admissible ...' So, today, Patrick would clearly have been right, although at the time the Hillmon case was still controversial.
9 *Commercial Advertiser*, 27 March 1902. See also *Regina* v. *Smith* (1992) 75 C.C.C. (3d) 257 (SCC).
10 See C. Sifakis, *Encyclopaedia of American Crime* (New York: Facts on File 1982) at pp. 351–2; R.H. Rovere, *Howe and Hummel, Criminal Lawyers* (New York: Paperback Library 1963).
11 *American*, 27 March 1902.
12 *Evening Journal*, 28 March 1902.
13 *American*, 28 March 1902.

### PART FIVE: APPEAL

### Section 66: Leaving the Tombs

1 *Sun*, 27 March 1902.
2 *Times*, 30 March 1902.
3 *Times*, 20 April 1902.
4 *Times*, 30 March 1902.
5 S. 491 of the 1881 Code.
6 See the *American*, 31 March 1902, referring to s. 4 of c. 330 of the Laws of 1901.
7 *Evening Journal*, 31 March 1902.
8 *World*, 6 April 1902.
9 *Journal*, 1 April 1902.
10 Rice Papers, Transcript of Sentencing Hearing, Additional Papers.
11 S. 492 of the 1881 Code.

## Section 67: To Ossining

1 See 'Passing of the Famous Sing Sing State Prison,' *Times*, 22 December 1907; L.E. Lawes, *Twenty Thousand Years in Sing Sins* (London: Constable 1932); D.J. Rothman, *Conscience and Convenience: The Asylum and Its Alternatives in Progressive America* (Boston: Little, Brown 1980); *Attica: The Official Report on The New York State Special Commission on Attica* (New York: Bantam 1972).

2 See (1901) 23 *American Monthly Review of Reviews* 272; *cf.* the favorable report on Sing Sing in 1902 by the State Commission on Prisons of New York for 1902 (the Eighth Report): (1903) 9 *American Journal of Sociology* 424. See also the report of a group of experts in 1905 recommending that Sing Sing be replaced by a new prison across the Hudson River: *Times*, 26 January 1905, (1906) 15 *Charities* 680.

3 1888 Laws of New York 778, 780: 'The punishment of death must, in every case, be inflicted by causing to pass through the body of the convict a current of electricity of sufficient intensity to cause death, and the application of such current must be continued until such convict is dead.'

4 C. Sifakis, *Encyclopaedia of American Crime*, pp. 237 *et seq.* ('Electric Chair') and p. 392 ('Kemmler, First Victim of Electric Chair'); J.R. Acker, 'New York's Proposed Death Penalty Legislation: Constitutional and Policy Perspectives' (1990) 54 *Albany L. Rev.* 515, particularly at pp. 517 *et seq.*; note, 'The Madness of the Method: The Use of Electrocution and the Death Penalty' (1992) 70 *Texas L. Rev.* 1039.

5 *Evening Journal*, 9 April 1902.

6 L.N. Robinson, *Penology in the United States* (Philadelphia: Winston 1921) at p. 255.

7 See Roland B. Molineux, *The Room with the Little Door* (New York: Dillingham 1903).

8 This description is drawn from the *Times*, *Evening Journal*, *Herald*, and *World*.

## Section 68: Probate

1 Rice Papers, File 65.2.

2 *Times*, 8 June 1942.

3 F.L. Wellman, *The Art of Cross-Examination*, 4th ed. (New York: Macmillan 1936).

4 See J.H.H. Gaute and R. Odell, *Murder 'What Dunit'* (London: Pan Books 1984) at pp. 305-7; C. Boswell and L. Thompson, *The Carlyle Harris Case* (New York:

Collier Books 1961). Details of the case were supplied to me by Larry Fleischer of New York City, who is writing a book on the case.

5 *Times*, 17 April 1902.

6 *Journal*, 24 April 1902.

7 *Commercial Advertiser*, 24 April 1902.

8 Rice Papers, File 65.2.

9 Rice Papers, Testimony of Probate Proceedings, Additional Papers.

10 Rice Papers, File 37.3.

11 Rice Papers, File 32.6.

12 *Times*, 19 September and 23 October 1902.

## Section 69: Motion for a New Trial

1 *Times*, 13 June 1902.

2 In 1902 New York penitentiaries would probably have had only a single source of power. Note the description by Theodore Dreiser of the dimming of the lights in *An American Tragedy* (p. 773 of the Signet Classic edition), a story based on the case of Chester Gillette, who was executed in Auburn in 1906. Subsequently, it would seem, execution chambers acquired their own separate power sources. See Sifakis, *Encyclopaedia of American Crime* p. 238: 'the lights never dim in the rest of the prison, because the chair is always powered by a separate source.'

3 S. 360 of the Laws of 1902. Formerly it was one year: s. 521 of 1881 Code.

4 *Times*, 11 October 1941; *City of New York Bar Association Reports*, vol. 79, 1942, p. 367. For a discussion of Rabbi Kaufmann Kohler and of the relationship between Jews and American law, see the excellent study J.S. Auerbach, *Rabbis and Lawyers: The Journey from Torah to Constitution* (Bloomington: Indiana University Press 1990).

5 See ss. 465 and 466 of the 1881 Code. See now ss. 440.10 *et seq.* of the Criminal Procedure Law ('motion to vacate judgment'). See generally L.B. Orfield, *Criminal Appeals in America* (Boston: Little, Brown 1939) at pp. 498 *et seq.*; M.L. Friedland, *Double Jeopardy* (Oxford: Clarendon Press 1969) at pp. 275–7; R.W. Vinal, *New York Criminal Practice Handbook* (Albany: New York State Bar Association 1991) at p. 737.

6 *Times*, 16 July 1954.

7 *Times* 6 December 1902.

8 Trial Transcript, pp. 2773 *et seq.*

9 *Commercial Advertiser*, 6 December 1902.

10 *Times*, 17 December 1902.

11 Trial Transcript, pp. 2928 *et seq.*

12 *Commercial Advertiser*, and

*Evening Telegram*, 27 November 1902.

13 Trial Transcript, pp. 3019 *et seq.*

14 *Commercial Advertiser*, 17 December 1902.

15 Rice Papers, 'People's Brief in Opposition to Motion for New Trial,' Additional Papers.

16 See s. 465 of the then Code of Criminal Procedure.

## Section 70: Preparing for the Appeal

1 *Journal*, 14 December 1902.

2 *Evening Telegram*, 2 December 1903.

3 *Times*, 24 February 1903.

4 Trial Transcript, pp. 3055-6.

5 *Brooklyn Citizen*, 31 May 1904.

6 Rice Papers, File 31.4.

7 *American*, 25 July 1903.

8 Hill Papers, Box 14, File 5.

9 *Times*, 25 July 1934; *City of New York Bar Association Reports*, vol. 58, 1935, p. 325; *Dictionary of American Biography*, Supp. 1, pp. 472-3.

10 *Times*, 9 and 10 April 1903; *Tribune* 9 April 1903; *Evening Post*, 8 April 1903.

11 New York *Daily News*, 9 April 1903.

12 *Tribune*, 9 April 1903, and *Times*, 10 April 1903.

13 *Times*, 4 February 1905. For a discussion of the disciplinary power of the New York Bar Association, see R.L. Abel, *American Lawyers* (New York: Oxford University Press 1989) at pp. 142 *et seq.*

## Section 71: Upholding the 1896 Will

1 The subject of a former judge arguing cases in court is not directly covered in the American Bar Association's *Model Rules of Professional Conduct and Code of Judicial Conduct* (New York: ABA 1989).

2 *In Re Rice's Will* 81 N.Y. Supp. 68 (1903).

3 Rice Papers, File 31.4.

4 At p. 72.

5 *In re Rice's Will* 68 N.E. 1123 (NYCA 1903).

6 S. 2653(a) of the Probate Code.

7 Rice Papers, File 31.4.

8 *Ibid.*

9 Rice Papers, File 41.4.

10 Rice Papers, File 69.5.

11 Rice Papers, File 41.4.

12 *Houston Post*, 5 April 1905.

13 At p. 118.

14 *Evening Sun*, 5 April 1905.

15 Rice Papers, File 69.5, enclosing clipping from the New York *Evening Post*, 5 March 1904.

16 Lipartito and Pratt, *Baker and Botts in the Development of Modern Houston* at p. 56.

17 *Ibid.*, at p. 57.

18 *Houston Post*, 29 October 1903.

### Section 72: David B. Hill

1 *Times*, 12 August 1930.
2 Hill Papers, Box 9, File 64.
3 Hill Papers, Box 14, File 5.
4 *Ibid.*
5 *Times*, 11 December and 21 October 1910; *Encyclopaedia of American Biography*, vol. 1, 1892, at pp. 453–4; H.J. Bass, *'I Am a Democrat': The Political Career of David Bennett Hill* (Syracuse University Press 1961); D.S. Alexander, *Four Famous New Yorkers* (Long Island: Ira J. Friedman 1923). For thorough discussions of New York politics during this period, see R.L. McCormick, *From Realignment to Reform: Political Change in New York State, 1893–1910* (Ithaca: Cornell University Press 1981); R.F. Wesser, *A Reponse to Progressivism: The Democratic Party and New York Politics, 1902–1918* (New York: NYU Press 1986).
6 The property is now the Wolferts Roost Country Club: see the privately published *The History of Wolferts Roost Country Club* (Albany 1985). The house burned down in 1926.
7 *Albany Times Union*, 26 March 1902.
8 Hill Papers, Box 14, File 5.
9 Hill Papers, Box 14, File 6.
10 Hill Papers, Box 14, File 7.
11 Hill Papers, Box 14, File 6.
12 *Herald*, 22 May 1904.
13 *Houston Chronicle*, 10 December 1904. An inspection of the *Star of Hope* journal at the Library of Congress in Washington, however, did not reveal any articles using his name or using what I believe to be his prison number.
14 *Herald*, 4 May 1903.
15 *American*, 21 October 1904.
16 *Herald*, 22 May 1904.
17 Hill Papers, Box 14, File 6.
18 *Times*, 29 August 1904; Alexander, *Four Famous New Yorkers* at pp. 431 *et seq.*
19 *Times*, 29 August 1904.
20 *Times*, 16 September 1904.
21 *Times*, 17 September 1904.
22 Alexander, *Four Famous New Yorkers* at p. 448.
23 *Times*, 28 August 1904.

### Section 73: The Medico-Legal Society

1 Hill Papers, Box 14, File 7.
2 *Ibid.*
3 *Times*, 12 October 1943.
4 *Houston Post*, 19 November 1904.
5 *Times*, 23 February 1918; *National Cyclopaedia of American Biography*, vol. 13, p. 204; S. Fiske, *Off-hand Portraits of Prominent New Yorkers* (New York: Lockwood 1884).
6 Hill Papers, Box 14, File 8.
7 *Tribune*, 16 February 1905, and Hill Papers, Box 14, File 8.
8 *American*, 17 February 1905.
9 *Evening Sun*, 20 February 1905.

## Section 74: The Court of Appeals

1 Hill Papers, Box 14, File 7.
2 *Times*, 13 December 1946.
3 *Times*, 7 September 1905;
   *National Cyclopaedia of American
   Biography*, vol. 37, p. 96.
4 New York: Houghton, Mifflin
   1889.
5 The ABA rules, for example, simply prohibit a judge from accepting employment 'in connection
   with any matter in which he had
   substantial responsibility prior to
   his leaving, since to accept employment would give the appearance of impropriety even if none
   exists': see Canon EC 9-3 of the
   ABA *Model Code of Professional Responsibility and Code of Judicial Conduct* (New York: ABA 1986).
6 Hill Papers, Box 14, File 8.
7 S. 541 of the 1881 Code states
   that the 'defendant need not personally appear in the appellate
   court.'
8 Hill Papers, Box 14, File 8.
9 See the 1992 pamphlet *Court of
   Appeals, State of New York*, distributed by the Court of Appeals, and
   the New York State Bar Association's handbook, *Appeals to the
   Court of Appeals* (2nd ed., 1991).
10 *Times*, 24 May 1922; *National
   Cyclopaedia of American Biography*,
   vol. 13, p. 444.
11 See, for example, the correspondence between Hill and O'Brien in
   1908 in the Bixby Papers, Box 18,
   New York State Library, Albany.
   Judge Vann was also an old friend:
   *ibid.*, letter from Hill to Vann, 16
   September 1910.
12 *Times*, 19 May 1909.
13 *Times*, 29 June 1915.
14 *American*, 15 March 1905.
15 *American*, 17 March 1905.

## Section 75: Judgment of the Court of Appeals

1 F. Bergan, *The History of the New
   York Court of Appeals, 1847–1932*
   (New York: Columbia University
   Press 1985) at p. 275.
2 *People* v. *Patrick* (1905) 74 N.E.
   843 (NYCA).
3 At p. 844.
4 At p. 850. See J.H. Wigmore,
   *Evidence*, 3rd ed., vol. 7 (Boston:
   Little, Brown 1940) at p. 335.
5 At p. 854.
6 See Wigmore, *Evidence*, vol. 8,
   p. 632.
7 S. 542 of the Code of Criminal
   Procedure.
8 *People* v. *Patrick*, at pp. 857–8.
9 At. p. 859.
10 At p. 860.
11 At p. 861.
12 At p. 862.
13 At p. 872.
14 *World*, 11 June 1905.
15 Hill Papers, Box 14, File 9;
   *American*, 20 June 1905.

## Section 76: Reargument

1 Hill Papers, Box 14, File 9.
2 Hill Papers, Box 14, File 10.
3 *Times*, 3 October 1905.
4 *Times*, 28 October 1905; *People* v. *Patrick* 75 N.E. 963 at 964 (NYCA 1905).

5 ABA, *Model Code of Judicial Conduct* (New York: ABA 1990), Canon 3 E(d)(ii) and F, which permits a judge to continue if there is disclosure and consent of the parties.

## Section 77: Further Steps

1 *People* v. *Patrick* 75 N.E. 963 at 964 (NYCA 1905).
2 Hill Papers, Box 14, File 11.
3 Hill Papers, Box 14, File 10.
4 Hill Papers, Box 14, File 9.
5 Hill Papers, Box 14, File 8.
6 Hill Papers, Box 14, File 10.

7 Hill Papers, Box 14, File 9.
8 'The Patrick Case,' *Medico-Legal Journal*, September 1905.
9 Hill Papers, Box 14, File 10.
10 Hill Papers, Box 14, File 11.
11 *Ibid.*

## Section 78: The Texas Trail

1 Hill Papers, Box 14, File 9.
2 Hill Papers, Box 14, File 10.
3 Hill Papers, Box 14, File 13.
4 Hill Papers, Box 14, File 9.

5 Hill Papers, Box 14, File 10, for this and following quotes in this section.

## Section 79: Resentencing

1 See ss. 503 and 504 of the 1881 Code.
2 Hill Papers, Box 14, File 10.
3 *Times*, 23 October 1905.
4 *Times*, 8 November 1905.

5 *American*, 7 December 1905.
6 *Times*, 7 December 1905.
7 *American*, 7 December 1905.
8 *Ibid.* and *Evening Journal*, 7 December 1905.

## PART SIX: FURTHER STEPS

### Section 80: Another Stay

1 *Times*, 8 December 1905.
2 *Houston Post*, 28 January 1906.
3 *Times*, 24 January 1906.
4 *Galveston News*, 22 December 1905, Hill Papers, New York City Public Library.
5 *Times*, 22 December 1905.
6 Hill Papers, Box 14, File 11.
7 Hill Papers, Box 14, File 12.
8 Hill Papers, Box 14, File 11.
9 *Times*, 22 March 1913.
10 *Times*, 11 May 1933; *City of New York Bar Association Reports*, 1934, vol. 55, p. 353.
11 See C. Sifakis, *The Encyclopaedia of American Crime* (New York: Facts on File 1982).
12 *Times*, 16 October 1909. *National Cyclopaedia of American Biography*, vol. 11, p. 485.
13 Hill Papers, Box 14, File 11.
14 See F.W. Miller *et al.*, *Criminal Justice Administration: Cases and Materials*, 4th ed. (Westbury, NY: Foundation Press 1991) at pp. 1232 *et seq.*
15 Act of 31 January 1928, chapter
14. See generally L.B. Orfield, *Criminal Appeals in America* (Boston: Little, Brown 1939), chapter 14, 'Federal Criminal Appeals.'
16 Hill Papers, Box 14, File 11.
17 *Times*, 24 November 1919; *National Cyclopaedia of American Biography*, vol. 9, p. 349; *Dictionary of American Biography*, vol. 4, pp. 179–80.
18 Hill Papers, Box 14, File 8.
19 *Times*, 22 December 1905.
20 *Herald*, 24 December 1905.
21 *Times*, 28 December 1905.
22 *Times*, 30 December 1905 and 3 January 1906.
23 *Times*, 13 and 14 January 1906.
24 *Houston Post*, 7 January 1906.
25 *Times*, 14 January 1906.
26 Chapter 213 of the Laws of 1887.
27 *Times*, 16 January 1906.
28 *Times*, 20 January 1906; New York *Morning Telegraph*, 21 January 1906.
29 *Evening World*, 19 January 1906.
30 *Times*, 16 January 1906.

### Section 81: Another New Trial Motion

1 *Houston Post*, 28 January 1906.
2 *Supra*, section 69.
3 Hill Papers, Box 14, File 12.
4 *Times*, 10 February 1906.
5 *Evening Sun*, 21 February 1906.
6 *Herald*, 20 February 1906.
7 *Times*, 22 and 27 February 1906.
8 *Evening World*, 22 February 1906.
9 *Times*, 21, 22, and 28 February 1906.
10 *World*, 25 February 1906.
11 *Herald*, 28 February 1906.

## Section 82: More Witnesses

1 District Attorney files, Affidavits and Notice of Motion for New Trial.
2 *Times*, 27 February 1906.
3 *Evening World*, 22 February 1906.
4 *Times*, 27 February 1906.
5 *Herald*, 22 February 1906.
6 *Herald*, 1 March 1906.
7 *Tribune*, 4 March 1906.
8 *Times*, 3 March 1906.
9 *Times*, 22 February 1906.
10 S. 835 of the Code of Civil Procedure of 1877, as amended by chapter 564 of the Laws of 1896.
11 *Evening Journal*, 2 February 1906.
12 See, for example, C.T. McCormick, *Evidence*, 3rd ed. (St Paul: West Publishing 1984) at pp. 221–2: 'it is now generally agreed that the privilege is the client's and his alone ... even in those states which ... codified the rule in terms of inadmissibility of evidence of communications, or of incompetency of the attorney to testify thereto.'
13 *Tribune*, 23 February 1906.
14 Hill Papers, Box 14, File 12.
15 *World*, 30 April 1906.

## Section 83: Still More Evidence

1 *Times*, 11 April 1906.
2 *Herald*, 1 March 1906.
3 District Attorney File, Affidavits and Notice of Motion for New Trial.
4 Hill Papers, Box 14, File 12.
5 *New York Press*, 18 February 1906.
6 District Attorney File, Affidavits and Notice of Motion for New Trial, for this and other testimony.
7 *Herald*, 2 May 1906.
8 *Times*, 29 May 1922.
9 *Times*, 24 May 1906.
10 *Ibid*.
11 Hill Papers, Box 14, File 12.

## Section 84: Goff's Ruling

1 Hill Papers, Box 14, File 12.
2 S. 450.70 of the Criminal Procedure Law.
3 *Tribune*, 14 April 1906.
4 *Tribune*, 30 May 1906.
5 See, for example, *Times*, 1 August 1905; *Evening Post*, 20 January 1906. See also (1903) 17 *Harv. L.* *Rev.* 317; (1903) 3 *Col. L. Rev.* 433; (1904) 4 *Col. L. Rev.* 356; *The Nation*, vol. 77, 19 November 1903.
6 Justice Brewster, April 1903 (reference misplaced).
7 *Evening Post*, 20 January 1906.
8 *Times*, 1 August 1905.

9 See generally M.L. Friedland, *Double Jeopardy* (Oxford: Clarendon Press 1969), chapter 9.
10 Hill Papers, Box 14, File 12.

11 *New York Law Journal*, 18 June 1906.
12 *New York Mail*, 12 June 1906.

## Section 85: Writ of Error

1 William Rufus Day Papers, Library of Congress, Manuscript Division, Box 21.
2 *Times*, 13 July 1923; *Dictionary of American Biography*, vol. 3, pp. 163–5; J.E. McLean, *William Rufus Day: Supreme Court Justice from Ohio* (Baltimore: Johns Hopkins 1946); J.F. Watts, 'William R. Day' in L. Friedman and F.L. Israel (eds.), *The Justices of the United States Supreme Court, 1789–1969* (New York: Chelsea House 1969) at pp. 1773–89.
3 *Leigh* v. *Green* (1904) 193 U.S. 79.

4 See, for example, *Gibson* v. *Mississippi* 162 U.S. 565 (1895) at p. 585: 'It was incumbent upon the state court to see to it that the accused had a fair and impartial trial ...'
5 Hill Papers, Box 14, File 12.
6 William Rufus Day Papers, Library of Congress, Manuscript Division, Box 21.
7 *Brooklyn Republican*, 23 December 1905.
8 *Evening Journal*, 26 March 1906.
9 *Evening Journal*, 24 June 1907.
10 Hill Papers, Box 14, File 12.

## Section 86: More Experiments and Petitions

1 See *People* v. *Ringe* 90 N.E. 451 (NYCA 1910), upholding the law, chapter 572 of the Laws of 1905.
2 (1906) 24 *Medico-Legal Journal* at pp. 329–30.
3 *Ibid.* at p. 321.

4 *Times*, 22 September 1906.
5 *Times*, 21 September 1906.
6 Hill Papers, Box 14, File 12.
7 Chapter 213 of the Laws of 1887.
8 *Times*, 19 July 1937.
9 *Times*, 21 September 1906.

## Section 87: The New Governor

1 Hill Papers, Box 14, File 13.
2 *Times*, 13 February 1907; *National Cyclopaedia of American Biography*, vol. 13, pp. 551–2.

3 *Times*, 26 September 1906.
4 *Times*, 28 August 1948; *National Cyclopaedia of American Biography*, vol. 39, pp. 1–7; R.F. Wesser,

*Charles Evans Hughes: Politics and Reform in New York, 1905–1910* (Ithaca: Cornell University Press 1967); M.J. Pusey, *Charles Evans Hughes* (New York: Columbia University Press 1963).

5 *Times*, 29 August 1906.
6 *Times*, 22 August 1906.
7 *Times*, 28 September 1906.
8 *Fort Worth Record*, 7 October 1906.
9 Hill Papers, Box 14, File 13.

### Section 88: Application for a Pardon?

1 *World*, 25 November 1906.
2 Hill Papers, Box 14, File 13.
3 *Ibid.*
4 Hill Papers, George Arents Research Library, Syracuse University.
5 *Evening Journal*, 27 November 1906.
6 Hill Papers, Box 14, File 13.
7 *Times*, 18 October 1924.
8 Hill Papers, New York City Public Library.
9 *Times*, 26 November 1906.
10 *Ibid.*
11 *Evening Telegram*, 26 November 1906.
12 Hill Papers, Box 14, File 13.

### Section 89: Governor Higgins

1 *Herald*, 7 December 1906.
2 *Herald*, 14 December 1906.
3 Hill Papers, Box 14, File 13.
4 W.T. Hewett, *Cornell University: A History*, vol. 2 (New York: University Publishing Society 1905).
5 Hill Papers, Box 14, New York City Public Library.
6 Hill Papers, Box 14, File 13.
7 Hill Papers, Syracuse University.
8 Hill Papers, Box 14, File 13.
9 *Albany Argus*, 23 September 1906.
10 *Times*, 7 June 1909.
11 Hill Papers, Syracuse University.
12 *Ibid.*
13 Hill Papers, New York City Public Library.
14 *Mail*, 18 December 1906.
15 Hill Papers, Box 14, File 13.
16 *American*, 17 December 1906.
17 *Times*, 21 December 1906; *Public Papers of Governor Higgins* (Albany).
18 *Times*, 21 December 1906.

PART SEVEN: CONCLUSION

Section 90: Reactions

1 *Times*, 22 December 1906.
2 *World*, 21 December 1906.
3 Hill Papers, Box 14, File 13.
4 *Binghamton Press*, 4 May 1907. See also M.J. Pusey, *Charles Evans Hughes*, vol. 1 (New York: Columbia University Press 1963) at pp. 198–9.
5 *Times*, 21 December 1906.
6 *American Lawyer*, vol. 14, December 1906, p. 539.
7 *World*, 22 December 1906.
8 *Times*, 22 December 1906.
9 *Times*, 21 December 1906.
10 *Charities*, 10 February 1906, vol. 5, pp. 680–2.
11 *Times*, 5 December 1907, 13 April 1908, 9 July 1908, 12 July 1908, 9 December 1908, 28 December 1911, 15 January 1912.
12 See the descriptions of Sing Sing by former wardens, L.E. Lawes, *Twenty Thousand Years in Sing Sing* (London: Constable 1932), and T.M. Osborne, *Society and Prisons* (New Haven: Yale University Press 1916), and by Prisoner #1500, *Life in Sing Sing* (Indianapolis: Bobbs-Merrill 1908); see also contemporary accounts, particularly the *Times*, 26 January 1905, 21, 22, and 23 December

1906, 19 July 1907; *World*, 22 December 1906; *New York Press*, 22 December 1906; *American*, 23 December 1906; 'An Inside View of Sing Sing' (1908) 33 *Arena* 328–32; 'The Awful Condition of Sing Sing Prison' (1901) 23 *American Monthly Review of Reviews* 272.
13 See, for example, the *World*, 24 December 1905 and 12 March 1906; *New York Press*, 23 and 30 July 1905.
14 The 1888 Yates Law in New York prohibited any prison-made products on the state markets. See generally K.L. Hall (ed.), *Police, Prison, and Punishment* (New York: Garland 1987) at pp. 254 *et seq.* (articles by B. McKelvey and M.B. Miller)
15 *Times*, 22 December 1906.
16 See Lawes, *Twenty Thousand Years in Sing Sing* at p. 109; D.J. Rothman, *Conscience and Convenience: The Asylum and Its Alternatives in Progressive America* (Boston: Little, Brown 1980) 129.
17 *Times*, 22 and 23 December 1906.
18 Lawes, *Twenty Thousand Years in Sing Sing* at pp. 24 and 42.

## Section 91: Hughes' Tenure Begins

1 *Times*, 22 December 1906.

2 *New York Mail*, 5 June 1907.

3 *Brooklyn Eagle*, 11 February 1907.

4 *Medico-Legal Journal*, vol. 25, 1907, p. 503.

5 *Ibid* at p. 461.

6 *American X-ray Journal*, 1898, vol. 3.

7 *Sunnyside*, 1 February 1907.

8 See Ely Liebow, *Dr. Joe Bell: Model for Sherlock Holmes* (Bowling Green University Press 1982).

9 *The Sunnyside*, 15 May 1907. Letters were signed by Joseph Bell, John Chiene, William Turner, H.D. Littlejohn, and A. Conan Doyle. All of these doctors are mentioned in Ely Liebow's fine book, *Dr. Joe Bell: Model for Sherlock Holmes*.

10 Liebow, *Dr. Joe Bell: Model for Sherlock Holmes*. I am grateful to embalmers Edward and Gail Johnson of Chicago for bringing to my attention Conan Doyle's connection with the case.

11 P. Costello, *The Real World of Sherlock Holmes: The True Crimes Investigated by Arthur Conan Doyle* (London: Robinson 1991). There is a specific chapter on American cases that interested Conan Doyle. Nor is it mentioned in a book of Conan Doyle's letters to the press: see J.M. Gibson and R.L. Green (eds.), *Letters to the Press: The Unknown Conan Doyle* (London: Secker and Warburg 1986).

12 'The Disappearance of Lady Frances Carfax' in *His Last Bow*: see p. 977 of Doubleday's *The Complete Sherlock Holmes*. Much has been written on the famous Adelaide Bartlett case of 1886, in which Mrs Bartlett was acquitted of murdering her husband in London by administering liquid chloroform.

It is interesting to note that O. Henry has a spoof on Sherlock Holmes in a short story in the *World* in 1904 in which the 'great New York detective' Shamrock Jolnes refers to a case very much like the Rice case. Shamrock Jolnes is made to say: 'There is only one case of importance on hand now. Old man McCarty, one hundred and four years old, died from eating too many bananas.' The culprit, Jolnes suggests, is 'the mafia.' See 'The Adventures of Shamrock Jolnes,' *World*, 7 February 1904, published in the collection *Sixes and Sevens* in 1911; see also D. Stuart, *O. Henry* (Chelsea, Mich.: Scarborough House 1990) at p. 162.

13 C. Sifakis, *Encyclopaedia of American Crime* (New York: Facts on File 1982) p. 246.

14 *Times*, 3 July 1938; see also *Auburn Citizen Advertiser*, 5 March 1920, 16 February 1927, 2 July 1938; *Who Was Who in America 1897–1942*, vol. 1, p. 510.

Some present-day scholars, however, describe him as a 'charlatan': see the unpublished, undated, paper by Jim Fisher of Edinboro University of Pennsylvania, 'Courtroom Charlatan.' See also J. Fisher, *The Lindbergh Case* (Rutgers University Press 1987); F. Russell, *Tragedy in Dedham: The Story of the Sacco-Vanzetti Case* (New York: McGraw-Hill 1962).

15 Hill Papers, Box 14, File 7.
16 *World*, 21 December 1906; *Sun*, 14 November 1908.
17 *World*, 21 December 1906.
18 Hill Papers, Box 14, File 14.
19 *Ibid*.
20 Bixby Papers, Box 18, New York State Library, Albany.

21 F. Meiners, *A History of Rice University: The Institute Years, 1907-1963* (Rice University Studies 1982).
22 *Galveston News*, 30 December 1906.
23 *Houston Chronicle*, 30 June 1907.
24 *Houston Post*, 30 December 1906.
25 *Houston Post*, 27 January and 24 February 1907.
26 Rice Papers, File 98.9.
27 A Train, 'The Patrick Case Complete' (1907) 64 *American Magazine* 97.
28 *American*, 7 May 1907.
29 *Evening Journal*, 7 May 1907.
30 *World*, 17 January 1907.
31 *World*, 22 July 1907.

### Section 92: Court Proceedings

1 *Catalogue of the University of Texas for 1885-6* (Austin: State Printing Office 1886), p. 13.
2 *Times*, 29 November 1924.
3 Petition to the US Circuit Court for Southern District of New York, US Supreme Court File 491/21287.
4 See *Urquart* v. *Brown* 205 U.S. 179 (1907); see also *Ex Parte Spencer* 228 U.S. 652 (1913). Federal habeas corpus jurisprudence was not significantly liberalized by the Supreme Court until *Brown* v. *Allen* 344 U.S. 443 (1953). The court, however, is now cutting back on the possibility of using habeas corpus: see, for example,

*Coleman* v. *Thompson* 111 S. Ct. 2546 (1991). See generally L.H. Tribe, *American Constitutional Law*, 2nd ed. (Mineola, NY: Foundation Press 1988) at pp. 162 *et seq.*; P. Bator, 'Finality in Criminal Law and Federal Habeas Corpus for State Prisoners' (1963) 76 *Harv. L. Rev.* 441; H.J. Friendly, 'Is Innocence Irrelevant? Collateral Attack on Criminal Judgments' (1970) 38 *U. Chicago L. Rev.* 142; M.M. Arkin, 'Rethinking the Constitutional Right to a Criminal Appeal' (1992) 39 *U.C.L.A.* 503.
5 *King's Handbook of New York City* (Boston: King 1893), pp. 255-6.

6 US Supreme Court File 491/21287.

7 *Ibid.*

8 *Ibid.* and *Times*, 19 October 1908.

9 Hill Papers, Box 14, File 14.

10 Act of 10 March 1908, chapter 76 of 35 U.S. Statutes 40. See *Bilik* v. *Strassheim* 212 U.S. 551 (1908).

11 *Herald*, 10 November 1908.

12 W.L. King, *Melville Weston Fuller: Chief Justice of the United States, 1888-1910* (New York: Macmillan 1950); H.B. Furer, *The Fuller Court, 1888-1910* (New York: Associated Faculty Press 1986); I. Schiffman, 'Melville W. Fuller' in L. Friedman and F.L. Israel (eds.), *The Justices of the United States Supreme Court, 1789-1969* (New York: Chelsea House 1969) at pp. 1471-95.

13 See L.M. Friedman, 'State Constitutions and Criminal Justice in the Late Nineteenth Century' (1989) 53 *Albany L. Rev.* 265.

14 (1908) 211 U.S. 78. The case, however, opened up possibilities for future incorporation: see D.J. Bodenhamer, *Fair Trial: Rights of the Accused in American History*

(New York: Oxford University Press 1992) at p. 83: '*Twining* v. *New Jersey* signaled the way for the eventual nationalization of federal guarantees for the criminally accused.'

15 367 U.S. 643 (1961).

16 *Ex Parte Patrick* 212 U.S. 555 (1908).

17 US Supreme Court File 491/21287.

18 *Times*, 12 September 1913; *Dictionary of American Biography*, vol. 4, pp. 200-1; *National Cyclopaedia of American Biography*, vol. 16, pp. 353-4; L.H. Pink, *Gaynor: The Tammany Mayor Who Swallowed the Tiger* (Freeport, NY: Books for Libraries 1931).

19 *Times*, 4 February 1909.

20 Hill Papers, Box 14, File 14.

21 *Times*, 3 February 1909.

22 *Times*, 29 March 1929.

23 Hill Papers, Box 14, File 14.

24 *Times*, 6 March 1909.

25 *Times*, 19 September 1924.

26 *Times*, 5 June 1909.

27 *Times*, 3 December 1909.

28 *Times*, 26 December 1909.

## Section 93: Meyers and Short

1 R. O'Connor, *Courtroom Warrior: The Combative Career of William Travers Jerome* (Boston: Little, Brown 1963) at p. 286.

2 *Times*, 20 July 1907 and 30 March 1947.

3 Hill Papers, Box 14, File 13.

4 *Ibid.*

5 NY District Attorney's files.

6 Rice Papers, Additional Papers, correspondence re prosecution of Meyers and Short.

7 NY District Attorney's files, Report and Recommendations of District Attorney's Office upon Indictment for Forgery, March 1910.

## Section 94: J.B. Brockman

1 *Times*, 19 December 1910.
2 Hill Papers, Box 14, File 14.
3 *Ibid.*
4 Rice Papers, Pardon File.
5 *Times*, 18 and 19 December 1910.
6 *Houston Post*, 26 and 27 October 1910; L.J. Marchiafava, 'The Houston Police: 1878-1948' (1977) 63 *Rice University Studies* 1 at p. 10.
7 *Houston Post*, 26 October 1910.

8 *Ibid.*
9 *Houston Chronicle*, 26 October 1910.
10 *Times*, 18, 19, and 20 December 1910, for this and following quotes.
11 *Houston Chronicle*, 19-22 April 1911.
12 *Houston Chronicle*, 2 April 1918; *Houston Post*, 3 April 1918.

## Section 95: Governor Dix

1 Rice Papers, Pardon File.
2 M.J. Pusey, *Charles Evans Hughes*, vol. 1 (New York: Columbia University Press 1963) at pp. 268-71.
3 *Times*, 7 January 1913.
4 *National Cyclopaedia of American Biography*, vol. 23, pp. 226-7.
5 *Times*, 12 October 1910.
6 J.W. Forrest and J. Malcolm, *Tammany's Treason: Impeachment of Governor William Sulzer* (Albany 1913) pp. 23-6.
7 Rice Papers, Pardon File.
8 *Ibid.*
9 S. 2653(a) of Code of Civil Procedure.
10 Rice Papers, Pardon File.
11 Meiners, *A History of Rice University*.
12 R.A.M. Stern, G. Gilmartin, and J.M. Massengale, *New York 1900: Metropolitan Architecture and Urbanism, 1890-1915* (New York:

Rizzoli 1983) at pp. 116-19, 401-2.
13 *Times*, 25 February 1912.
14 Rice Papers, File 100.1.
15 Rice Papers, File 100.3.
16 Rice Papers, Pardon File.
17 *Sunnyside*, May 1911.
18 Rice Papers, Pardon File.
19 *American*, 30 November 1912.
20 *Times*, 28 November 1912.
21 *Times*, 18 December 1910.
22 *In re Patrick* (1910) 120 N.Y. Supp. 1006 (S.C. App. Div. 1st Dep.), interpreting Judiciary Law, Laws of 1909, ch. 35, s. 88; *Times*, 2 January 1910.
23 Rice Papers, Pardon File.
24 *Times*, 4 May 1911.
25 *Times*, 28 November 1912.
26 Forrest and Malcolm, *Tammany's Treason* at p. 25; R.C.E. Brown, *History of the State of New York*, vol. 4, *1896-1920* (Syracuse University Press 1922) at p. 225; R.F.

Wesser, *A Response to Progressivism: The Democratic Party and New York Politics, 1902–1918* (New York: NYU Press 1986).

27 Meiners, *A History of Rice University* at pp. 47–9.
28 *Times*, 11 October 1912.
29 *Times*, and *American* 28 November 1912.

## Section 96: Leaving

1 *Times*, 28, 29, and 30 November 1912.
2 *World*, and *Times*, 28 November 1912.
3 *World*, 29 November 1912.
4 *Times*, 29 November 1912.
5 Rice Papers, Clippings, unidentified newspaper.
6 *Times*, 30 November 1912.
7 *American*, 30 November 1912.
8 *Denver Post*, 28 November 1912.
9 *Times*, 28 November 1912.
10 *New York Press*, 28 November 1912.
11 *Times*, 1 December 1912.
12 *American*, 6 December 1912.
13 *Times*, 28 November 1912.
14 *Commercial Advertiser*, 28 November 1912.
15 *Sun*, 28 November 1912.
16 *St. Louis Republic*, 30 November 1912.
17 *Times*, 30 November 1912.
18 *Times*, 29 November 1912.
19 Rice Papers, Pardon File.
20 *Times*, 5 December 1912.
21 Rice Papers, Pardon File.
22 Rice Papers, File 100.4.
23 Rice Papers, Pardon File.
24 *Denver Post*, 28 November 1912.
25 New York *Outlook*, 14 December 1912.
26 F.B. Crossley, 'The Pardon of Albert T. Patrick' (1913) 3 *Journal of the American Institute of Criminal Law and Criminology* 675. There was considerable interest in the pardoning power around that time: see W.W. Smithers, 'Nature and Limits of the Pardoning Power' (1910) 1 *J. of Crim. Law* 549; C.J. Bonaparte, 'The Pardoning Power' (1910) 19 *Yale L.J.* 630; J.D. Barnett, 'The Grounds of Pardon in the Courts' (1910) 20 *Yale L.J.* 131; W.W. Smithers, 'The Use of the Pardoning Power' (1914) 52 *Annals of the American Academy of Political and Social Sciences* 61. See generally K.D. Moore, *Pardons: Justice, Mercy and the Public Interest* (New York: Oxford 1989).
27 *Times*, 2 December 1912.
28 See the Executive Law Provisions, Laws of 1971, c.545. See also section 4 of the New York Constitution: P.J. Galie, *The New York State Constitution: A Reference Guide* (New York: Greenwood Press 1991) at pp. 102–3.
29 *Sun*, 28 November 1912.
30 *Times*, 7 December 1912.
31 *Houston Chronicle*, 28 November 1912.

## Section 97: Tulsa, Oklahoma

1 *Tulsa Daily World*, 19 December 1913.
2 *Times*, 22 and 23 June 1914 and 20 January 1915. Letter from Byrne to Baker, 28 November 1914, in Rice Papers, Pardon File.
3 *Times*, 29 April 1916.
4 See Forrest and Malcolm, *Tammany's Treason*; Wesser, *A Response to Progressivism* at pp. 99 *et seq.*
5 *New York Press*, 7 January 1913.
6 *Times*, 7 January 1913.
7 *Times*, 25 November 1914.
8 *Times*, 24 February 1913.
9 *American*, 22 November 1914.
10 *Houston Telegram*, 22 November 1914.
11 M.S. Sprague, *Money Mountain: The Story of Cripple Creek Gold* (Boston: Little, Brown 1953).
12 *Houston Telegram*, 22 November 1914.
13 *Tulsa Democrat*, 22 November 1914.
14 *Tulsa Democrat*, 23 November 1914.
15 *Houston Telegram*, 22 November 1914.
16 *Times*, 23 November 1914.
17 *Sun*, 23 November 1914.
18 *Times*, 24 November 1914.

## Section 98: Later Career

1 Rice Papers, Pardon File.
2 *Times*, 25 December 1916.
3 Thomas W. Gregory Collection, Library of Congress, and Patrick File, Woodson Research Library, Rice University.
4 *Houston Press*, 23 February 1926.
5 Simon Kaplan, Tulsa Public Library Archives.
6 References to this and the later Supreme Court proceedings can be found in US Department of Justice, File 234631, which contains the Transcript of Proceedings before the Board of Governors of the State Bar of Oklahoma: In re Albert T. Patrick, 29 March 1930; *Oklahoma State Bar Journal*, vol. 1, 1930; *Times*, 23 April, 11 June, and 25 November 1930. See also H.W. Taft, *Legal Miscellanies: Six Decades of Changes and Progress* (New York: Macmillan 1941). I am very grateful to Professor Peter B. Kutner of the College of Law, University of Oklahoma, for his help with this aspect of the case.
7 *Houston Press*, 23 February 1926.
8 The fourteen-story building has now been integrated with the award-winning thirty-six-story Reading and Bates Building.
9 Department of Justice, File 234631.
10 *Ibid.*

11 *Times*, 23 January 1950.

12 Department of Justice, File 234631.

13 J.B. Thoburn and M.H Wright, *Oklahoma: A History of the State and Its People*, vol. 4 (New York: Lewis Historical Publishing 1929) at p. 593.

14 *Ibid.*, vol. 3 at p. 58; R. Harlow, *Oklahoma Leaders: Biographical Sketches of the Foremost Living Men of Oklahoma* (Oklahoma City: Harlow Publishing 1928).

15 Kenneth P. Scheffel of the Bentley Historical Library of the University of Michigan informed me (letter of 17 April 1992) that 'he was directed to appear ... to explain his sentence to prison for larceny, and on June 13, 1903, upon failure to appear, the faculty voted unanimously by ballot to expel him.'

16 Transcript of Proceedings before the Board of Governors of the State Bar of Oklahoma: In re Albert T. Patrick, 29 March 1930 at p. 30.

17 Harlow, *Oklahoma Leaders* at p. 121.

18 *Oklahoma State Bar Journal*, vol. 1, no. 5, August 1930, at p. 4.

19 *Times*, 27 June 1954.

20 *Times*, 8 June 1959.

21 *Times*, 12 August 1945.

22 50 S. Ct. 349 (1930).

23 *Burdick* v. *U.S.* (1915) 236 U.S. 79; see S. Williston, 'Does a Pardon Blot Out Guilt?' (1915) 28 *Harv. L. Rev.* 647.

24 The Judiciary Law of 1909. See Taft, *Legal Miscellanies* at p. 184.

25 *Ibid.*

26 51 S. Ct. 88 (1930).

27 *Legal Miscellanies*, at p. 185.

## Section 99: Final Exits

1 *American*, 18 December 1912.

2 *Times*, 20 November 1937.

3 *Times*, 10 November 1924.

4 *Times*, 19 May 1909.

5 *Times*, 29 June 1915.

6 R. O'Connor, *Courtroom Warrior: The Combative Career of William Travers Jerome* at p. 113; *Times*, 14 February 1934.

7 *Times*, 8 September 1919.

8 *Times*, 8 November 1937.

9 J.W. Gerard, *My First Eighty-three Years in America: The Memoirs of James W. Gerard* (New York: Doubleday 1951) at pp. 81–2. *Times*, 7 September 1951.

10 *Times*, 17 June 1914.

11 *Times*, 5 November 1942.

12 *Times*, 24 November 1925.

13 *Times*, 27 and 28 November 1921; *Watertown Daily Times*, 28 November 1921.

14 *Times*, 21 October 1910.

15 *Times*, 11 May 1933.

16 *Times*, 11 October 1941.

17 *Tulsa Daily World*, 25 September 1938.

18 *Wetumka Gazette*, 16 February 1940.
19 *Tulsa Daily World*, 25 September 1938.
20 *Tulsa Daily World*, 12 February 1940.
21 *Times*, 3 August 1941; *Houston Post*, 3 and 4 August 1941.
22 *Houston Chronicle*, 3 August 1941.
23 *Houston Post*, 3 October 1937.
24 Rice Papers, James A. Baker clippings.
25 *Houston Post*, 3 October 1937.
26 *St. Louis Globe-Democrat*, 7 December 1942.
27 1 February 1919.
28 *Missouri Republican*, 12 June 1919.
29 Letter dated 24 February 1989, from Paul G. Anderson, Archivist, Washington University School of Medicine.
30 I am grateful to Luis and Rosa de Schwarz, the present owners, for this information. Rosa de Schwarz is the Honorary Consul of Peru.
31 *Times*, 13 January 1956. I have been unable to locate his will or his descendants.
32 30 August 1928.
33 Will dated 29 May 1924 and subsequent probate.
34 *Baytown Sun*, 17 November 1954.
35 *Baytown Sun*, 18 November 1954.
36 *Baytown Sun*, 2 December 1954.
37 *Coffeyville Journal*, 11 October 1965.
38 Telephone conversation with her niece, Emma H. West, of Duncan, British Columbia, on 27 January 1992.
39 *Who Was Who*, p. 402.
40 *Orlando Sentinel Star*, 13 April 1980.
41 Telephone conversation with Emma H. West on 27 January 1992.

## Section 100: My Exit

1 Letter to the author dated 15 October 1992.
2 Letter to the author dated 3 November 1992.
3 Letters to the author dated 17 December 1992 and 5 January 1993.
4 Letter to the author dated 13 January 1993.
5 Letter to the author dated 27 January 1993. See also Ms Masson's subsequent paper presented at the annual meeting of the American Society of Questioned Document Examiners in September 1993: 'The Rice Case: An Early Document Case from a Historical Perspective.'
6 See section 8.
7 *The Trials of Israel Lipski: A True Story of a Victorian Murder in the East End of London* (London: Macmillan 1984; New York: Beaufort Books 1985).
8 *The Case of Valentine Shortis: A*

*True Story of Crime and Politics in Canada* (University of Toronto Press 1986).

9   At p. 204.

10   See S.R. Gross, 'Expert Evidence' [1991] *Wisconsin L. Rev.* 1113.

11   New York Criminal Procedure Law, s. 50. See generally the symposium 'The Granting of Witness Immunity' (1976) 67 *J. of Crim. Law and Criminology* 129; Law Reform Commission of Canada, Working Paper 64, *Immunity from Prosecution* (Ottawa 1992).